APQ LIBRARY OF
PHILOSOPHY

APQ LIBRARY OF
PHILOSOPHY

TWO CENTURIES OF PHILOSOPHY IN AMERICA

EDITED AND WITH AN INTRODUCTION BY

PETER CAWS

PUBLISHED BY BASIL BLACKWELL

© American Philosophical Quarterly 1980

ISBN 0 631 11781 4

British Library Cataloguing in Publication Data

Two centuries of American philosophy.
 – ('APQ' library of philosophy; 7).
 1. Philosophy, American
 I. Caws, Peter   II. Series
 191   B851

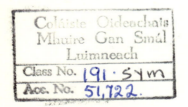
Set printed and bound in Great Britain
by Billing and Sons Limited
Guildford, London, Oxford, Worcester

CONTENTS

PART III:
THE AMERICAN PHILOSOPHICAL EXPERIENCE

PART IV: PUBLIC ISSUES
A. POLITICAL

PART IV: PUBLIC ISSUES

B. MORAL

ACKNOWLEDGMENTS

The papers gathered in this volume were all, with the exception of the Introduction, presented at the Bicentennial Symposium of Philosophy held in New York City from October 7–10, 1976. The Bicentennial Symposium would not have taken place had it not been for the interest, support and collaboration of a large number of people over a period of several years. Two names should be mentioned in connection with preliminary explorations towards some sort of philosophical recognition of the year 1976: those of Maurice Mandelbaum, chairman of the Board of Officers of the American Philosophical Association from 1968 to 1974, and George McLean, O.M., Secretary of the American Catholic Philosophical Association. In particular it was George McLean's presentation to the National Endowment for the Humanities, in connection with a possible World Congress of Philosophy, that laid the groundwork for the negotiations that issued in the Bicentennial Symposium.

Our debt to the National Endowment for the Humanities, which provided the bulk of the funding for the Symposium, and to the Rockefeller Foundation, which matched its generosity, is gratefully acknowledged. Financial contributions were also made by the IBM Corporation and by UNESCO, in the latter case specifically for the provision of travel funds to delegates from the Third World, and these organizations too deserve our thanks.

The work of planning was carried out in offices provided by the Graduate School of the City University of New York, and thanks are due to its president, Harold M. Proshansky, for making this possible. In preparing both for the Symposium itself and for the publication of this volume the director, subsequently the editor, enjoyed the collaboration of a working committee—first an Organizing Committee, then an Editorial Committee—whose members cheerfully converged on New York, or took time out at professional meetings, to lend their advice and judgment. Credit for the event and the volume really belongs to Richard De George, Jude Dougherty, Lewis Hahn, John Lachs, John McDermott, George McLean, Nicholas Rescher, John E. Smith, and H.

Standish Thayer, who in various combinations constituted the avatars of this committee and read everything that was submitted, as well as re-reading, after the Symposium, the papers that had been presented in order to cut the resulting volume down to its present size.

The office was staffed for most of its life, until well after the Symposium itself, by Ruth Davis, an indefatigable research assistant with a keen eye and a resourceful spirit. Practical matters on the spot were competently and imaginatively taken care of by Dr. Carol Phillips, while Patricia Turrisi organized single-handedly and with great talent the exhibition and meeting at Arisbe, Peirce's house in Milford, Pa. Finally, among the intelligent and willing helpers in the preparation of the manuscript special thanks are due to Elaine Salaverry and Frances Cutler.

PETER CAWS

January 1979

NOTES ON CONTRIBUTORS

E. JAMES CROMBIE teaches philosophy at the Université Ste-Anne, Pointe-de-l'Eglise, Nova Scotia, Canada, having previously taught at the University of Saskatchewan and Dalhousie University. His graduate and undergraduate studies were at the University of Waterloo, Ontario, except for a year at the Université de Montreal.

RICHARD T. DE GEORGE is University Distinguished Professor of Philosophy at the University of Kansas. He is President of the American section of the International Association for Philosophy of Law and Social Philosophy, Chairman of the Conference of Philosophical Societies, and author or editor of eleven books, including *Ethics, Free Enterprise and Public Policy.*

CHARLES JOHN DOUGHERTY was born in New York City in 1949, received a B.A. in philosophy at St. Bonaventure University and an M.A. and Ph.D. in Philosophy at the University of Notre Dame. He is currently assistant professor of philosophy at Creighton University in Omaha, Nebraska, where he specializes in American Philosophy and medical ethics. Articles by Professor Dougherty have appeared in *Philosophy Today, Teaching Philosophy, New Scholasticism, Ethics in Science and Medicine,* and *Linacre Quarterly.*

JUDE P. DOUGHERTY is Dean of the School of Philosophy of The Catholic University of America and editor of the *Review of Metaphysics.* He is the author of *Recent American Naturalism* and, with L. Dupre and others, of *Approaches to Morality.*

RONALD DWORKIN is Professor of Jurisprudence at Oxford University and Professor of Law at New York University. He was educated at Harvard and Oxford Universities. His recent works include *Taking Rights Seriously.*

ABRAHAM EDEL is Research Professor of Philosophy, University of Pennsylvania, and Distinguished Professor Emeritus of Philosophy, City University of New York. He was educated at McGill, Oxford, and Columbia (Ph.D.) and taught philosophy at the City College, New York, 1931–73. He is author of *Ethical Judgment, Science and the Structure of Ethics, Method in Ethical Theory, Aristotle, Analyzing Concepts in Social Science,* among others, and co-author of *Anthropology and Ethics, The Quest for Moral Understanding.*

ELIZABETH FLOWER is Professor of Philosophy at the University of Pennsylvania. She was educated at Wilson College, Bryn Mawr College and the University of Pennsylvania (Ph.D.) and has taught or lectured at Barnard College, Hamilton College, and the National Universities of Chile and Colombia. She was a Fellow at the National Humanities Center, 1978–9. Her writings are in ethics, philsophy of law and social philosophy, and she is co-author (with Murray Murphey) of *A History of Philosophy in America.*

WILLIAM K. FRANKENA has just retired after teaching at the University of Michigan since 1937, where he was Roy Wood Sellars Professor of Philosophy. He is the author of *Ethics (1963, 1973), Three Historical Philosophies of Education* (1965), and many essays in ethics and philosophy of education, some of which are reprinted in *Perspectives on Morality,* edited by K. E. Goodpaster. In 1974 he was Carus Lecturer.

A. C. GENOVA is Professor and Chairman of the Department of Philosophy at the University of Kansas. He has published a variety of journal articles in the areas of philosophy of language, philosophy of logic, metaphysics, ethical theory and the philosophy of Immanuel Kant—especially on Kant's *Critique of Judgment.*

NICHOLAS F. GIER is Associate Professor of Philosophy at the University of Idaho. He was educated at Oregon State University and the Claremont Graduate School. His publications are in the area of American theology and process philosophy, and include "Process Theology and the Death of God" in John Cobb, ed., *The Theology of Altizer* and "Prehension and Intentionality" in *Process Studies.* His "Wittgenstein and Forms of Life" will appear in *Philosophy of the Social Sciences* in Fall, 1980.

MORRIS GROSSMAN is Professor of Philosophy at Fairfield

University, Fairfield, Connecticut, where he has taught philosophy and the humanities. He received the Ph.D. from Columbia University. He has written on Santayana, aesthetics, American philosophy and philosophical methodology. His avocational interests include music, poetry, chess and tennis.

LEWIS E. HAHN is Distinguished Visiting Professor of Philosophy, Baylor University, and Research Professor Emeritus, Southern Illinois University at Carbondale (since 1977). He is Chairman of the Editorial Advisory Board of the Dewey Publication Project at SIU-C. Author of *A Contextualistic Theory of Perception*, he formerly held positions at the University of Missouri at Columbia, Princeton University, and Washington University, St. Louis.

VIRGINIA HELD is Professor of Philosophy at the City University of New York. She is the author of *The Public Interest and Individual Interests* (1970), and an editor of *Philosophy and Political Action* (1972) and *Philosophy, Morality and International Affairs* (1974). She has recently edited *Property, Profit, and Economic Justice* (1980).

ROSCOE HILL is Associate Professor of Philosophy and an Associate Dean of the College of Arts and Sciences at the University of Denver. He was educated at Carleton College and the University of Chicago (Ph.D.) and has taught at Carleton College, the University of Illinois (Chicago Circle), Yale University, and the University of Denver. His publications are in the areas of ethics and legal philosophy.

ROBERT L. HOLMES was educated at Harvard University and the University of Michigan (Ph.D.), has taught at the Universities of Michigan and Texas, and is now Professor of Philosophy at the University of Rochester. He was a Fellow at the Center for Advanced Study, University of Illinois, in 1970–71, and a Fellow at the National Humanities Institute, Yale University, in 1976–7.

SIDNEY HOOK is Senior Research Fellow at the Hoover Institute, Stanford University, and Emeritus Professor of Philosophy, New York University. He was educated at the City College of New York and Columbia University, and has also received several honorary degrees. His recent works include

Pragmatism and the Tragic Sense of Life and *Revolution, Reform and Social Justice.*

BRENDA JUBIN is President of Bevis Press and an assistant editor of *The Philosopher's Index.* She received her Ph.D. from Yale University, where she also taught and served as dean of Morse College. Her research interests are nineteenth-century British and American philosophy.

JOHN J. Mc DERMOTT is currently Professor and Head of Philosophy and Humanities at Texas A&M University. His teaching is primarily in the fields of American Philosophy, Contemporary Culture and Urban Aesthetics. The editor of scholarly editions of the writings of William James, Josiah Royce and John Dewey, he is presently on the Advisory Council for the critical edition of the Collected Works of William James. Professor Mc Dermott has taught and lectured at a variety of American universities and international symposia, and in 1970 was the recipient of the national E. Harris Harbison Award for Gifted Teaching.

MIHAILO MARKOVIC is Professor of Philosophy at the University of Belgrade and the University of Pennsylvania. He was educated at Belgrade and London Universities and has published works on logic, dialectics, and humanism. His most recent publications include *From Affluence to Praxis: Philosophy and Social Criticism.*

REX MARTIN is Professor of Philosophy and former Chairman of the Department at the University of Kansas, in Lawrence. His fields of major interest are political philosophy (in particular, rights), philosophy of the social sciences, and philosophy of history. He recently published *Historical Explanation: Re-enactment and Practical Inference* (1977).

WINFIELD EUGENE NAGLEY has been a Professor of Philosophy at the University of Hawaii, Manoa campus, since 1951. He served continuously as Department Chairman for 14 years, building the faculty in Eastern, Western and Comparative Philosophy from three members to its present size of 16, and established the doctoral program in those fields.

JOHN PASSMORE was born and educated in Australia. He is Professor of Philosophy in the Australian National University, and formerly was Senior Lecturer in the University of Sydney and Professor of Philosophy in the University of Otago, New Zealand. He has been visiting fellow in Oxford and Cambridge, visiting scholar in the Institute of Education, London, and visiting professor at Brandeis, and has lectured extensively in the USA, England, Japan, Denmark and Germany. He is former President of the Australian Academy of Humanities, and is Fellow of the Australian Academy of Social Sciences and foreign member of the British Academy, the American Academy of Arts and Sciences, and the Royal Danish Academy of Sciences and Letters. His most recent book is *Science and its Critics*.

ANDREW J. RECK, Professor and Chairman of the Department of Philosophy at Tulane University, has taught at Yale University and Fordham University. The author of works on American philosophy, the history of philosophy, metaphysics, and social and political philosophy, he has published *Recent American Philosophy* (1964), *The New American Philosophers* (1968), and *Speculative Philosophy* (1972). He has served as president of several philosophical societies, has received awards from the American Council of Learned Societies and the American Philosophical Society, and has been a Fulbright Scholar at St. Andrews, a fellow of the Howard Foundation, and a visiting fellow of the Huntington Library.

RICHARD RORTY studied at the University of Chicago and at Yale, and has taught at Princeton since 1961. He has written about philosophy of mind, philosophy of language, and metaphilosophy. His *Philosophy and the Mirror of Nature* appeared in 1979.

HERMAN J. SAATKAMP Jr. is Professor of Philosophy at the University of Tampa. He received the Ph.D. from Vanderbilt University. He is General Editor of the Santayana Edition and co-author of *George Santayana: A Bibliographical Checklist, 1880–1980*. He has published articles on Santayana and Whitehead.

JOHN E. SMITH is Clark Professor of Philosophy at Yale University. He is a former President of the Metaphysical Society of America, the Hegel Society and the American Theological Society.

Among his books are *Purpose and Thought: the Meaning of Pragmatism; Reason and God; The Spirit of American Philosophy; Experience and God* and *Themes in American Philosophy.*

TIMOTHY SPRIGGE, who is now Professor of Logic and Metaphysics at the University of Edinburgh, taught philosophy at the University of Sussex from 1963–79, apart from one year at the University of Cincinnati. His publications include *The Correspondence of Jeremy Bentham* (Vols. 1 and 2), *Facts, Words and Beliefs* and *Santayana: An Examination of his Philosophy.* He is now working on a comparative study of William James and F. H. Bradley, and has a special interest in the "golden age" of American philosophy.

JOHN J. STUHR is Assistant Professor of Philosophy and Paul Garrett Fellow at Whitman College, Walla Walla, Washington. He was educated at Carleton College and Vanderbilt University (Ph.D.). His dissertation was on John Dewey's philosophy of experience. He has published articles on American philosphy, ethics, metaphysics, and philosophy of education, and has received awards for excellence in teaching.

H. S. THAYER is Professor of Philosophy, The City College of the City University of New York. He has held a Guggenheim Fellowship, a National Endowment for the Humanities Fellowship, and membership in the Institute for Advanced Study, Princeton. He is author of many works on pragmatism including *Meaning and Action: A Critical History of Pragmatism* (1968, revised 1973, new edition in press), and of books and articles in the history of philosophy and science.

JUDITH THOMSON is Professor of Philosophy at the Massachusetts Institute of Technology. Among her recent publications is *Acts and other Events* (1977).

BRUCE WILSHIRE is Professor of Philosophy at Rutgers University and Convener of the Committee for Pluralism in Philosophy. He has been co-executive secretary of the Society for Phenomenology and Existential Philosophy and is the author of *Romanticism and Evolution; William James and Phenomenology; Metaphysics: An Introduction to Philosophy; William James: The*

Essential Writings; and *Role Playing and Identity: The Limits of Theatre and Theatrical Metaphor—A Philosophical Study.*

PETER CAWS (editor) is Professor of Philosophy at Hunter College and the Graduate School, City University of New York, and chairman of the Committee on International Cooperation, American Philosophical Association, in which capacity he directed the Bicentennial Symposium. He was educated at the University of London and Yale University. His recent publications include *Sartre*, in the series "The Arguments of the Philosophers."

INTRODUCTION:
PHILOSOPHY AT THE BICENTENNIAL

In a society of three-toed sloths it seems likely that celebrations of notable events would occur every thirty-six years, rather than every hundred. This contingency of our numbering system is only slightly less striking than the historical contingency that led to what Winston Churchill used to call the revolt of English gentlemen against a German king, whose outcome was the United States of America. While the fact that the signing of a piece of paper in Philadelphia could in fact constitute the birth of a new nation is in itself of profound philosophical significance, that significance attaches to the performative and constitutive actions involved (declaring, pledging and the like) and to the status of what is thus performed and constituted (a revolution, a republic) rather than to the details of the actual event—certainly not to its date.

It may well be asked, then, why philosophers, whose business would seem to lie with the necessary and the universal, should pay any attention at all to such accidental products of evolution and politics as the Bicentennial of the American Revolution. They rightly, it may be felt, took the occasion in 1976 to celebrate the two-hundredth anniversary of the death of David Hume, but had less excuse for a government-financed symposium simply to recall the final impatience of the thirteen colonies with the heavy taxes and repressive policies of a remote and unsympathetic regime. And yet it has been a popular view that there was something peculiarly philosophical about the American Revolution, that it represented the practical implementation of the rational ideas of the Enlightenment tempered with the solid empiricism of Locke. It has been an equally popular view that there is something peculiarly American about at least one major philosophical tradition, that of pragmatism. These views may be simplistic, but they have a kind of natural plausibility: it certainly appears that if the Revolution owed less to political tradition than most historical events it must have owed more to political philosophy, and if pragmatism owed less to Europe than most philosophical schools it must have owed more to America.

The problem of the relation between philosophy on the one hand and the American experience on the other has a kind of insistence

1

that it seemed natural to honor at the Bicentennial, when the American side of the question came in for so much attention. The Bicentennial Symposium was conceived less as a matter of celebrating the achievements of American philosophers—although it was that—than of reconsidering America as an idea in modern thought, and posing the question of the status of regional or national philosophies. The concept of a "new world" is still an attractive one, and the thought of attaching it to a new century reassuring in a time whose sources of hope may seem to be dwindling. America has stood for the excitement of the new ever since its discovery; the metaphor extended in the seventeenth and eighteenth centuries to all forms of novelty and exploration, even the erotic ("O my America, my new-found land!" was Donne's apostrophe to his mistress's body), and in spite of the fact that the United States is now among the world's oldest continuous political entities, rather than among its newest, it has managed to preserve some of the openness towards the future that was characteristic of its beginnings.

To European philosophers in the seventeenth century America seemed an unspoiled place, one in which it was possible to start afresh with natural resources but without historical burdens. For Hobbes it was the last stronghold of the state of nature,[1] for Locke the model of a fertile land whose bounty precluded the greed of private property: "Thus in the beginning all the world was America," he says, and adds: "and more so than that is now; for no such thing as money was anywhere known."[2] (What happens to natural riches with the introduction of money is another philosophically interesting question, which is outside the scope of this essay although it too is part of the American story. It is worth noting parenthetically the touching confidence of the Founders in the incorruptibility of American institutions by money: Madison, in the *Federalist Papers*, speaking of the risk that members of the House might be bought off by the President or by members of the Senate, says of the latter: "their private fortunes, as they must all be American citizens, cannot possibly be sources of danger.")[3] There was then no question of such a thing as American philosophy. Do *places* produce philosophies? Can philosophy be national and still remain philosophical?

The focus of attention in the Bicentennial Symposium was intended to be "philosophy in the life of a nation," to indicate at once the primacy of philosophy as such and its potential involvement with any national life, not just America's. But inevitably the subject was seen for the most part as an American philosophy whose existence was assumed. Had Plato been asked to comment on the special characteristics of Greek philosophy, he might have found the question puzzling. And yet he was quite accustomed to regional variations in style and language. Visiting philosophers and Sophists are habitually referred to in his writings under the names of their native cities—Gorgias of Leontium, Hippias of Elis—and in various dialogues we learn of specific local peculiarities: the notorious taciturnity of Lacedaemonian philosophizing is described in the *Protagoras*, and in the *Theaetetus* it is said of the Ephesians that, following their great countryman Heraclitus, they like to keep everything, including philosophical argument, in a state of uncertainty and flux. There are broader cultural traits as well, whose relevance to philosophy is less clear (although it might be considerable): the Boeotians approve of unnatural love, the Carthaginians are given to intoxication.

The question is, are there comparable traits in American culture or argumentative habits that stand out as similarly characteristic, and that might be important for understanding American philosophy? Perhaps the model of Ephesus or Sparta is better than that of Greece, and perhaps it corresponds better to St. Louis, Missouri, and Cambridge, Massachusetts, than to America. Certainly the Hegelians who founded the *Journal of Speculative Philosophy* in St. Louis in 1867, with its motto "Philosophy can bake no bread, but she can procure for us God, freedom and immortality," came from a very different tradition from the pragmatists in the great years of the Harvard philosophy department and its provincial dependencies. Even the acknowledged giants of what might be called classical American philosophy— Peirce, James, Royce, Santayana, Dewey—do not, taken together, form anything like a homogeneous class or maintain anything like a coherent doctrine. This might be expected in a country that has been known to pride itself on its "pluralism," on its receptivity to all ideas and all comers. But pluralism, while it is a virtue in its own way, is only part of what is characteristically American in philosophy, and I think there is another level that needs to be considered and on which a different virtue of philosophy in America, a virtue which might represent the best kind of involvement with the life of a nation, comes to light.

George Sarton, the historian of science—who used to like to compare New York to Alexandria, because the Mediterranean crossing from the old world of Athens to Alexandria, given the shipbuilding and navigation of the period, seemed to him to resemble the Atlantic crossing from Europe to America—remarks that "the intensity of a national culture should be represented by two factors, the first symbolizing the general educational level, and the second the exceptional merit of a small elite of pioneers."[4] It is the latter that usually predominates in histories of philosophy, which are as a rule, understandably enough, histories of the doctrines of the great philosophers. But the "general educational level" has its own significance when the question is not one of the sequence of doctrines but of their impact on national life—or, even better, of the impact of the habits of mind that the entertaining of the doctrines represents. Conceived as they were at the apogee of the Enlightenment, the principles on which the United States was founded included the efficacy of education and the perfectibility of man. That nothing is explicitly said about either in the founding documents does not weaken this claim, but rather strengthens it. In Plato's *Republic* the most important issue is the sort of persons who are to live in the state, and the manner of their education; the issue was certainly no less important in the eighteenth century, and its being passed over in silence means simply that the Founders had a kind of natural confidence in the regulation of such matters by the practical virtues of openness and rationality that they themselves embodied. They assumed that some form of education would be universal, just as the suffrage was to be universal.

Jefferson indeed worked out a scheme for public education in Virginia which was designed not only to produce a competent electorate but also to select and train the best minds for public service. In this he was implicitly following the advice of Plato about the philosopher-king, the main force of which, after all, was not so much to make philosophers kings as to ensure that "the kings and princes of this world have the spirit and power of philosophy."[5] (We tend to forget, because of the stigma attached after the Revolution to former titles of nobility, that those titles were for the most part merely descriptive of positions of prominence, and that republican principles excluded neither the positions nor the titles as such, but only the fact that they were hereditary. The President of the United States is *de facto* both monarch and prince, these being nothing more than the Greek and Latin terms for the one who holds the first place.) Jefferson, it is true, would have been appalled at the thought of an affinity with Plato; in a letter to Adams in 1814 he says of the *Republic*: "While wading thro' the whimsies, the puerilities, and unintelligible jargon of this work, I laid it down often to ask myself how it could have been that the world should have so long consented to give reputation to such nonsense as this?"[6]

For the present purpose it is less important to trace the specific content of philosophical influences on the Founders—as Bailyn has pointed out they depended far more on the politics of Rome than on the philosophy of Greece, and the classics appear in their work as "illustrative, not determinative, of thought"[7]—than to draw attention to the example they set and the expectations they entertained. Certainly the level of analytic reason they habitually exhibited was a good deal higher than in most other political circles at the time, or, for that matter, in the same circles since. And the "general educational level" that could absorb the *Federalist* as part of its daily newspaper set a high standard for popular participation in politics. It may be said that contemporary newspapers in other parts of the world were just as weighty, and that the local press has since declined (it is hard, for example, to imagine today the serialization of a treatise on political philosophy even in *The New York Times*). Admittedly the expectations were not always fulfilled, the general level not always maintained. There was nevertheless something about America than ministered to curiosity and enthusiasm about ideas, and which translated itself into a persistent feature of the American educational landscape.

Perhaps it had as much to do with the absence of a prior history as with any positive condition—the absence at any rate of history perceived as an obstacle to the new. Crèvecoeur's description of the European's transformation into an American tends to the melodramatic but has the ring of truth: "He no sooner breathes our air than he forms schemes and embarks in designs he never would have thought of in his own country. There the plenitude of society confines many useful ideas, and often extinguishes the most laudable schemes which here ripen into maturity."[8] Among other things America permitted a naive argumentativeness that did not fear academic ridicule and that often led to achievements as solid as those of conventional scholars elsewhere. There is no better example of this than Franklin, whose delight in controversy is evident in his account of disputations with his friend Keimer: "I used to work him so with my Socratic method, and had trepann'd him so often by questions apparently so distant from any point we had in hand, and yet by degrees lead to the point, and brought him into difficulties and contradictions, that at last he grew ridiculously cautious, and would hardly answer me the most common question, without asking first, '*What do you intend to infer from that?*'"[9]

Franklin was one of the founders of the University of Pennsylvania; it was inevitable that, after all, the free attachment to inquiry should be institutionalized. But it is in the institutions that Sarton's first level of culture is embedded. What has sometimes been called "academic philosophy" as a term of belittlement, and berated for its irrelevance to the great issues of the time,[10] is in fact the strongest and most persistent mode of entry of philosophy into the life of the nation; it sustains Sarton's second level but has a momentum of its own. It would be easy to overrate its influence on national life—but it would also be easy to underrate that influence; instruction in philosophy at the undergraduate level has been more pervasive in the United States than anywhere else, and it has been traditionally taught as inquiry rather than as doctrine. The tradition has even produced at least one minor novel, Owen Wister's *Philosophy Four*,[11] which in spite of a certain snobbery and even anti-intellectualism catches admirably the spirit of the "Introduction to Philosophy."

To have been introduced to philosophy, to have a casual, yet progressively more distant, acquaintance with it, may not ensure political or moral wisdom in the citizenry—it may for that matter have the disadvantages of tasting the Pierian spring. But it is worth remembering that Socrates needed the youth of Athens, even if he was accused of corrupting it, and that it has always been the students of philosophy—including those who became its masters—who have kept the discipline alive. (We owe modern philosophy, in the person of Descartes, to the Jesuit fathers of La Flèche, however traditional their teaching may have been.) Education is designed for the young, but they are not its only nor always its prime beneficiaries; the higher the "general education level" in philosophy the more likely, other things being equal, is the subsequent emergence of original philosophical work.

Most of the contributors to the Bicentennial Symposium are from the American academic world. They came not so much to reflect all that is going on there in the way of philosophical thinking—hardly anything, for example, is said in the book about Quine or Putnam or Davidson or Kripke—as to reflect on the phenomenon of philosophy in America. Many of them focussed on the achievements of the "small elite of pioneers," which is one reason why I have allowed myself to stress the other side of Sarton's dichotomy in the foregoing remarks. Some took the opportunity provided by the historical moment to revisit the Revolutionary period; the reader will find here important original contributions to the debate about the sources and strategies of philosophical reasoning on the part of the revolutionaries. But others—and I include among these most of the participants from abroad—raised fundamental questions that transcend the American experience while forming an integral part of it: questions about political categories, about the relationship of philosophy to high culture, about education itself, and morals, and technology. It was the hope of the organizers of the Symposium that the lively and open spirit of the eighteenth century, its sense of the immediate relevance of philosophy not only to politics in America but to the life of nations everywhere, might be recaptured. In the event there seemed to be a general feeling that something like this had, in however modest a fashion, been achieved.

To celebrate philosophy in America, even at its Bicentennial, is not to echo any chauvinistic claims about an American way of life, but to stress the way in which philosophy has entered into some aspects of American life, and the way in which we may hope it will inform the life of a new world, of which America will be part and is still, in spite of the failures of its own history, an image—faint, perhaps, in contrast to the optimistic zeal of the Revolution, but still offering a live alternative to some more recent ideological models. If Locke could say that in the beginning all the world was America, there have also been, it is true, those who have prophesied with gloom that in the end, too, all the world will be America: Americanized, flooded with American mass culture and American technology. But it may be that in these respects, as in the Revolution itself, America was only, and accidentally, a few steps ahead along a path the rest of the world was sooner or later to follow in any case, whose end is not yet in sight and whose direction may be changed by rational action. This book is a witness to the fact that philosophy has had, and an affirmation of the belief that it ought to have, an essential role in the following of that path.

NOTES

1. Thomas Hobbes, *Leviathan*, Part I, Chap. 13: "For the savage people in many places of America, except the government of small families, the concord whereof dependeth on natural lust, have no government at all; and live at this day in that brutish manner. ..."

2. John Locke, *Second Treatise of Government*, Chap. 5, par. 49.

3. James Madison, *The Federalist*, no. 55.

4. George Sarton, *A History of Science: Hellenistic Science and Culture in the Last Three Centuries B.C.* (Cambridge, Mass., Harvard University Press, 0000), p. viii

5. Plato, *Republic* 473.

6. Lester J. Cappon, ed., *The Adams-Jefferson Letters* (Chapel Hill, University of North Carolina Press, 1959), p. 432.

7. Bernard Bailyn, *The Ideological Origins of the American Revolution* (Cambridge, Mass., Belnap Press of Harvard University Press, 1967), p. 26.

8. J. Hector St. John (Pseud. for Michel Guillaume Jean de Crèvecoeur), *Letters from an American Farmer* (London, 1782). Excerpted in *The Annals of America* (Chicago, London, etc., Encyclopedia Britannica Inc., 1968–), II, 589.

9. Benjamin Franklin, *Benjamin Franklin, His Autobiography*, The Harvard Classics, Vol. I (New York, P. F. Collier & Son, 1909), pp. 36–7.

10. See e.g. Lewis Feuer, "American Philosophy is Dead," *The New York Times Magazine*, April 24, 1966, p. 30.

11. Owen Wister, *Philosophy Four: A Story of Harvard University* (New York, Lippincott, 1901).

PART I: ORIGINS

SOME PHILOSOPHERS AND THE
DECLARATION OF INDEPENDENCE

ANDREW J. RECK
Tulane University, New Orleans, Louisiana

As philosophers we are temperamentally attracted to the theory that ideals play important roles in history. In the case of the American Revolution we have good reason to take pride. Elsewhere I have described the American Revolution as primarily an ideological struggle—that is to say at the very least, a conflict between combatants who acknowledge the significance of ideas and even use them as weapons.[1] During the struggle for American independence a major cluster of ideas, circumscribing the doctrine of natural law and natural rights, was acknowledged and employed. These ideas come from the philosophers. In the eighteenth century, the Age of Reason and Revolution, the Enlightenment, philosophy replaced religion not only for the scientific understanding of nature but also for the discovery of those natural principles which were held to govern morality and politics. The ideas of the modern natural law thinkers, who in turn rested on classical authorities, among whom Cicero ranked first, make up the primary philosophical background of the American Revolution. In the eighteenth century the pamphlet was the major form of political expression; and the issues of the American Revolution were fought out in the first place in an historically unparalleled polemical literature of pamphlets. Supplemented by newspaper letters (often later collected and published as pamphlets) and the journals and documents of committees, assemblies, and congresses, pamphlets constitute the secondary philosophical background of the American Revolution. Within this polemical literature, the inherited philosophical ideas are set to work on practical issues, resulting not only in remarkable interpretations of the old but also in the genuine origination of new ideas. The pamphleteers were no strangers to philosophy, and often their argumentation, even when most passionate, displays a noteworthy knowledge of philosophy and an exceptional skill in logical dialectic. Thus in 1765, apprehensive of the effects of the Stamp Act on public education, John Adams, under the pseudonym Novanglus, declared in the "Dissertation on the Canon and Feudal Law," first published in the *Boston Gazette*: "A native of America who cannot read and write is as rare an appearance as a Jacobite or a Roman Catholic, i.e. as rare as a comet or an earthquake.—It has been observed that we are all of us, lawyers, divines, politicians and philosophers."[2]

The pamphlets of the American Revolution are filled with citations of philosophical authors. Bacon, Hooker, Machiavelli, Hobbes, Locke, Filmer, Harrington, Bolingbroke, Pufendorf, Grotius, Hoadly, Hutcheson, Lord Kames, Reid, Beattie, Hume, Montesquieu, Rousseau, Burlamaqui, Vattel, Voltaire, Beccaria, Domat—all are mentioned and quoted. Add ancient authors, like Cicero and Aristotle, and the list grows. Fundamentally, the pamphleteers, loyalists as well as patriots, subscribed to the Enlightenment philosophy of natural law and natural rights. As the Harvard historian Bernard Bailyn has correctly remarked: "Writers the colonists took to be opponents of Enlightenment rationalism—primarily Hobbes, Filmer, Sibthorpe, Mandeville, and Manwaring—were denounced as frequently by loyalists as by patriots; but almost never, before 1776, were Locke, Montesquieu, Vattel, Beccaria, Burlamaqui, Voltaire, or even Rousseau."[3] In the pamphlets of the leading American participants—James Otis, John Dickinson, Daniel Dulany, Richard Bland, Josiah Quincy, James Wilson, John Adams, Thomas Jefferson, and Alexander Hamilton, the modern philosophical authors who were most influential during the course of events leading to independence, to judge from the frequency with which they are cited and quoted on the topic of natural law and natural rights, are Hugo Grotius, Samuel Pufendorf, John Locke, and Jean Jacques Burlamaqui.[4] What divided the patriots from the loyalists was a crucial difference of interpretation of natural law and natural rights in regard to the American situation.[5] Both agreed that there exist universal natural principles, accessible to reason, common sense, or moral sense, which govern practical affairs just as the laws of nature, spelled out by Newton, govern the physical universe. Whereas the loyalists held that natural law was incarnate in the British constitution, which lodged sovereignty in Parliament, defined as King, Lords, and Commons together, the American patriots found an imperfection in the British imperial system which denied them their rights since they could not be represented in the British Parliament. Finding no guidance in the philosophers they read, they devised their own solution to the problem; they suggested a political organization which anticipated the British Commonwealth

DECLARATION OF INDEPENDENCE

of Nations, and failing to persuade the King, they reluctantly decided on independence.

Among the pamphleteers writing in England, two philosophers, heirs of Locke's empiricism and political liberalism, contributed significantly to the American side of the argument. They were Richard Price (1723–1791) and Joseph Priestley (1733–1804). Priestley fired the earlier shot.

Scientist, philosopher, theologian, Priestley was also a political radical who sympathized with the American patriots before and during the American Revolution and who, because of his support of the French Revolution, fled mob violence in Birmingham to settle in America, where he personally befriended Thomas Jefferson. As early as 1769, perhaps as a result of his association with Benjamin Franklin, Priestley had published *The Present State of Liberty* in defense of the American side. In 1768 he had published *An Essay on the First Principles of Government*, in which he presented the general political philosophy from which he condemned British and justified American actions. In the 1771 edition of this essay, he declared "that there must have been gross inattention to the very first principles of liberty, to say nothing worse, in the first scheme of taxing the inhabitants of America in the British parliament."[6] In this essay, which bears the influence of Rousseau more than Locke, natural law is wholly swallowed up by natural rights; the focus is, as its subtitle indicates, on the nature and types of liberty.

Priestley's first principles of government are utilitarian. Accepting the theory that men, originally in a state of nature where their individual powers are dissipated "by an attention to a multiplicity of objects," combine to form society and consequently government, Priestley described government as "the great instrument in the hand of divine providence" which makes possible the "progress of the species toward perfection" (pp. 2–3). Embracing the reality of progress, he affirmed that "whatever was the beginning of the world, the end will be glorious and paradisaical, beyond what our imaginations can now conceive" (p. 5). And to evaluate the performance of governments he raised high the utilitarian standard in terms which Jeremy Bentham is reputed to have applauded: "the good and happiness of the members, that is the majority of the members of any state, is the great standard by which every thing relating to that state must finally be determined" (p. 13). Distinguishing the types of liberty, Priestley defined political liberty as consisting "in the power, which

the members of the state reserve to themselves, of arriving at the
public offices, or, at least, of having votes in the nomination of
those who fill them" and civil liberty as "that power over their own
actions, which the members of the state reserve to themselves, and
which their officers must not infringe" (p. 9; italics removed).
Since he declined to affirm that "the good of mankind requires a
state of the most perfect political liberty" (p. 15), he defended the
mixed British constitution, which contains an hereditary monarch
and Lords in addition to an elective House of Commons. But he
emphasized that all office holders, including kings and nobles, are
servants of the people and hence are "accountable to the people for
the discharge of their respective offices" (p. 23). Hence he insisted
that the people have an inalienable right to punish and even depose
their kings. He did not think that the people should or would
lightly exercise their right to revolt. Too many difficulties surround
the endeavor to redress grievances by force of arms, so that
"nothing but very great oppression" could incite people to hostile
opposition to their government. "The bulk of a people," he
continued, "seldom so much as *complain* without reason, because
they never think of complaining till they *feel*; so that, in all cases
of dissatisfaction with government, it is most probable, that the
people are injured" (p. 32). Priestley, therefore, regarded the
revolutions against Charles I and James II and the execution of the
former to have been just. Against the objection that a deposed
monarch cannot be tried and punished except by appeal to *ex post
facto* laws which are, by consequence, unjust, Priestley appealed to
principles, pertaining to the nature and ends of society, which are
"prior to the establishment of any laws whatever" (p. 37). Worse
than the foreign invader, a king or other magistrate who subverts
the laws of his country, Priestley contended, commits the most
atrocious sort of crime and deserves to be resisted, deposed, and
punished. "In a case, therefore, of this highly criminal nature, *salus
populi suprema est lex.* That must be done which the good of the
whole requires" (p. 38). Priestley esteemed it "a maxim, than
which nothing is more true, that every government, in its original
principles, and antecedent to its present form, is an equal republic;
and, consequently, that every man, when he comes to be sensible of
his natural rights, and to feel his own importance, will consider
himself as fully equal to any other person whatsoever" (pp. 40–41).
Men delegate their powers to magistrates and legislators, who are
then held accountable. As Priestley declared, "No man can be
supposed to resign his natural liberty, but on *conditions*" (p. 44).

In regard to civil liberty, Priestley subordinated it to the public good. He maintained that, since "the happiness of the whole community is the ultimate end of government ... all claims of individuals inconsistent with the public good are absolutely null and void" (p. 57). He wrote: "The very idea of property, or right of any kind, is founded upon a regard to the general good of the society, under whose protection it is enjoyed; and nothing is properly a *man's own*, but what general rules, which have for their object the good of the whole, give to him" (p. 41). Aware of the "real difficulty in determining what general rules respecting the extent of the power of government, or governors, are most conducive to the public good" (p. 57), Priestley proposed that the extent of government be restrained and in effect gave the widest latitude to civil liberty compatible with the public good as already known. He wrote: "We are so little capable of arguing *a priori* in matters of government, that it should seem, experiments only can determine how far this power of the legislature ought to extend; and it should likewise seem, that, till a sufficient number of experiments have been made, it becomes the wisdom of the civil magistracy to take as little upon its hands as possible" (p. 58).

Upon the same general principles of liberty and government, Richard Price (1723–1791), a moral philosopher whose distinctively original theory was constructed upon revised Lockean epistemological conceptions and who wrote widely and effectively on contemporary political and economic problems, published his *Observations on the Nature of Civil Liberty* (London, 1776), followed by *Additional Observations on the Nature and Value of Civil Liberty* (London, 1777).[7] Large parts of both these pamphlets are devoted to analyzing and attacking British policies against America. Price parted from Priestley, who was a thoroughgoing materialistic determinist and who endeavored to refute him, inasmuch as Price grounded all types of liberty in a metaphysical kind which he termed "physical liberty" and defined as "the principle of Spontaneity, or Self-determination, which consistutes us *Agents*; or which gives us a command over our actions, rendering them properly *ours*, and not effects of the operation of any foreign cause" (I, p. 3). On this basis other types of liberty are distinguished, of which moral liberty and civil liberty merit special attention. Price defined moral liberty as "the power of following, in all circumstances, our sense of right and wrong, or of acting in conformity to our reflecting and moral principles, without being controuled [*sic*] by any contrary principles;" and civil liberty as "the power of a *Civil Society* or *State* to govern itself by its own discretion; or by laws of its own making, without being subject to any foreign discretion, or to the impositions of any extraneous will or power" (I, p. 3). While Price accepted Priestley's meanings in defining and distinguishing civil liberty as distinct from political liberty, he employed the terms somewhat differently (II, p. 13, note a). For Price civil liberty is a more generic concept than it is for Priestley; it subsumes three subtypes of liberty:

> The Liberty of the *citizen*—The liberty of the *government*—And the liberty of the *community.*—A *citizen* is free when the power of commanding his own conduct and the quiet possession of his life, person, property, and good name are *secured* to him by being his own legislator. ...—A *government* is free when constituted in such a manner as to give this *security.*—And the freedom of a community or nation is the same among nations, that the freedom of a citizen is among his fellow-citizens.—It is not, therefore, ... the mere possession of Liberty that denominates a citizen or a community free; but that security for the possession of it which arises from ... a free government ...; and which takes place, where there exists no power that can take it away. (II, pp. 13–14).

Within the context of argumentation over the principles at issue in the American Revolution, Richard Price formulated a maxim customarily ascribed to Immanuel Kant, the maxim of the autonomy of the human agent in morality and also in any political system based on moral foundations: "In every free state every man is his own Legislator" (I, p. 6). When the state is too large for the direct participation of every individual in the making and executing of the laws, liberty is served only by a system of representation in which law-makers and magistrates exercise powers delegated by the citizens on conditions of trust. Lacking the advantage of Kant's later thought, Price reached his position by drawing upon earlier seventeenth and eighteenth century thinkers: Locke, Molyneux, Hutcheson, Hume, Rousseau, and Montesquieu. He applied their philosophies to the developing American Revolution. Some highlights are noteworthy.

The basic line of argumentation, raised by the American colonists during the Stamp Act crisis, and adopted by Price throughout his pro-American pamphlets, was the Whig contention, rooted in Lockean principles, that the right to property is incompatible with taxation without consent or representation. Otherwise there was nothing a man could call his own. Since the American colonists were not and, by virtue of the realities of geography in the eighteenth century, could not be represented in Parliament, they should not be taxed by Parliament. During the course of the revolutionary epoch, this claim was generalized into the thesis that Parliament had no authority over the colonies whatever, because to be bound by laws to which one does not consent or in the making of which one does not participate is tantamount to slavery. Here Price cited the pamphlet of the Irish Protestant, member of Parliament, mathematician, and correspondent of John Locke—William Molyneux. For Molyneux's pamphlet, *The Case of Ireland's Being Bound by Acts of Parliament in England Stated* (Dublin, 1698), had mixed considerations of history and law with Lockean principles of political philosophy to repudiate the authority of the English Parliament over Ireland on constitutional grounds which three-quarters of a century later the American patriots retraced,[8] though often disclaiming any parallel between their situation and Ireland's. Further, Price quoted from Francis Hutcheson's *System of Moral Philosophy* to the effect that it is unnatural for "a large society, sufficient for all the good purposes of an independent political union," to remain "subject to the direction and government of a distant body of men who know not sufficiently the circumstances and exigencies of this society;" or to suppose that "this society [is] obliged to be governed solely for the benefit of a distant country."[9] As Hutcheson continued in Price's quotation, "it is not easy to imagine there can be any foundation for it in justice or equity. The insisting on *old claims* and *tacit conventions*, to extend civil power over distant nations, and form grand unwieldy empires, without regard to the obvious maxims of humanity, has been one great source of human misery" (II, p. 75, note a). Price amplified:

> In the section from whence this quotation is taken, Dr. Hutcheson discusses the question, "When colonies have a right to be released from the dominion of the parent state?" And his general sentiment seems to be, that they acquire such a right, "Whenever they so increased in numbers and strength, as to be sufficient by themselves for all the good ends of a political union."—Such a decision given by a wise man, long before we had any disputes with the colonies, deserves, I think, particular notice. (II, pp. 75, note a–76).

So firm was Price's conviction that participation in one's own government either directly or through representation is the *sine qua non* of liberty that he believed that peace in Europe, if it is to be attained without the despotic hegemony of one nation-state over the others, requires the establishment of a confederation under the governance of a European Senate in which all the member states would be represented and which would have legislative authority over objects of their common interests (I, pp. 8–9). Furthermore, he proposed this model for the political organization of the British Empire—a Senate superior to the British Parliament and to the colonial assemblies, but in which they would participate through representation (I, p. 28).

As the American side, including native patriots and British Whigs and radicals, converged in the contention that the colonies should not be subordinate to Parliament, the Tory side, including American loyalists and British Tories and Whigs, hardened in their position that in a well-ordered political system there is but one supreme power and in the British system that power is Parliament. The political doctrine of the absolute supremacy of Parliament received its most influential statement in the *Commentaries* of Sir William Blackstone, whom the colonists highly respected and therefore, as in the case of James Wilson, set out painstakingly to refute on this point. Having cast off the authority of Parliament over them, the colonists confronted the question of the mode of their subordination to Great Britain. And in pamphlets as early as the Stamp Act crisis—e.g., by Richard Bland in 1766—it was maintained that the colonies were linked to the mother country merely by their allegiance to the British monarch. This doctrine is well articulated in Thomas Jefferson's remarkable pamphlet, *A Summary View of the Rights of British America* (Williamsburg, 1774). Writing "in the language of truth" and avoiding "those expressions of servility which would persuade his majesty that we are asking favors and not rights," Thomas Jefferson addressed the king as "chief magistrate of the British Empire," presenting "complaints which are excited by many unwarrantable incroachments and usurpations, attempted to be made by the legislature of one part of the empire, upon those rights which God and the laws have given equally to all."[10] The vehemence of Jefferson's language in subordinating the king to the sovereignty of the people is noteworthy. He described the king as "no more than the chief officer of the people, appointed by the laws, and circumscribed with definite powers, to assist in working the great machine of government erected for their use, and consequently subject to their superintendance" (p. 121). And Jefferson went further still, placing blame on the king as well as on Parliament for infringements of the rights of British Americans, criticizing "the conduct of his majesty" and marking "out his deviations from the line of duty" (p. 129).

It was the historical role of an Englishman, Thomas Paine, only recently settled in America, to smash the idolatry of monarchy as the tenuous link, accepted by American political theory in 1775, between the American colonies and Great Britain. His pamphlet, *Common Sense* (Philadelphia, 1776), presented the first unqualified argument for American independence; it spread like wildfire throughout the colonies. As introductory to his argument for American independence, Paine first discussed the origin and design of government in general and subjected to severe criticism the much vaunted British constitution, attacking the monarchy and hereditary succession. In the entire British constitution he found only the materials of the House of Commons praiseworthy. This political philosophy, which Paine crudely but vigorously stated, is unoriginal republicanism harking back to the Puritan Revolution in England and kept alive by a long line of Commonwealthmen from that time to the American Revolution.[11] Paine's message superbly fitted the times, dispelling at last the colonists' obeisance to royalty. As he exclaimed:

> ... where, say some, is the King of America? I'll tell you, friends, he reigns above, and does not make havoc of mankind like the Royal Brute of Great Britain ... [I]n America the law is king. For as in absolute governments the King is law, so in free countries the law ought to be king; and there ought to be no other.[12]

The Declaration of Independence was therefore anticipated by the patriot pamphlets, expressing a philosophy which stems from European antecedents. Containing an implicit theory of the British Empire, it enunciates a general philosophy of government, both under the aegis of "the Laws of Nature and of Nature's God" which are invoked in its opening paragraph.

The Declaration of Independence implies that the British Empire is, in the words of Carl Becker, "a confederation of free peoples submitting themselves to the same King by an original compact voluntarily entered into, and terminable, in the case of any member at the will of the people concerned."[13] This theory is adumbrated in the entire document, surfacing fragmentarily in the first paragraph and presupposed by the long list of specific charges against George III. Furthermore, it was actually stated in the rough draft of the Declaration, in its penultimate paragraph, which says: "[W]e have reminded them [our British brethren] ... that in constituting our several forms of government, we [Americans] had adopted one common king, thereby laying a foundation for perpetual league & amity with them: but that submission to their parliament was no part of our constitution, nor ever in idea, if history may be credited."[14]

The Declaration of Independence states felicitously its general philosophy of government in the second paragraph. It presents the natural principles of politics which to the enlightened mind, Tory or patriot, seemed self-evident in the eighteenth century. It proclaims the values of human equality derived from God, of individual natural rights to life, liberty, and the pursuit of happiness, and of the people's right to be governed only on their own consent, to resist and revolt against a government which violates their rights, and to institute new government. The phraseology is so Lockean that its author has been accused of plagiarism, but as Morton White has pointed out in his penetrating interpretation of American philosophical thought, *Science and Sentiment in America*, Jefferson believed that he apprehended his moral and political truths not by means of Lockean reason but by the moral sense, not by the head but by the heart.[15] Furthermore, to the charges of plagiarism, Jefferson, while denying that he had copied from any book or pamphlet when writing the Declaration, insisted that he never intended to invent new ideas or to express sentiments never before expressed but "to place before mankind the common sense of the subject, in terms so plain and firm as to command their assent ... Neither aiming at originality of principles or sentiments, nor yet copied from any particular and previous writings, it was intended to be an expression of the American mind."[16]

NOTES

1. See my article, "The Philosophical Background of the American Revolution," *Southwestern Journal of Philosophy*, V (1974), 179–202.

2. Reprinted in Thomas Hollis, ed., *The True Sentiments of America* (London, 1766), p. 126.

3. Bernard Bailyn, *The Ideological Origins of the American Revolution* (Cambridge, Mass., Harvard University Press, 1967), p. 29.

4. See my paper. "Natural Law in American Revolutionary Thought," Review of Metaphysics, XXX (1977), 686–714.

5. For a fascinating revelation of the common ground and critical differences in fundamental moral and political philosophy between the American patriots and the loyalists, see Thomas Hutchinson, "A Dialogue between an American and a European Englishman (1768)," edited by Bernard Bailyn, *Perspectives in American*

History, XI (1975), 343–410. An exception is the loyalist Jonathan Boucher; he rejected the Enlightenment doctrine of natural law and natural rights and favored Filmer over Locke. See his *View of the Causes and Consequences of the American Revolution* (London, 1797), especially p. 530.

6. Joseph Priestley, *An Essay on the First Principles of Government; and on the Nature of Political, Civil, and Religious Liberty, including Remarks on Dr. Brown's Code of 'Education', and on Dr. Balguy's Sermon on Church Authority* (2nd ed.; London, 1771), p. 23. All citations incorporated in the text are to this edition.

7. Bound together and published as Richard Price, *Two Tracts on Civil Liberty, The War with America, and The Debts and Finances of the Kingdom: with A General Introduction and Supplement* (London, 1778; reprinted New York, Da Capo Press, 1972). Citations will be made to this edition, with the earlier essay designated as I and the later as II.

8. See Charles Howard McIlwain, *The American Revolution: A Constitutional Interpretation* (New York, The Macmillan Company, 1924), pp. 45ff.

9. Francis Hutcheson, *System of Moral Philosophy* (London, 1755), II, Chap. 8, pp. 308–309.

10. Julian P. Boyd, ed., *The Papers of Thomas Jefferson* (Princeton, N.J., Princeton University Press, 1950), I, 121. Citations to this pamphlet are to the Boyd edition.

11. See Caroline Robbins, *The Eighteenth-Century Commonwealthman* (Cambridge, Mass., Harvard University Press, 1961).

12. Thomas Paine, "Common Sense," in Carl Van Doren, ed., *The Writings of Thomas Paine* (New York, The Modern Library, n.d.), pp. 37–38.

13. Carl Becker, *The Declaration of Independence* (New York, Vintage Books, 1958), p. 130.

14. Julian P. Boyd, *op. cit.*, I, 426.

15. Morton White, *Science and Sentiment in America* (New York, Oxford University Press, 1972), p. 67. See also my paper, "Head and Heart, The Mind of Thomas Jefferson," presented as a lecture at the Institute of American Philosophy, Fordham University, September 23, 1976, and to be published by Fordham University Press.

16. Carl Becker, *op. cit.*, pp. 25–26. See my paper, "The Declaration of Independence as an 'Expression of the American Mind,'" *Revue internationale de philosophie* nos. 121–22 (1977), 401–437. See also Robert Ginsberg, "Early British Controversy on the Declaration of Independence," *Studies on Voltaire and the Eighteenth Century*, CLI–CLV (1976), 851–893.

RELIGIOUS LIBERALISM AND THE FOUNDING FATHERS

NICHOLAS GIER

University of Idaho, Moscow, Idaho

"It does me no injury for my neighbor to say there are twenty gods, or no god. It neither picks my pocket nor breaks my leg."
—Thomas Jefferson, "Notes on Virginia."

"Among all our presidents from Washington downward, not one was a professor of religion, at least not of more than Unitarianism."
—Bird Wilson, Episcopal Minister, October, 1831.

INTRODUCTION

Many misconceptions abound concerning the relation of religious belief and the American Revolution. Some view the birth of the American Republic as completely compatible with the Christian religion and as the culminating event of Christian history. While it is true that many conservative Christians were patriots—John Jay, Patrick Henry, Alexander Hamilton, and Samuel Adams to name a few—many others openly supported the British cause. In other words, there were many earnest Christians who saw the Revolution as contrary to God's will. In his "Tory Believers: Which Higher Loyalty?" Mark Noll has ably shown that "Tory believers" were not merely confined to Anglicans, but also included Methodists, Baptists, Presbyterians, and Congregationalists.[1] Using such arguments as Paul's injunction "to be subject to principalities and powers, to obey magistrates" (Titus 3:1), Christian loyalists claimed solid support from Scripture in refusing to engage in a political revolution which they thought would end in anarchy.

The other major figures of the American Revolution were not, contrary to popular belief, religious conservatives. But many of today's liberals go too far in calling them atheists, agnostics, or even deists.[2] George Washington, John Adams, Thomas Jefferson, James Madison, Thomas Paine, and Benjamin Franklin were religious liberals who were heavily influenced by the new science and rational philosophy of the European Enlightenment. Although each of these men was a believer in God, their religious philosophy as a whole went contrary to the conventional religion of the day.

The term "deist" is a common label attached to liberal religious thinkers of the eighteenth century. The fact is, however, that with the exception of Paine, none of our subjects called himself a deist in the sense of English or French deism, that theological movement in Europe which is generally assumed to have started with Herbert of Cherbury and ended with Voltaire. When referring to his own religious views, Jefferson uses deism as the simple Latin homologue of theism. In the letter to Benjamin Rush, Jefferson states that the Jews' "system was deism; that is, the belief in one only God."[3] He goes on to argue that Jesus "corrected the deism of the Jews" by giving "juster notions of [God's] attributes and government" and by providing a superior ethics. In his famous correspondence with Adams he refers favorably to the "deism taught us by Jesus of Nazareth."[4] Standing in stark contrast were the continental deists (plus Paine), who would have nothing to do with the Bible, Jesus, or his teachings.

In his *Autobiography* Franklin relates that he was converted to deism at an early age but later gave it up, mainly due to its inability to distinguish vice from virtue. Franklin was a thoroughly practical philosopher and could not accept what he claimed to be the empty "metaphysical reasoning" of the deists.[5] Adams, although definitely a religious liberal, explicitly argues against the views of Bolingbroke, Blount, and Voltaire. Of Bolingbroke he says that "his religion is pompous folly; and his abuse of the Christian religion is as superficial as it is impious."[6]

In 1704 Samuel Clarke, a staunch critic of deism, was able to delineate at least four types: (1) deists who denied providence and claimed that God had no relationship to the world except for its creation and predetermined laws; (2) deists who denied providence in moral affairs but allowed it with regard to natural events; (3) those who believed that God did have a role in human lives but held no belief in an afterlife; and (4) those who believed in providence in morals and nature and an afterlife.[7] The most widespread notion about what deism is corresponds most closely to the strict deism of (1). If this is true, then it would be inadvisable to call any of our subjects deists, because the evidence places them squarely in category (4). It is clear that the effects of the Enlightenment on American thought were mostly limited to a moderate phase in which Lockean empiricism and Newtonian science were readily reconciled with some form of liberal religion. If we are to call them deists, our subjects (except for Paine) were "constructive" deists rather than "critical" deists, i.e., those who were openly anti-Christian and anti-Bible.

All in all I believe that the label "religious liberal" is a far better way of characterizing the religious thought of these founding fathers. I am of course using the term "liberal" in its original sense as derived from the Latin adjective *liberalis*, which means "pertaining to a free person." Classical liberalism is the general philosophy that opposed the authoritarian governments of eighteenth century Europe. The leaders of both the American and French Revolutions represent the first full embodiment of this liberalism. In the area of religion this liberalism took the form of free and unconventional thought about God; and, as we shall see, a rejection of most of the doctrines of orthodox Christianity. It also meant an ethical view which was heavily influenced by European free-thinking and which had a strong utilitarian bent. Our subjects definitely preferred reason and utility to revelation in deciding matters of religion and ethics.

The religious liberalism of these founding fathers has four main characteristics. The first is a belief in God, but not necessarily the God of orthodox Christianity. Among the religious liberals I shall discuss, the concept of God ranged from the God of Nature of Thomas Paine, through the impersonal Providence of Washington, Jefferson, and Franklin, to the Biblical God of John Adams. Because their God was unorthodox, some of these men were called "atheists." This of course was totally undeserved and unfair.

One of the most predominant aspects of the liberal god was its impersonality and indefinite attributes. Scriptural and doctrinal characterizations of God as a person with specified attributes were rejected in favor of a concept of God derived from human reason. Although firm in their insistence on the use of reason in matters of religion, the liberals were also keenly aware of its limits. The power of human reason does allow us to secure an argument for the existence of God (usually the teleological argument), but it does not allow us to speculate about his particular attributes. This quote from Paine is a good example of the preceding point: "We can know God only through his works. We cannot have a conception of any one attribute, but by following some principle that leads to it. We have only a confused idea of his power, if we have not the means of comprehending something of its immensity. We can have no idea of his wisdom, but by knowing the order and manner in which it acts."[8]

The liberals contented themselves with a general notion of God's justice, omniscience, and omnipotence. Included in this doctrine of God is the distinction between particular and general providence, a concept best expressed in the works of Bolingbroke, who was thoroughly read by Jefferson, Adams, Franklin, and perhaps Washington. The doctrine of particular providence, that God was intimately involved in caring for each individual in detail, seemed to threaten human free-will. Seeing this danger to human autonomy, Bolingbroke proposed that God lays out the general framework for human action but does not interfere at an individual level. In our section on Washington we will find that the first president definitely believed in this view.

A second characteristic of the liberal view was grounds for despair and rejection among the orthodox. The liberals held a strict separation between Christian doctrine and Christian ethics. De-emphasizing adherence to doctrine or creed, they held the fundamental ethical principal that Christians as well as non-Christians should accept one another and act virtuously. It is not mere affirmation of dogma that makes a person religious; rather, it is a person's ethical and moral conduct. This led the liberals to the inevitable conclusion that it is possible for an atheist to be moral.

None of the liberals believed in the major doctrines of orthodox Christianity. As we will see in subsequent sections, they rejected some or all of the following doctrines: the Trinity, the divinity of Jesus, the virgin birth, the Bible as the literal word of God, predestination, Hell, Satan, and *creatio ex nihilo.* The only doctrine, other than a belief in God, that they held was the immortality of the soul and some sort of afterlife. Even with regard to the latter, we find some curious variations on the traditional belief. In his most sober moments, Jefferson, like Locke and Bolingbroke, decided that the question of an afterlife of rewards and punishments could not be decided by reason alone. On the face of it, it appeared to be an offense to God's perfection and its only possible value was to incite humans to do good deeds in this life.

Adams was much more traditional in his belief in another life but, surprisingly enough, speculated that it would not be eternal. At the age of eighty Adams stated: "I believe, too, in a future state of rewards and punishments, but not eternal."[9] Franklin, arguing from the conservation of matter (both Jefferson and he were thorough-going materialists), firmly believed in an afterlife—one however not of bliss or perfection but "with all the inconveniences human life is liable to ..."[10] Paine's view of the afterlife is perhaps the most peculiar: "My own opinion is, that those whose lives have been spent in doing good and endeavoring to make their fellow-mortals happy ... *will be happy hereafter*; and that the very wicked will meet with some punishment. But those who are neither good nor bad, or are too insignificant for notice, will be dropped entirely."[11] For thinkers who were supposedly conscious of the limits of reason, some of this speculation was definitely out of bounds.

The third characteristic of a religious liberal is an unqualified affirmation of the separation of church and state. Our founding fathers had fresh knowledge of the disastrous effects of European governments which chose to dictate religious belief and support one religion against others. Therefore the words "God" and "Christianity" do not appear anywhere in the Constitution, primarily because of the influence of these religious liberals at the Constitutional Convention of 1787. The Constitution (as amended) explicitly states that no office holder shall submit to a religious test and that no church may receive any form of support from the federal government.

The fourth characteristic which epitomizes religious liberalism is a fundamental belief in religious liberty and religious tolerance. While it is true that many early Americans were supportive of religious tolerance for the various forms of Christianity, it was only our religious liberals, especially Franklin, Jefferson, and Madison, who fought for and eventually attained full religious freedom for atheists and non-Christian believers. According to our founding fathers, America should be a country where peoples of all faiths, including those who profess no religious belief, can live in peace and mutual benefit. Full religious liberty means not only freedom *of* religion, but freedom *from* religion. James Madison summed up this ideal in this apt motto: "Conscience is the most sacred of all property."[12]

BENJAMIN FRANKLIN (1706–1790)

Benjamin Franklin was a leading disciple of the European Enlightenment and America's first Renaissance man. He was a person of complete versatility, who made original contributions in many areas of science and humanities. As to matters of religion, Franklin was America's first great liberal. Preferring to study on Sundays, he seldom went to church. When he did attend, he was generally disappointed, because, as he observed in his *Autobio-*

graphy, the preachers seemed more intent upon making people good Calvinists than good citizens.

In the Pennsylvania Constitution of 1776, there were clauses concerning religion to which Franklin took strong exception. The document contained a general statement of religious freedom and tolerance, but it was the specific qualifications for office holders that angered Franklin. An official was compelled to "acknowledge the being of God," and to affirm the following: "I do believe in one God, the Creator and Governor of the Universe, the rewarder of the good and the punisher of the wicked; and I do acknowledge the Scriptures of the Old and New Testament to be given by divine inspiration."[13] Franklin lost this battle at the convention and had to be content with a compromise over the status of Roman Catholics.

Franklin had doubts about orthodox Christianity very early in life. "I was scarce fifteen," he states, "when, after doubting by turns of several points, as I found them disputed in the different books I read, I began to doubt of Revelation itself."[14] He did not accept the Trinity or the deity of Christ.[15] He thought, like many religious liberals, that Jesus was a great moral teacher.

He refused to believe the Calvinist doctrine of the depravity of humankind which Jonathan Edwards had expressed so well as an "ineffable wickedness" and "an abyss infinitely deeper than Hell." Franklin believed that humans were basically good, albeit fallible, and that they could lead a good, moral life with the aid of their own reason and with a minimum of divine intervention. What he found most lacking in the sermons of the day was an emphasis on morality and good deeds. For him a religious faith which was not productive of good works was worthless. In a letter to Joseph Huey, he states: "I mean real good works, works of kindness, charity, mercy, and public spirit; not holiday-keeping, sermon-reading or hearing, performing church ceremonies, or making long prayers, filled with flatteries and compliments, despised even by wise men, and much less capable of pleasing the Deity."[16]

Franklin did believe in God, whom he addressed in his modest prayers as "O powerful Goodness, bountiful Father, merciful Guide." He argued that every person has a natural inclination to acknowledge the "infinitive power and Creator of nature." The worship of God should elevate one to "rational joy and pleasure" and to good works. Franklin apparently includes the word "rational" here to distinguish his view from more emotional forms of religion which stress God's total grace and humankind's total helplessness. Franklin believed that this type of religion tended to lead people away from the world and to become indifferent to what happens.

The otherworldliness of the creeds of his day was directly antithetical to Franklin's emphasis on the good, rational life here and now. If Franklin were alive today, he would definitely be a "modernist" and a proponent of the "social gospel," the belief that the role of religion is to transform the immediate lives of all people, whatever their place in life and whatever their religion.

In his writings, Franklin displayed the ultimate in religious tolerance. He used freely the term "God," but in his famous "Creed and Liturgy" there is no mention of Jesus Christ. He felt that the division of religion into many competing denominations was unfortunate. This state of affairs had divided people one against the other and had prevented them from confronting the real challenges of humankind.

There is a famous dictum by Franklin that shows the real core of his religious views. It reads: "... Vicious actions are not hurtful because they are forbidden, but forbidden because they are hurtful. ..."[17] This is a fundamental criticism of orthodox religion, be it Christian, Muslim, or Jewish. A person obeys the laws of God, not merely because they are commanded on authority alone, but because human reason sees the basic goodness and utility in following those laws.

Franklin's view on obedience to law is fundamental for the protection of human liberty, the main theme of the American Revolution. The American Constitution, with its provisions for a freely elected Congress and a system of checks and balances, eliminates the rule of an absolute sovereign who would force compliance to laws which were irrational and arbitrary. Franklin seems to imply the same for the rule and law of God. God was not an absolute sovereign and did not create humans so weak and so morally destitute that they would meekly submit to his arbitrary choices (e.g., predestination). No, God created us free, autonomous, and rational; and he made laws which are compatible with human reason. In the same way that we tend to agree and comply with the laws of Congress, we should agree and comply with the rational legislation of God. In fact, according to the English philosopher John Locke, who strongly influenced our founding fathers, the laws of the state should reflect the natural laws of God.

Jonathan Edwards, the great American Calvinist, often used thunder and lightning as an example of God's arbitrary use of power. The contrasting image is Franklin, rationalist and scientist, standing in a storm with a kite and a key on the string. Edwards' world was an irrational one in which people found themselves unfree, dependent, and humbled; but people were self-reliant, inquisitive, and proud in the rational world of Ben Franklin.

THOMAS PAINE (1737–1809)

Although not a native American, Thomas Paine did more for the success of the American Revolution than any other thinker. As Lafayette once said, "Free America without Thomas Paine is unthinkable."[18] Practically every literate American read Paine's "Common Sense." The illiterate, among whom were many of Washington's soldiers, were indirectly inspired by it. Paine was truly revolutionary America's *vox populi*.

A later book by Paine, *Age of Reason: Being an Investigation of True and Fabulous Theology*, was also widely read in America, but this time Americans, in an incredible display of religious intolerance, turned against the great patriot. Paine quickly realized that, contrary to his prediction, the revolution for complete religious liberty and freedom of thought had not followed upon the heels of the political revolution. Even a religious liberal like John Adams rejected him; the sponsor for his return to America, Thomas Jefferson, shunned him out of political expediency; and his own Quakers refused to bury him.

Paine's reputation did not improve as Americans, who knew *Age of Reason*, looked back in retrospect. Theodore Roosevelt called Paine "that dirty little atheist" and provided this additional description: "There are infidels and infidels, but Paine belonged to the variety ... that apparently esteems a bladder of dirty water as the proper weapon with which to assail Christianity."[19]

If one reads *Age of Reason*, one must agree that Paine's criticism of Christianity is not a model of diplomatic scholarship. The tone of the book is aptly portrayed in this statement concerning the virgin birth: "... Jesus Christ, begotten, they say, by a ghost, whom they call holy, on the body of a woman, engaged in marriage, and after married ... a theory which, speaking for myself, I hesitate not to disbelieve, and to say, is as fabulous and as false as God is true."[20]

Behind irreverent rhetoric like the above, there are some interesting and, for some who read it, compelling points. First, Paine makes it clear that he is not an atheist. In fact, he claims that his book is designed to counter the effects of atheism. In his opinion, Christianity is founded on such poor arguments that it, rather than subduing atheism, unwittingly promotes its spread in the world.

The first axiom of Paine's theology is that there is God and his creation and "no more."[21] What he meant by this "no more" is this: no idolatry of the Bible as the Word of God, no deification of Jesus the man and moral teacher, no miracles, no angels, no Hell, no original sin, no Trinity and no Virgin Mary. All of these additions to the first axiom are erroneous or mythical, and are actually detrimental to the cause of religion.

Perhaps the most interesting points that Paine makes are the objections he raises against the concept of Revelation. Orthodox Christians take the entire Bible as pure Revelation, a direct and immediate message from God. Paine observes, however, that most of the Bible is straightforward historical fact or fancy that is not of this character at all. When Revelation is purported to have occurred, as in the case of Moses, God was speaking to one person and one person only. Revelation is always in the first person and therefore it is, by legal definition, only hearsay if the message goes beyond the single person.

For Paine true Revelation is nature itself. Human language cannot serve as God's medium; it is too fragile and inadequate. Nature, however, is "an ever-existing original which every man can read. It cannot be forged; it cannot be counterfeited; it cannot be lost; it cannot be altered; it cannot be suppressed. It does not depend upon the will of man whether it shall be published or not; it publishes itself from one end of the earth to the other. It preaches to all nations and to all worlds; and this word of God reveals to man all that is necessary for man to know of God."[22]

The full implication of this theory is Paine's declaration that the true language of religion was the language of science. Paine sums up his religious creed in this statement: "The Almighty Lecturer, by displaying the principles of science in the structure of the universe, has invited man to study and imitation. It is as if He said to the inhabitants of this globe, that we call ours, 'I have made an earth for man to dwell upon, and I have rendered the starry heavens visible, to teach him science and the arts. He can now provide for his own comfort, and learn from my munificence to all, to be kind to each other.' "[23]

Such was the new gospel of the great patriot, Thomas Paine. But because of this new gospel, Paine was vilified by a people whom he had helped to become free.

GEORGE WASHINGTON (1732–1799)

More myths have been created about our first president than about any other American. Mason Locke Weems, an Anglican minister, was the inventor of the notorious cherry tree story and many of the tales pertaining to Washington's religiosity. Professor Paul Boller of the University of Massachusetts has laid to rest all of these fabrications in his excellent book, *George Washington and Religion*. I am indebted to his thorough research for some of the major points of this section.

Washington was not an intellectual but a man of action. He was not naturally given to deep reflection or detailed analysis of thought or belief. While Adams and Jefferson spent their last years reading philosophy and theology, and frequently writing to each other about it, Washington retired to the country and occupied himself with strictly non-intellectual pursuits. It was James Madison's opinion that Washington never "attended to the arguments for Christianity, and for the different systems of religion, [n]or in fact ... [had he] formed definite opinions on the subject."[24]

There is virtually no evidence in Washington's writings to indicate a firm commitment to the Christian religion. He always has something positive to say about religion in general. But there are a few remarks in his private correspondence and diaries which have a touch of cynicism. He once wrote in his diary that he would have liked to have collected his rents on Sundays, but he declined because the people living on his land were "apparently very religious."[25] Writing to Lafayette with regard to religious toleration, he states: "Being no bigot myself, I am disposed to indulge the professors of Christianity in the church with that road to Heaven, which to them shall seem the most direct, plainest, easiest, and least liable to exception."[26]

It seems that the only deep interest Washington had in the direction of religion was an enthusiasm for freemasonry. He was a nominal Episcopalian who attended church irregularly (ceasing after his retirement) and who never participated in Communion. While president he was once openly criticized from the pulpit by his pastor, James Abercrombie, for setting a poor example by not celebrating the Lord's Supper.[27]

Although Washington never refers to any specific readings in philosophy or theology, his religious liberalism is clearly apparent in numerous references made to the deity in his writings and speeches. In all of his voluminous writing only once does he speak of Jesus Christ and this single incident, a speech to the Delaware Indians, was most likely penned by an aide more orthodox than Washington. On the manuscript of another speech to Indian leaders, we can clearly see the word God crossed out and the phrase "the Great Spirit above" in Washington's handwriting.[28]

Washington never refers to a personal God—the most frequent appellation being "Providence," one of the most impersonal terms for the divine. The doctrine of general providence, outlined in the introduction, is clearly implied in many of the passages interpreting historical events as divinely ordained. It is always the patriots in general, not specific individuals, who are guided by God's providence. There is a certain amount of fatalism also embodied in much of this writing on God's actions in the world. A God that gave specific responses to all human petitioners would not be the God of reason or the creator of nature's inexorable laws. The general plan is somehow set and it would be irrational for God to change it. This view does not appear to change throughout Washington's life. In 1776 he stated: "I will not lament or repine at any acts of Providence, because I am in great measure a convert to Mr. Pope's opinion that whatever is, is right ...";[29] and in 1797 he still agreed: "But [it] is not for man to scan the wisdom of providence. The best he can do is to submit to its decrees. Reason, Religion, and Philosophy teaches us to do this. ..."[30]

Dr. Benjamin Rush, medical scientist and friend of Franklin, reported to Thomas Jefferson that upon leaving office Washington met with a group of clergy who submitted a number of questions for Washington to answer. Since he had never made any public affirmation of Christianity, one of their questions was whether or not he was a Christian. Washington very kindly answered all of the questions except that crucial one.[31]

The tolerance that Washington showed for all Christian denominations was another sign of his religious liberalism. There is the famous incident when Washington prevented his soldiers from burning the pope in effigy on Guy Fawkes Day. When once looking for new servants, Washington emphasized that any good workmen would be acceptable, be they "Mohametans, Jews, Christians of any sect, or ... atheists."[32]

Washington firmly believed in the separation of church and state. Probably the most striking and controversial expression of this principle, in which Washington played a part, appears in the Treaty of Tripoli. Article Eleven of this treaty begins: "As the government of the United States is not in any sense founded on the Christian religion. ..."[33] Later on, in times of religious emotionalism, this article raised many eyebrows among the orthodox. But in 1796, a time of religious rationalism, President Washington approved it and the treaty was ratified by the Senate in 1797 without a single objection.[34]

All in all, the evidence shows that George Washington was a religious liberal who believed in God as impersonal Providence. He probably did not believe in any of the doctrines of Christian orthodoxy. As Paul Boller concludes, "If Washington was a Christian, he was surely a Protestant of the most liberal persuasion."[35] In a famous sermon delivered in 1831, Bird Wilson declared that Washington was no more than a Unitarian.[36]

During the early 1950's, definitely an era of religious emotionalism, Congress passed without debate a bill authorizing the construction of a "Capital Prayer Room." One of the religious relics of this edifice is a stained-glass window portraying George Washington kneeling in prayer at Valley Forge. Paul Boller has shown conclusively that the prayer incident at Valley Forge is "utterly without foundation in fact."[37] Furthermore, many people witnessed the fact that Washington, in contrast to most American worshippers of the time (including Martha Washington), did not kneel for prayer in church.[38]

It is clear from what we know of his character and philosophy that this Congressional gesture, although made with the best of intentions, would have been a great embarrassment to Washington. (The cherry tree story was bad enough.) He was a very private person, especially in matters of religion, and he would have been scandalized at the prospect of a state-supported prayer room with his supplicating figure as the main attraction. There is an observation by Washington's adopted daughter which makes for a very appropriate conclusion: "He was not one of those who act or pray 'that they may be seen of men.' He communed with his God in secret."[39]

THOMAS JEFFERSON (1743–1826)

Thomas Jefferson was one of the most outstanding minds in American history. He was a consummate statesman and thinker. His intellectual prowess could have easily qualified him for a professorship in classics, political science, philosophy, or theology. Judging from the emphasis in his writings, it is conceivable that he might have chosen theology and Biblical studies if he had followed an academic career. Paul Blanshard, in *God and Man in Washington*, states that "although he was not a church member, Jefferson was probably more interested in religion than any of our other presidents."[40] It is highly ironic then to find that Jefferson was criticized in the election of 1800 as "an atheist and leveler from Virginia." Again we find the religiously orthodox completely unable to understand or to respect religious liberalism.

In 1787 Jefferson wrote a fatherly letter of advice to his nephew Peter Carr. This provides a valuable insight into the critical method Jefferson himself might have used to come to his own views on religion. The first and principal rule concerns the role of reason: "Fix reason firmly in her seat, and call to her tribunal every fact, every opinion. Question with boldness even the existence of God."[41] The second rule concerns the Bible and follows from the first rule. Using reason, one should examine the Bible critically. If one considers it a human creation, it will then contain both truth and error. For example, the critical eye will come across events that seem contrary to nature's laws. Reason, says Jefferson, will exclude those as myth.

Jefferson came out of this critical investigation with a belief in God intact, but with a disbelief in most, if not all, Christian doctrine. He did not believe that Jesus was God; Jesus claimed only "human excellence." He did not believe in the virgin birth or the Trinity. Jefferson found the Trinity especially unintelligible. In a letter to James Smith in 1822 he states: "The Athanasian paradox that one is three, and three but one, is so incomprehensible to the human mind, that no candid man can say he has any idea of it. ..."[42] He tells Smith to keep this rejection of the Trinity confidential, so that his reputation would not be further defamed by those who thought that strict compliance to Christian doctrine was the mark of a religious person.

Jefferson still claimed to be a "real" Christian, because he maintained that the major emphasis of Jesus' message was good deeds and not unintelligible creeds. He still thought that Christianity was the best possible religion because of its ethics and its celebration of the human mind. In a letter to Moses Robinson in 1801, he affirms: "... the Christian religion, when divested of the rags in which they have enveloped it, and brought to the original purity and simplicity of its benevolent instructor, is a religion of all others most friendly to liberty, science, and the freest expansion of the human mind."[43]

Jefferson attempted to distill the "original purity and simplicity" of the philosophy of Jesus in a book called *The Life and Morals of Jesus of Nazareth*, commonly known as the "Jeffersonian Bible." Jefferson selected those verses which showed Jesus as a man and a great moral teacher. Carefully excised were any verses that supported the traditional doctrines, Christ's divinity, the virgin birth, the Trinity, and Hell. These doctrines were the political additions by priestly men who wished to increase the power of themselves and the church. "The greatest enemies of the doctrines of Jesus," Jefferson wrote to John Adams, "are those calling themselves the expositors of them, who have perverted them for the structure of a system of fancy, absolutely incomprehensible, and without any foundation in his genuine words."[44] After all, Jefferson might well have argued, it is not necessary to believe in the divinity of Jesus in order to love one's neighbor.

One of the greatest corruptors of the teachings of Jesus was, in Jefferson's opinion, John Calvin. In a letter to John Adams in 1823, he has nothing but contempt for Calvin. Calvin was a "demon and malignant spirit," and he created a religion of "demonism." After listing Calvin's errors, e.g., God's predestination of the elect and the depravity of humans, he contends: "It would be more pardonable to believe in no God at all, than to blaspheme Him by the atrocious attributes of Calvin."[45]

In the election of 1800, as I have noted above, Jefferson's religious views were a major campaign issue. Jefferson's political opponents, the Federalists, tried to discredit him because of his religious liberalism. Rumors were spread that Jefferson would confiscate all the Bibles in the land and substitute his own version. Alexander Hamilton suggested devious political means to block Jefferson's election in New York in order to prevent "an atheist in religion and a fanatic in politics from getting possession of the helm of state." John Jay, then governor of New York and a Federalist, fortunately rejected Hamilton's suggestion.

Jefferson's opinion on prayer in public schools was very similar to the views of our own liberal Supreme Court Justice William O. Douglas. Following the principles of religious liberty which he and Madison had fought for, he concluded that prayer in the schools should be strictly voluntary and there should be a separate room for that purpose. Justice Douglas' own proposal is similar, but with the proviso that the worship facility be financed from non-tax sources.[46]

Jefferson believed in the separation of church and state so

strongly that he and Andrew Jackson are the only presidents who declined to make the traditional presidential proclamation to celebrate Thanksgiving Day.[47] Washington had started the tradition during his first term. He thought that the proclamation was only a "recommendation"; therefore he had felt that he had not violated the principle. Jefferson argued, however, that the state should not officiate in anything religious, including a day of thanksgiving and prayer.

In many places in his writings, Jefferson suggests that we judge a religion not on the basis of its scripture or its doctrine, but on the ethical result of its practice. In a letter to Miles King, Jefferson states: "I must ever believe that religion substantially good which produces an honest life. ..."[48] Jefferson's utilitarianism is not of the same theoretical purity as that of Bentham or Mill, as he believed that God endowed all men with a moral sense of judging right from wrong. But as Adrienne Koch has observed: "Jefferson held the theory of moral sense in an unorthodox form, giving ground to historical change and social 'refinement' of our moral judgments."[49] In true utilitarian style, Jefferson extols the "social advantages" of the moral-sense theory. There are conceivably many exceptions to any moral rule and when such "is wanting, we endeavor to supply the defect by education, by appeals to reason and calculation ... [e.g.] demonstrations by sound calculation that honesty promotes interest in the long run."[50] Koch concludes that, with some qualifications, Jefferson emerges as "a full-fledged altruistic utilitarian."[51]

Perhaps the ultimate test for such a utilitarian would be the question: Can the atheist be moral? In at least two passages in Jefferson's writings the answer is clearly affirmative. The first is found in the letter to Thomas Law cited above. Here Jefferson respects the atheism and firmly defends the morality of the French *philosophes*, Diderot, D'Alembert, D'Holbach, Condorcet, who "are known to have been among the most virtuous of men. Their virtue then must have had some other foundation than the love of God." The second reference is in the letter to his nephew Peter Carr which was mentioned above. Jefferson quite frankly suggests the possibility that the young Carr, using the critical method he proposed, might become an atheist. The following is Jefferson's advice: "If it ends in a belief that there is no God, you will find incitements to virtue in the comfort and pleasantness you feel in its exercise, and the love of others which it will procure you."[52]

This is a statement of an ideal, the ideal of the most perfect religious tolerance. Such supreme tolerance was only possible in the context of the natural religion of the liberals and their clean divorce of ethics from religious doctrine. Jefferson believed that this ought to be the goal of all American religious life: that Americans have complete religious liberty, freedom *from* as well as *of* religion. Jefferson soon discovered, even in his own personal experience, that this ideal was far from being realized. He was to experience the aspersions cast upon his character in the election of 1800, and the abuse to which his friend Paine was subjected when he returned to America.

JOHN ADAMS (1735–1826)

A first impression of our second president may lead us to conclude that he does not belong with the religious liberals discussed in this essay. The Adams family had a strong Calvinistic background, and John Adams was a regular churchgoer and Bible reader. After seeing Franklin in action in Paris, Adams stated that Franklin "has no religion ... [and] all the atheists, deists, and libertines as well as philosophers and ladies are in his train."[53] Furthermore, Adams reacted violently to Paine's *Age of Reason* and scolded him in person for stating such "ridiculous" things about the Old Testament.

Adams held a firm belief in God and contended that such a belief was necessary for morality. He also recognized the role of human reason in morality, but in contrast to Jefferson and Franklin, he de-emphasized human perfectibility through reason alone. He believed in God's providence and in miracles, and he thought that the Bible contained "the most perfect philosophy, the most perfect morality, and the most refined policy."[54] Adams explicitly stated that the principles of the American Revolution were the same as the general principles of Christianity.[55]

But this same Adams signed the Treaty of Tripoli with its notorious Article Eleven which began: "As the Government of the United States is not in any sense founded on the Christian Religion. ..." Is this not a direct contradiction to the views expressed above? If we understand clearly what Adams means by general Christian principles, the contradiction dissolves. Like the religious liberals of his time, Adams believed that the essential message of Jesus was ethical, not doctrinal. Truth, justice, liberty, and brotherhood are the principles of Christianity, and it is these which Adams felt coincided with the principles of the American

Revolution. The American Revolution was certainly not fought on the basis of Christ's divinity, the Trinity, or the virgin birth. Therefore, to return to the Treaty of Tripoli, it would have been perfectly legitimate to state that the U.S. government is founded on Christian principles of liberty and justice, but not on the dogmas of orthodox religion.

Adams became disillusioned with his strictly Calvinist upbringing early on; and, as this entry in his diary indicates, he began to loathe going to church: "... and Sundays are sacrificed 'to the frigid performances' of disciples of 'frigid John Calvin.'"[56] It is also apparent that some people around him sensed his dissatisfaction and knew of his liberal views. In a diary entry of 1756, Adams (then 21) recounts a discussion he had with a Major Greene about the divinity of Christ. Major Greene's argument left Adams completely unconvinced, as can be seen in his marginal note: "Thus mystery is made a convenient cover for absurdity."[57]

Adams believed firmly in the first principle of religious liberalism: that Christian morality is separate and distinct from Christian doctrine. Like Jefferson, Adams was convinced that in the Bible one can find ethics only. As he states: "Where do we find a precept in the Gospel for ... Creeds, Confessions, Oaths ... and whole cartloads of other trumpery that we find religion encumbered with in these days?"[58]

Adams was a solid intellectual and enjoyed exchanges with people like Benjamin Rush and, later on, with Thomas Jefferson. He read the classics, philosophy, and theology voraciously and initiated studies in the areas of the sociology of religion and comparative religion. He thought that we should study the other religions of the world thoroughly and accept these other views if they could prove themselves in the court of reason and common sense.[59] He concluded that anyone practicing Christian morality should be called a Christian, even though that person may not believe in Christ's deity or the Trinity. In a letter to Jefferson in 1813, he puts it very simply: "Yet I believe all the honest men among you are Christians, in my sense of the word."[60]

Adams felt so strongly about the importance of morality that he held that virtue, not liberty, is the first principle of government.[61] The responsible use of freedom cannot flourish without a foundation in morality. Adams argued that human kindness stems from being good and doing right, rather than simply doing what one pleases. Adams' priority of virtue would not set well with modern libertarians, who stress the right of people to do as they please as long as they do not kill, assault, rob, or defraud. None of our founding fathers would have agreed with this.

Adams, although nominally a Congregationalist, moved more and more in the direction of Unitarianism in his later life. This is clearly evident in his correspondence with Jefferson, where it seems to be Adams, not Jefferson, who is most enthusiastic about Unitarianism. With the political wounds of the past healed, Jefferson and Adams discovered many points of agreement on religion. They both ridiculed "frigid" John Calvin and expressed dismay at those who thought the Trinity or the deity of Jesus to be intelligible propositions. Neither, however, ever made any public statement about his unorthodox views.

At the age of eighty, Adams composed an elegant summary of his religious faith: "My religion is founded on the love of God and my neighbor; on the hope of pardon for my offenses; upon contrition; upon the duty as well as necessity of supporting with patience the inevitable evils of life; in the duty of doing no wrong, but all the good I can, to the creation of which I am but an infinitesimal part ... I believe, too, in a future state of rewards and punishments, but not eternal."[62]

JAMES MADISON (1751–1836)

Our fourth president, along with Thomas Jefferson, did more than any other American to promote the principles of complete religious liberty. The problem of religious intolerance vexed Madison "the worst of anything whatever." Madison believed that one owns one's thoughts and conscience in the same way that one owns private property. Following the philosophy of John Locke, our founding fathers believed that by mixing labor with things, by making or buying, a person has a natural right to hold those things as private property. Madison concluded that the same holds for a person's thoughts and opinions, be they political, economic, or religious. As Madison stated in 1792: "As a man is said to have a right to his property, he may be equally said to have a property in his rights."[63] An American would have the right to believe in a king, or to disbelieve in God. Madison seems to imply that a person even has the right to hold the false belief that private property is not a natural right.

The state constitutions of Revolutionary America contained many clauses that did not conform to the Madison formula. Many states had provisions that discriminated against Roman Catholics.

Many states had "established" churches, that is, one denomination that was state-supported. In the Franklin section we saw that Pennsylvania required office-holders to be orthodox Christians. Similar religious tests for officials were found in New Jersey, Delaware, North and South Carolina.[64] In contrast, the federal Constitution (as amended) expressly forbade the establishment of religion and the use of religious tests for office-holders. Many states, however, continued with established churches and religious tests.

In Virginia, where Madison and Jefferson were to make their great contribution, the Episcopal Church was established. During 1744 Baptists and other sectarian Christians were being persecuted and arrested. With regard to this situation, Madison wrote: "That diabolical, hell-conceived principle of persecution rages among some; and to their eternal infamy, the clergy can furnish their quota of imps for such business. This vexes me the worst of anything whatever. There are at this time in the adjacent county not less than five or six well-meaning men in close jail for publishing their religious sentiments ... "[65]

Primarily because of the valiant efforts of Madison and Jefferson, the Episcopal Church was gradually disestablished in Virginia. There were still efforts, however, by some to get some state support for the teaching of the Christian religion. In 1785 a bill was introduced to this effect and found supporters in such men as Patrick Henry and John Marshall. Jefferson and Madison strongly opposed it.[66] The bill would have essentially re-established Christianity in general as the religion of the state, and thereby discriminated against Jews and other non-Christians. Madison and Jefferson specifically objected to the wording that made Christ "the Holy Author of our religion" because of the implicit exclusion of non-Christians.[67]

As a result of the vigorous debate on this bill, Madison composed in 1785 his famous "Memorial and Remonstrance against Religious Assessments." In it he states: "The religion then of every man must be left to the conviction and conscience of every man; and it is the right of every man to exercise it as these may dictate. This right is in its nature an inalienable right." His support of non-Christians and atheists is implicit but clear: "Whilst we assert for ourselves a freedom to embrace, to profess, and to observe the religion which we believe to be of divine origin, we cannot deny an equal freedom to those whose minds have not yet yielded to the evidence which has convinced us."[68]

During his presidency, Madison stood firm on his principles, including the principle of the separation of church and state. Madison objected to state-supported chaplains in Congress, and to the exemption of churches from taxation.[69] Both traditions have persisted until the present despite Madison's criticisms. Oddly enough, President Madison did give official sanction to Thanksgiving Day, something which President Jefferson declined to do. In February of 1811, Madison vetoed a federal land grant to a Baptist church and a bill which would have established an Episcopal church in the District of Columbia.[70] In each veto message there is a stern reminder about the Constitution's explicit provision that the "Congress shall make no law respecting a religious establishment."

In his famous "Memorial and Remonstrance," Madison argues that the establishment of Christianity "is a contradiction to the Christian religion itself; for every page of it disavows dependence on the powers of this world: it is a contradiction to fact; for it is known that this religion both existed and flourished, not only without the support of human laws, but in spite of every opposition from them."[71] Throughout history we have found that where politics and religion intermingle, there has always been trouble. And both politics and religion have suffered because of it. In a letter of July, 1822, Madison states that "such indeed is the tendency to such a coalition, and such its corrupting influence on both the parties, that the danger cannot be too carefully guarded against ... religion and government will both exist in greater purity, the less they are mixed together."[72]

CONCLUSION

We have examined the religious views of six great Americans: the first four presidents, Benjamin Franklin, and Thomas Paine. We should keep in mind the fact that none of these thinkers could be called philosophers by any strict definition of that term. They were philosophers in the broad sense of having a love for ideas and an avid interest in the advances in reason and science. They were highly eclectic, sometimes inconsistent, and unsystematic. Koch describes Jefferson, probably the best thinker of the six, as "impatient with long intellectual stocktaking" and making "no energetic attempt to resolve the inconsistencies" of his ethical views.[73] None of them begin to qualify in the area of conceptual analysis or systematic metaphysics. But in the lives and works of these great Americans, we find some of the finest expressions of religious tolerance, love of reason, and adherence to principle. As we enter America's third century, let us keep in mind Madison's motto that "conscience is the most sacred of all property;" and that *all* Americans, regardless of political or religious persuasion, should be entitled, in Jefferson's words, to "the comfort and pleasantness ... and the love of others" which the free exercise of conscience will procure for them.

NOTES

1. *Christianity Today*, July 2, 1976.
2. See for example Edward Sorel's cartoon in *The Village Voice*, December 29, 1975. Sorel's protagonist is addressing Billy Graham with the following words: "Er ... I'm afraid I have ... er ... some disturbing news for you. Jefferson, Adams, Franklin, Payne [sic] and most of the other signers were either deists, agnostics, or ... atheists. Which explains, of course, why we didn't find any mention of God in the Declaration [sic] or Constitution."
3. To Benjamin Rush, April 21, 1803.
4. To John Adams, May 5, 1817.
5. Carl Van Doren, ed., *Benjamin Franklin's Autobiographical Writings* (New York, Viking, 1945), pp. 257–8.
6. L. H. Butterfield, ed., *The Diary and Autobiography of John Adams* (Cambridge, 1961), III, 264.
7. E. C. Mossner, "Deism," in *The Encyclopedia of Philosophy*, ed. Paul Edwards (New York, Macmillan, 1976), II, 327.
8. P. S. Foner, ed., *The Complete Writings of Thomas Paine* (New York, Citadel, 1945), I, 601.
9. Charles Francis Adams, ed., *The Works of John Adams* (Boston, 1850–56), X, 170.
10. Van Doren, *op. cit.*, p. 642.
11. Foner, *op. cit.*, II, 893.
12. *National Gazette*, March 29, 1792.
13. S. H. Cobb, *The Rise of Religious Liberty in America* (New York, 1902), p. 503.
14. Van Doren, *op. cit.*, p. 257.
15. *Ibid.*, p. 784.
16. To Joseph Huey, June 6, 1753.
17. Van Doren, *op. cit.*, p. 632.
18. Quoted in E. S. Bates, *American Faith* (New York, 1940), p. 269.
19. Theodore Roosevelt, *Gouverneur Morris* (Cambridge, 1888), p. 289.
20. Foner, *op. cit.*, I, 555.
21. *Ibid.*, p. 464.
22. *Ibid.*, p. 483.
23. *Ibid.*, p. 490.
24. Quoted in Paul F. Boller, Jr., *George Washington and Religion* (Dallas, 1963), p. 89.
25. Quoted in P. L. Ford, *George Washington* (Philadelphia, 1896), p. 79.
26. J. C. Fitzpatrick, ed., *The Writings of George Washington* (Washington, 1939), XII, 162.

27. W. F. Woodward, *George Washington: The Image and the Man* (New York, 1926), p. 144. See also Boller, *op. cit.*, pp. 33–34.

28. Boller, *op. cit.*, pp. 68–9.

29. To Joseph Reed, March 7, 1776.

30. To Henry Knox, March 2, 1797.

31. See Boller, *op. cit.*, pp. 80–86.

32. To Tench Tilghman, March 24, 1784.

33. Hunter Miller, ed., *Treaties and other International Acts of the United States of America* (Washington, D.C., 1931), II, 349–385. The full text of Article Eleven is the following: "As the Government of the United States of America is not in any sense founded on the Christian Religion; as it has in itself no character of enmity against the laws, religion, or tranquillity of Musselmen; and as the said States never have entered into any war or act of hostility any Mehomitan nation, it is declared by the parties, that no pretext arising from religious opinions shall ever produce an interruption of the harmony existing between the two countries."

There are some intriguing facts concerning this clause. The English translation was made by Joel Barlow, the American negotiator and signator, and has been taken as the official translation of the Arabic original. But here lies the rub. As Hunter Miller states: "The most extraordinary (and wholly unexplained) is the fact that Article Eleven of the Barlow translation, with its famous phrase ... does not exist at all [i.e., in the Arabic version]" (p. 384). Miller observes that there is no evidence at all in the diplomatic correspondence of the time that gives a clue about the reason for this clause in the English translation.

The initial and distinct impression the English version gives is that the Muslim leaders demanded such a strong statement of principle as a major concession by the U.S. (One could not have even imagined demanding the same from the theocratic ideologues of Tripoli. In the Arabic version each and every article begins with a praise to Allah!) But the Arabic version does not read like a concession at all. The Arabic that Barlow apparently made into Article Eleven is appended at the end of Article Ten in the Arabic version. All that is stated here is a principle of general religious tolerance: that Christians should respect Muslims when in America and vice versa. There is nothing at all in the Arabic to support Barlow's strong statement.

The solution to this problem, I believe, lies in the motives of Barlow himself, not in those of the Muslim theocrats. It is clear that Barlow's translation, which was ratified by the Senate, gave the Muslims more than they actually bargained for.

Barlow was a good friend of Thomas Paine and a religious liberal himself. In the preface to the second part of *Age of Reason*, Paine relates that he entrusted the original MS. of the book to Barlow for safe-keeping. (Paine was in a French prison at the time.) This is a strong indication that Barlow and Paine were in basic agreement about religion, perhaps including Paine's strong anti-Christian sentiments. It is only conjecture, but did Barlow believe so strongly in the separation of church and state that he deliberately mistranslated the text of the Treaty of Tripoli?

The mystery behind this clause may never be solved. Regardless of Barlow's motivations, there are these events which remain indubitably clear: President Washington accepted the draft of the treaty in Barlow's form, the senate ratified it with no debate (at least none has been recorded), and President Adams confirmed the Senate's ratification in June, 1797.

34. Charles and Mary Beard phrase Washington's role a little more forcefully by stating that President Washington "allowed it to be squarely stated. ..." The Beards, however, offer no documentation to support this point. See their *The Rise of American Civilization* (New York, 1930), vol. 1, p. 439.

35. Boller, *op. cit.*, p. 91. Boller also states: "On the other hand, if to believe in the divinity of Christ and his atonement for the sins of man and to participate in the sacrament of the Lord's Supper are requisites for the Christian faith, then Washington, on the evidence which we have examined, can hardly be considered a Christian, except in the most nominal sense" (p. 90). Boller also quotes from James Abercrombie, Washington's pastor, who states that "I cannot consider any man as a real Christian who uniformly disregards an ordinance [i.e., Communion] so solemnly enjoined by the divine Author of our holy religion, and considered as a channel of divine grace" (*Ibid.*).

36. *Ibid.*, p. 15.

37. *Ibid.*, p. 10.

38. Ford, *op. cit.*, pp. 82–3.

39. Jared Sparks, ed., *The Writings of Washington* (Boston, 1837), XII, 406. Sparks's editing and commentary are considered inaccurate, unreliable, and even fraudulent by professional historians today. Sparks was definitely building a pious monument and not writing objective history. This comment by Washington's daughter runs so much against the utmost piety that Sparks attempts to instill in Washington that I believe its credibility is thereby considerably strengthened.

40. Paul Blanshard, *Man and God in Washington* (Boston, 1960), p. 35.

41. A. A. Limpscomb, ed., *The Writings of Thomas Jefferson* (Washington, 1903), VI, 258.

42. *Ibid.*, XV, 409.

43. *Ibid.*, X, 237.

44. *Ibid.*, XV, 430.

45. *Ibid.*, XV, 425.

46. Blanshard, *op. cit.*, p. 14.

47. Cushing Strout, *The New Heavens and the New Earth* (New York, 1974), p. 97.

48. To Miles King, September 26, 1814.

49. Adrienne Koch, *The Philosophy of Thomas Jefferson* (Chicago, Quadrangle, 1943), p. 18.

50. To Thomas Law, June 13, 1814.

51. Koch, *op. cit.*, p. 29.

52. *The Writings of Thomas Jefferson*, VI, 260.

53. Page Smith, *John Adams* (Westport, Conn., 1962), I, 433.

54. *Ibid.*, II, 1078.

55. To Thomas Jefferson, June 28, 1813.

56. L. H. Butterfield, ed., *The Earliest Diary of John Adams* (Cambridge, 1966) p. 37.
57. L. H. Butterfield, ed., *The Diary and Autobiography of John Adams* (Cambridge, 1961), I, 6
58. *Ibid.*, p. 8.
59. Smith, *op. cit.*, II, 1079.
60. To Thomas Jefferson, September 14, 1813.
61. *The Works of John Adams*, IV, 193–4.
62. *Ibid.*, X, 170.
63. *National Gazette*, March 29, 1792. This article and many more of the original Madison texts are included in Saul K. Padover, ed., *The Complete Madison* (New York, 1953), p. 267.
64. See Cobb, *op. cit.*, pp. 490–505.
65. Padover, *op. cit.*, p. 298.
66. Cobb, *op. cit.*, p. 496.
67. Strout, *op. cit.*, p. 88.
68. Padover, *op. cit.*, pp. 300, 301.
69. Strout, *op. cit.*, p. 97.
70. Padover, *op. cit.*, pp. 307–8.
71. *Ibid.*, p. 302.
72. *Ibid.*, p. 309.
73. Koch, *op. cit.*, p. 14.

THINKING ABOUT INDIVIDUAL
LIBERTIES IN REVOLUTIONARY AMERICA

ROSCOE HILL
University of Denver, Denver, Colorado

One cannot help wondering how the American Revolutionaries derived the specific protections which were written into the Constitution and the Bill of Rights. They certainly did not pluck them out of the air, nor has anyone alleged that they resulted from Divine Revelation. As philosophers, we would like to be able to say that they resulted from philosophical reasoning of some sort, but we find that the labels we now use cannot, without anachronism, be applied to late eighteenth century America: Kantian deontology and Benthamite utilitarianism were then in early infancy, and such positions as Hegelian dialectic, Marxism, Pragmatism and emotivism were of course far off in the future. Some political philosophers were widely available and read in America—including Hobbes, Sydney, Locke, and Montesquieu—but they do not specifically and systematically discuss details such as the right of habeas corpus, the injustice of bills of attainder, the protection against unreasonable search and seizure, the necessity of grand jury indictments, the importance of trial by jury, the right not to incriminate oneself, etc. Not only is it impossible to find this list of rights stated, let alone philosophically grounded and defended, in the writing of any one political philosophy book read at the time, one cannot extract this list from the entire political philosophy bookshelf then available.

There is one last hope, though, which I wish to put aside before attempting to be constructive. Someone might argue that although the precise list of rights guaranteed by the Constitution and the Bill of Rights cannot be found explicitly stated by the political philosophers of the day, it is implicitly there. According to this view, the natural rights or social contract philosophies of the time, or some combination of the two, are able to generate in a virtually deductive manner the list of protections in the Constitution and the Bill of Rights. Despite some initial appeal, this view has problems: (1) if the protections were consciously arrived at in this way we would expect someone at the time to have done it, but no one did; (2) if they were not quite self-consciously arrived at in this way (after all, many men of affairs, and even scholars, writers and scientists, are not always fully aware of how they arrive at their beliefs and convictions), we would expect someone since to have done it for them—but no one has; (3) if it were possible to arrive credibly at this list in this way, we should be able to do so now—but I, at least, cannot. My difficulty with natural rights or social contract philosophy is not that they are out of fashion these days, nor is it that they are unable to provide the premises which *can* yield the list of protections in the Constitution and the Bill of Rights. I concede that natural rights and/or social contract can, given certain qualifications and assumptions, yield this list of protections, but I also insist that they can, given other qualifications and assumptions, yield a quite contrary list. What bothers me is not so much the fact, though it is a fact, that there were just as many Tories who also appealed to natural rights and/or social contract to justify restrictions on individual rights and liberties. What bothers me even more is my suspicion that this list of protections resulted from a very sophisticated, sincere and intelligent process of reasoning. But that eliminates the process of beginning with natural rights and/or social contract, and proceeding deductively to this list, for such a process is transparently circular—it can generate the desired list only if it starts with certain qualifications and assumptions, i.e., only if it covertly builds in that list at the beginning.

I want now to sketch a different process of reasoning which I believe more adequately accounts for the list of protections in the Constitition and the Bill of Rights. The label for this reasoning process comes from Aristotle. In the *Prior Analytics* (Bk. II, Ch. 24) he distinguishes between deductive reasoning ("reasoning from whole to part"), inductive reasoning ("reasoning from part to whole"), and reasoning by example ("reasoning from part to part"). My narrow claim is that the specific guarantees in the Constitution and the Bill of Rights resulted from the process of reasoning by example which I am about to sketch. (A wider thesis which I believe has some merit, but which cannot be tested here, is that responsible ethical and political thinking often conforms better to this reasoning by example model than to utilitarianism, Kantian deontology or pragmatism.)

Reasoning by example begins, of course, with examples—in this case, with examples of outrages whose recurrence is to be avoided and prevented. The American revolutionaries were well read in history, and especially impressed with the writings of the Whig historians, who viewed history—especially English history—as a slow process whereby individual rights and liberties were slowly triumphing over royal tyranny. The political-legal history of England provided many cases of outrageous tyrannical behavior which violated the rights of the individual. Americans knew of these cases through Emlyn's *State Trials* (by 1766 ten volumes had been published, and they were reprinted in 1776), through pamphlet accounts of the trials, and through colonial newspaper accounts of contemporary legal cases (such as the trials of Wilkes in London and McDougall in New York, and the writs of assistance debate in Boston). Indeed, there is not a single protection in the Constitution or the Bill of Rights which did not then rest on a long pedigree of outrageous violations in the previous 170 years of Anglo-American legal history (since the Stuarts assumed the throne in 1603). Regarding freedom of religion, there had been the persecutions of Puritans, Quakers and Catholics. Regarding the freedom of the press, there had been the prosecutions under the later Stuarts (of John Twynn, Benjamin Keach, Benjamin Harris and many others), and the seditious libel prosecutions during the eighteenth century, including the well-known trial of John Peter Zenger in New York (1735). Regarding the right of habeas corpus, perhaps the most familiar case was the Five Knights Case (1627), but over and over again the writ of habeas corpus was seen as an essential legal tool designed to protect individuals from indefinite imprisonment without charges even being filed. Regarding the right against self-incrimination, the Court of Star Chamber's proceedings actually required an oath, the hated oath *ex officio*, which committed a defendant to incriminate himself, and countless judges under the later Stuarts and even in the eighteenth century attempted to trick defendants into incriminating themselves. Regarding bills of attainder, Cromwell's Parliament persecuted James Naylor and executed such persons as Archbishop Laud and the Earl of Strafford, and in 1770 the New York legislature conducted a trial of Alexander McDougall because he had criticized the legislature in a broadside. Regarding unreasonable search and seizure, the two most notorious contemporary examples of the time were the Crown's use of writs of assistance in Boston, so eloquently denounced by James Otis in 1761, and the ruthless searches and seizures in 1763 which affected the Londoner John Wilkes and many others, following the publication of a criticism of the King's ministers in No. 45, *North Britain*. Regarding the insistence upon grand jury indictments, the detested Star Chamber procedures never required these, and the trial of John Peter Zenger was initiated without a grand jury indictment, as was the legislative trial of Alexander McDougall. The list could go on and on.

But it would be a mistake, and an injustice, to conclude from the above paragraph that the list of protections in the Constitution and the Bill of Rights was simply plucked from Anglo-American legal history, rather like ripe and obvious berries. There is more to it all than that, which is what I now wish to sketch. The reasoning by example which generated the protections in the Constitution and the Bill of Rights can be broken down into five elements:

I. The basic conceptual building block is a series of examples of outrageous tyranny which violated the rights of the individual. Some of these examples have been mentioned above, though hardly described in detail.

II. The precise description of these particular examples leads one to think of the villainy in somewhat more general terms (for refusing to take the oath *ex officio* John Lilburn was put to the lash, but the villainy would have remained had he been simply imprisoned for life; because John Wilkes was suspected of writing No. 45, *North Britain* his house was searched and his possessions seized under a general warrant, but the villainy would have remained had his house and possessions been burned to the ground). This is an obvious matter in morals: if it is wrong for A to use his right fist to hit the innocent B, then it is in most cases wrong for A to hit B with his left fist, too. Though every act of villainy may in some theoretical way be distinguishable from every other act, it is still the case that an act of villainy may, in every morally relevant sense, be indistinguishable from a number of other contemplated acts.

III. From the above two elements, it is possible to generate some rough maxims, such as "don't hit innocents," or "don't require people to take oaths which may commit them to incriminate themselves," or "don't issue general warrants," etc.

IV. The movement from the particular case to the more general case, and the movement from these to the rough maxim, is guided by an eclectic overlay of general doctrines regarding the nature of man and the state, the value of individual liberty and privacy, the importance of individual happiness and public utility, etc., etc. It is here that the eighteenth century doctrines of natural law and social contract can make their entrance, but it is in a secondary, subservient role—as the next item indicates.

V. The key characteristic of the process of reasoning by example is that the *intellectual bedrock* in this form of reasoning is the *example*. It is neither the maxims nor the general doctrines in the eclectic overlay. One does not, in this type of reasoning, begin with general principles and then deductively proceed to arrive at a judgment regarding a particular example. Instead, one begins with a particular case. That is the intellectual bedrock. All subsequent attention to general maxims and doctrines is logically secondary. That is what makes reasoning by example different from the deductive model.

If we apply the above five elements to late eighteenth century American thinkers, and if we remain fully cognizant of what they read, said, and wrote, I believe we can develop a much more adequate view than any other so far proposed, of the way they arrived at the list of protections in the Constitution and the Bill of Rights. I do not mean to claim that the framers and supporters of these documents were self-consciously aware that they were employing this method of reasoning by example, I only mean to suggest that this method provides the framework which best accommodates the arguments and justifications that have been left behind. This framework captures the complex sophistication of James Otis' attacks on writs of assistance, it does justice to James Madison's defenses of individual liberties, it helps explain George Mason's intransigent refusal to give his signature or support to a Constitition that lacked a Bill of Rights, etc., etc. These men's convictions were not derived from some deductive process, they came from a thorough acquaintance with historical examples of villainous tyranny and from a determination to develop legal strictures to prevent such tyrannous acts from being repeated. This is what Aristotle called reasoning from part to part: from the fact of past instances of villainy to the task of preventing similar cases in the future, via the intermediary of certain more general descriptions and doctrines regarding the villainy in question.

The nature of these general descriptions and doctrines is provided by Whig historians: royalty and governmental authority can too easily slip into tyranny which threatens the liberty of the subject, and so individual liberty must be protected by explicit legal guarantees. This view of course could be readily buttressed by certain sorts of natural rights and social contract doctrines, and by appeals to the inherent nobility and equality of men. These appeals were made over and over, but it is misleading to view them as first principles which deductively generated particular doctrines or laws. As indicated above, the prior and more fundamental intellectual bedrock was the historical cases themselves, and the mode of reasoning was not deductive but rather reasoning by example. The general doctrines arose out of awareness of certain historical cases and were interpreted accordingly. It is the cases that are the dog, wagging the tail of general doctrines—and not vice versa.

Even if I am correct in claiming that this method of reasoning by example best captures the way in which the American revolutionaries arrived at the specific protections in the Constitution and Bill of Rights, it may still turn out that reasoning by example is a deficient and defective form of practical reasoning. There are several reasons for doubting the adequacy of reasoning by example. First, Aristotle himself gives a most unpersuasive illustration of moving from (i) a particular example through (ii) a general doctrine or maxim to (iii) another particular: since (i) it was an evil ("it did not turn out well") for the Thebans to war with their neighbors the Phocians, therefore (ii) it is evil to fight against neighbors, and hence (iii) it would be evil for the Athenians to make war against their neighbors the Thebans. A belligerent Athenian general might quite rightly demand more compelling reasons than this for leaving the Thebans unmolested. Second, although the method of reasoning by example may have been once used to justify and protect individual liberties which we still hold dear, there is no necessity involved; given different historical cases and/or different general doctrines, this process of reasoning might generate quite repressive laws which would be much less acceptable to us. Finally, by placing general doctrines and fundamental propositions in a secondary role, the method of reasoning by example simply does not satisfy our itch for a deductive model. But whether these considerations amount to strengths or weaknesses for this method, as an appealing and responsible method for practical reasoning, is a topic for another time.

THE MATERIALISM OF JEFFERSON

WINFIELD E. NAGLEY
University of Hawaii, Honolulu, Hawaii

This paper articulates the intellectual forces that comprise the foundation of Jefferson's philosophy; specifically, the paper will set forth the meanings he gave to the term "materialism"; this is particularly an important task since "materialism" is a "color" word which often has unfavorable or special associations and connotations, philosophical or otherwise. Three forms which his materialism took will be examined in turn: classical materialism, Christian materialism, and scientific materialism.

I

Thomas Jefferson's classical education was of supreme worth to him; Jefferson's grandson illustrated this when he wrote that he had often heard his grandfather say that if he had to "decide between pleasure derived from the classical education which his father had given him and the estate he left him, he would decide in favor of the former."[1] Repeatedly in his own letters, Jefferson expressed deep gratitude for this classical education. Chinard wrote that "Homer, Euripides, Cicero were the masters who provided him [Jefferson] with strong moral standards."[2] Though Chinard perhaps overstated the case by omitting consideration of the influences of inborn temperament and the Anglican home upon Jefferson's values, he is certainly correct in stating how important Jefferson's classical predilections were in determining the values that he chose for commitment.

One of the few dominant classical themes which Jefferson emphasized was death, its inevitability and the few consolations man has in accepting its inevitability. From Homer, Jefferson drew courageous resignation and words of consolation to face the "riddle" of death. From Cicero, especially, came citations dealing with preparation of the mind for death: "Let us accustom ourselves to die"; "For this present life is really death"; "Whatever will happen, destiny must be overcome by bearing it"; and "All must die; if only there should be an end to misery in death."

These Greek and Latin quotations expressed the materialism of the Stoic and Epicurean tradition; it is more implicit than explicit, more fragmentary than systematic but it is there. One of the most explicit statments of this classic materialism Jefferson took from Cicero's *Tusculanae Quaestiones*, and it appears in one of his two "Commonplace Books":

> For if either the heart, or the blood, or the brain is the soul, then certainly the soul, being corporeal, must perish with the rest of the body; if it is air, it will perhaps be dissolved; if it is fire, it will be extinguished.[3]

This same view reappeared in Jefferson's other "Commonplace Book" according to Chinard, and in several of Jefferson's letters to John Adams.[4]

The theme of resignation—resting on a semi-submerged classical Stoic-Epicurean materialism—Jefferson stated in a letter to John Pope, written when he was twenty years old: Man must practice acceptance of the fact that perfect happiness is not the lot of the Deity's creatures. Indeed even the most fortunate meet calamity and misfortune. Man must fortify himself by assuming a "perfect resignation" to the will of Deity and such conduct may enable him to bear up under the burden of life. Then "Few things will disturb him at all; nothing will disturb him much."

It seems clear that Jefferson did not distinguish important theoretical differences between the Stoics and the Epicureans. The reason appears to lie in the fact that his level of analysis was not academic but served a practical purpose, namely, to incorporate such wisdom as he found in these schools into his own personal value structure. As Boorstin expressed it, Jefferson "lacked the unbalance of mind required to excel as a specialist."[6] Thus the Stoics and Epicureans seem inseparable resources in Jefferson's mind for joining actuality with philosophy, not only in his early years but also in his middle years when he was still an Epicurean materialist, à la Gassendi—in fact, throughout his life. In a letter to William Short in 1819 he wrote: "I too am an Epicurean"[7] and he set forth, "in the lapidary style," a "Syllabus of the doctrines of Epicurus." Jefferson maintained that the actual doctrines of Epicurus as set forth in Gassendi's *Syntagma* contained the summation of all that was rational in Greek and Roman moral philosophy. Not only did he find that Epicurus' doctrines contain all that was "rational" in the moral philosophy of Greece and Rome, but in the last years of his life facing his own approaching death he turned to classical literature whose "pages fill up the vacuum of *ennui*, and become sweet composers to that rest of the grave into which we are sooner or later to descend."[8]

II

In regard to Christian materialism, Thomas Jefferson was in conflict with the Hebraic-Christian tradition at two levels: one was institutional and the other philosophical. In neither case could this confrontation be described as anything other than open conflict with the hereditary spirit of the genteel tradition and an expression of the indigenous American liberal frame of mind.

Jefferson did not find any contradiction between holding a materialistic scientific cosmology—a mechanical atomistic model for describing experiences and predicting future events—yet also having a belief in God the Creator. The reason he found no contradiction between mechanism and deism appears to lie in the fact that he found matter and spirit to be incommensurate; the mind-body problem, the entire question of the relation of thought or spirit to matter, was for him an incomprehensible issue and he pleaded agnosticism. In a letter to John Adams, he discussed the fact that "Mr. Locke and other materialists" charge the "spiritualists" with blasphemy in that they deny the Creator the power of endowing some forms of matter with thought. Jefferson found such arguments beyond comprehension and thought that "ignorance"—undoubtedly echoing the celebrated pillow metaphor of Montaigne—was the "softest pillow" on which he could lay his head. He then, interestingly, remarked that if he had to choose sides, he would join that of Mr. Locke, preferring to swallow "one incomprehensibility rather than two." He continued this argument: "It requires one effort only to admit the single incomprehensibility of matter endowed with thought and two to believe, first that of an existence called spirit, of which we have neither evidence nor idea, and then secondly how that spirit, which has neither extension nor solidity, can put material organs into motion."[9] Jefferson concluded his letter observing that before long he and Adams might perhaps know the answers for themselves and they meantime had, after all, done injury to no man and good to their country.

The closing of the above-cited letter points to the central focus of Jefferson's religious views, namely their ethical and social significance. Jefferson indicates in a letter to William Short that he had sometimes considered translating Epictetus (no current translation being adequate in his view) "by adding the genuine doctrines of Epicurus from the *Syntagma* of Gassendi [in whose writings he had much interest], and an abstract from the Evangelists of whatever has the stamp of the eloquence and fine imagination of Jesus."[10] It is clear that the emphasis of this proposed compilation would have been upon ethics and wisdom, not upon Christian and Epicurean views of the character of the natural world.

The main argument offered by Jefferson for holding fast to his Christian materialism lay in the teachings of the church fathers of the first three centuries. He found they were "generally" if not "universally" materialists "extending ... even to the Creator Himself." Jefferson admitted that he did not know exactly when the "heresy of spiritualism" was introduced but believed it was probably by Athanasius and the Council of Nicaea. He quoted from second-hand sources on Origen, St. Macari, Justin Martyr and Tertullian. The quotations are tantalizing fragments, suggesting radical departures from traditional Christian doctrine; they were written in Greek or Latin, without analysis, in support of his materialistic thesis. For example: "Justin· Martyr says expressly 'The deity we say is immaterial, but no immaterial being exists.' "[11] Jefferson quoted Tertullian: "What then is God if not body? Who however would deny that God is body?"[12] Bishop Huet's commentary on Origen is cited by Jefferson in a passage echoing Epicurean materialistic theory: "God therefore, to whom the soul is similar, according to Origen, is in actual fact corporeal, but by comparison with such heavy bodies is incorporeal."[13] Jefferson added that he learned from authors he respected that St. Augustine, St. Basil, Lactantius, Tatian, Athenagoras, and others all concur in asserting the "materiality of the soul" and suggested archly that modern doctors of divinity would hardly "venture or wish to condemn their fathers as heretics."

Actually their heresy started, in Jefferson's eyes, when the Christian church adopted *"immaterialism,"* probably at the time of Athanasius and the Council of Nicaea. This *"immaterialism"* was "masked atheism" which Jesus taught nothing of; admitting that He did teach that God is a Spirit, Jesus did not define what a spirit is nor did he say "that it is not matter." The early church fathers, Jefferson argued, held spirit to be matter, "Light and thin indeed, an ethereal gas but still matter." He quoted again the same church fathers, mentioned in the previous paragraph, to support further his thesis against the heretical immaterialists.

Though Jefferson played the role of a thorough-going sceptic with respect to the assertions of the "spiritualists," his scepticism was none the less of a limited sort. He was most decidedly not a sceptic in regard to the existence and nature of ethical values, the reality of God as Creator, and the genuineness and usefulness of scientific knowledge. For Jefferson the problem of philosophical scepticism was not a serious one. He spoke of ridding himself of "Pyrrhonisms" by rejecting all organs of information but his senses; reliance on the senses freed one from engaging in "antiphysical" speculations which only uselessly occupy the mind and cause disquiet to it.

There is no discussion by Jefferson of the problem of Pyrrhonism even though he could hardly have been unaware of the subject not only with respect to Gassendi's important critique of Descartes but with regard to the larger problem of scepticism in French philosophy, as expressed by the *libertins*. Jefferson's agreement with Gassendi's Epicurean views and with his critique of Descartes's "immaterialism" would certainly support the assumption that Jefferson was familiar with the problems of the Pyrrhonists and the anti-Pyrrhonists in the French philosophical tradition. The fact that he cited Bishop Pierre-Daniel Huet's commentary on Origen further suggests Jefferson's familiarity with the issue of scepticism; it is hardly conceivable that he would not have been aware of the fact that Huet was a Pyrrhonist Christian as well as a devastating sceptical opponent of Descartes.[14]

Though Jefferson did not concern himself with this philosophical issue, he himself took a practical Pyrrhonistic stance of his own, avoiding philosophical debate.

> Nevertheless, I cannot forsee much utility in reviewing, in this country, the controversy between the Spiritualists and the Materialists. Why should time be wasted in disputing about two substances, when both parties agree that neither knows anything about either?[15]

The very fact that he employed the words "in this country" would further suggest his awareness of the problem of scepticism in other countries, which would include France. He specifically noted that this issue was found in India.

With this clash of spiritualist and materialist world views, then, Jefferson would have nothing to do. His own methodological materialism, his "constructive scepticism" as Gassendi stated it, asserted itself in a dramatic explosion of ideas mingling scepticism, hedonism, and fideism.

Vain man! mind your own business! Do no wrong; do all the good you can! Eat your canvas-back ducks! Drink your Burgundy! Sleep your siesta when necessary, and TRUST IN GOD![16]

III

Regarding scientific materialism, the third form of materialism found in Jefferson, his writings on the subject of science disclose an empirical cast of mind which primarily turned not to theoretical writings about matters of science and knowledge but found expression mainly in his own scientific activity as evidenced in his inveterate habit of gathering scientific information upon a limitless range of subjects, and in his reading about scientific discoveries. And all of this was accomplished while serving in succession Virginia and the new nation under the most trying and demanding conditions as legislator, war-time Governor, successful revolutionary, Ambassador to France, Secretary of State and President.

One of the most remarkable expressions of his scientific empiricism is to be found in his *Notes on Virginia*, where a striking impression is made on the reader by the encyclopedic range of scientific matters about which Jefferson had factual information: geography, climatology, geology, botany, anthropology, agriculture, natural history and much more. The central interest of Jefferson in the *Notes* was upon useful and practical facts as might be expected since his true interests were scientific and practical. There were two scientific controversies into which Jefferson entered that reveal his keenly sceptical and carefully empirical frame of mind, which also shows more than a touch of fantasy. One of the controversies was his vigorous opposition to the theoretical speculations of the prestigious Comte de Buffon and the other concerned the explanation of fossils which were found in the Virginia mountains.

Not only did Jefferson advocate and pursue the practice of science but he was also keenly interested in the philosophy of science. This interest did not merely "round out" his "spontaneous and home-grown" philosophical thinking, to use Koch's phrase,[17] but was an early, as well as late, serious concern as evidenced in his *Literary Bible*. Especially it must be recognized that in this matter, as in all matters, theory and practice never stood in a dichotomous academic relationship to each other in Jefferson's view of life but were used together in what Koch correctly recognized as a problem-solving activity.

On that most basic theoretical question that recurs in the theory of science, the problem of materialism, Jefferson characteristically went his own way. We have already seen that he had a strongly anti-metaphysical bias against the *philosophia perennis*—against all "spiritualists." He himself espoused "materialism" and his materialism was expressed in part by his commitment to Epicureanism and in part by his advocacy of Christian materialism; this Epicurean-deism suggests the influence of Gassendi although Jefferson's materialism can also be seen as an expression of what Santayana would term a natural materialism which everyone instinctively adopts.

The question of materialism arose in his mind with respect to science and again it becomes clear that his materialism was not the metaphysical world-view of a Hobbes or a Holbach; he was too anti-metaphysical in temperament, and any form of dogmatic mechanical materialism was unacceptable to his sceptical and empirical mind.

It is this empiricism which points to the meaning that scientific materialism had for Jefferson. Basically, Jefferson used the term "materialism" in three ways in his writings about science: First, as has been noted, he used "materialism" to contrast his view to that of "spiritualists" or "immaterialists." Thus in doing scientific work one is a materialist in the sense that one avoids meta-empirical causes and explanations. Second, by the term "materialism" Jefferson meant a methodological postulate for experimental scientific work. This is made clear by his approval of the materialism of Cabanis, which was clearly confined to scientific hypothesis, irrespective of whatever Cabanis's own cosmological position might have been. Materialism as a methodological postulate can be found also in Jefferson's enthusiasm for the work of Flourens on the physiology of the brain in which experiments on the nervous systems of vertebrate animals were described indicating the different behavioral effects produced by removing various portions of the brain. Jefferson remarked in the midst of his glowing account of this work, "I wish to see what the spiritualists will say to this."[18]

The third meaning of Jefferson's "scientific materialism" is that of a "sensationalistic positivism," to use Koch's terminology,[19] in which he maintained: "I feel therefore I exist."[20] He felt bodies other than his own and he felt them changing place. "I call them *matter* and on the basis of sensation, matter and motion ... we

may erect the fabric of all the certainties we can have or need ...
When once we quit the basis of sensation, all is in the wind."[21]

It is this "sensationalism" that freed Jefferson from "pyrrhon-ism," the more so because it was joined with Scottish realism which was a major influence upon him. "But I believe I am supported in my creed of materialism by the Lockes, the Tracys and the Stewarts."[22] This quotation shows very clearly that he leaned more toward the English materialists, who were reluctant to move in the direction of thoroughgoing systematic materialism in the manner of Holbach and who also sought to avoid the problem of pyrrhonism which so plagued the French tradition. And Jefferson's desire to join actuality with philosophy made him susceptible to the appeal of a realism which was not disturbed by the sceptical possibility that cognition rests merely upon custom or even upon irrational foundations.

IV

In conclusion, then, the foundation of the materialism of Jefferson is a fusion of several strands: first, classical Graeco-Roman materialism, which provided him with much of his ethical thought, his pursuit of tranquility and his consolation at the fact of death; second, Hebraic-Christian materialism, which provided him with the view of a Creator God, a teleological universe and ethical standards; and third, scientific materialism, which provided him with an empirical and sensation-oriented methodology. These three materialisms together comprise Jefferson's genuine philosophy, in Santayana's sense of a genuine philosophy, that is, one which inspires and expresses the life of those who hold it.

NOTES

1. Henry S. Randall, *The Life of Thomas Jefferson* (Freeport, New York, Books for Libraries Press, 1970), p. 18.

2. Gilbert Chinard, *The Literary Bible of Thomas Jefferson* (Baltimore, The Johns Hopkins Press, 1928), p. 35.

3. *Ibid.*, p. 72.

4. *Ibid.*, p. 17.

5. Andrew A. Lipscomb, ed., *The Writings of Thomas Jefferson*, 20 volumes (Washington, D.C., The Thomas Jefferson Memorial Association, XV), IV, 10. Hereinafter all references to this Memorial Edition will be cited as M.E.

6. Daniel J. Boorstin, *Lost World of Jefferson* (Boston, Beacon Press, 1948), p. 23.

7. M.E., XV, 219.

8. *Ibid.*, p. 209.
9. *Ibid.*, p. 241.
10. *Ibid.*, p. 221.
11. *Ibid.*, p. 267 (the author is responsible for this translation and the next two).
12. *Ibid.*
13. *Ibid.*, p. 266.
14. Richard H. Popkin, *The History of Scepticism from Erasmus to Descartes*, (Assen, Netherlands, Royal Van Gorcum Ltd., 1960), p. 204.
15. M.E., XV, 121.
16. *Ibid.*, p. 122.
17. Adrienne Koch, *The Philosophy of Thomas Jefferson* (Chicago, Quadrangle Books, 1964), p. 44.
18. M.E., XVI, 92.
19. Koch, *op. cit.*, p. 100.
20. M.E., XV, 273.
21. *Ibid.*, p. 274.
22. *Ibid.*

PART II:
ASPECTS OF A TRADITION

PEIRCE ON TRUTH*

H. S. THAYER

*The City College and Graduate School
of the City University of New York, New York, New York*

"The essence of truth lies in its resistance to being ignored."
(*CP*2.139)

I

Peirce's writings contain many references to and brief discussions of truth. What he has to say on these diverse occasions is not always very clear; nor is there an obvious unity and coherence in the views expressed. The reader is faced with the recurrent difficulty in understanding Peirce's intentions as to whether he is encountering thematically distinct and historically separate phases of thought, or if there is to be discovered beneath the fragmentary state of the writings an underlying consistency of procedures and a common objective.

Peirce's views on truth appear to have had a circuitous formation, reflecting and proliferating among aspects of a coherence theory, a theory of truth as correspondence of propositions with reality, and a pragmatic theory of true belief as the resolution of doubt by means of inquiry. It is not my purpose to discuss the question of whether one or several theories of truth are to be attributed to Peirce. I incline to think, with some hesitation, that despite a number of anomolous formulations, certain changes in emphasis and construction—effects, no doubt, of refactory difficulties and critical revision—there is one generally coherent and comprehensive sense in which Peirce understood the meaning of truth. The differences among his various statements on truth are due primarily, I believe, not to major changes of mind—and accordingly of theories—but to what seems to have been an attempt to explore several different ways of capturing and articulating one comprehensive theory of truth. The problem was how to arrive at a statement that was precise enough to be useful and informative while also retaining a sufficient generality so as not to exclude or fail to account for the characteristically varied

63

uses the notion of truth has enjoyed in the sciences, the arts, philosophy, and the common language.[1] The effort culminated in the formulation of the meaning of truth within the general theory of signs and sign interpretation.

It is Peirce's general theory of truth and some of its suggestive features, rather than the particular history of its development, that I propose to discuss.

The most familiar of his statements on truth are the following:

(A) The opinion which is fated to be ultimately agreed to by all who investigate, is what we mean by the truth, and the object represented in this opinion is the real (*CP* 5.407).

(B) Truth is that concordance of an abstract statement with the ideal limit towards which endless investigation would tend to bring scientific belief, which concordance the abstract statement may possess by virtue of the confession of its inaccuracy and onesidedness, and this is an essential ingredient of truth (*CP* 5.565).

Of the two (B) is a more careful and complete definition. As for (A)—which is from "How to Make Our Ideas Clear"—it occurs in a discussion devoted to the meaning of "reality," not truth. And in this respect, the notion of an opinion "fated" or "destined" to be agreed upon by all who investigate it, while having a role in the analysis of truth, is particularly important; for it formulates the criterion of what is meant by a "real" object. In speaking of an opinion "fated" to be agreed on, Peirce explained that he meant only what is sure to come about and cannot be avoided. He intended nothing more mysterious or superstitious than to say that a coin tossed often enough is "fated" to land heads one-half the number of trials. It meant "that which is sure to come true" (*CP* 5.407n). And he added that even if by some perversity an "arbitrary proposition ... be universally accepted" by the whole human race, still if investigation should be carried "sufficiently far," even by another race of investigators, the "true opinion must be the one which they would ultimately come to" (*CP* 5.408).

As will be seen below, this does not commit Peirce to requiring of a true opinion that it is, or must be, one that will be ultimately agreed to by all who investigate. For it is not necessary to our understanding of what we mean by some opinion being true that it *will* be agreed upon by those who investigate it; rather, for Peirce, the true opinion is one that *would* be so agreed upon. And there is an important difference between stating that something *will* be the case and that something *would* be the case.[2] Furthermore it is possible to believe truly that a coin would land heads one-half of a large number of trials, and to know what I *mean* by this belief being true (viz., that in the long run the ratio of heads to tails would approximate to one-half) without having to venture on the heroic but futile task of dedicating a lifetime to realizing this "fated" result.

We may remark, in passing, that the propriety of regarding (A) and (B) as definitive, or fundamentally representative of Peirce's conception of truth, is, of course, open to question. We do not have Peirce's authority for this supposition; nor, on the other hand, do we have his disapproval. It has been in the scholarly writing on Peirce that these statements have come to receive special attention. With the growing interest in Peirce's thought that commenced in the 1920's, and perhaps centered in M. R. Cohen's *Chance, Love, and Logic* (1923), which made some of the important material accessible then to readers, these statements gradually acquired the status of "received doctrine."[3] In 1939, in *Logic: The Theory of Inquiry*, Dewey gave these same statements a conspicuous place, recognizing their importance and expressing his endorsement of them.[4] But it is worth observing that while William James made generous acknowledgments to Peirce as the founder of pragmatism, it is Peirce's views on *meaning*, not *truth*, that interested him. He has very little to say about the latter (indeed nothing about truth in his most notable discussions of Peirce's ideas). And in his own accounts of pragmatic truth, although James frequently cites Schiller and Dewey, he at best makes only remote allusions to Peirce's doctrine of truth.[5] Thus while Peirce undoubtedly did hold a theory of truth in his own lifetime, this was not what gained him notice. His well-known renunciation of pragmatism for pragmaticism (about 1905, see *CP* 5.414) was, I suspect, among other reasons partly motivated by his consciousness of the disparity between his own conception of truth and the theories expounded by James and Schiller.

It is therefore with some diffidence that I will suppose one generally consistent theory of truth can be attributed to Peirce, concerning which (A) and (B) are, while sketchy, representative. We can derive, however, some comfort from the fact that the unpublished manuscripts exhibit developments of ideas that are frequently in harmony with (A) and (B), and sometimes closely similar in language and substance. In any case, the theory stated in (A) and (B) is original and interesting on its own account and has come to be regarded and discussed—whether altogether justly or not—as Peirce's theory. So we may pass from merely identifying the statements in question to an examination of them.

II

Three eminent philosophers, Russell, Ayer, and Quine, have registered severe criticisms of (A) and (B). Russell had several objections.[6] Concerning (A), which so far as I know he had come upon in Dewey's quotation in the *Logic* and not in Peirce's original article, he expressed perplexity shared by many readers over the notion of an opinion "fated" for agreement. (But we recognized earlier the innocuous sense in which, for Peirce, an opinion may be fated for agreement.) He was equally troubled about the word "ultimately" in Peirce's saying that there will be an opinion "ultimately agreed to by all who investigate." He remarks that if "ultimate" is intended chronologically, truth will depend on the opinion of the last man alive in his last minutes as the earth becomes too cold to support life. But Russell sees that it is more likely that what Peirce had in mind is "a series of opinions, analogous to a series of numbers such as 1/2, 3/4, 7/8 ... tending to a limit, and each differing less from its predecessor than any earlier member of the series does."[7] (This may be questioned as we will see.) Russell also found strange the notion of a "confession of inaccuracy" as essential to truth. Finally he wondered why Peirce believed there was ever an ideal limit towards which investigation would bring belief. He queried, is this an empirical generalization or unfounded optimism?

Quine regards (A) to be mistaken for several reasons, but for two especially.[8] He questions the assumption of there being one "ideal limit" or unique resulting theory as the outcome of continuously applied scientific method to belief.[9] He also comments: "There is a faulty use of numerical analogy in speaking of a limit of theories, since the notion of limit depends on that of 'nearer than,' which is defined for numbers and not for theories."

Ayer restates another of Russell's objections.[10] There are many particular events which, while candidates for true or false beliefs, are likely never to be recorded. Such, for example, would be beliefs as to the number of grains of sand on a beach, or, as Russell instanced, whether I had bacon for breakfast. Concerning such questions of belief Peirce's definition of truth appears to be inapplicable for "it can hardly be supposed that even in the scientific millennium a complete historical record will have been kept of every particular event." He, too, questions the apparent assumption of there being a continuous investigation of opinion, of an "endless investigation." A further difficulty raised by Ayer can be put this way: it is trivial to hold that there are no real things or laws that will escape being known by science, if it is assumed that investigation will continue into infinity. For if something *can* be known, it will "eventually" become known if you allow the eventuality to come under a process of discovery that can continue forever.[11]

These various objections raise two kinds of questions which, especially in dealing with Peirce's ideas on truth, are inseparable although distinguishable. There is first a question of accurately discerning Peirce's intentions; distinguishing if possible certain philosophic assumptions and convictions that he may have held and which color and affect what he says. And there is the problem of determining precisely what he does say and means to say. Before turning to what I think is the most serious error underlying the above criticisms, two observations which take these questions into consideration are worth making.

(1) Both Russell and Quine view (B) as suggesting that in the scientific investigation of belief, opinions or theories become ordered in a series analogous to a series of numbers tending to a limit. While this is a natural interpretation of what Peirce says, it is, I think, doubtful. Peirce does not, so far as I can find, expatiate on the point and so settle the matter for us. But I think it is quite likely that what he had in mind was not that a series of opinions (or theories) tends like numbers to a limit. His intention was rather to suggest that a continuous critical activity of investigation and testing would—like a series of numbers tending to a limit—render some asserted opinion ever more precise and accurate (and ever more definitely true or false). The persistent and "endless investigation," he says (in (B)), would "tend to bring scientific belief" to an "ideal limit." And in the same passage he says that it is an *"abstract statement"* (not a series of opinions or theories) that is in concordance with the ideal limit. It is the "endless investigation" of the belief represented by the abstract statement (i.e., the belief as stated) that tends towards the "ideal limit." It is, in short, *inquiry,* a complex of critical operations and activities shared by those who investigate, that is the continuous activity—a remark he makes shortly before stating (B) supports this interpretation. When we assert an abstract proposition, he says, the

truth of it depends on "that proposition's not professing to be exactly true." We hope that in the progress of science, "error will indefinitely diminish, just as the error of 3.14159, the value given for π, will indefinitely diminish as the calculation is carried to more and more places of decimals." But he adds, "What we call π is an ideal limit to which no numerical expression can be perfectly true." I understand this to suggest that continued "calculation," that is, continuous inquiry concerning some initially stated proposition, would indefinitely diminish its error. But this is not to claim that single opinions or whole theories can be arranged in a series like the decimal expansion of π, and made to approach a limit.

(2) Russell thought the main question to be raised concerning (B) was the assumption that an investigation would continue indefinitely and would result in ultimate agreement. The question is: is this belief well founded? We could press even further and ask: is the belief that investigation will continue indefinitely and produce an ultimate agreement itself subject to endless investigation and ultimate agreement? Is (B), Peirce's theory of truth, true on its own terms? Here I will say dogmatically, for brevity, that it is usually a mistake to demand of any theory or definition of truth that it must itself satisfy the conditions it legislates, that it should be included in its own scope. For a theory or definition of truth is not an expression of belief or a statement in the same sense as the beliefs or statements whose truth (or falsity) it is designed to formulate. But to return to Russell's objection.

It is clear that we cannot *know* (i) that an investigation will continue forever; or (ii) that an endless investigation will tend to an ultimate agreement. Peirce, however, *believed* both (i) and (ii) and gave reasons. He says there is no ground for disbelieving (i). He was, we may recall, a child of the nineteenth century, the century of "progress." We, living in the age of the nuclear bomb, may be somewhat less confident than was Peirce about the irresistible evolution of concrete reasonableness. He thought that intelligent life on earth would probably not continue indefinitely, but even if it disappeared, there is a likelihood of intelligent life existing in other parts of the universe. The community of intelligent inquiry is a cosmic disposition! His most empirical reason for affirming (ii) is the history of science. He thought that the history of science exhibited clearly a gradual tendency to increasingly systematic agreement over the acceptance and rejection of beliefs. We speak of the growth of scientific thought, and the word "growth" reflects these characteristics of the cumulative and logical unification of beliefs. Crises that might occur in scientific theory he would have explained, I think, as taking place within a wider context of settled beliefs and practices. Revolutions in science occur within frameworks and with references to a settled background of prior and collateral information that makes their advent, detection, and our appreciation of what is at stake possible.

There is an assumption which Peirce acknowledges: the number of questions will increase with the increase in knowledge; but the number of answers will also increase. This, he says, is because the method of providing answers will also increase in efficacy and precision. And in apparent inconsistency with (A) and (B) he was to comment that some questions may never be answered and some opinions are already "true"; they will have, thus, acquired the status of ultimate agreement.[12]

For his beliefs in (i) and (ii) Peirce was guided by metaphysical convictions concerning cosmic evolution and a progressive reasonableness persistent in the universe and effecting the realization of law and rational order. But, in addition, there was a form of reasoning, most readily exemplified in mathematics (especially in the theory of errors), which profoundly inspired Peirce and is essential to understanding his conception of endless investigation and the ideal limit.[13] The idea undoubtedly also had metaphysical significance for him in relation to what he regarded as cosmic reason. This paradigm of reasoning he once referred to as the "marvelous self-correcting property of Reason" which "belongs to every science" (*CP* 5.579). The self-corrective process is the essence of rationality. He regarded it as

> one of the most wonderful features of reasoning and one of the most important philosophemes in the doctrine of science ... namely, that reasoning tends to correct itself (*CP* 5.575).

III

The above are some of the empirical and philosophical considerations that Peirce adduces in behalf of (A) and (B) and other similar accounts of truth. All this is well known to readers of Peirce and requires no elaboration here. Still, I think it must be conceded that, excepting (1) some pages earlier, what we have just reviewed can scarcely be regarded as answering the objections raised by Russell, Quine, and Ayer.

What I now wish to suggest is that the foregoing are not *arguments* for Peirce's theory at all. His belief that ours is a rationally evolving universe, and that there is "fated" to be an enlightened ultimate opinion agreed to by those who investigate, are no doubt intimately related to the doctrine of truth as he conceived it. Indeed these ideas help explain why Peirce formulated his statements on truth in the manner of (A) and (B); they explain the idiom. But it is a serious mistake to suppose, as Russell, Quine, and Ayer have done (and in this they are not alone), that (A) and (B) state conditions that must be fulfilled by any one opinion (or belief) if it is to be true. What (A) and (B) say is not that to be true an opinion must necessarily be "ultimately agreed to by all who investigate" and be the "ideal limit" of an "endless investigation." Rather, (A) and (B) specify what it *means* to say that an opinion is true; the definitions state what conditions are entailed and *would* be fulfilled if an opinion is true. And this is to explain what is meant by ascribing truth to an opinion.

There is an important difference to be observed. If it is snowing, and I see that it is and form the opinion "It is snowing," my opinion is true. I do not mean that it is true because (or only if) it represents the ideal limit of endless investigation. For since no such investigation has occurred, the opinion will then be either false or neither true nor false—and this is absurd. Nor do I mean that the opinion will *in fact* ever be the subject of endless investigation. And in this respect Russell and Ayer are correct; there are many particular events and beliefs that in fact will never be recorded nor ever come under investigation to result in an "ultimate opinion." The point, for Peirce, is that what we mean by the truth of the opinion (e.g., that it is snowing) is that what it represents and asserts *would* be affirmed *if* it were subject to endless investigation. We also mean that an endless number of expectations of a certain description and numerous instances of it would be entailed by the truth of the opinion.

In developing the meaning of truth Peirce was, I think, following the same procedure he recommended for the explication of any general predicate (notably in "How to Make Our Ideas Clear"). If we mean by 'hard' "would not be scratched by many substances," we can form the translation and explication of the predication "x is hard" as follows: We specify a certain experimental situation, E (the apparatus and conditions for scratch-testing on x); the operation of testing, O; and the general result, R (x is not scratched by many substances in repeated tests). We may then say: "x is hard" *means*: if E and O, then R (x would not be scratched). Peirce's accounts of the meaning of truth exhibit analogous distinctions. To say x is true (where x is an opinion or statement) will mean: if E (the conditions for investigating x) and O (the operation of endless investigation of x), then R (x is fated to be agreed on by all who engage in O). We can state this last part of the description in another way suggested by Peirce, namely: if E and O, then the number of assentors to x approaches unity while the number of dissentors approaches zero.[14]

It is to be noticed that we are not here saying that if x is true, it is *because* an endless investigation results in an ever increasing assent and diminishing dissent to x among investigators. For no such investigation need occur; and even if it could occur, the investigation does not *make* x true (for in the same way, the operation of scratch-testing on x does not make x hard). Thus, all we are permitted to say is that the above conditional description makes explicit what we *mean* when we ascribe truth to some x.

The above sketch of Peirce's method of explicating the meaning of truth should also indicate how the idea of probability and the notion of meaning containing a reference to the future have roles in Peirce's definition of truth. For R represents a statistical fact: the distribution of assent and dissent in investigations tending to a limit (and that distribution, for Peirce, is like the tendency of a coin when tossed to come up heads one-half the number of tosses, as we noticed previously in II). Thus the meaning of "x is true" contains a reference to this future result (to innumerable confirming instances of "is fated to be ultimately agreed on by all who investigate").

It is thus necessary to distinguish the following.

(a) Why we think a belief is true. As to this, Peirce says we think a belief is true if we have no reason to doubt it, or it satisfies us, or it appears "unassailable by doubt" (*CP* 5.416). A further reason would be that the belief, as a premiss or a habit of reasoning, always (so far as we know) leads to satisfactory consequences, no dissatisfactory consequences having been encountered to follow from it.

(b) How we know a belief is true. Here we instigate tests and develop inferences. And while falliblism advises us that we never know fully that any of our beliefs is true,[15] we may have good reasons for thinking that some and indeed most of them are true.

(c) What we mean by ascribing truth to a belief.

In criticizing Peirce's definitions of truth, Russell, Quine, and Ayer treat (b) and (c) as comprising one question. They proceed, without any justification that I can discover, to confuse (b) and (c); to regard Peirce's definitions of the meaning of truth (that is, (c)) as involving and depending fundamentally on questions of (b), of how truth so defined could ever be known, or how we could ever come to know a belief is true. And because Peirce defines truth (for purposes of (c)) as a statement represented by an ideal limit of endless investigation, they object that this is not acceptable because *in fact* no actual investigation will be endless nor will it be likely to arrive at an ideal limit. This question of fact, of how such truths can be known is, if anything, possibly germane to (b); but it does not present a fatal difficulty for what Peirce discusses under (c). Peirce himself kept this distinction clear. He wrote:

> I do not say it is infallibly true that there is any belief to which [a] person would come if he were to carry his inquiries far enough. I only say that that alone is what I call Truth. I cannot infallibly know that there *is* any Truth.[16]

It is curious that his critics should fail to distinguish issues of (b) and of (c), for they are the very philosophers who have effectively pointed out on other occasions that the meaning of "truth" and the discovery of truth are not at all the same.

IV

Dewey was right in noticing the importance of (A) and (B) as fundamental statements of Peirce's theory of truth. But there are other formulations which, while not free of obscurity, are equally important. Many of these have a place—as perhaps all things were envisioned by Peirce to have a place—within the theory of signs. And he later expressed regret that he had omitted from the famous articles of 1877–78 a discussion of signs and of pragmatism as the method of interpreting signs.[17] We find a change, not so much in the meaning of truth, but in the development of specialized procedures of analysis and of concepts for expressing that meaning. As an alternative locution to the set of ideal conditions and operations forming the conditional explication by means of E, O, and R (as we represented these above), Peirce seems to have become more interested in the clarification of truth as a function of a certain kind of signs and the conditions they must satisfy through a procedure of interpretation.

When Peirce treats the meaning of truth in his theory of signs, he emphasizes the role of propositions. Truth, he says, belongs "exclusively to propositions" (*CP* 5.553). Propositions are

Dicisigns, "the kind of sign that *conveys* information" (*CP* 2.309; 2.320), and "professes to refer" or relate "to something as having a real being" (*CP* 2.310).[18] Every sign is a *representamen*, "something which stands to somebody for something in some respect or capacity," it "addresses" and acts in this capacity, and further "creates in the mind of that person" another sign, which Peirce calls the *intepretant* (*CP* 2.228).[19] A proposition is thus indicative and is equivalent to a sentence in the indicative mood (*CP* 2.315). The indicative function is explained by noting that a proposition contains a subject and predicate, and "the subject is a sign; the predicate is a sign; and the proposition is a sign that the predicate is a sign of that of which the subject is a sign. If it be so, it is true" (*CP* 5.553).[20] The proposition as a whole is "a sign which separately indicates its object" (*CP* 5.569). The *interpretant* of the proposition is the mental representation thus determined, "it represents the proposition to be a genuine Index of a Real Object ... for an Index involves the existence of its Object" (*CP* 2.315).

A true proposition will be one whose representamen, as interpreted, is indicative (and an Index) of real objects as so represented. Peirce states the point with emphasis: "Truth is the conformity of a representamen to its object, *its* object, ITS object, mind you" (*CP* 5.554).

Since signs are interpreted by signs, and the interpretant sign is another sign of the same object, the interpretant of a proposition will be another proposition. A true proposition is one for which "every interpretation of it is true" (*CP* 5.569). Any necessary inference from a proposition is also an interpretant. It is by developing the interpretants of propositions and their issue in perceptual experience that acceptance or refutation is made possible and truth or falsity is discovered:

> an interpretant of the proposition would, if believed, produce the expectation of a certain description of [a] percept on a certain occasion. The occasion arrives; the percept forced upon us is different. This constitutes the falsity of every proposition of which the disappointing prediction was the interpretant. ... A true proposition is a proposition belief in which would never lead to such disappointment. ... (*CP* 5.569)

The picture that emerges from this very crude and inadequate sketch of Peirce's view is of a system of knowledge and communication as a vast and intricate structure of propositions and sets of equivalently related propositions as partial interpretants. The distinctively pragmatic aspect has to do with the method of developing interpretations of propositions. And a prerequisite of the method is that it enables us to derive in a systematic fashion such interpretants of propositions as will eventuate in predictive judgments and percepts of a certain prescribed and definite character. For this method will be essential to determining the *meaning* of signs as well as to determining their *truth*. The derivations issue as "precepts" and formulae "prescribing what you are to *do* in order to gain a perceptual acquaintance with the object of the word" (*CP* 2.330) or proposition. While for valuable practical purposes the interpretations are limited, theoretically they are never exhaustive or complete; there is no last analysis or final interpretation. Or perhaps, if there is a final interpretation of propositional signs, it will not be found in scientific thought but, Peirce suggests, in the esthetically good, the ultimate achievement and highest translation of all thought (*CP* 5.594).

Thus while the theory of truth found in (A) and (B) was absorbed in a wider theory of signs, the theory of signs culminates in a transcendental esthetic. Moreover, it was from the esthetic that Peirce conceived his proof of the truth of pragmatism. The line of thought moved back and forth or took a cyclical course.

While I regard Peirce's outlook to be primarily a form of philosophic naturalism, there are certainly propensities to transcendentalism incurrent in and crossing through the naturalistic grain. Even (A) stands to (B) as truth conceived in the spirit of experimental naturalism to a *semiotic* (*CP* 2.227) with offshoots into idealism. Affinities with Royce could be cited, and Peirce once remarked on the close alliance of pragmaticism and Hegelian absolute idealism (*CP* 5.436). Still, the transcendentalism might be given a Kantian rendition, referring to interpretative principles whose application is not a departure from all experience, but whose relevance and function are not confined to any one limited portion or single aspect of experience, and which have the whole varied domain of experience for their object. In this sense the theory of signs appears to be a transcendental construction.

In inspecting Peirce's theorizing about truth we seem to have found an illustration of the main thesis of Professor Goudge's book.[21] I am not certain that the conflict in this case is irresolvable. While Goudge's thesis may require certain refinements and modifications, it remains, nonetheless, a valuable guide to our understanding of Peirce's thought and the problems that affected its troubled and incomplete development. And we are enabled to appreciate all the more perceptively Peirce's remarkable acumen, imaginative power, and richness of philosophic vision—the rarest of capabilities but which never quite achieved complete focus or realization. That destined incompleteness which he believed to be a positive virtue and essential ingredient of truth in the unfolding of reason in communal and public forms was just as surely to be Peirce's private tragedy.

NOTES

* This paper is dedicated to Thomas A. Goudge. With some minor changes and an additional paragraph, it is to appear in a *Festschrift* for Professor Goudge edited by John C. Slater, Fred Wilson, and L. J. Sumner, and published by the University of Toronto Press.

1. Thus in the article on "Truth" for J. M. Baldwin's *Dictionary of Philosophy and Psychology* (New York, Macmillan Co., 1905). The definition, which I give as (B) below, is shown to apply to logical, normative, and practical subject matters. For these passages, see Vol. V, paragraphs 565–573, of the *Collected Papers of Charles Sanders Peirce*, 8 volumes: Vols. I–VI, edited by C. Hartshorne, and P. Weiss, Vols. VII and VIII edited by A. W. Burks (Cambridge, Mass., Harvard University Press, 1931–1958). All references in the present paper to this edition, designated as "*CP,*" will follow the usual practice of citing volume number and paragraph number.

2. The term "would" is a very important item in Peirce's discussions of dispositional traits, metaphysical possibility, his "scholastic realism," and his theory of probability. I have commented on this in *Meaning and Action: A Critical History of Pragmatism* (Indianapolis–New York, The Bobbs-Merrill Company, Inc., 1968), pp. 113–120.

3. But points of doctrine are, in this case, open to question; for a problem ever present to a commentary on any of Peirce's ideas is how to establish connections and priorities between the published and the manuscript material, and to determine which (of often several drafts and revisions) are the authoritative statements, i.e., most representative of Peirce's intention. Perhaps the controlling context for the determination of Peirce's ideas is his general theory (or theories) of signs, with its relation to his tripartite categorical scheme and the existential graphs. Here, to aggravate our problem, there is a vast collection of manuscript material raising difficult questions of chronology, stages of development, and the scope and direction of Peirce's philosophizing. For these reasons one must applaud the efforts now being taken, under Professor Max Fisch's direction, to make more of these materials available in chronologically accurate and complete texts.

4. John Dewey, *Logic: The Theory of Inquiry* (New York, Henry Holt and Company, 1938), p. 345.

5. William James, *Pragmatism* (Cambridge, Mass., Harvard University Press, 1975), pp. 106–107; or *The Meaning of Truth* (Cambridge, Mass., Harvard University Press, 1975), pp. 88–89.

6. "Dewey's New Logic." In P. Schilpp. ed. *The Philosophy of John Dewey.* ("The Library of Living Philosophers," Vol. I [Evanston and Chicago, Northwestern University Press, 1939]), pp. 135–156.

7. *Ibid.*, p. 145.

8. Quine, *Word and Object* (Cambridge, Mass., M.I.T. Press, 1960), p. 23.

9. Quine's objection on this score has been carefully and critically discussed by

Robert Almeder in "Fallibilism and the Ultimate Irreversible Opinion." *American Philosophical Quarterly*, Monograph No. 9 (1975), pp. 33–54.

10. A. J. Ayer, *The Origins of Pragmatism* (San Francisco, California, Freeman, Cooper & Company, 1968), p. 27.

11. *Ibid.*, p. 26.

12. *CP* 8.43 "... upon innumerable questions, we have already reached the final opinion."

13. These matters are dealt with in my *Meaning and Action*, pp. 105–120. See note no. 2.

14. These points are argued in more detail in my *Meaning and Action*, pp. 90–92; 118; 129–132. See note no. 2.

15. *CP* 1.14 : "There are three things we can never hope to attain ... absolute certainty, absolute exactitude, absolute universality."

16. Letter to Lady Welby, Dec. 23, 1908. Irwin C. Lieb, *Charles S. Peirce's Letters to Lady Welby* (New Haven, Conn., Whitlock's Inc., 1953), p. 26.

17. This has been pointed out by Max Fisch in a paper, "The 'Proof' of Pragmatism," forthcoming in the *Festschrift* for Professor Goudge, University of Toronto Press.

18. It should be noticed that proposition signs are not confined to linguistic signs. A portrait of a man with his name under it or a photograph can be propositions. *CP* 2.320; 5.569.

19. On *representamen* see also *CP* 1.564.

20. See *CP* 5.435, where this is developed as the "essential proposition of pragmaticism." See also *CP* 2.316.

21. Thomas A. Goudge, *The Thought of Charles Sanders Peirce* (Toronto, University of Toronto Press, 1950).

PEIRCE ON OUR KNOWLEDGE OF MIND:
A NEGLECTED THIRD APPROACH

E. JAMES CROMBIE
Université Sainte-Anne, Pointe-de-l'Eglise, Nova Scotia

In his 1868 articles for the *Journal of Speculative Philosophy*,[1] Charles Sanders Peirce, in the context of a larger epistemological discussion, presents and argues for a theory of mind which has been largely disregarded by contemporary English-speaking philosophers, especially those who write on what is called the philosophy of mind. One of the consequences of this view of mind, which seems to have been the result of more than a little judicious weeding in the Kantian garden, is that "we have no power of Introspection, but all knowledge of the internal world is derived by hypothetical reasoning from our knowledge of external facts."[2] This position, however, is not to be confused with behaviorism, which says that knowledge of the internal world is derivable only from observation of behavior, a more restrictive position than Peirce's, although Peirce would of course agree with those behaviorists who deny that we have a special intuitive faculty of introspection, but would be willing to allow that in many cases the individual person is in a much better position to judge of his own state of mind than strangers who have only observations of his behavior to go on. Peirce's point is about the epistemological status of such judgments: it is *not* that judgments about one's internal state cannot be made with a high degree of assuredness, but that such judgments do not enjoy a *special kind* of assuredness not enjoyed by others.

Peirce's position, as has just been mentioned, is at least partly shadowed forth by Kant's. Kant likewise denies that we have any direct intuitive introspective access to the inner nature of our own minds, holding not only that "the representations of the *outer senses* constitute the proper material with which we occupy our mind"[3] but furthermore that we derive from "things outside us ... the whole material of knowledge, even for our inner sense"[4] and that the mind can know itself only insofar "as it is affected by itself."[5]

The usual procedure, however, among English-speaking philosophers of the past century has been, when treating of mind, to neglect these valuable hints[6] provided by Kant and developed by

Peirce and to adopt instead some variation on one of two basic themes, which Jerome Shaffer has characterized as the first-person and third-person approaches toward mind, respectively.[7]

The first-person type of approach is so named because it analyses mental terms as referring to the data of introspection. A first-person type analysis of mental terms thus renders their application to third parties somewhat problematical and runs afoul of the arguments against the possibility that the meaning of any word has to do with its reference to an essentially private item. In the words of Wittgenstein's parable, the beetle in the box "cancels out."[8] And even if the beetle did not "cancel out," it is a subject of controversy whether we can get a look at even our own beetle, with no less an authority than D. O. Hebb maintaining that we cannot;[9] so that if the logical difficulty about reference to the contents of private awareness could somehow be circumvented, there remains the empirical point that there is no private awareness of our own states of mind, or at least none that is more immediate than our awareness of the properties of, say, chairs, so that the entities allegedly referred to by mental terms are not available in any epistemologically *special* way, whether that special way be termed "immediate acquaintance," or "privileged access,"[10] and are not the objects of a special category of judgments unaffected by such usual sources of error as afflict, for example, perceptual judgments as to the state of the external world.

Alternatives to the introspective or "privileged access" approach Shaffer characterizes as being "third-person accounts" in that they all seem to involve some kind of reference to the world beyond the sphere of consciousness and differ from first-person accounts principally in that there is held to be, in third-person accounts, no greater theoretical difficulty—and frequently less difficulty in actual practice—in ascertaining whether a mental term applies to a third party than in deciding whether it applies to oneself, since such accounts analyze mental terms as referring to some overt, publicly identifiable feature of intelligent beings, such as their actual conduct or behavior or the current state of their brains and nervous systems.

Such analyses are fraught with difficulties and obscurities, as a perusal of recent literature in the philosophy of mind will testify. The consensus of philosophical opinion seems to be, however, that these difficulties can be ironed out through some variation on the third-person theme, whereas proponents of a purely first-person approach have been pretty well stymied by Wittgenstein's beetle (or his cancelled-out remains).

Thus a third-person account of some variety or other would seem destined to carry the day were it not for the *prima facie* implausibility of third-person analyses. It is notoriously difficult to convince a man afflicted with intense grief or pain, particularly when he is a non-philosopher, that when we speak of his "mental state," no reference to what he actually feels is involved but only to his jumping up and down or to his tears or, alternatively, to the current pattern of electrical charges and discharges among his neurons and synapses.[11]

Even the Wittgensteinian version of the third-person approach, which appeals to the rules governing the use of mental terms, is unlikely to strike our afflicted man as a completely satisfactory analysis of mental terms, although it is superior to other third-person analyses in that it makes some concession to the special concern and insight which the subject may have in his own case. Ordinarily, of course, on the Wittgensteinian account as on many others, we apply or refuse to apply mental terms on the basis of either overt behavior or other evidence as to future overt behavior. But there is a *further rule*, the Wittgensteinian would say, governing the use of such terms and according to which we should defer, barring exceptional circumstances, to the testimony of the person to whom the term is applied.[12] Our afflicted man, however, temporarily forgetting his grief and pain and becoming very philosophical, replies that while all this may be an advance over crude behaviorism or crude identity-theory analyses, the appeal to this further rule of deference to the speaker seems somewhat *ad hoc* and unmotivated. Clearly we do have such a rule of usage, but the Wittgensteinian, pointing at this rule of usage, seems to want to leave it at that. What prevents us, however, from asking *why there should be such a rule of usage*? Is this not a legitimate move in the language game? And, if not, why not? We do not defer to tape-recorders which loudly proclaim, "I am not plugged in; my batteries are dead; I am not in play-back mode." Why then should we defer to human speakers? Because they have "privileged access" to their own states of mind? Or because a speaker "just knows" whether or not certain mental terms are applicable in his case? But to affirm the latter, on the Wittgensteinian account, is to affirm no more than that we ought to defer to the speaker—since intuitive or immediate awareness of our own inner states cannot be invoked here. Their presence or absence, on the Wittgensteinian view, is simply not relevant to the correct use of the mental terms in question, as the parable of the beetle is designed to show.

Some way out of this quandary seems called for. I think Shaffer's attempt at a "compromise solution" will not work, however, depending as it does on a dubious theory of meaning expressed by means of a metaphor in which the rules of usage give the "logical address," so to speak, and the private experience, the "logical content."[13] The analogy is with street addresses and the people (or meter sticks) to be met with at them. But the beetle might not be at home and the language game can function even if the box is empty.[14]

But before we go on to consider Peirce's account of mind and mental terms, let us briefly summarize the preceding proposals for the analysis of mental terms by considering what, according to each proposal, would be the theoretically most reliable way for me to know my own mind, to know, for example, whether I am in pain. The introspectionist recommends that I should close my eyes and pay very close attention to my inner state. The radical metaphysical behaviorist suggests that I consult reports of my recent behavior. The identity theorist suggests that I train myself in the use of a yet-to-be-invented super fluoroscope by means of which I could observe my own brain-states. The Wittgensteinian suggests that I listen to what others and I myself *say* about my mental condition.

Finally, we come to Peirce's suggestion, which is to construe the existence and properties of an empirical self as inferrable from anomalies and contradictions in the world as it presents itself to us, from how our observations of the external world seem to be "affected" by something not belonging to that world: The landscape appears to me today to be somehow not so cheerless and hard as it did yesterday. But when I mention this "fact" to family and friends, it is universally maintained that today is, if anything, even more wretched and miserable than yesterday and the landscape is certainly not more inviting. Upon reflection, then, I find that I cannot identify any precise feature in which today's landscape differs from yesterday's, either in the color of the dead leaves against the sky or in the cold and the intensity of the wind. I therefore attribute to a change in my own inner state a change which I had at first thought to observe in external facts. This, then, is the general line which Peirce proposes as an alternative to the suggestion that the contents of our minds are open to direct, intuitive introspection.

No one questions [says Peirce] that, when a sound is heard by a child, he thinks, not of himself as hearing, but of the bell or other object as sounding. How [is it then] when he wills to move a table? Does he then think of himself as desiring, or only of the table as fit to be moved? That he has the latter thought, is beyond question; that he has the former, must, until the existence of an intuitive self-consciousness is proved, remain an arbitrary and baseless supposition. There is no good reason for thinking he is less ignorant of his own peculiar condition than the angry adult who denies that he is in a passion.[15]

How many times, to insist on this last point, have we heard the following piece of dialogue: "Me, excited? *Who's* excited? It's you who're getting excited!" It is, as Peirce remarks, a mark of returning reason that a man will admit that he was angry.[16]

If a man is angry, [says Peirce,] he is saying to himself that this or that is vile and outrageous. If he is in joy, he is saying "this is delicious." If he is wondering, he is saying "this is strange." In short, whenever a man feels, he is thinking of *something*. Even those passions which have no definite object—as melancholy—only come to consciousness through tinging the *objects of thought*.[17]

But Peirce goes even further. Not only does he suggest that the knowledge we have of our inner selves is by a sort of hypothetical inference from what first enters consciousness as a judgment or series of judgments as to external fact,[18] but he goes so far as to maintain that the whole notion that there is an empirical self[19] which is the subject of my judgments and emotions is likewise reached by a species of inference from "external facts" and is in fact reached at about the time that we learn to distinguish between judgment and emotion, between fact and mere appearance.[20]

Returning, then, to our child who has just perceived a table as "fit to be moved," we observe first of all the importance which the child attaches to his body even before he may be supposed to have a notion of self and hence of "mine" and "yours." This body to which he attaches so much attention is identified not so much as his body as the *central* body, for the reason that "only what *it* touches has any actual and present feeling; only what *it* faces has any actual color; only what is on *its* tongue has any actual taste."[21] Furthermore, "the child ... must soon discover ... that things which are ... fit to be changed are apt actually to undergo this change, after a contact with that peculiarly important body called Willy or Johnny."[22]

During this time we may imagine that the child is proceeding to learn the language,

> that is to say, a connection between certain sounds and certain facts becomes established in his mind. He has previously noticed the connection between these sounds and the motions of the lips of bodies somewhat similar to the central one, and ... thus connects ... language with bodies somewhat similar to the central one. By efforts, so unenergetic that they should be called rather instinctive, perhaps, than tentative, he learns to produce those sounds. So he begins to converse.
> It must be about this time [Peirce continues] that he begins to find that what these people about him say is the very best evidence of fact. So much so, that testimony is an even stronger mark of fact than *the facts themselves*, or rather than what must now be thought of as the *appearances* themselves. ... A child hears it said that the stove is hot. But it is not, he says; and, indeed, that central body is not touching it, and only what that touches is hot or cold. But he touches it, and finds the testimony confirmed in a striking way. Thus, he becomes aware of ignorance, and it is necessary to suppose a *self* in which this ignorance can inhere. ...
> But, further, although usually appearances are either only confirmed or merely supplemented by testimony, yet there is a certain remarkable class of appearances which are continually contradicted by testimony. These are those predicates which *we* know to be emotional, but which *he* distinguishes by their connection with the movements of that central person, himself (that the table wants moving, etc.). These judgments are generally denied by others. Moreover, he has reason to think that others, also, have such judgments which are quite denied by all the rest. Thus, he adds to the conception of appearance as the actualization of fact, the conception of it as something *private* and valid only for one body. In short, *error* appears, and it can be explained only by supposing a *self* which is fallible.[23]

A number of things should be insisted upon with regard to this argument of Peirce's. The first is the important role which is attributed to the learning of *language* and contact with other human beings in coming to awareness of self. The second is that his account seems to fill in what was missing from the sort of account of mental concepts given by Wittgensteinians, namely it motivates the rules of usage which had appeared as an absolute before. The belief in self is seen to be a product of that kind of mental act which at its loftiest and most self-conscious involves the postulation of theoretical entities[24] but which in its middle varieties finds me concluding that there are birds outside my window judging from the chirruppy racket, even though I can't see any, and in its lower reaches includes perceptual judgments of the ordinary sort.

A third point to be mentioned is that whether Peirce's account will stand in all its details is less important here than that it seems that, whatever the faults of this particular account may be, they can be rectified and some account or other *along these lines* should prove correct. It is the point regarding the *kind* of account which could be given and checked out by empirical inquiry which is of philosophical interest. The identity-theorist, it should be remembered, does not precisely specify exactly which brain states correspond to which mental terms, nor does the Wittgensteinian do more than provide sketches of the sorts of rules of usage that he takes to be the embodiment of whatever meaning mental terms may have. So that we may see Peirce as indeed providing a distinct variety of philosophical account of mental terms. Furthermore, Peirce's account seems to fit neither of Shaffer's general classifications of approaches to mind. It differs from a third-person approach in that it involves inference from the nature of one's *own* experience, but differs from the first-person approach in that the experiences in question concern the outer and not the inner world.

Much more remains to be said of Peirce's view of mind and personhood. "The mind," he suggests, "is a sign developing according to the laws of inference"[25] and "the fact that every thought is a sign, taken in conjunction with the fact that life is a train of thought, proves that man is a sign: so, that every thought is an *external* sign, proves that man is an external sign. ... Thus my language is the sum total of myself."[26] A forthcoming paper by Konstantin Kolenda deals with this further development of Peirce's view of mind and its relation to Heidegger's approach to much the same subject.[27]

NOTES

1. Charles Sanders Peirce, "Questions Concerning Certain Faculties Claimed for Man" and "Some Consequences of Four Incapacities," in *The Collected Papers of Charles S. Peirce*, 8 volumes, Vols. I–VI edited by Charles Hartshorne and Paul Weiss; Vols. VII and VIII edited by A. W. Burks (Cambridge, Mass., Harvard University Press, 1931–1958), 5.213–317 esp. 5.225–237, 5.244–249, and 5.291–292. Further references to this edition are given with the usual abbreviation *CP*.

2. *CP* 5.265.

3. Immanuel Kant, tr. Norman Kemp Smith, *Critique of Pure Reason* (second impression with corrections; New York, St. Martin's Press, 1933), B67. (References are to page numbers of the A and B editions in the margin of the Kemp Smith translation.)

4. *Ibid.*, B xl, n; cf. B520/A491–2, B 701/A 673.

5. *Ibid.*, B 69. Elsewhere, Kant says that "consciousness in itself is not a representation distinguishing a particular object, but a form of representation in general; for of it I can only say that I am thereby thinking something." (A 346/B 404 with divergence from Kemp-Smith's translation.)

6. Roderick M. Chisholm takes note of Kant's contention that that which thinks "is known only through the thoughts which are its predicates" (A 346/B 404), but with a view to disapproving of it. *Cf.* "On the Observability of the Self," in *Language and Human Nature*, ed. Paul Kurtz (St. Louis, Warren H. Green, Inc., 1968), pp. 153 and 153n.

7. Jerome A. Shaffer, *Philosophy of Mind* (Englewood Cliffs, Prentice-Hall, 1968), p. 14.

8. Ludwig Wittgenstein, tr. G. E. M. Anscombe, *Philosophical Investigations* (3rd edition; New York, Macmillan, 1968), I, 293; also 271. Peirce makes a similar point when he observes that "if there be a man to whom red things look as blue ones do to me and *vice versa*, that man's eyes teach him the same facts that they would if he were like me" (*CP* 5.261). A feeling, "as a feeling, is merely the *material quality* of a mental sign" (*CP* 5.291).

9. D. O. Hebb, "To Know Your Own Mind," in *Images, Perception and Knowledge*, Western Ontario Series in the Philosophy of Science, forthcoming.

10. William Alston, "Varieties of Privileged Access," in *Empirical Knowledge*, eds. M. Chisholm and J. Swartz (Englewood Cliffs, Prentice-Hall, 1973), pp. 376–410. (Alston's article originally appeared in the *Am. Phil. Q.*, VIII (1971), 223–241.) Alston, while agreeing (pp. 393–394) that our knowledge of our own mental states may not be "immediate" in any spatial ("right up next to") or causal (no intervening causal links) sense, contends that in a third "more distinctively epistemic sense" (p. 394) some of our self-knowledge is immediate in that it is not *based on* or *justified by* any other knowledge. "... It seems overwhelmingly plausible to suppose," writes Alston, "that what warrants me in believing that I feel disturbed, or am thinking about the mind-body problem, is not some other knowledge that I have" (p. 396). Alston holds that a "first-person-current-mental-state-belief (FPCMSB)" is "self-warranted" in a sense in which the mere fact that I *have* such a belief *justifies* me in having it (cf. pp. 404, 399, etc.). The difficulty in this position lies in specifying the kind of justification involved in a way which is sufficiently strong, on the one hand, to permit a demarcation between the sort of justification Alston has in mind and the justification which attaches to any belief of mine about matters of daily concern, merely in virtue of my actually holding them— and sufficiently weak, on the other hand, to avoid absurdity when confronted with the well-known instances of unconscious mental activity as well as of ignorance and error with respect to our own mental states. Don Locke, incidentally, attempts to accommodate current philosophical paradigms with this latter requirement, by limiting his claim of privileged status to those processses which are "essentially conscious ... which means that they cannot be said to occur unless the person to whom they are ascribed knows that they occur" (Don Locke, *Myself and Others: A Study in Our Knowledge of Minds* (Oxford, 1968), p. 17). But this is reminiscent of the ontological argument: Who is to say whether conscious processes, as defined, exist? And there are further problems which arise as a result of attempting to stipulate that I cannot be said to be conscious of x unless I am conscious that I am conscious of x, etc.

11. J. J. C. Smart, "Sensations and Brain Processes," in *The Mind/Brain Identity Theory*, ed. C. V. Borst (London, Macmillan, 1970), p. 55–56. Smart, of course, is careful, when he claims that sensations, etc., are brain processes, not to claim that there is an identity of *meaning* between sensation-words and words usually taken to denote neurological happenings. Smart's thesis is thus not to be taken as an analysis of mental terms. Implicit in his thesis, however, is the view that if our knowledge of neurology were sufficiently improved we could, without any

reduction in the number of true statements of non-linguistic fact we could make, eliminate sensation words altogether!

12. Alston, who is not quite a Wittgensteinian, reports (*op. cit.*, p. 403) a stronger formulation of this as a possible defence against criticisms of certain versions of the "privileged access" thesis: "... It is 'part of their meaning' that FPCMSB's are self-warranted. It is impossible, in *our language*, to make sense of the supposition that such a belief should not be warranted." Alston does not seem to criticize this position, but it is not clear that he adopts it either.

13. Shaffer, *op. cit.*, pp. 28–33.

14. Wittgenstein, *op. cit.*, I, 293. Cf. note 8, above.

15. *CP* 5.230.

16. *CP* 5.247.

17. *CP* 5.292.

18. For an account of the evolution of Peirce's thought and terminology with regard to "external facts" and judgments as to external fact, *cf.* E. James Crombie, *Peirce, Cognition, and the Modes of Inference*, M.A. thesis at the University of Waterloo, Ontario, 1970, p. 44.

19. The empirical self is, for Peirce, to be distinguished from the "absolute ego of pure apperception" (Cf. *CP 5.235 and 5.225*).

20. *CP* 5.233.

21. *CP* 5.229. (Italics added.)

22. *CP* 5.231.

23. *CP* 5.232–234.

24. David Bloor, "Is the Official Theory of Mind Absurd?" in *Br. J. Phil. Sci.*, XXI (1970), 167–183. Bloor, following Fodor, suggests as a criticism of Ryle that "the everyday and technical language of psychology, our ascriptions of mental conduct concepts, should be understood by likening them to the process of postulating theoretical entities in science." But Bloor's and Fodor's approach seems nonetheless to fall under the designation of a "third-person" approach, given their tendency to construe, e.g., desire as an explanation of behavior (in others) rather than primarily as accounting for anomolous perceptions (in oneself). Bloor's argument against Ryle is interesting in that he draws a parallel between the reasoning of early opponents of atomic theory (atoms are unobservable, have no explanatory power when unpacked, etc.) and Ryle's criticisms of the "official theory" of mind.

25. *CP* 5.313.

26. *CP* 5.314.

27. Konstantin Kolenda, " 'Man is a Sign'; Peirce and Heidegger," Texas Tech. Press, forthcoming. Read at NAAP meeting in New Orleans, March, 1976.

C. S. PEIRCE'S CRITIQUE OF PSYCHOLOGISM

CHARLES J. DOUGHERTY

Creighton University, Omaha, Nebraska

In 1903 Peirce, recalling his earlier article (1878) "How to Make Our Ideas Clear" and the account of belief and truth contained there, wrote

> My original article carried this back to a psychological principle. The conception of truth, according to me, was developed out of an original impulse to act consistently, to have a definite intention. But in the first place, this was not very clearly made out, and in the second place, I do not think it satisfactory to reduce such fundamental things to facts of psychology ... all attempts to ground the fundamentals of logic on psychology are seen to be essentially shallow.[1]

Peirce is here accusing himself of psychologism, the doctrine that the science of psychology provides the theoretical justification for the laws of logic. An examination of Peirce's writings on logic after this psychologistic period[2] reveals a number of arguments against that doctrine. We can isolate the following.

1. Psychology is an experiential or positive science. Logic, on the other hand, contents itself "... with considering what would be the case in hypothetical states of things."[3]
2. Logic, unlike psychology, is a normative discipline. Its application is conditioned upon acceptance of *right* reasoning as a norm. Logic assumes an element of choice, of control.[4]
3. Right reasoning means reasoning that accords with the facts as they are, not as we may think they are. Logic, therefore, is not the science of how we do think, but the science of how we ought to think *in order to be in absolute conformity with fact.*[5]
4. The logical notion of inference is a broader category than human consciousness. This claim is supported by the existence of what Peirce called "calculating machines," those machines which turn out data having a correct inferential relation to the data turned in.[6]
5. Psychology is primarily concerned with human judgments. Logic is primarily concerned with propositions. "To explain

the judgment in terms of the 'proposition' is to explain it by that which is essentially intelligible. To explain the proposition in terms of the 'judgment' is to explain the self-intelligible in terms of a psychical act, which is the most obscure of phenomena or facts."[7]

6. Psychologism is circular. "Now, the only sound psychology being a special science, which ought itself to be based upon a well-grounded logic, it is indeed a vicious circle to make logic rest upon a theory of cognition so understood."[8]

7. Peirce held that psychology itself was not a very secure or developed science. He claimed that "... psychological conceptions are not sufficiently matured to afford a safe foundation for any part of logic. ..."[9]

8. Finally, psychology is an inductive science. It is therefore unfit for the task of justifying the laws which govern deductive logic. Inductions rely on fact gathering, infer only with probability and typically amplify our knowledge. Deduction does not rely on fact gathering (certainly not in any sense similar to induction), infers apodictically and does not amplify our knowledge. These two forms of argument must not be conflated.[10]

This is Peirce's critique of psychologism. Much could be and ought to be said about the validity of this critique and the several arguments comprising it. That is not what I plan to do here. Having demonstrated that Peirce did in fact have a critique of psychologism whatever its merits, I want to explore the deeper epistemological significance of psychologism. Before we quit these arguments entirely, however, one observation is in order. Arguments 1, 2 and 3 (respectively) allege that logic is hypothetical, normative and brings us into absolute conformity with fact. An adequate account of logic's validity will have to reconcile these diverse claims. Let us bear this in mind when we approach Peirce's alternative to psychologism.

Perhaps the foremost proponent of psychologism, and certainly the philosopher most frequently associated with it by Peirce, is John Stuart Mill. His classical statement of that doctrine appears in his work *An Examination of Sir William Hamilton's Philosophy.* There Mill stated:

It [logic] is not a science distinct from, and coordinate with, Psychology. So far as it is a science at all, it is a part, or branch, of Psychology; differing from it, on the one hand as a part differs from the whole, and on the other, as an Art differs from a Science. Its theoretical grounds are wholly borrowed from Psychology, and include as much of that science as is required to justify the rules of the art.[11]

The psychology Mill is referring to here is associationist psychology, specifically as developed by David Hartley, Thomas Brown and Mill's father, James Mill. This psychology was an attempt to create a new scientific system out of some general epistemological assumptions that run through the British empirical tradition and are especially evident (allowing for minor variations) in the philosophies of Locke, Berkeley and Hume. Let us attempt to describe some of the general assumptions.

One of the classical assumptions of British empiricism is that each individual enters the world of experience as a blank tablet. There are no innate ideas, the slate is clean. All ideas are a product of experience's effect on that tablet. The mind is regarded as essentially passive and receptive, experience acting on it and shaping it

Experience itself is composed of sense impressions and ideas derived from them. The most simple ideas are images of the sense impressions which they individually represent. They differ from the original impressions only by degree. More complex ideas are not derived directly from sense impressions but are aggregates of simple ideas which are so derived. Sense impressions are atomic. Each is an individual unique in itself save for its resemblance to other impressions in the past. These resemblances, along with the order and regularity of certain groups of sense impressions, account for the mind's tendency to move from one idea to another similar to it. The mind associates ideas on the basis of past order, regularity and resemblance among the sense impressions from which the ideas derive.

These are the major insights of associationist psychology: a receptive mind moving from idea to idea on the basis of associations perceived among the incoming sense impressions. This model is essentially two termed, mind and sense impressions. The former is passive with respect to the latter.

Given this analysis of the knowing situation several important considerations follow. All knowledge will be founded upon the renderings of sense. Derivative knowledge claims will be composed out of the more basic deliverances. All knowledge will be only as secure as the initial knowings. These initial knowings will be known directly, i.e., without a medium. Most importantly the method for judging the validity of any particular knowledge claim will be reductive. Complex notions will be shown to be valid when they have been shown to be reducible *in toto* to their origins in sense impressions.

Associationist psychology was conceived by Mill to be an empirical study of the associations the mind makes among ideas and of the genesis of both complex ideas from simpler ones and of simple ideas themselves from sensations. Associationist psychology would, among other things, offer an empirical method of judging the validity of any idea. The laws of logic are themselves ideas and must have been derived from sense experience like any other ideas. Associationist psychology would therefore be in the position to justify the laws of logic. This is the doctrine of psychologism.

Peirce's rejection of psychologism can now be seen in a larger context. He rejected nearly all of the epistemological assumptions of which psychologism is a part.

For Peirce the knowing situation is irreducibly triadic. Knowing is not an immediate intuition. It requires a medium. That medium is an act of interpretation. The mind is confronted by some impressions and it actively interprets them in terms of its own experience.

The lowest level instance of this is the perceptual judgment. Peirce calls the sensory aspect of the perceptual judgment the percept. Strictly speaking we have no knowledge of the percept since it passes in the absolute present.[12] Our most primitive knowing is the knowing of the percept *as* something. We have at this point already classified the ephemeral percept under some general category from our past experience.[13] This classification is unconscious and indubitable at the instant that it occurs, but since it is conjectural or hypothetical in nature it is eminently fallible and revisable after additional experience.

The three aspects of the knowing situation for Peirce then are the percept, the general classification and the interpretation of the percept under the general classification. These three aspects are "given" as an essential unity and correspond to the phenomenological categories of secondness, firstness, and thirdness, respectively. These three aspects can never be separated in fact but they can be separated in thought by the process Peirce calls precision.[14] This process allows us to precind the first from both the second and the third.[15] In terms of the perceptual judgment this means that we can mentally isolate the general aspect of any experience and regard it in itself as an *ens rationis*[16] or a Platonic Idea.[17]

Any relationships which these general ideas have among themselves will be evidenced in all experience since these generals are aspects of any possible experience. The most abstract relationships which these generals share are the laws of logic. The laws of logic can then be seen to relate to a hypothetical world of ideas and to be guaranteed, so to speak, to always conform us to the facts—the facts being partly (aspect-partly) composed of these ideas. Furthermore logic is normative since it will divide all possible propositions into the true (or possibly true) and the false. The latter class of propositions will be those which incorporate into their unity of thirdness some firstness or general idea which violates a relationship it has with other general ideas. ("This is a round-square," for example, is known to be false separate from any empirical testing.) Logic is at once hypothetical, normative and brings one into conformity with fact. Psychologism is thus avoided completely. The laws of logic can be validated in a formal analysis of relations among general ideas in their precinded firstness and yet known to apply to all experience since firstness will always compose an aspect of any experienced unity.

Peirce's rejection of psychologism, then, is a consistent extension of his rejection of the empiricist epistemology which underlies it. The knowing situation is not dualistic, it is triadic. The mind is not a passive recipient but an active interpreter of experience. There are no foundational bits of knowledge which we know intuitively and out of which all other knowledge is constructed. All knowing is a conjecturing about the present in terms of generals learned in the past. Validation lies in the future, as only future experience can tend to confirm hypotheses. There is no certainty in knowing in its complete thirdness sense. Logical certainty is certainty only of our own firstness contribution to the triadic knowing situation. Of knowing in its full empirical sense there is only high probability based on success in both thought and action, a success always subject to review in light of future experience.

In 1900, just three years before Peirce rejected the psychologistic leanings of his earlier writings, Edmund Husserl made a startlingly similar confession.

> I began work on the prevailing assumption that psychology was the science from which logic in general, and the logic of the deductive sciences, had to hope for philosophical classification. For this reason psychological researches occupy a very large place in the first (the only published) volume of my Philosophy of Arithmetic ... I became more and more disquieted by doubts

of principle, as to how to reconcile the objectivity of mathematics, and of all science in general with a psychological foundation for logic.[18]

Husserl then went on to offer his justly famous critique of psychologism and in particular of John Stuart Mill. Husserl claimed that psychology may not provide a justification of logic because logic is certain,[19] exact,[20] a priori,[21] implies no matters of fact[22] and divides a given domain normatively.[23] Psychology, by contrast, is probable, vague, inductive, existential in reference and descriptive. If we allow Peirce's claim that logic brings us into absolute conformity to fact to be a means of expressing logic's certainty and that psychology's vagueness is an aspect of its insecurity as a science then Peirce's critique contains every substantial element of Husserl's.

Furthermore, Husserl follows his critique of psychologism by a lengthy investigation into and rejection of the epistemological assumptions lying behind psychologism. These are typically those of British empiricism. A similar relationship between rejection of psychologism and rejection of certain empiricist assumptions can be seen in Peirce's thought.

Finally, if we look at the alternative epistemology which Husserl offers in the *Logical Investigations* we can see empiricism's dualism being replaced by a triadic relation. Husserl claims that all possible experience is intentional. The most basic of all intentional acts, the one upon which every other intentional act is founded, is what he calls an objectifying act, an act of constituting some object as an object for consciousness. "Each concretely complete objectifying act," writes Husserl, "has three components: its quality, its matter and its representative content."[24] Representative content is sensory material and is clearly similar to Peirce's notion of the percept, the aspect of secondness. Matter for Husserl is an essence, the general idea under which the representative content is classified. This is clearly Peirce's firstness aspect. Quality is the nature of the act of constituting representative content under an essence as an object of assertion, belief, fantasy, doubt, etc. This notion of quality bears resemblance to Peirce's notion of thirdness since it is an act of combining the other two members into a unitary interpretation. Husserl's own justification of logic is correspondingly similar to Peirce's: laws of logic are high order relationships among essences which compose the matter of any possible objectifying act.[25]

All of the above references to Peirce's works have been to papers written after 1896. All of the references here to Husserl have been to his *Logical Investigations* (1900–1902). For the sake of this comparison Peirce and Husserl are contemporaries. Although there was no interaction between these philosophers we have uncovered a great deal of similarity. Both had psychologistic periods which they came to recognize and reject. Both replace the empiricists' dualistic epistemology with a triadic one. This allows both men to develop an alternative account of logic's validity. Both of these accounts hold logic to be a system of meaning relationships which hold among general ideas. These general ideas are aspects of every knowing situation. For each philosopher the total knowing unity is bound by the meaning restrictions which bind the general ideas as parts.

There is one further historical observation which may shed some light on these affinities. In the year 1901, Husserl first used the term phenomenology (Phänomenologie). The very next year, 1902, is Peirce's first recorded use.[26] For Husserl and Peirce the practice of this new discipline relied on a methodological technique similar in both cases and similarly different from any method available to British empiricists. Husserl called his method *boundless free variation*. Peirce called his *precision*. For both this method was a way of isolating in thought that which was not capable of isolation in fact. Any given unity could be analyzed in terms of relationships between aspect-parts whereas the empirical tradition allowed only decomposition, i.e., reduction, into piece-parts. It is my speculative opinion that this methodological advance by these two men at roughly the same time is crucial to understanding the other similarities noted. Only by the development of a more subtle instrument of analysis could Peirce and Husserl both have revealed a third element in the knowing situation: an actively interpreting human mind.

Even if this speculation of mine is helpful in understanding the other epistemological parallels between Peirce and Husserl we are left with the task of accounting for the relatively simultaneous development of these two methods of boundless free variation and precision. I can think of no better way to penetrate this remarkable coincidence than by appeal to one of Peirce's own speculations, viz. that there exists a continuity of mind, "an apparent agapasm in the history of thought."[27]

NOTES

1. Charles Sanders Peirce, *The Collected Papers of Charles S. Peirce*, 8 volumes. Vols. I–VI edited by Charles Hartshorne and Paul Weiss; Vols. VII and VIII edited by A. W. Burks (Cambridge, Mass., Harvard University Press, 1931–1958), 5.28. Further references to this edition are given with the usual abbreviation *CP*.

2. The year 1896 seems to have been a turning point in this respect. See, e.g., M. G. Murphey, *The Development of Peirce's Philosophy* (Cambridge, 1961), p. 355.

3. *CP* 2.65.

4. *CP* 2.165, 2.182, 4.540, 5.109.

5. *CP* 2.50, 2.52, 5.85, 5.126.

6. *CP* 2.56, 2.54, 2.59, 2.66, 4.551.

7. *CP* 2.309, 1.561, 2.148, 2.252, 5.424.

8. *CP* 3.432, 2.51, 2.210, 5.485, 8.167, 8.242.

9. *CP* 2.43, 2.42.

10. E.g., *CP* 2.766.

11. John Stuart Mill, *An Examination of Sir William Hamilton's Philosophy* (4th ed.; London, 1872), pp. 461–2.

12. *CP* 2.27, 2.141, 5.116, 7.653.

13. *CP* 5.151, 5.156, 5.157, 5.181, 5.183, 5.186.

14. The spelling of this term varies in Peirce's writings.

15. *CP* 1.353. (It also permits separation of second from third, but not third from second and first or second from first.)

16. *CP* 1.83, 3.642, 4.463.

17. *CP* 2.228. (Peirce also calls this the *ground*.)

18. Edmund Husserl, *Logical Investigations*, 2nd German ed., trans. J. N. Findlay (New York, 1970), p. 42.

19. *Ibid.*, p. 98.

20. *Ibid.*, p. 98.

21. *Ibid.*, p. 121.

22. *Ibid.*, p. 104.

23. *Ibid.*, p. 130.

24. *Ibid.*, p. 740.

25. *Ibid.*, p. 144. Also see Edmund Husserl, "A Reply to a Critic of My Refutation of Logical Psychologism," tr. Dallas Willard, *Personalist*, LIII (1972), 11.

26. Herbert Spielgelberg, "Husserl and Peirce's Phenomenologies: Coincidence or Interaction?," *Philosophy and Phenomenological Research*, XVII (1957), 164.

27. *CP* 6.315.

I gratefully acknowledge the assistance of Professors C. F. Delaney and Gary Gutting, both of the University of Notre Dame, in the preparation of my doctoral dissertation, which is the basis for this paper.

SOME INTERESTING CONNECTIONS BETWEEN THE COMMON SENSE REALISTS AND THE PRAGMATISTS, ESPECIALLY JAMES

ELIZABETH FLOWER

University of Pennsylvania, Philadelphia, Pennsylvania

The history of ideas is often as interesting for what it reveals of problems that did not enter the mainstream as for those that occupied the center of the stage. This is particularly so when the issues underlie the practice of an age but are made virtually inaccessible by the presuppositions with which it was working.

One such problem—surprisingly late in reaching center stage—concerns goal-oriented and purposive activity, planning and cognitively directed action, the relation between knowledge and action, and learning by self-conscious critique. These only began to be treated head on toward the end of the nineteenth century and into the twentieth under the pressures of the complexity of linguistic competencies, computer programming, and the renewed interest in intentional behavior and cognitive studies generally, which once again joins philosophy and psychology in common pursuits.

Interest in such problems is a hallmark of pragmatism and accounts for much of its American flavor. I want to hold that the distinctive manner of approaching this nest of problems has its roots in a rather special way of reading Locke, one cultivated by Scottish common sense realists but thoroughly naturalized on American soil.

Locke's *Essay* worked with a singularly limited view of human capacities and activities. On the whole, the classic British tradition followed Locke's view of that nature as basically passive in knowing, reproducing the combinations of elements under tyranny of the order given in experience of nature, pulled and pushed by pleasures and pains. Reasonable and guided action remains a mystery. Insofar as that view was enriched by the mainstream of British philosophy, it was (Berkeley excepted) largely through a growing appreciation of sensibilities, aesthetic and moral as in Hume and Adam Smith, or of the complexities of the associative mechanism, as in Hartley and James Mill. The model was seldom challenged, nor were the activities of which men were patently capable often reviewed. Indeed, Hume's own psychology could not explain either the writing of a sustained treatise or the executing of his planned economic reforms.

Now the Americans followed these developments with care, for they were (virtually) all Lockeans of some kind. They exploited all the Lockean options, from classic empiricism to materialism. And there was even, as in Frederick Beasley, a back-to-Locke movement, to take him straight. But these alternatives were at variance with manifest features of the life Americans were living. After all, they were carving out cities, pushing back frontiers, designing and realizing institutions. It is not surprising therefore that their major sympathies were enlisted by the Scots, taken broadly to include all those involved in the Scottish enlightenment, from Hutcheson to Hutton and even Hume (especially his Histories), the scientists and inventors of the day, but most particularly the trio central to common sense realism—Thomas Reid, Dugald Stewart, and Thomas Brown—who were attempting to keep alive a dynamic view of human powers. Often enough our histories of philosophy have treated them as having driven the realist strain in Locke to a dead end or, in Sir William Hamilton (their last representative), to have prepared the way for British neo-Hegelianism. Unfortunately, their bad press is often due to their nineteenth century self-appointed representatives such as McCosh of Princeton, who tangled with Mill over Hamilton's philosophy, and Porter of Yale.

The fact of Scottish influence on American thinking is not at issue, neither the broader Scottish enlightenment nor the narrower realism. It is not implausible that the Presbyterian structure of indirect representation, and the dynamics (at least in theory) of power flow in contrast to checks and balances, had a role in the unique features of the Constitution, molded as it was by James Wilson and Witherspoon (native Scotsmen) and Madison, the latter's graduate student. Rather less debatable is the reform of Scottish universities which, beginning early in the eighteenth century, allowed for specialization and encompassed the professional schools of law and medicine with the universities. This too was transferred in person either by the immigration of Scots or the Americans who were educated in Scottish universities.

Reid, Stewart and Brown were edited, published, abridged, pirated and cited from one end of this country to the other. The editions of *Encyclopedia Britannica* as designed by Stewart with their full-length supplements on topics ranging from metaphysics to moral philosophy, including economics and demography, were used as texts. Intimate connections were further cemented by personal contacts, especially of Franklin, Jefferson, Rush, and by such influential academics as William Smith, Samuel Johnson and William Smart of the colleges of Pennsylvania, Columbia and William and Mary.

Materials sufficient to establish the case for the direct influence of common sense, both Scottish and American, on pragmatism (and naturalism) would take us far beyond the limits of a paper such as this. That story remains to be filled out. It would most certainly carry us through Francis Bowen who, though stodgy as James insisted, still purveyed sophisticated Scottish problems to his Harvard students, coloring even the mood in which they read Kant. Merely the connections with James would require a monograph. I shall be content here to suggest the continuity of James's problems with the orientation developed by common sense realism, especially with respect to the problems mentioned at the outset.

Let us start by suggesting some of the issues to be found in James, especially in the *Psychology*, that took shape among the Scots and were further fashioned by American discussions. James himself recognized the roots of his psychology in the development of the tradition that began with Locke. He writes, "There is no new psychology, only the psychology of Locke, together with some further refinements in introspection, physiology, and evolution" *(Talks to Teachers)*. Certainly, like Locke, he regards psychology as a natural science of mental life, its phenomena and their conditions, but the refinements were massive. They included a thorough-going challenge to faculty psychology and to association-ism, an emphasis on the activity of the knower in constructing a stable world out of the flux of experience and the choice even then among alternate ones. The neurophysiology that he exploited helped tie voluntary action to perception, and evolution raised in a respectable way the questions of goal-seeking purposes and the utility of knowledge in directing responses as well as in survival. Refinements in introspection enstated an enormous phenomenal domain which included among others the vague and peripheral experiences of relation, of self, of activity. The innovation of James in these matters is perhaps best summarized in the features of consciousness that were taken by Wittgenstein and Whitehead and Schutz among others as the core of the revolution in psychology that James fathered. As will be recalled, consciousness (or awareness) is continuous, continuously changing, personal cognitive (i.e., referential) and selective (i.e., active).

Thomas Reid, the founder of Scottish philosophy in the narrower sense of common sense realism, is enjoying something of a revival today and an understanding of what he was trying to do is filtering down out of a century of misunderstanding. Starting as everyone did from Locke, he was taking the turn away from Berkeley's immaterialism; but he nonetheless utilized Berkeley's *New Theory of Vision* as a scientific account in his effort to recover a place for science from the debilitating challenge of Hume. Locke's *Essay* was perceived by Reid, as by the other realists, more as a scientific study of how we know than as an epistemology requiring speculative defense. The charge that their realism is weakly defended (which it doubtless is) misses this focus. They were exploring the science of knowing and perceiving as a general part of the science of man, just as they sought the properties and utility of chemistry or physiology; they examined the nature and powers of government as they might those of steam. From the start in America as well as in Scotland they had a kind of buffer against Hume's scepticism, finding Hutton's *Inquiry* with his view of probable but corrigible science more believable. Doubtless in the background is a kind of theological comfort—not so much that God wouldn't deceive us, as that He allows such competence as makes the obvious progress of science possible.

By common sense principles Reid did not mean horse sense or ordinary good judgment nor did his realism baldly assert a mind-independent external world and veridical perception of its objects. His defense of common sense principles is rather a defense of Newton and Locke and of the developing sciences, particularly chemistry and physiology. It was also an acknowledgment of the activities of thinking and planning which had found no place in Lockean theory. After Locke he was hesitant to label these as "innate," for he agreed with Locke that there is no content save what sensible experience provides. It is not content but operations which are innate, and operations not only have a heavy role in structuring knowledge but their laws are also open to observation, especially by way of the study of behavior and language.

Reid's position rests on a sophisticated account of perception as distinct from sensation; his central problem is how sensations become transformed into the (meaningful) perceptions which are judgmental and cognitive and carry an outward and objective reference. He denies that we have such loose and relationless elements as Locke's sensations or Hume's impressions from which as experience we compound an object. We do not have visual sensations as such, our perceiving is functionally a seeing of objects; we do not know concepts, our concepts are a knowing of objects. (He parts company here with a copy theory as a model.) Like James, Reid believes that we seldom if ever experience pure sensations mere or unstructured feelings; a pure sensation is a fiction of psychologists.

Sensation functions importantly as a sign conducting us to something in the world. Generally this interpretive feature is so automatic that we only distinguish the sign from what it signifies with difficulty. Our vocabulary contains no distinguishing terms to carry out the separation. When a man talks of the smell of a fish he generally intends a public quality in the fish; but he may use the same expression to refer to a private experience, i.e., the smell-as-subjective-feeling. These two are of course very unlike, but we locate the quality (in the fish or in awareness) as urgency requires. Strongly distasteful sensations are likely to be located within us. (Cf. James's analysis of sliding predicates, such as the weary road, and carrion.) All this is, of course, non-inferential; even in the language of art we do not see lines or hear notes and then proceed to infer some emotion, say grief; the grief is felt directly if it is felt at all. The sign has thus triggered into a system of meaning or language. The sign-signified relation is not a causal one; there is nothing in the sign as merely experienced which betrays the nature of the thing signified.

His distinction between perception and conception, once it gets beyond the standard contrast of particular and discerned samenesses and differences of individuals, has some interesting pragmatic premonitions. To conceive means to be able to predicate or apply a term unambiguously, but we must possess some sort of criterion of applicability in advance in order to make the judgment. Conceptions and perceptions evolve mutually; "categories" emerge only in the activity of judging and are modified by their utility.

Reid's list of principles of common sense is fairly complex. It includes necessary logical principles, assumptions about the uniformity of nature which he regards as constitutive of any inquiry (including Hume's) and contingent principles. Among the last, interestingly, he includes personal identity and continued existence over time. Of course this is not demonstrable but, just as the externality of objects is reflected in the grammatical distinction between subject and predicate, so also is the difference between self and object given in experience and reflected in all languages. Both the notion of self-identity and the stable world of objects depend on a kind of continuity in experience itself beyond what the associationist theory provides. Reid moves from "trains of association," advancing the metaphor to "fountains," and finally adds the flourish of the "stream of thought."

And if the stream of thought were not Jamesian enough, there is Reid's central emphasis on the active powers of man. He saw man as not only active in thought, but active in the natural world. A good bit of behavior is explicable in causal terms, but such explanation leaves untouched the patent facts of translating sensible and physiological stimuli into awareness and meaningful perception as well as how plans can be deliberately chosen and executed. The relations of agency and act, designer and system, producer and product, must all be distinguished from mechanical cause; they are experienced as phenomena of a different order and involve different relations. This dimension does not make human deliberation and action unapproachable by psychology; what it requires are fuller laws adequate to the phenomena.

Associative laws, though they do apply, are insufficient. Man is a natural being in the world of nature; just as we need knowledge of the physical world to bend it to our purposes and make it serve our ends, at the very least we require knowledge of those very interests and purposes in some advanced and sophisticated psychology, which is more than a mere department of physics or astronomy.

Reid's discussion of the active powers and his voluntarism formed part of the lectures which he delivered toward the end of his career, when the amiable protagonist Hume had been replaced by the pugnacious Dr. Priestley. Reid had not answered Priestley's early *Examination* (1774), but he did not come to grips with that author's materialism and determinism. When Priestley came to America, he brought this polemic with him, though the debate with the realists here was considerably muted, doubtless partly because Jefferson had sympathies with both sides. As a matter of fact, Reid found an ally in Richard Price, Priestley's friend and co-religionist. Price and Reid both denied the adequacy of the utilitarian reduction of morality to mere happiness, and of mental phenomena to association; both add the activity of the moral agent in a normative or regulative conscience, making duty the peer of happiness. Reid and Price, allied in moral opinions with Butler, were enormously influential in New England as regards these matters, although it was Price, through his intimacy with Channing, who touched the development of Unitarianism, while Reid was left in the common pool as a resource for the orthodox and the unorthodox alike.

Dugald Stewart, Reid's successor at Edinburgh, differed from Reid by refining common sense principles in ways that reflected his interest in mathematics, formal languages, and linguistics. Doubtless piqued by Priestley's and Kant's criticism of common sense as mere appeal to the vulgar, Stewart identifies it with those processes involved in and necessary to all reasoning, argument, and inquiry. He hoped, by examining mathematical reasoning as the paradigm, to coopt for common sense the kind of universality and necessity so often the step-child of empiricism. He sought to identify the rules by which we move from suppositions to conclusions, that is, to make explicit those undemonstrable relations by which a conclusion follows necessarily from its premises. Such principles are contributions of the mind, but their universality and utility convince us that they are harmonious with the order of nature. Still, such rules as guide transformations within a system are formal and guarantee nothing in the way of actual experience or existence. Stewart is very modern in distinguishing pure hypothetical systems from interpreted ones. He notes that the first are limited only by imagination and consistency, while the second, assigned empirical reference, are never more than probabilistic and contingent. He points out that even in the latter there may be alternate conceptualizations or theories over the same set of observations. Still, it is theory which provides the context in which such observations become meaningful. Theory and observation develop hand in hand. There must always be room for correction and replacement in the light of ongoing experience. There may even be rival and equally consistent hypotheses covering a single set of observations. In that case, the choice between them will turn on considerations of utility, elegance, and simplicity. Stewart illustrates the point by reference to the time when Copernican theory was overtaking the Ptolemaic. No difference of observation was really in contest, what was at issue was how the world was to be described, and the decision turned on considerations of simplicity.

Knowledge cannot be adequately analyzed in terms of sensation alone. From the latter we cannot derive the formal rules of inference, nor other principles such as the tendency to clarify, to order, and to assimilate experience and inquiry. Critical mental activities are attending and conceiving. Attending is active, of course, and reduces experientially to felt effort. When we are attending to one thing, the threshold of other stimuli may be raised or lowered: thus focus closes out surrounding noise, while love may heighten music. Conceiving presupposes the ability to isolate properties and to represent an absent object which has previously been perceived, but it does not provide a transcript of anything since even perception itself is modified by interest, the prefabrication of language, and other subtle aspects of our social environment. Language, taken in its broadest sense, preserves past experience and aids in ordering the world, but it is critical also for mediating between particular experiences and the likenesses and dissimilarities. Stewart's emphasis on the determining force of interest, choice and purpose in the building of a stable world out of alternate possible ones, and his view of the corrigibility of empirical knowledge, bring him very close to a conceptual pragmatism.

Brown's work is also suggestive of much to be found in James's psychology, including a thorough-going naturalism. He emphasizes the flow of experience and its activity, and he even agonizes over the relation between physiology and psychology. He was maverick enough for J. S. Mill to have claimed him for the main line of associationism that joins the Hartley-Priestley tradition to Mill and Bain, but, like the other realists from Hutcheson to Stewart, he found that the account of the association of ideas as it had been developed was insufficient to explain the palpable features of experience. Brown starts from the traditional theory determined to get as much mileage out of it as possible, but he reduces the relations of contiguity, resemblance and cause and effect to a single law of contiguity. Still, he could not ignore the apparent violations of such "laws": a single vivid experience, for example an execution, maintains itself over a multitude of colorless perceptions whatever the connections established by frequency, and even here there are marked individual differences, both only between different individuals and between the individual at different times.

Brown places association on a much wider base than merely ideas; it ranges over "feelings," that is, all sorts of internal and external affections, emotions, as well as cognitions. Thus the whiteness of untrodden snow and the innocence of an unpolluted heart are associated not by frequency but by engendering a common emotion. Brown prefers the term "suggestion" to denote simply the antecedence of one feeling and the sequence of another.

Of course, like the other realists before him, he built on Berkeley's *New Theory of Vision*, but his debt is far more than the term "suggestion." The sign-meaning relation is like that of stimulus and response and is analogous to language in that the relation between signs and things symbolized is neither logically necessary nor causal. But Brown develops a theory of natural signs which is essential if we are to learn how to regulate action for preservation. Thus sensible experience involves a kind of systematic organization that critically involves anticipation. This is already the antechamber of a pragmatic theory of verification.

Brown brings stronger physiological resources than Berkeley's to give a convincing account of the intimate relation of ideas to motor activity and of the latter to the construction of an external world. Physiologists like Whytt and the Bells had already shown that sensory as well as motor nerves are critical in controlled and voluntary movement. Brown calls on the experiences of felt resistance (not in one instance but differentially) with the memory of a temporal order of succession to explain how we construct a world of permanent and external objects. This construction is not inference, since organization occurs even at the perceptual level, for we see it in patterns and meaningful relations from the start. Departing from Hume he takes relations, which are a prerequisite for perceiving resemblances, to be directly experienced. These include analogies, which lie at the heart of science, as well as what James later called transitive states, that is, feelings of "and," "of," "fringe of continuity." Without such continuity consciousness would be reduced to a single point. Most important, departing from classic associationist theory, he allows for overlappings instead of time slices; thus there are even moods and constant purposes which, enduring over a period, may color a train of thought. Further, feelings may often fuse in a kind of creative synthesis, making a composite which has little resemblance to its constituents. Thus, in the James example, the taste of lemonade is not the sum of separate elements. Mental states are themselves indivisible wholes.

It is clear that the kind of dynamic theory Brown is sponsoring will help him in establishing self-identity. The self is not a faculty, but is found in the flow of experience, in the ways of annexing one experience to another. Self-identity becomes essentially a set of *my* memories having coherence in change, in just the way objects have a kind of permanence even when they are altering through time.

Selves and objects are constructions out of sets of events that preserve resemblances.

Similar considerations are involved in his moral theory. The complex fusion of emotion and association (suggestion) allows him, like Priestley, to overcome the utilitarian problem, viz. how each self-seeking individual comes to adopt as his goal the general good of society. Our humanity is learned through a social process; we transfer pleasure and moods to their sources: the pleasure we get from drinking milk becomes united with the idea of the mother who gives it to us. In general, we extend to a whole class of actions those approvals and disapprovals that arise in particular instances. However, at the last moment Brown balks at a complete utilitarianism, preferring to cast his lot with Hutcheson, Reid, and Stewart in championing a "moral sense." Of course this is no faculty but the perception of a special kind of "moral" relation between agent and act and situation. Brown lent his weight and influence in America to the notion of a social philosophy that would seek reform, not only by altering the individual, but by changing the environment. The function of knowledge is practical:

> It is of importance for us to know, *what* antecedents truly precede *what* consequents; since we can thus provide for the future, which we are hence enabled to foresee, and can, in a great measure, modify and almost create, the future to our-selves ...
>
> [*Phil. of the Human Mind*, 78]

Interesting in its own right is the kind of structural similarity between Reid, Brown and Stewart on the one hand and James, Dewey and C. I. Lewis on the other. James on the whole seems much closer to Reid; Brown adds an evolutionary and functional consideration; while Stewart's interest in alternate formal conceptual systems, the testing of them in experience, and the preference of one over another on pragmatic grounds takes the role of Lewis. (In connection with this last, there is an interesting survival of the Ptolemy illustration, including phrasing, in his "Pragmatic Element in Knowledge." Of course there is no indication that Lewis had read Stewart, but we may all remember how favorite examples of our teachers are inherited, including the cadences.) Intriguing, too, is the pre-shadowing of differences, for example between Dewey (and Brown) and Lewis (and Stewart) in the ways they see experience mustered to meet new cases.

WILLIAM JAMES'S THEORY OF TRUTH PHENOMENOLOGICALLY CONSIDERED

BRUCE WILSHIRE

Rutgers University, New Brunswick, New Jersey

I think a more profound questioning of philosophical assumptions concerning truth can be found in William James than has been carried on by most of his critics in America. But his probings can often be spotted and retrieved only after taking an approach to the truth question different from what prevails in America today; in this instance I take the phenomenological approach of Martin Heidegger. I do not mean to imply that Heidegger's ideas are just the same as his. I do mean that taking his viewpoint helps us to raise afresh key issues, and to see the distinctive approach to them taken by James, e.g., on the issue of the status of propositional truth.

In "The Essence of Truth" Heidegger inquires into the possibility of the "agreement" of intellect (or statement) with the thing to be known. No crude sense of "agreement" will do, e.g., a true statement about round coins is neither round nor metallic. A statement agrees when it asserts that the thing is what it really and genuinely is. But to claim to know what it really and genuinely is is to claim to know it is a true *thing*—a thing which agrees with its idea or form.

Thus Heidegger traces the somewhat hidden roots of contemporary discussion of truth to its quite completely hidden source in the scholastics: Truth as the agreement of created thing to the divine intellect guarantees the possibility of agreement between the human intellect and the created thing. The thing and the true human statement about it are in equal conformity with *the* idea: all coheres in the divine creative plan.

But our secular age, knowing that it has lopped off all belief in divine intellect and plan, thinks that it has cut the medieval roots as well. It has not, thinks Heidegger. The result is a self-closing circularity of thought about truth in which intellect is taken only in the sense of human intellect. Thus to assert the conformity of thing to intellect or idea is assumed to be merely an awkward and somewhat misleading re-statement of the conformity of intellect to

104

thing. For all we could mean by the thing itself is just what we mean by *our* true idea of it. Following Heidegger, one might say that only the ghost of God remains in this contemporary notion of the omni-competence of human ideas.

Thus the current belief in the autonomy of epistemology. But this is a delusion, thinks Heidegger, for truth as rightness cannot be explained on this basis except by *simply* postulating, at a certain level, agreement between ideas and things, and this begs questions of what things are—of beings in their Being. It also thinks mistakenly that explanation of truth is independent of the explanation of the nature of man as the vehicle and perfecter of intellect.

Hence Heidegger attempts to dig beneath the medieval roots so as not merely to repeat, in disguised and mutilated form, what grows from them. His radical, non-theological modification of the idea that truth is the conformity of thing to idea takes the form of his search for the truth of Being, with Being understood as that source of intelligibility without which no being could be thought to be anything. He denies that what is expressed by statements—propositions—are the ultimate bearers of truth. He implies that the term "proposition"—ambiguous as between subjective and objective "domains"—fudges the truth relationship by smearing first in the direction of mind, then in that of things, thus begging questions of the relationship of thought and thought's object and of mind and Being.

Heidegger's approach is a phenomenological one; it re-situates truth. He asks, when is the truth of a proposition evident? He answers, when it discovers for us that about which it is a proposition. When it discovers it in its self-manifestation, in its identity. We cannot say that truth is primordially a property of a proposition, because before we can verify any proposition, that about which it is a proposition must be evident, i.e., *truly* revealed.[1]

One might wish to speak of mental states as the bearers of truth. Then Heidegger's response would be that for a mental state to correspond to, and be true of, a physical thing, they must already have met. And this can be seen to be possible only when we understand the very reality of a thing to be disclosive, revelatory. That is, the *is* of that which-is, the Being or intelligibility of any being, must be understood phenomenologically, and as that which is metaphysically prior to, and neutral between, mind and matter. Things must be intended as intendable ("meanable") if any verifying experience is to be understood to be identical in its intention with the identity of the thing known.

The parallel in James is quite close: his "pragmatic" theory of truth makes sense only within the framework of his metaphysics of pure experience. Pure experiences are those which are metaphysically prior to, and neutral between, mind and matter. Pure experience "leans on nothing" James says. Truth emerges only within the real as simultaneously both reliable guidance for the knower and a quite literal "building-out" of the thing itself known—a development of its sphere of influence. Truth lies "between" the knower and the known, in "interaction."

Heidegger's and James's thinking is ethical in a radicalized classical sense. It thinks out of and into man's belonging in the whole. It thinks man's relationship to the whole without postulating thoughtlessly in advance the independent identity of the terms related, e.g., without postulating man as a subject, a repository of sensations. Thus Heidegger writes, in "Letter on Humanism," "That thought which thinks the truth of Being as the original element of man as ex-sisting is already itself at the source of ethics."[2] Or, in his first book on Kant, he states that man's belonging to Being makes the relation between subject and object possible, hence it cannot be reduced to the latter.[3]

If we are not distracted by sheer terminology, I think we can see that a central thrust of James's thought becomes clear only when we read it as similarly "ethically" oriented.[4] It is struggling to articulate a perpetually opening and open-ended common ground of meaning—vague on its fringes—out of which are precipitated the very notions of knower and known. His thought (for the most part) rules out the possibility that if the two are defined as actualities in advance of their relation in the ground any general ideal could link them later. For general ideas are always ready at work in the ground, and the question is with what justification. Knowledge by description cannot function independently of knowledge by acquaintance (as he understands the distinction, not Russell).

To compare the assumptions of some of the stock critiques of James's theory of truth with the theory's own assumptions is instructive. It has been charged (1) "That an idea 'works' cannot be a criterion of its truth, because even false ideas work, i.e., make us happy." This critique assumes that thought is a psychical state which works when it involves pleasure or vital feeling. These are not James's assumptions. Thoughts themselves have their own satisfactions and dissatisfactions independently of the satisfactions of the thinker, although when the meaning of the thought itself predicts the satisfaction of the thinker—as do ideas in aesthetics, ethics and religion—it is not logical to divide the satisfactions. Or, it has been charged (2) "Truth cannot 'happen,' as James says, for this means that what the truth is true of cannot happen until the truth about it is achieved. Thus, for example, yesterday, when it is finally known tomorrow, can only be tomorrow." But given James's notion of an ongoing temporal world, given *as* a temporal span, and much too thick and temporally multi-dimensioned to be equated with any set of descriptions, this is precisely what James could not have believed. As he himself discerned, lying behind the charges is the "instinctively accepted" idea that "propositions are true if they copy the eternal thought" of "extramental realities."[5] That is, the charges make surface sense only if truth and reality are simply—"lazily"—conflated, only if the nature of Being is begged by supposing that the truth about it is already possessed by the eternal thought. Only by playing God, or claiming a special revelation, can we juxtapose the reality of yesterday with the "mere working" of our ideas about it today.

What his critics have not grasped, he says, are the actual conditions which situate inquiry.[6] A thing picked out to be known must already be counted a "relatively more fixed part" of experience which is a force either of "advance" or "resistance" to one's cognitive purposes. Truth consists of "working in" relatively less fixed parts of experience. The truth is an imputation of some quality or activity to the thing *qua* enduring "substance" which is "graftable" onto it, which "takes," which is absorbed into and coheres with the complex of the thing's emerging aspects. A true idea is a good idea. Our experience is true when the things meant in it are developed in a revelation that preserves as much as possible what they were. Thus *things* could also be said to be true when their revelation develops truly, consummately and coherently within our experience.[7] For what is true is things-experienced, or experience-of-things, not experience alone nor things alone, whatever that might mean. Things are true when they consistently conform to ideas that are being tested even as they test these things within the inarticulable whole of interaction. If we call this "ethical" source of intelligibility "Being," along with Heidegger, then things are true when they conform to the truth of Being. This is Heidegger's radical modification of the scholastic's view that things are true when they conform to their Idea in God's mind.

Being appears across an horizon of human temporality and concern.

For James, all the conditions of the coherence and meaningfulness of the experienceable world are conditions for the preserving development which is truth. He writes, "Julius Caesar was real, or we can never listen to history again. Trilobites were once alive, or all our thought about the strata is at sea ... In all this, it is but one portion of our beliefs reacting on another so as to yield the most satisfactory total state of mind."[8] James believed that the past is "built-out" by the future.

Consonant with Heidegger's situational or phenomenological approach to the nature of truth in which he asks, When is the truth of a proposition evident?, James maintains that all truth is knowledge of the truth. Truth which is all, and only, virtual does not exist. Of course, it is possible to say what is true without knowing that it is true, e.g., without counting I say there are 178 oranges on a tree, and there are just that many. But James's point is that the *only* thing that we can *mean* by saying that I speak the truth is that *if* persons counted, 178 would be all they could consistently get. Actual truth does not pre-exist its discovery, but is added by our meanings and operations which conserve and further connect the world. It is a function both of things which get known and the knowing, for it is limited by our ability to mean and to care. And through it all, general ideas test *and* are tested endlessly.

James's project is at bottom metaphysical: to determine the structure of the world in terms of its experienceability. What is it for something to count for us as "one," as "real," as "mental," etc., and how can we determine this without falling into the trap of begging questions of Being by simply conflating conceptual and existential structure? James speaks of truth as "an unstayed wilderness."

If James's theory of truth is studied independently of his metaphysics of radical empiricism it will be taken subjectivistically, thus mistakenly. His early attack on Spencer pivots on the point that even on the theory that the truth of an idea is determined by whether the being who holds it will survive (which theory is false), even here the criterion is survival—that which is not yet actual, so quasi-ideal. Genuine criteria of truth are norms and ideals, not corresponding to anything actual in the world, generated to be sure by pre-deliberate interests ("interest is the apriori factor in cognition," he writes), but these interests are instinct with their own criteria, which are not necessarily commensurate with the egoistic demands of the particular being whose interests they are. A human idea is true if *it* survives. Our interests are, in various ways, theoretical.

To be known, what is actually there in the world has to correspond to these ideal norms; it is not just that statements or thoughts have to correspond to things; the parallel to Heidegger should be noted. But this does not subjectivize the world, for interests and purposes were not subjectivized to begin with. The interest of the interacting organism is the context of any inquiry, so it cannot be exhausted in the dissecting focus of any or all inquiries; hence introspective psychology, for example, can never delimit the ground of interest. The limits of interest and of the imagination are literally unimaginable. And only if we naively conceive truth to be eternally standing propositions which mirror all actual states of affairs will we infer mistakenly that since, for James, truth is within an attitude, from a point of view and partial, it is therefore subjective. For James, truth is partial, from a point of view and objective, the only kind there is. When we recall that for him interest illuminates a field of experience, a "much at once" which is ultimate for the time being as a totality, the kinship to Heidegger's *Gestimmtheit*, attunement, is more than marginal.

Knowing will affect the known *at least* to the extent of altering the consequences it effects in interacting creatures who know it. This altered interaction cannot be limited to something that just occurs in their minds. Nor can it be limited to what occurs in their bodies—if body is understood in physiological terminology only. The reality is the whole cognitive relationship of knower and known. What we can conceive the very thing itself to be is a function of an interaction which can *itself* be conceptually pinned down with no absolute precision. James here implicitly approaches Heidegger's idea that Being, the context that determines the intelligibility of all inquiries into beings, cannot itself be denoted or mapped in its parameters as can particular beings. Nor can the conditions of its application be (more or less) specified as can general concepts. It is more "open textured" than are specifically "open textured concepts."

James's attack on the "psychologist's fallacy" is an attack on the practical attitudes which influence the theories of empirical psychologists as well as common men. The fallacy consists in constricting the description of a thought to what the observer thinks the thought is about practically, i.e., to the clear conclusion it may be about to come to, or to the thing "in itself" in the world which causes it, or, what may be the same, to the things included in its range which the organism having the thought must cope with or suffer from. The thought's vast object as thought itself thinks it, with all its rings of intensity and clarity, its dimensions of flow and levels of relationships, is masked from view.

To conclude: Heidegger's rethinking of truth stems from his reappraisal of the early Greek notion of *aletheia*, unforgetfulness, or less literally, disclosedness. The truth is achieved when a being can disclose itself. The thing's disclosure is its truth: it discloses itself for what it is. But unlike the view of later Greeks, this is not a disclosure of its participation in an eternal form. It is disclosed when it is "gathered" within a "totality of circumspective concern."[9] This concern is never fully objectifiable nor predictable, and in the selecting, emphasizing and grouping of a thing—which together with the receptive moment of cognition is its disclosure— we will never be aware of all that has been left out, unselected, undisclosed. Truth involves, for the philosopher, the awareness that disclosure involves concealment. To "gather," then, is not just to gather the thing into sets (if we wish to speak this way about the generic), with the sets themselves gathered together logistically in advance, and then to verify by sense experience, say, the thing's inclusion in the set. For these sets and sets of sets are gatherings that are tested open-endedly in the very process of testing what is gathered into them. The ironical fault of all traditional logistic metaphysics, says Heidegger, is that things must be contracted in the genus in order to be contrasted in the species, with these gatherings and separatings frozen opaquely in place. Any calculus of properties or predicates runs the risk of *a priorism*—a rigidity and exclusiveness unaware of itself.

For Heidegger, our sense of a being being anything is determined by our sense of Being, but this is determined by how we already belong to Being in openness and freedom—and not just by a concept of Being or by a supremely general word, "Being." Or— differently put—it is determined by our interaction within the totality of that which-is, and this is never completely objectifiable or thematizable. There is no foothold for the intellect outside of our belonging to Being, and within it there are irreducibly non-verbal elements. Nor can epistemology be separated from a fundamental *Ontologie*. Somewhat comparably to Gabriel Marcel's idea of mystery, we cannot raise the question of the truth of Being without distorting to some extent the very conditions requisite for the answer; for to raise the question is already to have answered it—in some way.

Although James does not trace his theory to the Greek idea of truth as the dis-closedness of the thing, several of his points suggest a view similar to Heidegger's reinterpretation of this idea: (1) Knowledge by acquaintance is irreducible to knowledge by description, and it must be mediated by experiences which are neutral *vis-à-vis* mind or matter; (2) We know a thing when we make satisfactory contact with it—with "satisfactory" admitting of no definition because its modes are so various; (3) General ideas *qua* general purposes and concerns and the criteria native to them—to which *things* must coincide or conform if they are to be known—are tested openendedly in the very process of testing, and these ideas comprise no hierarchy generable in advance by a calculus. All this suggests Heidegger's idea that truth emerges within a "totality of circumspective concern," and involves direct contact with the thing in its contexts; it is not just a property of propositions.

James's inquiries into truth, I submit, are pulled by a similar proto-ethical and supra-logistical sense of our belonging to a totality. But he makes neither the problem of being nor that of totality consistently thematic, nor does he frame a thoroughgoing critique of the intellect. We get the impression, then, in his last works, e.g., *A Pluralistic Universe*, that he has, in utter exhaustion, simply given up on the intellect; that he can frame no idea of the intellect other than the logistic one, and this he cannot accept. Many of his insights end equivocally and inconclusively, therefore, and even leave the impression of subjectivism or mysticism. He does, however, point to new horizons in philosophy.

NOTES

1. Moreover, given a definite concern, e.g., with the state of repair of a house, a mere "look!" or a gesture will reveal that a window is broken. No proposition at all is needed. There is mute perception too.

2. Martin Heidegger, *Philosophy in the Twentieth Century*, eds. William Barrett and Henry Aiken (New York, Harper and Row, 1971), III, 219.

3. Martin Heidegger, *Kant and the Problem of Metaphysics*, trans. J. Churchill (Bloomington, Indiana University Press, 1962), p. 243.

4. Recall James's keynote statement, "The true is the good in the way of belief."

5. "Humanism and Truth," in *William James: The Essential Writings*, ed. Bruce Wilshire (New York, Harper and Row Torchbook, 1971), p. 271.

6. *Ibid.*, 268.

7. It is not unheard of to attribute truth and falsity to things. In *Metaphysics*

1024-b-22 Aristotle regards things as false which exist, but which either appear not to exist, or which appear to be other than they are. This implies that things are true which appear to be what they are. But in 1027-b-25, he contradicts himself; truth and falsity are only in thought, not in things.

8. "Humanism and Truth," *op. cit.*, p. 274.

9. These locutions are used in his *Introduction to Metaphysics*.

ROYCE, PRAGMATISM, AND THE EGOCENTRIC PREDICAMENT

ROBERT L. HOLMES

University of Rochester, Rochester, New York

R. B. Perry provides us with the following carefully drawn contrast between Royce and James. Pointing out that Royce was the son of an immigrant who moved to California in the 1840's, where Royce was born in the small mining town of Grass Valley, he says that:

> It thus transpired that, although Royce's was the characteristic American experience, it was left to James to develop an indigenous American philosophy, the first, perhaps in which the American experience escaped the stamp of an imported ideology. Royce, bred and reared amidst what was most unique and local in American life, imported his philosophy from the fashion makers of continental Europe; while James, uprooted almost from infancy and thoroughly imbued with the culture of Germany and France, was a philosophical patriot, cutting the garment of his thought from homespun materials and creating a new American model.[1]

Now I want to suggest that while this accurately reflects one side of Royce's philosophy, there is another side which bears a close affinity to what is unique in American philosophy, namely, pragmatism; and furthermore, that this latter influence came increasingly to reinforce Royce's overarching idealistic conception of reality. But my aim will not be solely to make this observation; it will in addition be to highlight certain aspects of Royce's philosophy which seem to me to be of continuing philosophical interest in their own right.

The features of Royce's philosophy relevant to both of these aims can best be seen in the context of what Perry called the egocentric predicament.[2] This, in Perry's view, is a methodological predicament confronting the epistemological idealist. Idealism he defines as the assertion of the proposition that anything and everything is defined by the relationship of consciousness (perceiving, remembering, willing, desiring, etc.) in which it stands to an ego or subject. This proposition's truth must be proved if idealism is to be established, and it is the attempt to do this that runs headlong into the egocentric predicament. For to establish the truth of this proposition, one must specify the nature of the modification of things by this distinctive relation, and this, he says, it is impossible to do. We cannot, obviously, look for instances of things outside of this relationship, for as soon as we observe, investigate, or even think about a thing we immediately reinstitute the relationship in question to it. Nor will it do to compare objects which stand in this relationship with *another* subject with those which do not, since we ourselves will all the while be standing in the relationship in question to those objects. We cannot establish even with probability that things exist only as one term in this relationship, since the only inductive argument applicable to the case is Mill's Method of Agreement, and that by itself is inadequate. Therefore, Perry argues, we can neither justify logically the conclusion that nothing exists unperceived by inference from the premise that nothing can be known outside of being perceived, nor justify empirically the step from one to the other. Hence idealism cannot be proved.

Perry was right, of course, to highlight the problem confronting the idealist. What he did not note, however, was that the problem cuts both ways, and that to the extent that his analysis is correct, it shows equally why the realist cannot make good his case for his own theory. For the same considerations which make it impossible for the idealist to prove that things don't exist unperceived make it impossible for the realist to prove that they *do* so exist. The upshot of the argument, given the shared assumptions on each side, is that the issue is incapable of resolution and the debate between idealism and realism is at an impasse.

Now Royce, I want to suggest, had indeed come to grips with the egocentric predicament, and in fact had done so in advance of the appearance of Perry's essay in 1910. But he did so in the only way possible—and in the way represented by some recent philosophy—and that is by denying certain of the assumptions shared by both sides to the debate.

Chief among these is the notion that the agency in the knowing situation is essentially passive; that he is merely the recipient of data impressed upon him from outside, and must, whether by causal inference, a priori deduction, or mere faith, make the transition from these data to externally existing objects—or, failing that, somehow construct objects out of these data according to their patterns of sequence and association. Royce recasts the problem in a way which alters its basic character from the outset. While he retains much of the same terminology, and speaks of "ideas" and their correspondence with things in the world, he invests the notion of ideas with a new significance. They no longer stand for the usual sense-data impressed from outside upon a passive subject. They come to stand for purposes, plans of action, projects emanating from an active self engaged with concrete problems arising from specific needs. Volition and need become the key terms.[3] One's engagement with the outer world is not through the intermediary of sense-data, but through responses to the immediate, brute fact of practical needs which seek satisfaction. It is these needs which are the immediately given in experience. And it is these which control our will in the construction of the world about us. We do not, as certain realists would have it, "merely find outer objects as independent of our will, and as nevertheless possessed in all their independence of their various predicates, qualitative, relational, substantial, individual. We find them possessed of characters, only insofar as we ourselves cooperate in the construction, in the definition, in the linkage of these very predicates, which we then ascribe to the objects."[4] That a particular configuration of pieces of wood answers to certain needs explains why it is conceptualized as a chair; just as the interests served by so doing explain why ever larger groups are taken to constitute families, societies, or nations. Were there some need to do so—however bizarre it might seem to us—a particular chair, the NATO Alliance and the constellation Andromeda could conceivably come to constitute an object. It is the exigencies of our active, practical nature which inform our world of experience, and it is the success or failure to satisfy these needs which at every level determines the adequacy of our concepts.

This success or failure, however, must be socially verifiable. Truth is public. Only science, as an open, social enterprise, gives us knowledge of nature. In reiterating this point Royce departs from much of tradition in his view that we can never understand the possibility of truth, much less know what is in fact true, if, with Descartes, we suppose it to be a matter of private experience. Like Peirce in his critique of Cartesianism, or Wittgenstein on private languages, Royce is convinced that a dead end awaits attempts to understand either our knowledge of an external world or the possibility of truth (or, in Wittgenstein's case, the conditions of the significance of language) while retaining the assumption of the privacy of experience.

We can now see that several pragmatic elements in Royce's theory are readily apparent. His restructuring of the basic situation said to give rise to the egocentric predicament proceeds from the same basis as Dewey's instrumentalism: the confrontation of persons with practical aims and interests with problematic situations. And in Royce, no less than in Dewey, there is a disdain for dualisms, and in particular a breakdown of a sharp distinction between theory and practice, knowledge and action. "Even affirmation and denial," he says,

> ... have typical outward expressions in conduct. A thought which has no conscious reference to a deed, which involves no plan of conduct ... which neither accepts nor rejects but only passively contemplates, is no thought at all, but is a vacant staring at nothing in particular by nobody who is self-conscious.[5]

Closely associated with this conception is his assignment of a preeminent role to the concept of purpose. In fact, his definition of "idea" in *The World and the Individual*[6] is expressly in terms of purpose, and it is this notion which is a chief determinant in investing ideas with significance, much as for Peirce the notion is important for the very elucidation of "meaning" itself. Finally, the conception of an interest-controlled construction of the physical world by the subject cannot fail to be suggestive of Dewey's account according to which similarly practical motives categorize and shape the flux of experience.

However, if this suffices to emphasize the strong pragmatic strain in Royce's philosophy, it does not yet explain how this strain supports his idealistic metaphysics, or what has happened to the egocentric predicament. And it is Royce's manner of establishing the linkage between the views we have so far considered and his central metaphysical thesis which brings out what, at the outset, I indicated I take to be of greatest philosophical interest on its own. His path here is not easy to follow, however, and in this limited space I can only sketch its course.

Returning now to the role of need and interest in our understanding of the world, we see that Royce stresses the insufficiency of one's own limited point of view in the process of judging and believing. We simply are not satisfied with Protagorean relativism according to which we can say no more than that "This judgment is true for me." For among our needs is the need for a *warrant* for our beliefs; for confirmation of them from points of view other than our own. This need gives a priority to our belief in other persons over our belief in an external physical world.[7] For the very conditions of objectivity and permanence essential to an understanding of the physical world presuppose a community of experience, and it is such a community that underlies our knowledge of nature.[8] What we are warranted in claiming to know of the outer world must be knowable by others. There is, in short, an ineradicably social character to our knowledge.

More specifically, our judgment that some fact of nature is the case has two components. It does indeed say that one believes that x is the case. But in addition it says that x is *to be* believed; that it *ought* to be believed.[9] There is, in other words, a normative element in our factual judgments about the world, an ethical underpinning to our empirical knowledge. Whereas for James truth is a species of goodness, for Royce it is a species of obligation. A true judgment is one which ought to be believed. This dualistic analysis of factual propositions has its counterpart in ethics and value theory. In Dewey's account of value, for example, to say that x is desirable is to say not only that it is desired, but that it is to be desired—this marking the distinction, for him, between de facto and de jure values. And more recently, in C. L. Stevenson's well-known model for explicating normative language, to judge that x is good is to say "I approve of x; do so as well." Now, while the Roycean "this is to be believed" is not altogether dissimilar from the Stevensonian "do so as well," there is an important difference between the two, one which provides the impetus to Royce's search for the Absolute. It is that whereas for Stevenson the judgment that something is good need in no way be affected by the fact that no one *in fact* does so as well, for Royce the need for confirmation of our judgments from points of view other than our own requires that one be prepared to revise or reject those beliefs and judgments which are not sustained by our fellow persons. The very notions of objectivity and permanence with which our concept of knowledge of nature is infused demand that we view nature as a realm of common experience. The closer analogy here—again within the realm of ethics, and again in the thought of a contemporary American philosopher—is in the conception of the social and objective character of moral judgments found in W. K. Frankena, who proposes that to judge that something is right from the moral point of view is to judge that it will be similarly appraised by others who adopt that point of view, where one must be prepared to reconsider his judgment if this assessment is not sustained.

Suppose, then, that my judgment of some particular matter of fact is confirmed by yours, and both of ours by that of another whose point of view, as it were, encompasses ours, and perhaps by ever-enlarging points of view to the point that it is attested to by the whole community of competent inquirers. Is what is so agreed upon thereby true, and its object reality, as Peirce maintained? No, according to Royce. No mere multiplication of points of view suffices. For no matter how many such inquirers (or judges as he calls them) we may introduce, so long as they are only finite, it always makes sense to ask: "Is their view of the *ought* the view that they *ought* to hold? Are their conscious ways of judging this object only the expression of their social, but still relative, temporary, passing, unstable point of view?"[10] Do we not, Royce might have asked, have a nagging feeling that perhaps Peirce's whole community of inquirers might be wrong? Is that at least not a possibility? Have we not merely transferred the problem of how error is possible within the privacy of a single experience to the level of common experience, without in principle altering its character? It is in his answer to these questions that Royce parts company with the pragmatists. For he sees in the logic of this line of thought compelling recognition of an all-encompassing point of view which, because it can be superseded by no other, and comprehends in a single insight all points of view, meets fully the conditions of what any point of view concerning particular oughts ought to be. Only if there is such a point of view, or, as he would put it, a Self which has such a point of view, have we met the logical conditions for the possibility of error, and thereby the conditions for the possibility of truth. The fallibility of empirical knowledge, he might have said, either compels the acknowledgement of such a conclusion, or it leads ultimately to skepticism. Royce, in short, is a pragmatist who remains committed to the quest for certainty.

Royce has not, to be sure, found a way out of the egocentric predicament, for if our earlier assessment is correct, there is no way out. But he has proposed a way around the impasse it creates by so construing the underlying problem of knowledge that the predicament does not arise. By stressing purposes, needs, and interests—those of persons already *in* problematic situations— Royce, like Dewey, takes as his starting point a conceptualization according to which we are already out of the predicament. What we find in Royce is not so much an egocentric predicament as what we might call an anthropocentric predicament, one in which it is the collective experience of mankind that defines the outer limits of our knowledge of the world. Is this question-begging against those whose interpretation of the problem is framed in terms which lead to Perry's predicament? Yes and no. Yes, in the sense that it displaces their theories without having shown them to be incorrect. No, in the sense that this ultimately is the way of all consistent, competing philosophical theories. So long as the assumptions which, if correct, would falsify our opponents' theories are not too conspicuous and in the forefront of our arguments, we tend not to regard them as question-begging, though in principle they are every bit as much so as the illustrative examples from elementary logic texts. Does this mean, then, that our philosophical theories do not and cannot provide us with any vantage point from which to judge them, other than in terms of internal consistency? Are they like works of art which can really only be contemplated and admired but not ranked as more or less nearly approximating truth? Here we might take our cue from Royce's analysis, and acknowledge that only from a vantage point—a point of view, if you like—which embraced not only the perspectives represented by the philosophy which has been done in the past, but also the perspectives of all the philosophy that will and might be done, and which synthesized in one insight all of this knowledge in the light of an understanding of the true nature of the reality which they seek to reveal, could one answer this. And so perhaps the case for philosophical truth itself stands or falls with the plausibility of some such analysis as Royce's.

NOTES

1. R. B. Perry, *In the Spirit of William James* (Bloomington, Indiana University Press, 1958), p. 25.

2. R. B. Perry, "The Ego-centric Predicament," *The Journal of Philosophy, Psychology, and Scientific Method*, VII (1910), 5–14, reprinted in W. G. Muelder, L. Sears, and A. V. Schlabach, eds., *The Development of American Philosophy*, 2nd edition, pp. 331–37.

3. See Josiah Royce, "The Eternal and the Practical," Presidential Address, the American Philosophical Association, Dec. 30, 1903. Published in the *Philosophical Review*, XIII, (1904), 113–42. Reprinted in W. G. Muelder, L. Sears, and A. V. Schlabach, eds., *op. cit.*, pp. 243–57. Page references to the latter.

4. *Ibid.*, p. 248.

5. *Ibid.*, p. 246.

6. *The World and the Individual.* Gifford lectures delivered before the University of Aberdeen. First Series (New York, Macmillan, 1901), pp. 22f.

7. *The World and the Individual*, Second Series, pp. 165–174.

8. *The Spirit of Modern Philosophy* (New York, W. W. Norton & Co., Inc., 1967), Lecture XII.

9. "The External and the Practical," pp. 252–56.

10. *Ibid.*, p. 256.

THE "YES" AND "NO" CONSCIOUSNESS

BRENDA JUBIN

Bevis Press, Cheshire, Connecticut

In his 1902 presidential address to the American Psychological Association, Josiah Royce urged psychologists and logicians to turn their attention to the "delicate and fundamental" questions surrounding the "yes" and "no" consciousness.[1] The "yes" and "no" consciousness, Royce explained, is "the selection or suppression of a certain possible response to an object"; it is "the consciousness wherein we are aware of accepting or inhibiting certain acts—acts through which we treat two or more objects as belonging to one class, or as belonging to classes that exclude each other."[2] As such, it is an integral part of all judgment, all thought. And yet, Royce asserted, in spite of its enormous importance, the "yes" and "no" consciousness remained a psychological mystery and an open logical issue. It was not that the subject had been totally neglected. In 1894 Royce had himself devoted an essay to some psychological aspects of the "yes" and "no" consciousness, and the logical literature was, of course, vast. Still, many vital questions had not, to Royce's mind, been satisfactorily answered—among them, the question of how we can accept the law of double negation and still hold that affirmation and negation are determinately different forms of thought. This problem became a dominant theme in his later logical writings.

Royce began his investigation with naive confidence. There are, he claimed, absolute logical truths which are determined by the self-sustaining forms of our thought activity. One such truth is that "there is a determinate difference between the assertion and the denial of a given proposition." This truth is absolute because it expresses a difference between two forms of thought which sustains itself through every attempt to inhibit it. "One who says: 'I do not admit that for me there is any difference between saying yes and saying no,'—says 'no,' and distinguishes negation from affirmation, even in the very act of denying this distinction."[3] Royce's reasoning here is confused and self-serving: confused, because not admitting a difference is not equivalent to denying a difference; self-serving, because the test for the absoluteness of the truth that there is a determinate difference between affirmation and negation hinges on accepting the very distinction in question. Nonetheless, he was convinced that there is a determinate difference between affirming P and denying P *because* it is an absolute logical truth that affirmation and negation are determinately different forms of thought.

Royce's confidence, however, was soon shaken. In his article on negation, he pondered the purely logical nature of the not-relation and concluded that, whether we take the relation between a proposition and its contradictory, between a mode of action and its contradictory, or between two terms X and not-X, the not-relation is in all cases symmetrical and bi-univocal. That is, if the proposition P is the negation of the proposition Q, then Q is the negation of P. And if Q contradicts P, and another proposition X also contradicts P, then Q and X are formally equivalent propositions. Now "obviously connected" with these characteristics of the not-relation, Royce continued, "is the familiar principle that the negation of the negation of a proposition is equivalent to the proposition itself; or, as it is often said, a double negation is equivalent to a simple affirmation."[4] From this, however, it follows as an "indubitable logical fact" that "there is no distinct class of propositions [or judgments] that are essentially affirmative, and thereby opposed to or to be distinguished from a class of propositions [or judgments] that are essentially negative ... every affirmation is *ipso facto*, from the logical point of view, a negation, since judgments, as well as propositions, essentially go in pairs of contradictories."[5] Moreover, logically speaking, there is no consciousness which is distinctively positive and none which is distinctively negative. "It is vain ... to say, 'For my part, I prefer to avoid negations and to confine myself to such positive affirmations as I can make'; it is vain to attempt to confine oneself to 'merely affirmative' thinking; for to affirm is to deny the contradictory of whatever one affirms. It would be equally vain for one, in a sceptical mood, to declare that his favorite attitude is that of negation or denial; for whoever denies any proposition affirms its contradictory, so that every denial is, in its logical meaning, an affirmation."[6] From a logical point of view, affirmation and negation are not determinately different forms of thought; the "yes" consciousness is at one and the same time the "no" consciousness.

Royce wanted to accept the law of double negation, but he recognized that it conflicted with the demands of philosophy and the teachings of experience. Casting his dilemma in practical terms, he pointed to the acknowledged "contrast between the negative mode of commands illustrated by the Ten Commandments and the positive attitudes of the will expressed in the Sayings which tradition attributes to Christ" and to the familiar pedagogical advice, "'Tell the children, in a persuasive way, what to do; but do not insist upon telling them what not to do, unless you are obliged to do so.'"[7] And yet, how are we justified in distinguishing between affirmative and negative modes of commands since "whoever says, 'Do this,' logically speaking, counsels us not to refuse to do this, not to do the contradictory act."[8]

Royce's answer was not altogether free from ambiguity and confusion. He seemed to take refuge in the fact that the not-relation, as it occurs in our lived experience, is always associated with other relations "triadic, tetradic, and, in fact, polyadic, with various degrees of complexity." By virtue of its association with these relations, "what is, from a certain point of view or in certain respects, to be regarded as the not-relation ... comes to appear in other respects no longer symmetrical, and frequently no longer dyadic."[9] To take Royce's example, we may divide the world of debtors into two classes: the solvent and the insolvent. These two classes of debtors are, for formal logic, the mere negation of each other and thus are symmetrically related. But, Royce argued, once the not-relation is associated with unsymmetrical relations within a particular universe of discourse (such as the world of financial obligations considered legally or socially), it takes on unsymmetrical characteristics itself. In the case at hand, although it is true that the solvent debtor is not insolvent and that the insolvent debtor is not solvent, it is also true that the solvent debtor has the power to pay his debts whereas the insolvent debtor is deprived of this power, which he presumably needs or wants. That is, the not-relation is associated with "a definable or empirically obvious distinction in value, dignity or desirableness" between having and lacking the power to pay one's debts.[10] Because of this association, "because the debtor wants to pay his share, or because the law may put him in peril if he does not do so," Royce concluded, "the universe of discourse of the solvent and insolvent debtors comes to be not merely a world which is classified, but a world in which solvency, as something positive, is contrasted with insolvency, as something which involves privation."[11]

Royce intended his analysis of the distinction between solvent and insolvent debtors to serve as an illustration of "how, in general, affirmation and positive and constructive attitudes of will and modes of knowledge are defined."[12] It is not clear, however, that his illustration is entirely apposite to the problem at hand. For the main point to emerge from this analysis is that, although the logically symmetrical not-relation is the necessary basis of every thought and every deed, nothing can, in the final analysis, be the mere negation of anything else. Or, as Royce put it, "'pure negation' can play no part in our concrete thinking and life."[13] In life we are always guided by certain values and interests, in accordance with which "the logically symmetrical not-relation becomes unsymmetrical, and furnishes a pair of terms or propositions of which one is more fruitful, more instructive, or in general more valuable than the other."[14] But how, from the fact that our rational and volitional objects stand in unsymmetrical relations to one another, can we infer the character of the subjective "yes" and "no" consciousness—the character, that is, of our contrasting attitudes or states of mind? And how, even if the "yes" and "no" consciousness is viewed objectively and identified with contrasting assertions and deeds, can we show that these assertions and deeds have determinately different logical structures?

"For reasons," Royce wrote, "which may be mainly practical, and which may also be of great theoretical importance in more or less exact sciences, and may be bound up with the most various enterprises and incidents of life, conduct, and knowledge, we accept as an 'affirmative' attitude or assertion, or as a 'positive' deed or state of mind, one of two contrasted objects each of which is the negation of the other."[15] Read literally, this passage is philosophical nonsense, for it identifies a state of consciousness (such as an affirmative attitude) with an object of consciousness (e.g., the class of solvent debtors). Royce's point, however, is not, as he misleadingly asserts, that we accept an object as a state of mind or even (though this is more in keeping with his voluntaristic idealism) that we accept an object as an act of mind. His point is rather that the practical value or fruitfulness of our intentional object serves as a sign of our state of mind and that, in addition, it helps to determine the logical character, affirmative or negative, of our act of mind. An intentional object which, for a given purpose and within a limited universe of discourse, has more practical value than its contrasting object is a sign of an affirmative attitude and helps to determine the affirmative character of our volitional act.

An intentional object which is less valuable than its contrasting object indicates a negative attitude and a negating volitional act.

But—a more serious problem—what does Royce really mean here by contrasting objects? Are they, as he asserts and as his example of solvent and insolvent debtors indicates, the negation of each other, X and not-X? There are two difficulties with such a view. First, if we accept this definition of contrasting objects, we cannot offer a satisfactory account of erroneous, grammatically affirmative judgments or of immoral, grammatically affirmative commands. To judge that $2+2=5$ is to will a proposition that has less value than its contradictory, but surely we would not thereby conclude that the person making the judgment has a negative attitude or that "$2+2=5$" is a negative judgment. To command another to steal is to will a course of action that has less value than its contradictory, but we would be conflating ethical and logical issues if we were to say that this command is negative whereas the command "Do not steal!" is affirmative. Second, if contrasting objects are logical contradictories, Royce cannot accomplish the task he set for himself: to provide a warrant for distinguishing between the affirmative and negative modes of formally equivalent expressions. He can do this only by positing a valuational difference between objects, one of which is either the negation of the contradictory of the other or the contradictory of the negation of the other.

Yet on this interpretation of Royce's view, the distinction between affirmation and negation seems forced. Claiming, for instance, that the proposition "$2+2=4$" has more value than the negation of its contradictory, "It is not the case that '$2+2\neq 4$,'" is not compelling. The former might be more simple and direct, but otherwise the two propositions do not seem to differ in their mathematical fruitfulness. And if the valuational difference between these propositions is obscure, the difference between affirmation and negation is equally obscure. Royce's valuational account of the "yes" and "no" consciousness would thus appear to be shipwrecked.

One reason that Royce's theory, on this interpretation, has failed is that it makes a claim to universal applicability. Yet Royce explicitly ruled out this possibility. "There can be," he wrote, "no negation purely in general" (and hence there can be no "yes" and "no" consciousness purely in general) because "negation ... gets a definite meaning only when one can name or define of what, in a given case, something is the negation."[16] The not-relation may have different properties, depending on whether its object is a possible course of action, a proposition, a kind or class of being, or what Royce described as "a highly general type, grade, or state of being." For instance, when negative theology regards God as the negation of the finite world, this "negation differs, historically at least, and in some important respects both logically and metaphysically, from the ordinary negation of the logical textbooks, whose object is a class or a kind of being."[17] So, from the standpoint of Royce's living logic, affirmation and negation are not fixed attitudes which the mind can take towards any kind of object; they are not absolute forms of thought. On the contrary, we can determine the logical character of affirmation and negation only if we know the ontological character of the object which is being affirmed or denied. Royce's own examples throughout his article on negation indicate that his own aims were limited; he was concerned not with affirmative and negative expressions in general but rather with one particular kind of expression: moral, pedagogical, and religious commands.

Moreover, the notion of fruitfulness must be studied against the backdrop of Royce's philosophy of loyalty and his theory of interpretation. Although, on this occasion, Royce referred to loyalty only briefly and made no explicit mention of interpretation, his whole treatment of the not-relation presupposes the larger framework of his later philosophy. His analysis is sketchy, but the supportive examples suggest the general thrust of his argument: i.e., that, for the most part, the resultant attitude of the person to whom a command is addressed determines the mode, affirmative or negative, of that command. For instance, Royce was certain that "encouraging advice" given to children will "awaken them by winning suggestions" while negative commands will inflame "their already existing disposition to rebel against our counsel."[18] Affirmative commands (which Royce illegitimately equated with "winning suggestions" or "encouraging advice") usually inspire loyalty; negative commands, by contrast, tend to inspire disloyalty. Royce knew that there are exceptions to this rule, i.e., that the effectiveness of a command does not always depend on the mode in which it is cast. Where the addressee feels no sense of community with the addressor, an affirmative command may be totally ineffective. Royce contrasted the people at the foot of Mt. Sinai with Christ's followers. "The Ten Commandments," he noted, "appear to make their appeal to an already more or less evil-minded, rebellious or wayward people, whom the thunders of the law are to terrify into submission. ... On the other hand, the Sayings and the Sermon on the Mount give their counsels in a universe of discourse where the unsymmetrical relations between the Father and His children, between the Shepherd and the lost sheep, already inspire confidence, a tendency to harmony with one's counsellor, and a disposition to regard him as one who speaks with a peculiar and winning 'authority'."[19] The addressee's disposition to loyalty is thus an important factor in determining the effectiveness and, by implication, the logical mode of a command.

Royce recognized that, with traditional logical categories, one could not adequately describe the "yes" and "no" consciousness. He therefore brought ontological, valuational, and social considerations to bear on the problem, developing a logic of interpretation which would be sensitive to the workings of living reason. Even with this impressive array of philosophical weaponry, Royce did not give a definitive account of the "yes" and "no" consciousness. He knew that, at best, his analysis could justify only the minimal claim that, for the most part, within the realms of ethics, theology, and pedagogy, affirmative and negative modes of commands can be distinguished by studying the attitudes they inspire. Even this minimal claim may be incorrect, resting as it does on a questionable psychological hypothesis. Nonetheless, it is not without importance. For it points to the fact that the not-relation, as it occurs within our experience, is always used for particular purposes and has consequences which "make a difference." If the purposive and consequential character of the not-relation is ignored, the "yes" and "no" consciousness will remain a philosophical mystery.

NOTES

1. Josiah Royce, "Recent Logical Inquiries and Their Psychological Bearings," reprinted in *Royce's Logical Essays*, ed. Daniel S. Robinson (Dubuque, Wm. C. Brown Company, 1951), p. 27.

2. *Ibid.*, pp. 26 and 31.

3. Royce, "The Problem of Truth in the Light of Recent Discussion," reprinted in *Royce's Logical Essays*, p. 91.

4. Royce, "Negation," reprinted in *Royce's Logical Essays*, p. 183.

5. *Ibid.*, pp. 183–185.

6. *Ibid.*, p. 184.

7. *Ibid.*, pp. 186–187.

8. *Ibid.*, p. 197.

9. *Ibid.*, pp. 189–190.

10. *Ibid.*, p. 192.

11. *Ibid.*, p. 193.

12. *Ibid.*, p. 194.
13. *Ibid.*, p. 195.
14. *Ibid.*, p. 196.
15. *Ibid.*, p. 195.
16. *Ibid.*, p. 179.
17. *Ibid.*, pp. 180–181.
18. *Ibid.*, p. 200.
19. *Ibid.*, pp. 200–201.

REALITY REVISITED:
THE CONTROLLED AMBIGUITY OF
SANTAYANA'S REALMS

MORRIS GROSSMAN

Fairfield University, Fairfield, Connecticut

Philosophy's search for the "really real" is only gradually being abandoned. For example, Justus Buchler's concept of "ontological parity" involves such an attempt, and Buchler says, "It is misleading to ask whether what is exhibited (in philosophy) is a structure of 'ideas' or a structure of 'existence'."[1] It seems to me that Santayana's ontology represents the first major attempt in philosophy to depart from orders of reality. The following discussion seeks to show this, and to indicate the paradoxes and ambiguities that are associated with such an enterprise. For reasons of brevity and focus, I deal exclusively with the realms of matter and essence.

The realm of matter, for Santayana, is the realm of existence or of existent things. The realm of essence is the realm of entities (we need such a substitute word here) which do not exist but which are real. In encountering concepts like existence and reality, if we are to understand Santayana aright we must guard against traditional responses to these words and discern the actual baggage with which Santayana weighs them. For in resting in these two primary—equally primary—ways of being, and in distinguishing between them, Santayana deliberately evades any obvious linkage of splendor, importance or moral authority with the one or the other. This primal and ultimate neutrality with respect to the realms is philosophically the most significant element in the manner of their choice. Santayana attempts to avoid what he sees as the errors of traditional philosophy, i.e., the making of distinctions and classifications on the basis of hidden moral preferences. In making his own distinctions, in marking out his own realms, Santayana is *not* setting up the *ens realissimum* (the most real of things) or the *summum bonum* (the highest good). Neither of the realms can be so characterized. Santayana's ontology is designed to do away with the confusions of past philosophy— particularly the tendencies to assimilate the power of fact to the authority of value, and to engage in categorial summitry.

Santayana had once hoped to do a book on the mistakes of philosophy, and among the earliest mistakes was Platonism. He sees in it the casuistry of a "moralizing physics," a false conjunction of excellence and existence, a misconstrual of the relationship between fact and value. Plato disliked sensual and worldly things and he liked recondite intellectual ones. On this account (to put it a bit crudely) he attached higher being and existence to intellectual ones. Such projection or hypostatization of preferences is what Santayana keenly wishes to avoid, even, as we shall see, to the extent of conceding the tentativeness of his own categories and realms.

In the Western tradition, theological philosophizing outplatonized Plato in the tendency to identify all being, or the most real of being, with all power and goodness. The ontological argument so-called is based on the premise that other things being equal, to exist is better than not to exist. Even philosophical systems without ordinary theological emphasis, like Spinoza's and Hegel's, tend to press the equation of highest being or existence with highest value.

Santayana departs from such traditional, rationalistic and theological views of the universe. For him such philosophies actually dehumanize man (and unwittingly humanize the universe) by elevating man's autonomous power of generating and appreciating ideals into the conceit of attained cosmological success. Such philosophies turn the wishable horse of the beggar into a proclaimed Pegasus. The world might have been a better place if fact and value were not rivals for our attention, if our hopes and ideals, well conceived, were provided us by an accommodating universe. But thinking that the universe is so, wanting it to be so when it is not, leaves it a worse place than it is when we properly see the ambiguous conflicts and disparities between the is's and the ought's. By recognizing that the actual and the possible are neither of them ultimately privileged nor ultimately coincident—not mysteriously one in some reach of things we say we cannot fathom—we can care about this tragic sundering in the primal order of things and act to undo it as far as is in our power. It expresses a concern for modifying what needs modification by proposing a universe that is amenable to moral effort. It could be perversely argued that picturing the universe as Santayana does, does indeed satisfy a moral desire—the desire to make moral effort significant and difficult, and the desire to perpetuate righteousness and care. From this paradox, the paradox of firmly denying a primal order of reality and excellence, there is no extrication (as we shall see) apart from its articulated acceptance.

It is necessary to get closer to Santayana's ontology in order to show just how moral concerns interweave with existential details. As we have indicated, there are two sorts of reality in Santayana's scheme, existence and being, but neither one, *per se*, is the lesser or the greater. Value does not belong univocally to either. Here Santayana departs from the platonists and theologians at one extreme, and from coarse materialists at the other extreme. There is value in both existence (the realm of matter) and being (the realm of essence) and also negative value or disvalue in both. The values of existence are associated with its irrationality, its surdness, its external relations, its fecundity, its awesome power of generation. But existence also generates wantonly, it produces tragic conflicts of purpose, it is indefinite, mindless, awesome and irrational. (Note that we can use some of the same terms to describe the good and evil aspects of existence.) Santayana encounters matter with as much moral neutrality as he can muster. The identification of the realm of matter is not a projection of feelings of fear or admiration, nor an indication of unconditional approval or disapproval.

Nor is the realm of essence a limiting haven for the humanly or cosmically best. Men live with the aid of hopes, ideals, values, logical constructs—and these are avenues to non-existent essences. But just as essences can be lovely and wonderful objects of intuition, they can be ugly and distasteful. The values and disvalues that apply to matter also apply to essences. The opera *Don Giovanni* has an essence, but so do hair, dirt, cruelty, etc. Santayana feels none of the embarrassment that Socrates felt with respect to undesirable forms. Essences are democratic, infinite, equal qua essences, and the superiority of *Don Giovanni* to the essences of hair and dirt is a matter of human preference. Essences do not do things, they just are, definite and sometimes thinkable. Even the fact—if we can call it a fact—that they are timeless and powerless is morally neutral. Santayana's occasionally expressed fondness for contemplating essences is certainly not an unconditional partiality for all of them. Like matter, essences are not accorded any *a priori* fear or worship. Santayana somewhere says that it would be mad to worship essences. The realm of essence, rather than functioning as a hypostatization of some primal preference or aversion, to make clear that preferences and

aversions are just that—not convenient accommodations by nature
to our desires.

In naming the realms, and in making a choice of such high
ontological generality, can one at the same time be free of the taint
of human posturing and projection? The naming of the realm of
essence as a category of thought, as a proclaimed reality, as a
moral choice, is *that* moral choice which is completely transparent
to its own arbitrariness. Or, it is the choice so designed as to free
us of any illusions about choice. Or, it is the choice so exercised as
to prevent its own hypostatization and the creation of a "moralized
physics." Santayana accomplishes this by attributing being to
essences, but not existence to them, by making essences equal and
infinite—and by not setting up any implicit or explicit moral
hierarchy between being and existence. Santayana is profoundly
impartial with respect to being and existence—this is perhaps his
uniqueness as a philosopher—and the structure and definition of
the realms is carefully designed to exhibit and celebrate such
impartiality.

The function, then, of the realm of essence is to display ultimate
impartiality in the face of the paradox of the human partiality in
discriminating it. Santayana does discriminate it and in doing so
conveys by his performance, if not by overtly saying it, that he
regards it as good to do so. And it is good, provided that it is good
to care about ultimate detachment, and to mark out the backdrop
of undifferentiated indifference from which all preference and
aversion must emerge. For in recognizing that our preferences and
aversions have this enormous optionality, we might be freed of the
tendency to give false import to our desires and fears, and hence to
relinquish our fanaticisms about them.

It is a recurrent theme in Santayana that there is a need to
make choices that are human, limited, bound to time and place,
and that at the same time there is a need to extricate oneself from
human partiality. But this must apply, self-reflexively, even to the
human impulse to discriminate realms of essence and matter, and
to any tendency to attach great cosmological importance to such
discrimination. As we shall see further in the sequel, Santayana
ventures both to create an ontology, a generalized system of
metaphysics, and also to hold it in abeyance as preferred or special.
We might say that Santayana's ontology is that choice which
frames itself in an extended vision of the optionality and
arbitrariness of all choices.

A further point about the ambiguous self-reflexivity previously touched upon. The realm of matter is in one sense the class of all material and existing things in their elaborate external relations. The realm of essence is in one sense the class of infinite, non-existent, ideal or possible objects of intuition and discourse. But we can also say that the realm of matter (or the "realm of matter"—though it is significant that Santayana himself did not clarify or do away with ambiguity with such quotation marks, and in fact constantly interlinked things like nature and the idea of nature, beauty and the sense of beauty) is a category in Santayana's philosophy, an essence, a member of a class of such categories. Likewise the realm of essence is another such category, an essence among essences, a member of itself.

The categories of realms, taken as essences or logical constructs, provide Santayana with a convenient way to "shepherd his thoughts," as he put it, and to discriminate, in ways congenial to him, the things he chose to discriminate. As categories of thought, as more or less definable essences, the "realm of matter" and the "realm of essence" are themselves essences, and hence non-existent. In Santayana's words the contrast between essence and existence is not a division among existences, and so in that sense the realms can hardly be constitutive of an ontology. This is the stance that Santayana took in response to critics who did not find his categories congenial or satisfactory, and who preferred their own. He simply relinquished the faith and intent with which he approached his realms, even the realm of matter.

Could Santayana be serious in such relinquishings, and see the realms, to which he devoted so many years of effort, as optional and personal categories of thought? The answer is that Santayana could be serious in two ways, serious in acknowledging the optional imaginativeness of his philosophizing, and serious also in employing his categories with an intended scope that should carry them, for those who shared his vision, to the steadiness and wholeness of all that there is. This double seriousness, this controlled ambiguity, is at the heart of the smiling sadness of the entire Santayanian corpus. As has been suggested, only with his realms so chosen, and left so undefended against attack, could he have accomplished such remarkable duplicity of ontological function. The realms are Santayana's *synthetic a priori*, the "true but necessary" that perhaps finds its way into every philosophy.

The two ways of seeing that we have been talking about are ubiquitous to Santayana and constitute what has been called his binary or dramatic vision. He could intend his realms to carry him

to the "unvarnished truth" and he could also see his realms as
congenial essences of his own. It might be helpful to draw on
Santayana's own words as evidence of his capacity to renounce his
own ontology. Such "renunciation," although always implicit,
appears explicitly and poignantly in his concluding remarks at the
end of *Realms of Being*. In this footnote to his long work,
Santayana writes:

> In general, it would avoid misunderstanding to remember that
> essence, matter, truth and spirit are not, in my view, separate
> cosmological regions, separately substantial, and then jux-
> taposed. They are summary categories of logic, meant to
> describe a single natural dynamic process, and to dismiss from
> organized reflection all unnecessary objects of faith.[2]

That essence, truth and spirit are not separate cosmological regions
is fairly obvious, but that the realm of matter can be seen as a
"summary category of logic" is, as it were, another matter. As we
saw, what is said about matter in one sense is said about the
existent; this belongs to cosmology and *a fortiori* is part of bona
fide ontology. But we also saw, and now see again, the sense in
which the discrimination of the realm of matter is the delineation
of an essence. On this latter view, Santayana holds it to be the
philosopher's business to articulate, so to speak, the essence or idea
of existence, leaving it to scientists to get to matter more directly.
So even the realm of matter can be airily dissolved into a category
of logic. Santayana goes on to say in the section quoted:

> Essence is not an object of faith ... In regard to the realm of
> matter I propose no theories ... What I lay down about the
> realm of spirit involves no system of idealism ... no eschato-
> logy ... no philosophy of history ... In reconstructing the *moral*
> history of spirit ... there is the language of poetry and religion.

Poetry and religion are at once the stuff of dreams, the stuff of
philosophy, and all the "really real" we can rest secure in.
Santayana's summary dismissals of any residual dogmatic claims
in his ontology are reminiscent of a statement that appears twice in
the Santayana corpus, once in *Platonism and the Spiritual Life* and
again as the closing words of *The Last Puritan*:

> After life is over and the world has gone up in smoke, what
> realities might the spirit in us still call its own without illusion
> save the form of those very illusions which have made up our
> story?

Like Prospero (or Shakespeare) who at the end relinquishes his powers of enchantment, Santayana, the artificer of an elaborate ontology, dispenses with his masterful artifice at the very moment of its completion.

NOTES

1. Justus Buchler, *The Concept of Method* (New York, Columbia University Press, 1961), p. 166.

2. George Santayana, *Realms of Being* (New York, Charles Scribner's Sons, 1942), p. 831.

SOME REMARKS ON
SANTAYANA'S SCEPTICISM*

HERMAN J. SAATKAMP, Jr.
University of Tampa, Tampa, Florida

I

In *Scepticism and Animal Faith* Santayana develops a scepticism that is radical and complete. The literary form of Santayana's scepticism is Cartesian in style in that he begins by showing our ordinary beliefs are subject to criticism and doubt and then through a form of regress argument ends his scepticism on a note of certainty. This literary parallel with Descartes adds a strikingly dramatic quality to Santayana's clearly anti-Cartesian conclusion concerning the significance of the certainty obtained at the terminus of his sceptical regress. This certainty according to Santayana logically cannot be the foundation for any set of beliefs or knowledge claims. In his own characteristic fashion Santayana maintains both that there is something which may be characterized as indubitable and that such indubitability is a dead end. It is a dead end because it does not provide the basis or the standards for consciously reconstructing our knowledge from its foundations. With one hand Santayana gives to the strong foundationalist[1] (like Descartes) the concept of indubitability and infallibility that is required for their approach while with the other hand he takes away all the significance of such "self-warrant" that is essential to the foundationalist position. This not only is a neat trick but is quite relevant to contemporary analysis of foundationalist claims.[2] In order to present Santayana's position it is first necessary to give a brief account of the type of foundationalism he is arguing against.

II

In *Scepticism and Animal Faith* Santayana is arguing against the strong foundationalism exemplified in Descartes, but this does not mean that this form of foundationalism is the only one that Santayana's arguments can be marshalled against.[3] In its barest outlines one may say that strong foundationalism consists of at least five theses.

1. Every bit of knowledge is either mediate or immediate, and all mediate knowledge stands at the end of a chain of justification that rests upon immediate knowledge.
2. Immediate knowledge is indubitable and infallible, i.e., it is not subject to doubt or error in any conceivable case.
3. By regress arguments one can in fact discover such immediate knowledge.
4. Immediate knowledge is epistemic. That is, if a person has immediate knowledge of p, then he not only knows p, but he knows (immediately) that he knows p.
5. Once this immediate knowledge is discovered, one can begin to reconstruct one's knowledge from its foundations.

The benefits of completing a strong foundationalist program are numerous, but only three will be mentioned. First, the establishment of a strong foundationalist position would answer scepticism in the clearest, surest fashion. Secondly, one would not only have shown that there *is* knowledge, but one would also have shown the exact nature of and justification for knowledge. Thirdly, one would be able to carry out (at least, theoretically) a thorough program of reconstructing our knowledge from the foundations with the use of suitable inference rules.

III

A.   Santayana's disagreement with the strong foundationalist primarily stems from his denial that infallible and indubitable epistemic knowledge is at the terminus of a thorough-going sceptical regress. Santayana does maintain that one can discover a form of infallibility and indubitability at the end of a sceptical regress, but he denies that what is discovered is epistemic and therefore maintains it cannot provide the foundations for any reconstruction of knowledge on rational grounds. He argues that the ultimate terminus of a sceptical regress is a solipsism of the present moment. In maintaining this, Santayana's scepticism, like most traditional scepticisms, is parasitic. He assumes the rationalistic criterion of the strong foundationalist and seeks to find self-evident knowledge. In this pursuit he discards all beliefs and knowledge claims that are not demonstrably certain or self-evidently true, and he pushes scepticism to an end quite different from that maintained by the strong foundationalist. An explication of the exact steps of Santayana's sceptical regress would require far too much space for a short paper. However, it is the last step in this regress that is most significant and should receive close attention. The earlier stages are reminiscent of traditional positions noting that our cherished beliefs about the physical world, history, self-consciousness, and time are all subject to doubt.

In the final stages of his regress Santayana raises a question of transcendental criticism in asking whether or not there is any belief about experience alone that is absolutely certain, i.e., a belief not subject to any conceivable doubt or error. In the tradition of his time he examines the "given" in experience and maintains that when one attends only to the given, he attends to that which lies beyond both doubt and belief, and therein lies the certainty found by a sceptical regress. Admittedly, this is a peculiar kind of certainty since it is non-propositional and non-judgmental, but more will be said of this later. For now it is important to understand the central thesis of Santayana's approach because in *Scepticism and Animal Faith* this thesis becomes fused with other tenets of Santayana's philosophy (such as essence), but the central thesis can stand quite independent of many of these other tenets and of the difficulties associated with them. Briefly, this thesis is simply that there is something given in any instance of consciousness that is independent of our being conscious of it or believing in it; and if we can theoretically or in practice suspend our beliefs about the given, then we can understand that the reality of the given is simply what it is apart from our beliefs or doubts about it. The given is what it is and that is certain, but it is a certainty that is otiose with respect to laying down foundations for knowledge because it is a certainty based on the suspension of belief and not the establishment of it. This certainty is found only in the vacant awareness of a momentary given which characterizes the solipsism of the present moment.

Another way of making the same point is to say that if one is seeking that which cannot be doubted or be in error, then according to Santayana one is driven to the vacant awareness of what is given. The vacancy of the awareness guarantees there can be no doubt about the given, but that is because there is no belief to doubt, i.e., there is no foundational belief or knowledge that can be discerned in the certitude of the solipsism of the present moment because there is no belief whatsoever in such a solipsism. As Santayana writes, his solipsism of the present moment "was not an invitation to the public to become solipsists or a pretence that I had become one, but a demonstration that demonstration in matters of belief is impossible. ...."[4]

B.   Of course, Santayana describes the given as an essence. An essence is said to be eternal in that its being is not dependent on any time or location, and it is a universal and not a particular as in sense-data theories. Santayana was well aware of many of the difficulties associated with describing the given as an essence.

> These words ["essence" and "realms of essence"], and my whole presentation of this subject, were perhaps unfortunate. I have advanced an emancipating doctrine in traditional terms; the terms excite immediate scorn in modern radical quarters, while the emancipating doctrine horrifies those conservatives to whom the terms might not give offense. I am sorry: but this accident after all is of little consequence, especially as the same doctrine—loaded, no doubt, with other accidental lumber—is being propagated by various influential writers in uglier and more timely terms. The point is to reduce the evident to the actually evident, and to relegate all the rest to hypothesis, presumption, and animal faith.[5]

In more contemporary terms (but uglier and far less dramatic) Santayana's contention is that if we reduce our knowledge to the actually evident, we may discern an awareness that is infallible and indubitable; but this infallibility and indubitability character-ize such a restricted state of consciousness that it cannot be described as knowledge in any form and therefore cannot provide the basis for the reconstruction of knowledge on self-evident beliefs or knowledge claims.

C.   If this analysis of Santayana's sceptical regress is correct, then it is possible to distinguish the central thesis of his solipsism of the present moment from his fully developed doctrine of essences. In order to make this clearer let us adopt the distinction between a person who would be in a solipsism of the present moment and one who might be reflecting on such a solipsism, i.e., a philosophical observer. A person within a solipsism of the present moment can make no assertions or judgments about the object (essence) presently intuited (Santayana's term for bare consciousness) by him because any such assertion or judgment would be subject to error and therefore would not be infallible or indubitable. For Santayana it seemed clear that in order to make an assertion or a judgment about the given one would have to recognize the identity of the given and such recognition (such as "Blue now") is subject to error because "identity ... implies two moments, two instances, or two intuitions, between which it obtains."[6] If identity involves this sort of temporal relation, then it is conceivable that one may be mistaken about identifying that which *now* is intuited with what *was* intuited (if only an instant before). Perhaps another way of making a similar point would be to say that recognition and identification involve the application of concepts to the given and as such raise the possibility of a misapplication. Hence, for the individual within a solipsism of the present moment "all his heroic efforts are concentrated on *not* asserting and *not* implying anything, but simply noticing what he finds."[7] This "noticing" is only the blank stare of consciousness at the passing scene of the given. It is a non-judgmental attending to the self-identical given without any assertion, belief, or judgment.[8] As Santayana notes, a person in a solipsism of the present moment "would not be troubled by doubts, because he would believe nothing."[9]

However, Santayana is not trying to convince people to adopt the position of the solipsism of the present moment, rather he is interested in the significance of this terminus of a sceptical regress. A way of getting at this significance is to ask how a philosophical observer might describe the solipsism of the present moment; he, at least, could make assertions about it. Suppose one asks if an observer could describe the awareness of the solipsist as something like "Red patch here now." After all, if such a description is accurate and the described state of consciousness shared the infallibility and indubitability of the solipsism, then with suitable inference rules one might, at least theoretically, be able to reconstruct knowledge from such self-evident foundations. However, Santayana would emphatically deny that such a description is accurate. The solipsist is only vacantly aware of the given, and the most one could say is that there is something present to consciousness, perhaps a "this," that is only attended to and is not judged to be anything at all. If one asks what that something is, then Santayana maintains it is self-identical, it is what it is, and one may well be able to say "This is this" or perhaps "Red is red" if "red" is given no more significance than "this." As Santayana claims, "self-evidence, or contemplative possession of a datum, collapses logically into tautology, and is not knowledge. Intellection without dubious claims can be found only in some self-limiting sensation, intuition, or definition."[10] Hence, in *Scepticism and Animal Faith* Santayana maintains that in the order of evidence the first belief (not self-evident) that one possesses is the identity of given essences.

> Without this postulate [the identity of essences] it would be impossible to say or think anything on any subject. No essence could be recognized, and therefore no change could be specified. Yet this necessary belief is one impossible to prove or even to defend by argument, since all argument presupposes it. It must be accepted as a rule of the game, if you think the game worth playing.[11]

If this is a correct analysis, then any description of the actually evident beyond its bare presence and its self-identity is subject to doubt and is therefore not self-evident. "... if I consider what they [essences] are, and how they appear, I see that this appearance is an accident to them; that the principle of it is a contribution from my side. ..."[12] When Santayana uses the term "essence" to refer only to the actually evident, then one may say that the awareness of essences is indubitable and infallible in the vacuous sense of the essence being what it is. But when Santayana uses the term "essence" to describe other characteristics of the actually evident, these descriptions are not infallible or indubitable, or as Santayana would say they are objects of faith and not self-evident knowledge. Thus, the fully developed content of Santayana's doctrine of essences (eternal, internal relations, trophes, truth, as well as specific characterizations of particular essences such as yellow, triangle, geometic, etc.) may be distinguished from the central theme of his sceptical regress. This fully developed doctrine is as subject to criticism and doubt as any other, but he would maintain that the vacant awareness of the given found in the solipsism of the present moment, once understood, is rightly characterized by indubitability and infallibility.

IV

A.   Santayana's scepticism is radical and complete. In response to the strong foundationalist he denies there is any infallible or indubitable epistemic knowledge and in so doing denies the rudiments necessary for reconstructing our knowledge on foundationalist principles. But this should not be a surprise. Any radical sceptic worthy of the name sets out a program that is defined in such a way that no epistemological position could possibly answer it. For the radical sceptic asks that one construct an argument that concludes "there is knowledge" but does not permit one any premises in which there is knowledge, and without that one cannot get the argument started.[13]

Santayana's scepticism not only applies to strong foundationalism but to other forms of foundationalism as well. For instance, suppose that a sense data theorist were to argue that one does not need epistemic knowledge in order to reconstruct knowledge from its foundations. He might argue that one knows the immediate character of a sense datum infallibly and indubitably and that one need not assert that one knows (immediately) that he knows such. That is, knowing that he knows requires evidence that is fallible, but his immediate knowledge of the sense data is not. However, Santayana's approach is once again telling because of his argument that there is no knowledge of any form that is infallible and indubitable, even that of the immediate character of the actually evident found in the solipsism of the present moment. Hence, Santayana's position, if correct, can be marshalled against any reconstruction of knowledge that has any form of infallible and indubitable knowledge at its base.

B.   In contrast to foundationalism Santayana does not attempt to refute scepticism but accepts it.[14] This acceptance though is not a denial of knowledge.

> A great source of misunderstanding is the impression that scepticism means disbelief. But disbelief is not sceptical; it is *belief* in the falseness of a previous assertion. The true sceptic merely analyses belief, discovering the risk and the logical uncertainty inherent in it. He finds that alleged knowledge is always faith. ...[15]

Hence, for Santayana all knowledge is in some sense faith because it is subject to possible error and doubt. But that in no way means that knowledge is impossible, quite the contrary it is essential; and in his sense Santayana is a dogmatist. But he distinguishes two types of dogmatism.

> ... the initial kind of dogmatist, having only sensation and fancy to guide him, assumes that things are just as they seem or as he thinks they ought to be: and if this assumption be challenged, the rash dogmatist hotly denies the relativity of his knowledge and of his conscience. Now I have always asserted this double relativity; it is implied in my materialism. I am not, then, a dogmatist in this first popular sense of the word, but decidedly a sceptic. Yet I stoutly assert relativity; I am a dogmatist there; for I see clearly that an animal cannot exist without a habitat, and that his impulses and perceptions are soon directed upon it with a remarkable quickness and precision: he therefore has true and transitive knowledge. But I also see clearly that this knowledge, if it takes an imaginative or moral form at all, must

take a form determined by his specific senses and instincts. His true knowledge must then be, in its terms, relative to his nature, and no miraculous intuition of his habitat as it exists in itself.[16]

Thus, in relation to the foundationalist Santayana accepts a thoroughgoing scepticism while maintaining there is knowledge, and in the later chapters of *Scepticism and Animal Faith* he even maintains that it is possible to reconstruct knowledge on the basis of evidence[17] though there is no rational guarantee of the certitude of the reconstruction. All in all Santayana's scepticism is remarkable in that, if correct, it is a thorough defeat of any foundationalism based on infallible and indubitable knowledge and at the same time it serves to introduce Santayana's own description of knowledge.

NOTES

* Work for this paper was supported by grants from the Council for Philosophical Studies (1976) and the Penrose Fund of the American Philosophical Society (1977).
1. See William P. Alston, "Varieties of Privileged Access," *American Philosophical Quarterly*, VIII, no. 3, (July, 1971), 223–241 for a careful explication of the distinction between infallibility, indubitability, self-warrant, and other forms of favorable epistemic positions.
2. Though I shall not be able to show it within this short paper, I believe that Santayana's arguments are significantly related to contemporary formulations and criticisms of foundationalism. In particular I have in mind some of the work of R. M. Chisholm as found, for example, in *Philosophy* (Englewood Cliffs, New Jersey, Prentice-Hall, Inc., 1964); Bruce Aune's criticism of foundationalism as found in *Knowledge, Mind, and Nature* (New York, Random House, 1967); and some of the latest articles and papers by William P. Alston in which he explicates and develops a form of "weak foundationalism."
3. In Section IVA, I try to show how Santayana's argument applies to another form of foundationalism.
4. George Santayana, "Apologia Pro Menta Sua," in *The Philosophy of George Santayana*, ed. Paul A. Schilpp (New York, Tudor Publishing Company, 1951), p. 517.
5. Santayana, "A General Confession," *op. cit.*, p. 28.
6. Santayana, *Scepticism and Animal Faith*, (New York, Dover Publications, Inc., 1955), p. 8; see also Chapter XII.
7. *Ibid.*, p. 16.
8. John Lachs, "Belief, Confidence and Faith," *The Southern Journal of Philosophy*, X, no. 2 (summer, 1972), 277.
9. Santayana, *Scepticism*, p. 17.
10. Santayana, "Apologia," p. 515.
11. Santayana, *Scepticism*, p. 114.
12. *Ibid.*, p. 133.
13. William P. Alston, "Types of Foundationalism," pp. 24–25. Unpublished paper.
14. It would be interesting to examine how Santayana's acceptance of scepticism sets him apart from Royce and James.
15. Santayana, "Apologia," p. 515.

16. *Ibid.*, p. 511.
17. Santayana, *Scepticism*, pp. 110ff.

SANTAYANA'S UNNATURAL NATURALISM

JOHN J. STUHR
Whitman College, Walla Walla, Washington

In his critical review of Dewey's *Experience and Nature*, Santayana labels Dewey's position "half-hearted" naturalism.[1] In his reply to this attack, Dewey calls Santayana's version of naturalism "broken-backed."[2] This explicit confrontation between two great American philosophers is hardly unknown. Unfortunately, its philosophical importance is seldom grasped. This argument over the meaning and worth of naturalism in philosophy is more than a quibble over labels. Instead, it constitutes a source of fundamental importance for a proper understanding of the world-views of both Santayana and Dewey; it is also a striking example of an important feature and function of American philosophy in general—a valuable function often inadequately fulfilled today.

This ultimate value of the exchange cannot be obtained without a clear understanding of the positions involved. This is a difficult undertaking—indeed, it is one at which Santayana himself failed in large part. Let us see how this is so. Santayana understands naturalism to be that "spontaneous and inevitable body of beliefs involved in all animal life." It includes the beliefs of children who identify themselves with their bodies, and are interested in "mechanical contrivances and in physical feats." In short, it is that body of beliefs which "covers the whole field of possible material action to its uttermost reaches." It is in this "world of naturalism," Santayana continues, that philosophers, with all men, labor: "philosophical systems are either extensions (a supernatural environment, itself natural in its own way, being added to nature) or interpretations (as in Aristotle and Spinoza) or denials (as in idealism)."[3] Philosophical systems, that is, with all words, feelings, ideas, spirit, poetries, theologies, and so on, are "hung" on this material framework or universe of action. The "natural place" of such things is secondary and epiphenomenal. Accordingly, naturalism breaks down, for Santayana, when the mental or spiritual "are taken to be substantial on their own account, and powers at work prior to the existence of their organs, or independent of them."[4]

Now, Santayana states that Dewey is a naturalist in *just* this sense in some of his writing (though this sense of naturalism is not as precise as Santayana appears to think). Dewey's naturalism is not fullblown, however. According to Santayana, he grafts something consciously actual and spiritual upon the natural world: the immaterial foreground is made the dominant reality. In a famous passage, Santayana writes: "In nature, there is no foreground or background, no here, no now, no moral cathedra, no centre so really central as to reduce all other things to mere margins and mere perspectives. ... If such a foreground becomes dominant in a philosophy naturalism is abandoned" and "some local perspective or some interest is set up in the place of universal nature or behind it, or before it so that all the rest of nature is reputed to be intrinsically remote or dubious or merely ideal."[5] Santayana's point, then, is this: Dewey's philosophy *essentially* is one in which the immaterial and "unnatural"—events, histories, situations, qualities, uses and endings, preparations and culminations—are ontologically dominant and primary: this philosophy accidentally and secondarily is naturalistic because it just happens that the foreground of twentieth century America is "monopolized by enterprise and material activity" and the accompanying naturalistic assumptions.[6] The philosophy of America, Santayana thinks, is the philosophy of enterprise—of enterprise which moves "in the infinitely extendible boyish world of feats and discoveries—in the world of naturalism." Dewey, Santayana finds, is the spokesman of this culture; his naturalism is imposed by the character of the prevalent arts. As such, this naturalism is "half-hearted" and "short-winded." It is the reduction, Santayana concludes, of nature to the deployment of experience, of the world to a story or history, and of the real to the immediate (having of experience).

Supposing for the moment that Santayana has fully understood Dewey's position—which he has not—why is that position philosophically objectionable? Dewey's philosophy, like that of Santayana, surely was influenced by the many interwoven features of the culture of the day—by a culture of which it was a part. It is less sure that these features are primarily commercialism and industrialism in business, instead of experimentalism in science and democracy in government; the further claim that Dewey's philosophy is an attempt to justify all aspects of this commercialism is simply unfounded rhetoric. In any case, a philosophy— even a "half-hearted" naturalism—cannot be rejected *merely* by noting those factors, objectionable or not, which shaped in large part the character of its author. If Santayana's analysis of Dewey's position is to be accepted as criticism of that position—as Santayana intends—Santayana's own brand of naturalism must be adequately set forth and accepted. The weakness of Dewey's view simply is not self-evident, even in Santayana's "world of naturalism"; if it is a weakness, it is one in relation to the foreground or local perspective of Santayana's philosophy.

It is vital for present purposes, then, that Santayana's description or characterization of the "natural" material world be successful. What exactly does this "world of naturalism" commit us, "spontaneously and inevitably," to believe? Most basically, it commits us to a distinction of existents into two sorts: there is the active material world or framework—the separate chunks of space in distinct bits of time—and there is consciousness or spirit, constituted by intuitions—the foreground that binds, unifies, and makes meaningful the realm of active matter.[7] Now, what is Santayana's account of matter, the organ of spirit and the foundation of his naturalism? (Before turning to this, it is interesting to note that Santayana, contrary to his own pronouncements, most often accounts for spirit not in terms of an epiphenomenal foreground or dressing of a primary reality, but as an on-going inclusive unity of spirit and its products or world by which it is known. The accounts of spirit or reason in art, religion, science, government, and social practice are accounts of spirit as activity, in Aristotle's sense of that term as a temporal unity of means and end, of act and product, of subject and object.)[8] Santayana often avoids giving us an account of the material world, or rather his account is not an account at all.[9] He writes that this realm is unknowable and wholly without character. Encountering matter, he suggests, is a speechless kneeling before the unknown infinite. In his terminology, it is the totally indeterminate and formless counterpart of essence. The essence of matter, moreover, is not matter itself, but matterless and uninstantiated. Matter is a nature-less and unknowable surd. Nature, the field of material action, is thus unnatural or non-natural: at least for man, it is without nature or character.

This account clearly is inadequate and unacceptable. If matter is, as Santayana says, without form or character and is thus unknowable, the identification and designation of the realm of matter or "natural world" is without meaning or justification. Indeed, there can be no evidence or import of such existence, for it is without connection to the foreground of human life. Moreover, it is not clear how something which we cannot know and characterize can be characterized, by Santayana himself, in terms of a contrast to spirit and foreground. Santayana's version of naturalism thus seems little more than confused and unjustified faith.

If there is to be a meaningful account and evidence of matter, matter must be knowable and must have form or character. But such a characterization of matter results in a naturalism which rejects a sharp existential dichotomy between matter and form, matter and spirit, matter and essence. Again, despite his claim that matter is featureless and unknowable, Santayana's own brand of naturalism is often of this more defensible sort. Santayana's own confusion here is evident in his discussion of substance and matter.[10] This confusion is noted by Dewey: "In his concrete treatments of any special topic ... he seems genuinely naturalistic [in Dewey's sense of "half-hearted" naturalism]; the things of experience are treated not as specious and conventional, but as genuine extensions of the nature of which physics and chemistry and biology are scientific statements." "But when Santayana deals with systems of thought," Dewey continues, "his naturalism reduces itself to a vague gesture of adoring faith in some all-comprehensive unknowable in contrast with which all human life—barring this one gesture—is specious and illusory."[11]

Santayana's more informative account of matter emerges in discussions of specific issues, particularly in *Scepticism and Animal Faith* and *The Realm of Matter*, where the "world of naturalism" is the world of substance; substance is understood as the union of a specifying and determining form, and a slice of constitutive and creative material action or energy. The combination of essence and matter is the constitution of a particular existent; neither essence nor matter exist independently and self-sufficiently. This world of substance is the reality or material of our daily lives: it is the stuff of our loving, hating, striving, obtaining, failing, encountering, and re-making. But this material or stuff is not "matter" in Santayana's ontological sense of the term. Instead, matter is the creative source or producing agent of this natural world of substance; form is the resource from which this creative material action selects or "picks out." The union of these factors is the natural world of substance. Matter and substance, then, constitute an activity in Aristotle's sense of the term as unity of producing and product, of doing and deed. Just as Santayana describes spirit in terms of its fruits in our natural world, so he accounts for matter most successfully in terms of its consequences and establishments in our environment. In *The Realm of Matter*, for instance, it is clear that matter is not self-enclosed and without character: it is the context in which we act, a context which presupposes and is presupposed by our actions and purposes; it is the unified, continuous spatio-temporal milieu which surrounds, supports, and includes us. Thus Santayana goes so far as to say that there is no substance, no existence, essentially independent of this field or context of action.[12] This active reality, of course, is strikingly "unnatural" in Santayana's professed (first) sense of naturalism.

Exactly why it might be appropriate to call this nature "material" is not clear. Santayana's motives or prejudices are not my concern here. Nor is it my concern to detail the two strains of "naturalism" in Santayana's thought. I *am* concerned to note that his "whole-hearted" naturalism is empty and inadequate; it is also important to see that the second strain of naturalism, although very confused, is whole-heartedly "half-hearted." Despite its confusions and inconsistencies, it is this strain of naturalism which is the source of Santayana's most successful and insightful writing.

This strain or position, of course, is developed in greater detail, consistency, and self-awareness by Dewey. Santayana, in his "half-hearted" naturalistic moments, writes that all existence or substance is constituted by an agent in a field of action. Dewey writes that existence is constituted by selective interest in a context or background. He calls this existence "experience" (and thus struggles to differentiate his meaning of the term from that of "orthodox British mentalism").[13] This experience, according to Dewey, is eventful, historical, qualitative, practical, meaningful, and social. Moreover, it is "world-constitutive": there is nothing which can meaningfully be said to be existence which is not intrinsically a feature or aspect of experience; existence or nature is, as Santayana noted, experience (and not experienc*ing*) deployed. To so much as refer to existence unconnected with human experiencing is to connect that existence to that experiencing; this connection, moreover, is as real a feature of a given existent as any other feature. Experience, for Dewey as for James, is "double-barrelled": it includes the processes of experiencing and the objects of that experiencing. Experience is transactional: it is an inclusive unity and continuity of subject and object, of producer, process, and product. In Dewey's naturalism, then, the foreground is not ontologically dominant; rather it achieves an ontological equality with its subject-matter, with the material with which it interacts. Experiencing, thus, is of nature; in the inclusive unity of experience, Dewey unites what Santayana separates. Near the end of *Experience and Nature*, Dewey asserts that the human situation or foreground falls wholly within nature; as such, nature is understood not only as the object of experiencing, but the activity which is the union of experiencing and the subject-matter experienced.[14]

We are now in a position to grasp the philosophical and larger social importance of this "half-hearted" naturalism which understands reality in terms of unified, continuous activity. To identify this reality, with Dewey, as experience, is to profess naturalism in such a way as to call attention to the reality of human undertakings, the efficacy of human purposes, and the need for human intelligence. To do this is to remind the philosopher that his undertakings arise from and return to this environment of daily social practice. The philosopher should see to it that this return is marked by an enlightenment and enrichment of that daily living. This concern has been a trademark of the great American philosophers, regardless of the labels which they applied to their work.

The soundness of philosophical positions and the stakes of philosophical controversies cannot be divorced from intimate relationship with this value. A philosophy which focuses on this human experience achieves this value: as Santayana notes, it removes "external compulsions"; it also removes "external supports," and forces us to be responsible for the intelligent and satisfying re-shaping of our lives and environment.[15] Dewey's work is an inspiring example of this: in *Art as Experience*, for example, aesthetic experience is not only described but made accessible, extended, and deepened; in *A Common Faith*, the religious nature of our lives is not merely noted or defined, but expanded so as to pervade the farthest reaches of daily transactions. Such a "naturalism of the foreground" is a whole-hearted humanism: it is a philosophy in which the focus on natural ends directs us to the achievement of moral ends, of human values. This promise should turn us to the present difficulties and further development of this approach.

NOTES

1. George Santayana, "Dewey's Naturalistic Mctaphysics," in P. A. Schilpp, ed., *The Philosophy of John Dewey* (LaSalle, Illinois, Open Court, 1951), pp. 245–261.

This is, essentially, a reprint of Santayana's earlier article of the same title in *The Journal of Philosophy*, XXII (Dec. 3, 1925).

2. John Dewey, "'Half-Hearted Naturalism,'" *The Journal of Philosophy*, XXIV (Feb. 3, 1925), pp. 57–64.

3. Santayana, *op. cit.*, pp. 245–246.

4. *Ibid.*, p. 246.

5. *Ibid.*, p. 251. See also p. 250.

6. *Ibid.*, pp. 247, 252–253.

7. This view, of course, is central to Santayana's writings in general. See especially *The Realm of Matter* (Scribners, New York, 1930).

8. See *The Life of Reason* in Art, Religion, Science, Society, and Common Sense. See also the account[s] of the mental in *The Realm of Spirit* (New York, Scribners, 1940), and *The Idea of Christ in the Gospels*.

9. Santayana, *The Realm of Matter*, especially Chaps. 1 and 2.

10. *Ibid.*, Chap. 2, Chap. 10.

11. Dewey, *op. cit.*, p. 64.

12. Santayana, *The Realm of Matter*, Chap. 2. See also *The Realm of Spirit*, final chapter.

13. Dewey, *Experience and Nature* (Open Court, Chicago, 1925), Chap. 1. This is central to and present throughout Dewey's work.

14. For a detailed account, see my *Experience as Activity: Dewey's Metaphysics* (Ann Arbor, University Xerox, 1976).

15. Santayana, "Dewey's Naturalistic Metaphyiscs," pp. 258–259.

REFLECTIONS ON THE METAPHYSICS
OF JOHN DEWEY:
EXPERIENCE AND NATURE

SIDNEY HOOK
Hoover Institution, Stanford University, Stanford, California

In discussing the metaphysics of John Dewey at a conference devoted to the theme "philosophy in the life of a nation," the natural assumption is that his metaphysics in some way reflected or influenced our national life, if not directly then through its bearings on other aspects of his philosophy that did. From the point of view of most traditional conceptions of metaphysics which regard it as a deductive discipline that gives us knowledge of the grammar of existence or necessary truths about anything that is or may be conceived, or of Being *qua* Being, any such reflections or influence would be sufficient to condemn it. For it would seem to be evidence of some apologetic intent very much like those metaphysical systems of the past, criticized by Dewey himself, that imposed some parochial scheme of values on the cosmos in order to justify the *status quo* or facilitate a consolatory reconciliation with it.

Although many things are unclear about Dewey's philosophy, no one can reasonably dispute the assertion that he did not hold this conception of the nature of metaphysics. If anything, the view of philosophy he proposed when he abandoned Hegelian idealism for naturalism made of it "the critical method of developing methods of criticism"; and because its subject matter involved an inescapable concern with values, the unremitting critic of the social order.

Dewey's *Experience and Nature* is both the most suggestive and most difficult of his writings, the source of the most widespread objections by hostile critics, and of the most diverse interpretations by sympathetic critics. I shall try to restate what I regard as its main positions and relate them in passing not too arbitrarily to the central theme of the conference, philosophy in the life of a nation. There is no evidence that Dewey himself was aware of any relation between American national life and his metaphysics or that it figured in his intent in the way in which it did when he wrote books on specific social or political questions, like *Individualism-Old and New*, and *Liberalism and Social Action*. Although Dewey believed that all his central views hung together, he had no system in the traditional sense. One could reject the views expressed in *Experience and Nature* and accept those in *Democracy and Education* or *Freedom and Culture*.

Nor am I saying that, whatever the relation or connection between American life and Dewey's thought, it is the most important aspect of his philosophy—indeed, in my view it is quite peripheral. Dewey himself would claim that to the extent that his philosophical positions were significant and relevant, they reflected the human condition in our time rather than the American condition, although it might be argued with some plausibility that modern technological and cultural developments make the American condition and experience not unrepresentative of life in other Western industrialized nations, too.

Discussion today of Dewey's metaphysics in *Experience and Nature* must take note of the well-known fact that Dewey regarded the use of the terms "metaphysics" and "experience" as unfortunate. He was prepared to jettison both terms at the end of his long philosophical career in order to avoid misunderstanding. For "experience" he would have substituted "culture" in the anthropological sense. Culture is what characterizes man wherever he is found and differentiates *human* nature from animal nature. Human nature is cultural and historical rather than merely biological. Indeed, in a synoptic account of the history of philosophy in his unfinished new introduction to *Experience and Nature*, he contended that the relation between nature and human nature "was the standing if not always the outstanding problem," with which philosophy has perennially been concerned. He vowed on the eve of his ninetieth year "never to use the words [metaphysics and metaphysical] again in connection with any aspect of my own position" because, he complained, his use of the terms had been assimilated to the sense they bear, "in the classic tradition based on Aristotle."

Regardless of what word he used instead of "metaphysics," Dewey would have had to concern himself with the matters to which it referred in his previous essays, viz., "the nature of the existential world in which we live"[1] or, in many variations of the phrase, the study or "cognizance of the generic traits of existence."[2] After all Dewey has always argued and quite properly that the conduct of life, if it is to be intelligent, requires that we rely upon the relevant knowledge of the nature of nature. Otherwise all our plans and projects would be shipwrecked. Human nature is a part of nature, too, albeit a distinctive part, and must be studied in the same spirit and the same logic of inquiry, though not with the same techniques, as we study inanimate things and other animal behavior. These traits of nature and human nature function, as Dewey puts it, "as a ground map of the province of criticism." They are always relevant to what we do and above all in the area in which the basic philosophic choices are made that define wisdom. The distinctive function of philosophy for Dewey, to the extent that it can be marked off for emphasis but not separation from other disciplines, is *the normative consideration of human values*—most simply put, the quest for a good life in a good society.

If the knowledge of the nature of the physical, biological and social world is necessary to develop a reasonable way of life, why do we need anything more than the knowledge of the special sciences and common sense knowledge of ordinary affairs to guide us? After all, Dewey has affirmed on many occasions that empirical or experimental science is the paradigm of reliable knowledge, and has dismissed the view that any claim to philosophical knowledge could serve as a rival to, or surrogate of, scientific knowledge. Dewey's answer is that certain misconceptions about the nature of knowledge, the nature of man, and especially the nature of human experience have prevented the fruitful application of such knowledge to human affairs; that certain traditional assumptions, drawn from philosophies of the past, and whose categories to some extent have entered our language, have generated insoluble problems, introducing unbridgeable dualisms between subject and object, the real and the apparent, the physical and the mental, man and nature, things of experience and things in themselves, the individual and society. This has resulted in consequence in making man a stranger in the world and the operation of human intelligence a mystery.

According to Dewey there are certain fundamental traits or features of natural existence[3] which are studied by no specific scientific discipline, although implicitly recognized in some form by all of them as well as by common sense reflections, that are to be found in some "proportional union" in all situations. The "doings and undergoings that constitute experience" are marked by a union of the precarious and the assured, the perilous and the safe, the novel and familiar, or the irregular and the uniform. Dewey rings the changes on a long list of polarities.

Structure and process, substance and accident, matter and energy, permanence and flux, one and many, continuity and discreteness, order and progress, law and liberty, uniformity and growth, tradition and renovation, rational will and impelling desires, proof and discovery, the actual and the possible are names given to various phases of their conjunctions, and the issue of living depends upon the art with which these things are adjusted to each other.[4]

There seems little difficulty in accepting this characterization as holding for the human condition and its predicaments anywhere and everywhere. It may even strike one as a set of truisms, important truisms when counterposed to absurdities which would reduce or expand the meaning of these traits to a point where they had no intelligible opposite. Even if one contests Dewey's reading of the history of philosophy which interprets most regnant philosophies of the past as attempts to glorify the certain, the fixed, and the eternal, and degrading the probable, the contingent, and the temporal, the reading is intelligible. Nor is there much difficulty with Dewey's contention that the human condition and its predicaments fall entirely within nature. The difficulty begins with the further assertion that these traits and qualities that mark the human condition are the mark of nature, too. "The *world* is precarious and perilous,"[5] declares Dewey. "In nature itself qualities and relations, individualities and uniformities, finalities and efficacities, contingencies and necessities are inextricably bound together."[6] These generic traits "are manifested by existences of all kinds without regard to their differentiation into physical and mental."[7] They are "traits discovered in every theme of discourse since they are ineluctable traits of natural existence."[8]

These traits or qualities are not "subjective" in the sense of having a private locus that cannot be shared by others. They characterize states of affairs, are functions of an environment, their presence ascertainable in the same way as other facts are. For example, it is sometimes the case that a person feels anxiety or fear in a situation in which there is no danger, in which there is nothing to be fearful about. In such a case his fear is real enough, manifested by his behavior in walking gingerly, as if he were picking his way in a minefield, on a sidewalk streaming with pedestrians on all sides of him. The persistence of this fear or anxiety in the situation would be evidence that he was suffering a neurosis. On the other hand, there may be an individual who even in an actual minefield feels no fear or danger as evidenced by the fact that his behavior is no different from what it is, say, in a picnic field. Now if it is a genuine minefield in which he finds himself, we may call him fearless but to call him such presupposes that the situation itself is fearful or dangerous. It is in these contexts that Dewey says, "the world is precarious and perilous."[9]

This view has notoriously been a stone of stumbling to many of Dewey's contemporaries, notably Russell and M. R. Cohen. The difficulties for them reflect their differing view of the nature of experience. Fear for them is only a state of mind without any inherent connection with what exists or does not exist in nature. It has an exclusive private locus, like all tertiary and even secondary qualities, in the mind or nervous system of a specific person. Dewey regards this bifurcation between nature and experience as inherently untenable and as leading to conclusions that make our ordinary practical judgment incoherent. It does not account for the fact that in our judgments we can and do fruitfully distinguish between the experience of the person whose fear is justified in the situation and the experience of the person whose fear is unjustified. The fear is justified by what is truly fearful or dangerous *in the environment*. The fearfulness, the danger is objectively there, and we become aware of it; and if it isn't there, we don't create it by our neurotic fears. The dangerous possibility of a nuclear war is objectively rooted in the possession and proliferation of nuclear weapons by mutually hostile powers; would that it were only in our imagination ...

It was in the hope of avoiding the misunderstanding that resulted from translating his views of experience into those of his critics that Dewey proposed to substitute the term culture. For although it is still possible, instead of asking "whose experience?" when the term appears in philosophical discourse, to ask "whose culture?" when that term is substituted, the qualities of culture in the anthropological sense cannot plausibly be considered as private and exclusive. The manifold dependences of cultures, especially primitive cultures, on the environing physical world is so intimate that the precarious and hazardous character of existence, the world of empirical things, is a pervasive and omnipresent fact of life. Already in the first edition of *Experience and Nature*, Dewey makes illustrative use of the anthropological notion of culture.

It is important to realize that in *his* use of the term "experience" and in his proposed substitution of the term "culture," Dewey is not differing with his critics merely on matters of lexicographical or linguistic policy, as one of his persistent critics

asserts, but about an approach to the facts of personal and social
life which will illumine phenomena about which there is no dispute
in the ordinary affairs of men. M. R. Cohen once wrote:

> ... what on earth could Dewey have had in mind in his answer
> to me. Not only does he beg the question in assuming that the
> word *experience must* be used in his all inclusive instead of my
> restricted sense (a question of linguistic policy) but he does not
> seem to realize that the continuity between thought and other
> natural events is factual to be established by empirical evidence
> and not to be violently asserted or stealthily smuggled in by a
> definition, by using words, so that real distinctions are blurred.[10]

Dewey's standing reply, so to speak, to criticisms of this sort is
that first his conception of experience does recognize the distinction
between experienc*ing* and the experienc*ed* (that is why he calls it a
double ba-relled word), that far from *assuming* the continuity
between thoughts and natural events, it is a view fortified by the
cumulative results of the natural, biological-medical and cultural
disciplines From the standpoint of scientific empiricism—which
his critics profess to accept—thinking is a natural event or process,
a form of behavior in which some natural events are used to direct
and regulate other events. This approach explains why thinking
makes a difference to the world, and accounts for the fact that
thought can be practical which according to Dewey is a complete
mystery or his critics' traditional dualistic view.

Before developing these points I want to say something about
the possible changes that the shift from experience to culture might
make to Dewey's account of metaphysics. When we speak of
culture rather than experience it is not likely that culture in all its
relativities will be identified only as a mode of knowing, for it is an
affair of many types of doing and enjoying that are made possible
by the nature of things. Man never faces nature as a solitary center
of experience but as an acculturated organism, as part of a group
or community. It is easier to locate the objective features of social
life that determine the limits of normality. It is easier to see how
the threatening and supporting features of associated life depend
on the traits of the natural environment.

Nonetheless although the traits that are observable in social life
cannot be understood if we draw arbitrary lines between the
natural and the cultural, it will not do to suggest that the traits of
culture are no more than traits of nature as they appear in a social
context or that every social trait is found in nature in the same way
as in society. Granted that just as we do not have "to deny to

nature the characters that make things loveable and contemptible, beautiful, adorable and awful," so we do not have to deny to nature the characters that make social life cooperative and competitive, peaceful and warring. But just as we must avoid the implication that the characters in nature which make or contribute to making things loveable and contemptible are themselves *eo ipso* loveable and contemptible, so we must avoid the implication that the characters in nature which make societies peaceful or in conflict are themselves intelligibly at peace or in conflict with each other. Certain existential traits in culture and/or experience are evidential of other existential traits in nature but they are not necessarily the same traits.

Dewey is not a pan-psychist for whom the conditions of sentience are themselves sentient. Nor is he a dialectical idealist or a dialectical materialist for whom there is an objective dialectic in Nature. He is an evolutionary naturalist for whom all the qualities that emerge in human culture or experience require as conditions for their existence objective extra-organic natural traits. These traits are not given all together nor are they reducible to each other. Unless this much is made clear, it is a positive invitation to misunderstanding. Nature must be such "as to generate ignorance and inquiry," needs and wants, hunger and thirst but it does not itself possess these traits in the same literal sense. It is one thing to say that there is an element of randomness or contingency, order or irregularity in nature, that situations are indeterminate. But to say that a situation is *problematic* implies that it relates to a human or social predicament or at the very least to the presence of an element of sentience. Nature has no problems although the fact that *we* have problems tells us something about nature.

In my view, in revising *Experience and Nature* Dewey would have done well to modify his conception of metaphysics and to avoid the imputation that it is an independent discipline that gives us knowledge of the world that we cannot reach by any other study, and that what it gives us knowledge about are generic traits that are discoverable in any subject matter or every universe of discourse. I do not believe that there are any natural traits, physical, biological, personal or social, that are generic in this sense. Nor does it seem to me that Dewey's view requires that he interpret traits in this way. What he is really interested in is cataloging and analyzing those features of the world that have an important bearing on the human condition, on human hopes and possibilities, that are often taken for granted without being clearly articulated and sometimes ignored or even denied in the emphasis we give to other traits or in our failing to recognize the irreducibility of some feature of subject matter—and occasionally ending up by calling into question the very existence of the subject matter from which we have taken our point of departure. It is a world in which man learns that no matter how much power he acquires he cannot live or create like a God but that he need not therefore live like an animal or an automaton, that although he may not act wisely in what he does, he cannot act unnaturally—for even the unconventional is natural. To me this is what is conveyed by Dewey's metaphorical references to nature "supporting" or "frustrating" man or "withdrawing assistance" or "flouting its own creatures."

It may be objected that there are some generic traits that do turn up in all types or universes of discourse and which characterize all subject matters—for example individuality and continuity, unity and multiplicity, the novel and the familiar, the clear and the obscure, the distant and at hand, and a host of other polarities. These traits differ from those—like the perilous and the safe, the aleatory and the certain, the contingent and the necessary—which obviously are not applicable to all subject matters and universes of discourse. Nonetheless I believe it is demonstrable that with the first set of allegedly generic traits we are confronted with terms that stand for different meanings in the different fields in which they are in use. We are not dealing with an invariant meaning or trait but with a cluster of different meanings and traits. The trait—say individuality—that enables me to distinguish an individual number in a series of numbers is not the same as the trait that enables me to identify an individual shade of color or an individual person or an individual nation. As an abstraction the term "individual" like all others of its kind is systematically ambiguous until applied in a specific context.

Dewey himself is aware that the mere enumeration of generic traits of nature is not very helpful in understanding the world and guiding ourselves in their light. For with respect to the specific issues and challenges with which we must cope, it is "the degree and ratio they [these traits] sustain to one another" that make the difference to the outcome. "Barely to note and register that contingency is a trait of natural events," Dewey tells us, "has nothing to do with wisdom. To note, however, contingency in connection with a concrete situation in life is that fear of the Lord which is at least the beginning of wisdom."[11] We carry that wisdom forward when we allow for the contingent as we plan the affairs of life. How to do that properly requires much more knowledge than the knowledge of generic traits as in planning for contingencies in building an atomic energy plant or a new school in an earthquake region. If we cannot be wise, we can at least avoid being invincibly foolish. To be foolish is cocksurely to ignore or deny the element of the contingent in all the affairs of man, society and nature, and therefore to run the needless risk of being overtaken by surprise if not disaster.

As I read Dewey, or if I am charged with misreading him, as I would revise him, what he calls metaphysics or metaphysical truths constitutes a philosophical anthropology, a selection of those gross features of the world that impinge upon the theatre of human life, the background against which, and in intersection with which, human beings play out their roles. The script for their roles is written neither in the stars nor in the patterns of DNA. Most of it is drawn from the culture in which human beings find themselves but the lines are never final nor complete. Both the nature of man and of his culture is such that, although at the mercy of natural forces that may overwhelm and extinguish them, human beings can within modest limits, by virtue of intelligent behavior and luck, *reconstruct* some parts of the natural world, some of the institutions of their culture, and sublimate human passions so that they find expression in liberal and humane forms.

*   *   *   *

It is this reconstructive and redetermining role of man in culture and nature and therefore in modifying, however slowly, the nature of human nature that Dewey stresses most in his account of the interactions and transactions between the human organism and its environment. It explains his particular usage of the term "experience," and his rejection of the views of Russell, Cohen and the philosophical tradition that identifies experience with the private, the mentalistic and subjective.

Dewey's analysis of the Cartesian tradition from which modern epistemological and psycho-physical dualism stems is well known and need not be repeated here. His approach to the mind-body problem is biological—the material and the mental, the bodily and psychic, are not independent substances but "properties of particular fields of interacting events." The qualities of experience which on the traditional view are denied any existence outside mind, with the familiar incredible consequences of this root bifurcation—incredible because no one really acts on them—on Dewey's views are qualities of inclusive situations. The problems arising from dualism have led to blind alleys in whose mazes philosophers are still wandering.

We may briefly mention Dewey's treatment of the most celebrated of the epistemological problems that flows from the view that experience is narrowly restricted to what is given in sensation or perception. This generates the so-called problem of the existence of the external world: how can we infer from the immediately experienced objects of sense or sense data to the existence of anything outside or beyond that experience? From our visual, auditory, tactile and kinaesthetic data how do we get to an external and public world? Dewey offers a cogent analysis to prove that the question is self-defeating, that it cannot be intelligibly put without already presupposing that something, outside of that allegedly immediate experience, already exists. The nub of his argument is that the very identification of data as visual or auditory implies references to other bodies in space and time. That "color is visible or visual is a synthetic proposition." That I see with my eyes is as much an empirical proposition as that I think with my brain, not with my heart. Further, the assignment of temporal quality to sense data when they are characterized as immediate or momentary, here rather than there, involves reference to a series of things or events beyond the immediate experience, to make other times intelligible. Similarly, when we speak of "my or our own data" to identify the "I" or "our," it necessarily involves reference to a community and a system of language. Dewey concludes that we cannot significantly doubt the existence of the world but only the validity of some beliefs or assumptions about some things *within* it. There are echoes of Hegel and Peirce, to be sure, in this analysis but in no way does it entail their objective idealism.

More positive and less dialectical is Dewey's attempt to explain how thinking makes a difference to the world which is a mystery to all conceptions of experience that center it in consciousness as a substance or function isolated from the system of energies that constitute nature. If thinking merely mirrors or reflects the world as all traditional forms of the correspondence theory assume, how could we ever change the world by taking thought about it and its problems? Whatever one's philosophy, as human beings we are always urging the necessity of *reflective conduct* on our children, our students, our colleagues and public officials. No one really questions the possibility of thoughtful behavior, even when doubtful in any specific situation of its presence. Yet it could be claimed for Dewey that no one before him has come near to accounting for it without dissolving the whole world into a system of logical thought, and even then not being able to explain the specific failures and successes of thought. Here if anywhere it is plausible to believe that the transformation of the American wilderness into an industrial civilization in consequence of the applications of science and technology had some influence on Dewey's thinking about thinking. It is reflected in Dewey's conception of science and most suggestively expressed in his view, which has been scandalously caricatured, that from a liberal and humane point of view, science *in* application gives us knowledge in a pre-eminent degree. In a memorable passage he writes:

> Etymologically, "science" may signify tested and authentic instances of knowledge. But knowledge has also a meaning more liberal and humane. It signifies events understood, events so discriminately penetrated by thought that mind is literally at home in them ... What is sometimes called "applied science" may be more truly science than what is conventionally called pure science. For it is directly concerned with not just instrumentalities, but instrumentalities at work in effecting modifications of existence in behalf of conclusions that are reflectively preferred ... Thus conceived, knowledge exists in engineering, medicine, and the social arts more adequately than it does in mathematics and physics.[12]

Application here means operational or practical embodiment, not for personal satisfaction or commercial gain. It means that in applied science we are making the world more rational and life more reasonable, if the purposes for which scientific knowledge is applied are worthy of moral approval. Regardless of whether one shares this assessment of the character of applied knowledge, its existence must be accounted for. It cannot be done by dualistic views which put the natural world and human thought in separate domains. For the mind on such an approach can only be an idle spectator. Indeed, what else can the mind not rooted in nature do but stare impotently at the world or dream about it? And even the substance of its dreams indicates that it is not unrelated to natural events.

On Dewey's view human beings make inferences as naturally as they do other things. In the course of interaction a mutual modification takes place reflected in the product or outcome of the activity whether it is breathing or walking. Different modes or manners of experiencing considered as a series of activities affect the status of the subject matter experienced. Knowing, then, like any other natural process is a form of behavior but unlike other modes of experience, it operates through signs, symbols and meanings to reconstruct problematic, indeterminate situations into determinate ones. But the meanings used in knowing or inquiry at some point must lead to overt acts, a laying on of hands, so to speak, on things, to reorder or reconstruct the material or subject matter of the situation being inquired into.

This view has given rise to some hilarity among Dewey's critics. If the object of knowledge is modified in the course of our knowing it, how can we ever know it? When we seek knowledge about the moon, surely the moon remains unchanged in the course of our inquiry? Of course it does but to achieve confirmed knowledge about the moon something else is changed in the context and situation of inquiry—whether it be the position of an instrument or of the human body itself in the observations we make. The object of knowledge, the solution to the problem of inquiry, the objective if one calls it that, cannot be changed in the course of inquiry without stultification but when we are trying to find out or test an hypothesis about something we are doubtful about, the situation at some point must be reconstructed to give us a warranted conclusion. Reflection on the role of experiment in inquiry should make this clear. All existential knowledge for Dewey is experimental, which always involves an ordered change guided by some hypothesis. In passing, what was once considered a *reductio ad absurdum* implication of Dewey's theory has recently lost its sting, since as a result of some experiments on the surface of the moon, something about it too, as well as the positions of the observers and the experimental apparatus, was changed.

If thought is practical, which means for Dewey not that it is personally useful or a crutch to the will to believe but that it involves practice or experiment, then as determined as nature may be, it is not a closed or finished system, not a block universe but an open one. If, as Justic Holmes graphically puts it, "The mode in which the inevitable comes to pass is through effort," then at least to the extent that our effort has been spent, there is nothing altogether inevitable about the future or inevitable in all its respects and aspects. The world is open in the sense that there are some objective alternatives of development, that even when trends in nature or society are so overwhelmingly powerful that man cannot resist their cyclonic fury, the way one meets them or stands up to them is not foreclosed. We cannot as yet escape death, we can only postpone it. But the way we die may be more significant, if controllable, than the fact of death itself, not only in our own life but for the lives of others.

Whether the environing American society with its open frontier had a subconscious influence on Dewey's view of the open universe is hard to say. He himself recalls that during his early years "in imagination at least the country was still having an open frontier," that it was building a new society. Even more speculative is the presumption that his objective relativism expresses if not the actualities, the promise of American democracy. For his objective relativism recognizes no superior realms of being, no hierarchy of realities, but acknowledges equal existential status to all sorts of experience. "Illusions are illusions," he writes "but the occurrence of an illusion is not an illusion."[13] Errors abound in the world but they consist not in unreal or inferior existence or appearances— things are as they are experienced *as*—but in mistaken *inferences* from what is truly there to an assertion about its continued existence and behavior in a different spatial or temporal context. To truly be is to be reliable in a specific context. And perhaps it is not altogether fanciful to see in his refusal to assign a superior reality to causes—despite the role causes play in control—the American tendency to give as much, perhaps more, weight to what a person becomes as to what and where he comes from.

*   *   *   *

It seems almost obvious that Dewey's social and political philosophy and his "faith in the possibilities of intelligence and education as a correlate of intelligence" reflects the culture of his time. He modestly says: "I did not invent this faith. I acquired it from my surroundings as far as these surroundings were animated by the democratic spirit." Since these surroundings contained much more than the democratic spirit, including ideas, attitudes, and institutional practices at variance with that spirit, it would be more accurate to say that the life of the nation was more truly reflected in what Dewey was critical of, in what he took issue with, as he developed his thoughts. I am thinking of the exaltation of the individual and individualism in Dewey's lifetime, the absence or rather the insufficiency of social planning, and the failure to bring the resources of social intelligence to bear on the problems of social life. I want to say a few words about each.

As one would expect, Dewey rejected the standard and easy counterposition of the Individual and the Social as if they were fixed concepts or entities. Individuals are made not born—they are born only as particular organisms—and they are made by the multiple associations of which society consists. And as those associations develop historically, different individuals are created. Concern then must be with specific social institutions, political, economic, educational, in their effects in releasing and organizing personal capacities to their fullest desirable growth. We must always ask, and judge a society by the answer to the question: what kind of person is being created?

Just as the individual is an abstraction for an immense variety of responses, dispositions and susceptibilities developed in the relationships of persons to each other, so Society is an abstraction for all sorts of associations and institutions that regulate the joint experiences of human beings. The specific forms of these associations and institutions must be modified and planned whenever their functioning generates hardships which deprive any members of the community from enjoying equal opportunities—and sharing the goods and services on which the realization of these equal opportunities depend—necessary to develop as persons.

Planning today is a word in bad order because of the failure of some recent ill-conceived and half-hearted social programs. In a complex and dangerous world where not only what we do but also what we fail to do has consequences, planning is necessary in order to survive, particularly if there are powerful forces and nations in the grip of an ideology that encompasses the destruction of the open societies of the West. The fact that planning always has unintended and unanticipated consequences does not militate against its wisdom when we compare it with the consequences of not planning. That unintended consequences flow from our plans and actions is a ground for more careful and better planning. Modern medicine in prolonging human life has unintentionally prolonged and intensified human suffering. Who would therefore draw the moral that we should not continue to plan to eliminate disease? We need not, we cannot plan for everything. The question is always the specific one of what to plan, where and how. Dewey's slogan during the depression of the thirties, "Regiment things, not persons," may have been too simplistic, but he lived long enough to believe it was possible to plan to expand human freedom and, with an eye on the concentration camp economies of the world, to know what to avoid.

By the failure to bring the resources of organized intelligence to bear on social problems, Dewey means the failure to use scientific and rational methods of resolving social conflicts, of discovering the institutional changes required to extend the area of shared interests among the contestants, in the absence of which society is always in a state of incipient civil war. He undoubtedly oversimplified the difficulties of solving social problems even by extending "the methods of consultation, persuasion, negotiation and communication." Conflicting interests may count more heavily than shared interests. Until we discover ways of inducing man to rely on the values, attitudes and habits of intelligence, can faith in intelligence be an intelligent faith? Dewey's best answer is that although the use of scientific method, as he describes it, may fail no other method so far tried has succeeded.

Dewey denied he was a Utopian, denied that he believed all problems can be solved, or that intelligence will triumph in the strife of methods in resolving disputes or that it will save us from ruin or destruction. His more modest claim is that in a world where the only open frontier left to us is the moral frontier, in which all social problems must be considered moral and educational problems, he asserts that the methods of intelligence are worth trying. Certainly, they are worth trying but will they be tried? My own great difficulty with this is with his assumption that the presence of intelligence naturally carries with it, as it did in his life, the moral courage to act on one's own intelligent convictions. There is evidence that in this assumption he takes too much for granted. The courage of fanatics and fanaticism is notorious whatever we think of their morals. There is even the courage of the confused and the ignorant who do not see the pitfalls around them. But the courage—the moral courage—of the intelligent, without which wisdom is only a wistful possibility, is not itself entailed by the possession of intelligence. What is its source? How can it be developed? How can it prevail against the unintelligence of the courageous fanatic? To these questions Dewey offers no answers. Nor have I been able to find any other thinker who offers adequate ones.

NOTES

1. John Dewey, *Experience and Nature* (LaSalle, Ill., Open Court Pub. Co., 1929), p. 45.
2. *Ibid.*, p. 51.

3. *Ibid.*, p. 75.
4. *Ibid.*, pp. 75–6.
5. *Ibid.*, p. 42.
6. *Ibid.*, p. 421.
7. *Ibid.*, p. 412.
8. *Ibid.*, p. 413.
9. *Ibid.*, p. 42.
10. Letter to the writer, August 21, 1931.
11. Dewey, *op cit.*, p. 413.
12. *Ibid.*, pp. 161–162.
13. *Ibid.*, p. 20.

DEWEY'S VIEW OF EXPERIENCE AND CULTURE

LEWIS E. HAHN

Southern Illinois, University at Carbondale, Carbondale, Illinois

Experience is a focal concept for Dewey's philosophy, and he labored long and diligently to clarify it. Such major works as his *Art as Experience, Experience and Education,* and *Experience and Nature* deal with it; and some of his last writings, for example, his unpublished drafts of a new introduction for *Experience and Nature,* show his continuing concern for this key notion. (These drafts are in the John Dewey Papers, Special Collections, Morris Library, Southern Illinois University at Carbondale.)

For Dewey as for William James experience is a double-barreled fact which includes both the experienc*ed* and the experienc*ing,* both what is experienced and the ways in which it is experienced. It is *of* as well as *in* nature. It constitutes the entire range of man's relations to, or transactions with, nature at large or the universe. It is "something at least as wide and deep and full as all history on this earth, a history which ... includes the earth and the physical relatives of man."[1] It is an affair of intercourse, mutual adaptation, between a living organism and its physical and social environment, a matter of simultaneous doings and sufferings. It is "the peculiar intermixture of support and frustration of man by nature."[2] It carries principles of connection and order within itself. It is experimental and self-corrective.

Although Dewey offers an empirical approach, it is not the traditional empiricism; and to understand his view of experience one must take it within the context of a new world view which stresses change, becoming, innovation, rather than the immutable or permanent. It is not enough, I fear, simply to follow the Dewey-Bentley program of returning the term to its idiomatic usages without the interpretive guidance of the world view. At any rate, Dewey calls this view empirical naturalism, naturalistic empiricism, or naturalistic humanism. I prefer to call it contextualism, and I have discussed this view at length elsewhere.[3] In these other discussions I hold that in a contextualistic world view we find existence characterized not merely by change but also by such other generic traits as diversity, interaction or transaction, continuity, texture, strands, quality, fusion, reference or connection, and context. Analysis on this view is an affair of tracing patterns of change rather than one of reducing wholes to eternal elements.

One of the major advantages of this view for Dewey's account of experience, moreover, is that a Lockean or Cartesian dualism of an inner subjective realm as over against an outer objective world does not arise in it. Although for Dewey experience is the human side of reality and nature the non-human, they are not separate but continuous. In a draft for a new introduction to *Experience and Nature* Dewey speaks of the intimate connections and outstanding differences or distinctions between human achievements, failures, and strivings, "the subject matter collectively named by the word *Experience*,' and "what is marked off on the other hand as the non-human to which as such the name *nature* applies." Experience is the method for getting at nature, and nature empirically disclosed deepens, enrichens, and directs the further development of experience.[4]

Some of the major differences between Dewey's empiricism and the traditional empiricism turn about their respective interpretations of experience; and in "The Need for a Recovery of Philosophy" Dewey offers five points of contrast between his interpretation and what he calls the orthodox view, that accepted by both the traditional empiricists and their opponents.[5] In the first place, whereas on the orthodox view experience is primarily a knowledge affair, on Dewey's it is centrally intercourse between a living organism and its physical and social environment, an affair of had qualities, a transaction of enjoying and suffering, of doing and undergoing. Although any experience may become an object of knowledge or reflection, the knowing is always part of a larger basically non-cognitive interaction.

In the second place, for the traditionalist, experience is a psychical thing, infected throughout by subjectivity, an inner private collection of mental states set over against an outer physical world. For Dewey, on the other hand, experience flows in and through its objective environment, which supports or blocks it and is in turn modified by it. Experience is of a piece with the objective world which surrounds, maintains, and supports it—a situation significantly different from the traditionalist's picture of two separate and disparate realms separated by a cosmic chasm. Dewey repeatedly complains that his critics attribute to him the view he is criticizing; they forget or overlook the more "vital, concrete, and pregnant sense" in which he uses the term experience and substitute a kind of psychological abstract.

Thirdly, the proponents of the traditional view have been preoccupied with what is or has been "given" in a bare present, whereas for Dewey the salient trait of experience is its connection with a future. What is important, as he sees it, is not what has been or is given but rather what might be done to change what is given to further human purposes. An experimental form of experience requires a forward look, with emphasis on anticipation rather than recollection.

A fourth major point of difference between the two versions of experience turns about the traditionalist's commitment to parti-cularism, to discrete sense data or more or less isolated states of consciousness, sensations, impressions, or ideas. This view, according to Dewey, neglects connections, relations, and con-tinuities, supposing them to be either foreign to experience or dubious by-products of it. Dewey, like James, stressed relations and held that experience carries principles of connection and organization within itself. He emphasized the contextual, situational, transactional, or field character of experience. It was for him, as he repeatedly noted, "a matter of functions and habits, of active adjustments and re-adjustments, of co-ordinations and activities, rather than of states of consciousness," isolated impressions or ideas. (See, for example, "A Short Catechism Concerning Truth," *The Influence of Darwin on Philosophy*, p. 156.) As he declared in *Reconstruction in Philosophy* (Beacon Paperback, 1957, p. 91), adaptive courses of action, connections of doing and undergoing, and not discrete sensations, are the "stuff" of experience.

Fifth and finally, the supporters of the orthodox view oppose experience to thought in the sense of inference, but for Dewey experience is full of inference, as might be expected from his relational emphasis. For him, moreover, inference is not a mere recall of the past or a desperate and probably invalid leap beyond experience, but rather is an essential part of it. If one is to employ the direct support of the environment to effect indirectly changes that would not otherwise occur, to avoid the hostile and make more secure the favorable incidents, an imaginative forecast of the future, inference, is needed for guidance.

The nature of experience, on Dewey's view, however, is exhibited most clearly in aesthetic experience. In it, according to *Art as Experience*, we find experiences in their fullness and singularity, vivified, clarified, intensified, and integrated. In them the interactive character of experience comes out with special clarity. In Dewey's words, "In an experience, things and events belonging to the world, physical and social, are transformed through the human context they enter, while the live creature is changed and developed through its intercourse with things previously external to it.[6] There is an "intrinsic connection of the self with the world through reciprocity of undergoing and doing," and "all distinctions which analysis can introduce into the psychological factor are but difference aspects and phases of a continuous, though varied, interaction of self and environment."[7]

As late as 1951 Dewey could still say that he did not feel the need to take back any of the things he said about experience in the earlier text of Experience and Nature; but this statement was coupled with the declaration that "were the book that was published with the title Experience and Nature being written today, its caption would be Culture and Nature and the treatment of specific subject matters would be correspondingly modified". (This assertion and the remaining quotations in this paper are from John Dewey Papers, Special Collections, Morris Library, Southern Illinois University at Carbondale.) Although in theory he could still see justification for his previous use of the terms "experience" and "experiential," it seemed to him that there were both negative and positive grounds for changing to the term "culture."

He mentions at least four lines of justification for his earlier usage. In the first place, as over against the dualisms of subjective and objective, mind and the world, psychological and physical which have tended to dominate the systems and doctrines of modern philosophy, "there is much to be said in favor of using 'experience' and 'experiential' (as distinct from 'empirical') to designate the inclusive subject matter in which what is experienced is taken systematically into account as well as the ways in which it is experienced." Secondly, the appeal to experience seemed to him a wholesome and "much needed aspiration to get philosophy away from desiccated abstraction into an area that is vitally concrete."

A third justification has to do with the office or role of philosophy in its comprehensive aim, in its claim to make comprehensive sense of the full range of experienced facts. Since the comprehensiveness of its subject matter is what distinguishes philosophy from other intellectual or cognitive undertakings, "a linguistic expression is needed which specifically designates that property," and "experience" in its inclusive sense is one way of meeting this need. Somewhat differently stated, nature when viewed and treated as material of and for human experience seems "to satisfy the historic claim of philosophy to be concerned with what is comprehensive in scope and abundant and intense in content."

Fourthly, the appeal to experience was a commendable "protest against the attempt of previously accepted philosophies to neglect, to slight and slur over the possibilities of human life in locating what is comprehensive and basic in what was taken to be eternal, above time, immutable, far above change, and universal ..." Dewey was convinced that the rational ground and justification as well as the practical and factual base of the newer and more promising movements in modern philosophy were to be found in the "systematic recognition of *Process* as providing *the* comprehensive point of view from which to survey and report the natural world to which man belongs."

From these lines of justification it seems clear that Dewey had not changed his substantive views of experience. Why, then, was he considering abandoning the terms "experience" and "experiential"? A primary reason was the negative consideration that "the course of *historical* events within and outside of developments in philosophy formed an effective and solid obstruction to the words being understood in the sense intended—one namely in which ... they named *what* is *experienced* in full conjunction with the ways of experiencing that are involved in the very structure and constitution of *what* is experienced." In the course of history experience had become effectively identified with experiencing in the psychological sense, and the psychological had come to be thought of as the exclusively individual or the "intrinsically psychical, mental, private," the subjective as set over against the objective. In short, the course of history had resulted in what he had called in "The Need for a Recovery of Philosophy" the orthodox view of experience, a view against which he had been arguing all these years. But this account of experience has no place in the world view of empirical naturalism or contextualism.

There was, however, something new in the situation, and this constituted the positive ground for the proposed change from "experience" to "culture." Other historical developments in anthropology had conferred upon "culture" just the range and depth of significance of which "experience" had been progressively and effectively derived. Dewey, therefore, concluded that "as a matter of historical fact the only sense in which 'experience' could be understood to designate the vast range of things experienced in an indefinite variety of ways is by identifying its import or significance with that of the whole range of considerations to which the name 'culture' in its anthropological (not its Matthew Arnold) sense is now applied. It possesses as a name just that body of substantial references of which ... 'experience' as a name has been emptied. In addition 'culture' names a whole set of considerations which are of utmost significance in and for the enterprise of philosophy as intellectually inclusive." These include material artifacts and technologies, beliefs and practices, moral attitudes and scientific dispositions, the material and ideal in their reciprocal relations each upon the other. In addition "culture" also designates, "also in their reciprocal connections with one another, that immense diversity of human affairs, interests, concerns, values, which when specified piecemeal are designated *religious, moral, aesthetic, political, economic,* etc., etc., thereby holding them together in their human and humanistic unity—a service which ... f philosophy is to fulfill its ambition to be comprehensive, is of utmost importance for its status and development."

In short then, "culture" is to do what Dewey previously had hoped "experience" would do. This is a very suggestive idea, but whether the new term can perform this function any better than the old remains to be seen. The new term may help emphasize the social side of experience. Many found the older term slanted toward individuals in a biological matrix. Perhaps, moreover, substituting "culture" for "experience" will enable some readers to better understand Dewey's interpretation of experience and thus possibly make it more acceptable, but it does not seem to me that any substantive change in his outlook is involved. Accordingly, I think it unlikely that the new terminology will change the attitude of those who have been most critical of the old. As I see it, then, a basic defense or critique of his account of experience would still need to be offered in terms of an examination of this account in relation to the relevant facts and his comprehensive philosophy; and the case for it turns largely, not on the terminology used, but rather on how well one finds these facts illuminated by this world view. Since I find this view quite illuminating, it seems to me that we should be the poorer without his account of experience.

NOTES

1. John Dewey, *Experience and Nature* (LaSalle, Ill., Open Court Pub. Co., 1929), p. 8.

2. *Ibid.*, p. 2a.

3. For example, in *A Contextualistic Theory of Perception* (University of California Publications in Philosophy, XXII) pp. 6–19; in "Dewey's Philosophy and Philosophic Method" in Jo Ann Boydston, ed., *Guide to the Works of John Dewey* (SIU Press, 1970), pp. 15–60, esp. 40–51; and in "Contextualism and Cosmic Evolution-Revolution," in Rubin Gotesky and Ervin Laszlo, eds., *Evolution-Revolution* (New York, London, Paris, Gordon & Breach, 1971), pp. 3–39.

4. Dewey, *op. cit.*, p. 2a.

5. Dewey, *Creative Intelligence: Essays in the Pragmatic Attitude* (New York, H. Holt & Co., 1917), pp. 3–69.

6. Dewey, *Art as Experience* (New York, Capricorn Books, 1934), p. 246.

7. *Ibid.*, p. 247.

DEWEY ON RELIGION

JUDE P. DOUGHERTY

The Catholic University of America, Washington, D.C.

It would be naive to seek a fully developed philosophy of religion in the writings of John Dewey. Though there are few topics normally addressed by philosophers to which Dewey has not devoted at least some attention, he has not taken up, in any detail, those themes usually identified with the philosophy of religion, such as religious symbols, revelation, religious language, the logic of religion, the naming of God, and mysticism. There are reasons for this. Some stem from the built-in difficulties which every philosopher experiences when it comes to talk about religion. But the most important reason for silence flows out of Dewey's basic metaphysical and epistemological assumptions.

I am talking about the mature Dewey. For Dewey is one of those philosophers where the difference between the mature thinker and the youthful apprentice is almost the difference between men. It is the difference between two men because it is the difference between two schools of thought, an idealism in the early years and a materialistic naturalism in the later. In a way, Dewey's intellectual biography is the chronicle of his times, reflecting in the academic world a shift in belief from a fundamentalist Christianity in the last quarter of the nineteenth century to an outright secularism in the first quarter of the twentieth. In his mature years, as a philosophical naturalist. Dewey has concluded that there is no evidence for a transcendent realm. Nature is self-intelligible and the only reliable method of acquiring knowledge is that commonly designated "scientific." The key to his mature inquiry is the conviction that religion is mistaken in its claims to knowledge.

While Dewey cannot take faith at face value in terms of its cognitive claims, he can do two things: he can evaluate it in terms of its social effects, and he can analyze it to free it from its mistaken forms and display the religious impulse in its pure and unencumbered state, natural sentiment with a natural object. To some extent, he does both. Yet Dewey's final approach to religion is not so much that of the philosopher attempting to understand it, but rather that of the critic and reformer. His major work on the

174

subject, *A Common Faith*, must be considered a critique of religion. And the stance from which the critique is delivered is primarily, perhaps even necessarily, a sociological one. This is not to deny what we have just said, that Dewey's attitude toward religion has metaphysical roots. His naturalism leads him to affirm that there is no evidence for the existence of God. It is his anthropology and sociology which enable him to explain religion in terms of its purely natural orgins. And it is against certain adopted social canons that he evaluates its worth.

But Dewey was not always a naturalist, and it is instructive to begin at the beginning. The sources for Dewey's views on religion range from his homily on "The Obligation to Knowledge of God," delivered to the Student Christian Association at the University of Michigan in 1884, to the Terry Lectures delivered at Yale some fifty years later, and published under the title *A Common Faith*. In Dewey's early period, as a young instructor of philosophy and as faculty advisor to the Student Christian Association, he had occasion to deliver a number of lectures, perhaps more properly called sermons, that would grace any contemporary pulpit both for their charm and for their Christian orthodoxy. In the earliest of these, belief is presented as an obligation. Religion is not so much the payment of a debt to God as it is the deliberate acquisition of a vision, both a way of looking at things and a program for action.

In the first source mentioned, Dewey declares that "The scriptures are uniform in their treatment of scepticism. There is an obligation to know God, and to fail to meet this obligation is not to err intellectually, but to sin morally. Belief is not a privilege, but a duty ... Whatsoever is not of faith is sin."[1] He goes on to say:

> All knowledge is one. It is all of God ... and if any set of facts are regarded as something in themselves, out of all relation to God and God's creatures, it is no knowledge. The whole world of nature and history is worthless except as it is brought into relation with man's nature and activities; and *that* science or philosophy is worthless which does not ultimately bring every fact into guiding relation with the living activity of man, and the end of all his striving—approach to God. He that does the Will, alone has real knowledge.[2]

Not only is all knowledge one, but knowing and willing are intimately related. Knowledge does not originate in a faculty apart, separate from our will and desires. There is no knowledge of anything except as our interests are alive to the matter. We know only what we most want to know. Knowledge is not a colorless intellectua thing; it is essentially a moral thing. "We must seek in order to find, and we find that for which we seek. If the desires and will of man are for God, he will find God in all of his knowledge."[3] If there is not this attitude, man's knowledge, though it extend ever so far, will never reach God, for He has been shut out from the start.

By 1892, however, Dewey is well on his way to a purely secular interpretation of religion. In a lecture, "Christianity and Democracy," delivered at the University of Michigan, he makes a distinction between "cult and creed," on the one hand, and "revelation" as the ongoing discovery of the truth of life, on the other.[4] Looked at from the outside, religion seems to be cult and a body of doctrine. This is only appearance. Research into the origin and development of religion destroys the appearance. It shows the every religion has its source in the social and intellectual life of a community or race. Every religion is an expression of the mental attitudes and habits of a people; its rites, its cult, are but a recognition of the sacred and divine significance of these relationships.

Similarly in 1894, while the language remains Hegelian, the mood is unmistakably secular. In a lecture entitled "Reconstruction," Dewey suggests that because of the established results of modern science, the church must "reconstruct its doctrines of revelation and inspiration." In a like manner, it is important for the individual to "reconstruct, within his own religious life, his conception of what spiritual truth is and the nature of its authority over him. Science has made real to us, and is bound to make still more real, the actual incarnation of truth in human experience and the need for giving heed to it."[5]

By 1908 it is evident that the transition is complete. In the article "Religion in Our Schools," he characterizes religion as "secret, not public; peculiarly revealed, not generally known; authoritatively declared, not communicated and tested in ordinary ways."[6] There is "something self-contradictory in speaking of education in religion in the same sense in which we speak of education in topics where the method of free inquiry has made its way."[7] The wider and deeper knowledge provided by contemporary science undermines the religionist's traditional basis:

It is increased knowledge of nature which has made supra-nature incredible, or at least difficult of belief. We measure the change from the standpoint of the supra-natural and we call it irreligious. Possibly if we measured it from the standpoint of the natural piety it is fostering, the sense of the permanent and inevitable implication of nature and man in a common career and destiny, it would appear as the growth of religion.[8]

While Dewey is to attack supernaturalism in a number of major works published subsequent to "Religion in Our Schools," (*Essays in Experimental Logic*, 1916; *Human Nature*, 1922; *The Quest for Certainty*, 1929) it is in the Terry Lectures delivered at Yale in 1934 that we find the major expression of Dewey's mature view of religion. Dewey was 74 years of age when he gave those lectures, and though he was to write about religion again in several places before his death, it remains his definitive work on the subject. Regarding the Terry Lectures, Dewey was later to say that they were addressed chiefly to those who had already abandoned supernaturalism.

Dewey opens his slim volume, *A Common Faith*,[9] with the observation that men have been divided in history over the question of religion. The root of this division of men into two camps is, in his view, "the supernatural."[10] Religionists maintain that no belief can be genuinely called religious which is not connected with the supernatural. Among believers there is a range of positions, from those who hold that the Greek and Roman Churches, with their dogmatic and sacramental systems, are the only sure means of access to the supernatural, to the theist or mild deist. Between them are many Protestant persuasions who think scripture and conscience are adequate avenues to religious truth. Those opposed to religion believe that the advance of anthropological and psychological studies has adequately revealed the all too human sources of what has customarily been ascribed to the supernatural. The extremists in the latter group believe that with the elimination of the supernatural not only must historical religions be dismissed, but with them everything of a religious nature.

Having appraised the situation in this way, Dewey indicates that his procedures will be to examine the root causes of the division among men over the issue of religion—he proposes to attend to the ground for, and the consequences of, the identification of the religious with the supernatural, the reasons for this identification and the value of it. In doing so, he proposes another conception of the nature of the religious phase of experience, one that separates it from the supernatural and the derivations that have been added to it.

Cutting these away will, in his view, enable genuinely religious human experience to develop freely on its own account. To this end, in the first of the three chapters comprising *A Common Faith*, Dewey introduces a distinction between "religion" as a noun and the adjective "religious."[11] The purpose of this distinction is to provide a hermeneutical tool for salvaging that which is valid in experience designated "religious" from the encumbrances which have cropped up in association with such experiences as they have been explained by, and in the context of, various historic religions.[12] There is, in Dewey's estimation, a validity to what is globally designated religious experience. This can be had apart from the variety of historical religions which in fact have hampered the full play of such experiences.[13] If this valid core can be brought to light and appreciated, then men will stop thinking that they need religions to reap this fruit.

While Dewey does not deny that a religious attitude has many beneficent effects, he does deny that these effects are exclusive to religion. It is the claim of religions that they bring about a change in attitude, but the difficulty with institutions is that they take such an attitude and turn it into a religion. They change moral faith into speculative faith and dogma. Moral faith entails the conviction that some end should be supreme over conduct. Speculative faith, by contrast, attributes existence to that object and makes it a truth for the intellect. Moral faith subordinates itself to a goal which has a rightful claim over desires and purposes. It is practical, not intellectual. It goes beyond evidence, but it has only the authority of a freely admitted ideal, not that of a fact. Institutional religions take such an attitude, give personal reality to what was a moral ideal, and present this ideal as a final reality at the heart of everything that exists. Religion has no difficulty in doing this. Desire has a powerful influence on intellectual beliefs. Men tend to believe what they ardently desire. Besides, it is always easier to believe that the ideal is already a fact than to strive to make it so.[14]

Dewey regards the ideal as fundamentally more religious than its reification in formal religions. For the ideal points to possibilities, and all endeavor is better moved by faith in what is possible than in adherence to what is already actual. Furthermore, such an ideal can be denotive of activity on the level of nature. It is consonant with nature and does not divorce us from it. "Faith in the continued disclosing of truth through directed cooperative human endeavor is more religious in quality than is any faith in a completed revelation."[15] Thus, nature and man's experience within it become both the source and object of an ideal which is directive of life. Any activity pursued on behalf of an ideal end is religious in quality. The essentially unreligious attitude is that which attributes human achievement and purpose to man in isolation from nature and his fellows. To regard religious act in this way is to avoid the antagonism between religion and modern science.

It is worth noting that Dewey, at this stage, takes leave of James's approach to religious belief. James had been willing to grant some validity and meaning to a belief that produced satisfactory results in the life of the believer. Dewey is more cautious. He asks whether James employs the pragmatic method to discover the valuable in terms of the consequences of some religious formula which has its logical content already fixed, or uses his pragmatic method to criticize, revise, and ultimately constitute the meaning of the formula.[16] He is afraid that some may understand pragmatism in the first sense, and be disposed to attribute existential value to fixed dogmas which science has rendered untenable. If pragmatism is of any value in the religious sphere, its contribution is to replace faith in the supernatural order of traditional religion with faith in the religious possibilities of ordinary experience. There can be faith in intelligence, a devotion to the process by which truth is discovered, a commitment to science and to the worth and dignity of the human person. In this way, morality and religion will become an integral part of everyday living, emerging out of nature and renovating the nature out of which it has arisen.

Dewey has not been without his critics. John Herman Randall, Jr., historian of philosophy and in many respects sympathetic to Dewey, accuses him of a religious provincialism. Of Dewey he says, "He has sought the religious function in general; and he emerges as the spokesman of the habits of mind of the liberal American protestant christian of our generation."[17] He adds:

> To free the religious attitude from institutional embodiment in any religion sounds suspiciously like freeing art from embodiment in any particular work of art; and the religious man who never goes near a religious institution suggests the musical person who never touches a musical instrument or attends a concert.[18]

In another article, Randall draws a comparison between Dewey's treatment of art and his treatment of religion:

> In art, Dewey is quite aware that criticism not intimately acquainted with a variety of traditions is limited, onesided, and distorted. For him, art is the gateway to appreciating alien cultures, and his perception is both catholic and discriminating.

But religion must reject the past for the best in the present; and here his sympathies are both protestant and unimaginative. Art is to be enjoyed wherever it is found excellent; religion is not to be enjoyed, but to be emancipated from historic encumbrances the better to foster an intelligent humanism.[19]

Randall, is, of course, viewing Dewey from what is essentially his own romantic interpretation of religion. Randall, in the tradition of Schleiermacher and Ritschl, can regard religion as valuable from an ethical and aesthetic point of view, and can even call for intelligently fabricated theology. No less a naturalist than Dewey, he can still appreciate religion in its historical and contemporary manifestations, because of its elevating role.

In one respect, Dewey's position is more honest than Randall's. As a non-believer, Dewey has little use for religion or religious institutions, whatever roles they may have played in the past. Randall would allow religion to serve by inspiring men to perform the difficult good or providing an integration of their nobler impulses through appropriate symbols. But Dewey looks to religion neither for knowledge nor for motivation. Randall would use religion; Dewey would, in effect, abolish it. But in another respect, Randall's criticism is telling. It is possible for Dewey to remind those who have abandoned supernaturalism that they still have available to them all the elements of a profound religious commitment to the well-being of mankind. This does not, however, mitigate the responsibility of the philosopher of religion to make an attempt to understand the development, prevalence and functions of religion in society.

NOTES

1. *John Dewey, The Early Works*, ed. Jo Ann Boydston, Vol. I, 1882–1888 (Carbondale, The Southern Illinois University Press, 1969), p. 61. Anyone writing on the philosophy of John Dewey, particularly on aspects of his thought which draw upon his early writings, must acknowledge a debt to Jo Ann Boydston who, as Director of Co-operative Research on Dewey Publications at Southern Illinois University, is editor of the four-volume collection *John Dewey, The Early Works 1882–1898* and editor of *Guide to the Work of John Dewey*, an important bibliographical tool. Many of Dewey's early lectures and essays, particularly those on religion, were largely inaccessible, and consequently were unexamined by scholars, before their reprinting by the Southern Illinois University Press.

2. *Ibid.*, p. 62.
3. *Ibid.*, pp. 62–63.
4. John Dewey, *The Early Works*, Vol. IV, 1893–94, p. 3.
5. *Ibid.*, p. 103.
6. John Dewey, *Hibbert Journal*, Vol. VI (1908), p. 804.

7. *Ibid.*, p. 805.
8. *Ibid.*, p. 808.
9. John Dewey, *A Common Faith* (New Haven: Yale University Press, 1934).
10. *Ibid.*, p. 1.
11. *Ibid.*
12. *Ibid.*, p. 2.
13. *Ibid.*, p. 3.
14. *Ibid.*, p. 22.
15. *Ibid.*, p. 26.
16. See also Dewey's *Essays in Experimental Logic* (Chicago, University of Chicago Press), p. 313.
17. John Herman Randall, Jr., "The Religion of Shared Experience," in *The Philosopher of the Common Man, Essays in Honor of John Dewey to Celebrate His Eightieth Birthday* (New York, G. P. Putnam's Sons, 1940), p. 138.
18. *Ibid.*, p. 137. See also W. E. Arnett, "Critique of Dewey's Anticlerical Religious Philosophy," *Journal of Religion*, XXXIV (1954).
19. John Herman Randall, Jr., "Art and Religion as Education," *Social Frontier*, II (1936), 110.

PART III:
THE AMERICAN PHILOSOPHICAL
EXPERIENCE

RECEPTIVITY, CHANGE AND RELEVANCE; SOME HALLMARKS OF PHILOSOPHY IN AMERICA

JOHN E. SMITH

Yale University, New Haven, Connecticut

Anyone who has given thought to what might be meant by the phrase "American Philosophy" becomes aware at once of the dilemma which presents itself and which, like all significant dilemmas, resists a neat solution. By "American philosophy," it would seem, we must mean either an identifiable American position, outlook or system of thought, on the one hand, or a mere catalogue, an enumeration of all the types of philosophical thinking taking place on the American scene, on the other. In the first sense we would be pointing to a substantive "American" philosophy analogous, for example, to British empiricism or German idealism, whereas in the second sense, the adjective "American" would have a largely geographical connotation, conveying little more than the place or the environment within which a quite heterogeneous collection of philosophical issues have been discussed and philosophical positions articulated. I am inclined to think that there was in fact an indigenous American philosophy in the first sense to be found in the many-sided development of pragmatism beginning with the early papers of Peirce and continuing through the work of Dewey and Mead. Since, however, that classical development had run its course a decade or so before the middle of the century and was succeeded, on the academic scene at least, by new interests in language, semantics, epistemology and logic introduced through both British and Continental sources, it is no longer legitimate to speak of American philosophy solely in terms of the classical position. In saying this I do not mean to imply that the basic ideas of the pragmatists have simply disappeared; on the contrary, there is at present a new interest in their ideas both at home and abroad. I mean rather to call attention to the fact that so many new interests, positions and approaches have made their appearance in our midst that it is clearly impossible to speak of American philosophy as if it represented one substantive position or tradition. And indeed this is precisely what one should expect in a pluralistic culture such as our own.

In view of these considerations, it seems to me that the only way to do justice to a rather complex situation is to speak about "philosophy in America" with the aim of distinguishing some hallmarks which have become evident on the philosophical scene. In pursuing this aim, we shall be speaking neither of *an* American philosophy nor of an inventory of philosophical positions, but of something closer to a pervasive spirit in philosophical thinking manifesting itself in the interests and concerns of American philosophers and in their manner of approach to philosophical issues.

The hallmarks I have selected, receptivity, change and relevance, represent, I confess, a somewhat mixed bag. The first points primarily to an attitude, a style, a manner of approach; the second is simply a basic and predominant fact about the nature of things which carries with it an entire spectrum of philosophical problems to be resolved; and the third is a fundamental concern about the bearing of thought in all its forms on the problems of human existence, especially a concern for determining what idea or piece of knowledge counts and what doesn't count for the answering of a question or the solving of a problem. In attempting to make clear what I mean by each of these hallmarks, I shall avail myself of some representative illustrations drawn from developments of the past fifty or so years.

I. *Receptivity*

American thinkers have ever been open and receptive to points of view other than their own and they have welcomed the many different winds of philosophical doctrine from whatever quarter they have blown. This receptivity, to be sure, has called forth from foreign critics interpretations filled with ambivalence. Some have seen the willingness to enter sympathetically into philosophical positions conceived abroad as a sign of our uncertainty and insecurity stemming from a deep suspicion of the philosophical product grown in America. Both versions of C. D. Broad's notorious comment on this head come to the same conclusion in the end. According to one version, old and dying philosophies come to America for last rites and a proper burial, while according to another, such philosophies are resurrected, as it were, and start a new life as a form of "transatlantic truth." In both interpretations, the imported position is supposed to be the genuine article on a market that is without a serious domestic rival.

Polemical academic politics aside, however, there is another way of looking at the receptivity displayed by American thinkers; it calls attention to a broadly empirical outlook on the world, including the world of thought, and represents what Dewey called the experimental spirit, a refusal to be encapsulated in one position while remaining heedless of all others. This positive intepretation of receptivity which bespeaks a genuine concern for understanding what philosophers in other places are saying and not a desperate attempt to fill a philosophical void, is dramatically illustrated by the treatment accorded by American thinkers to the philosophy of existence in its own development from Kierkegaard to Sartre. And, as I shall suggest, this treatment is even more dramatic when it is compared with the corresponding response to American pragmatism in some other parts of the world. The selection here of the philosophy of existence as an example is not meant to ignore the manifestation of the same receptivity on the part of American philosophers to the phenomenological movement, both German and French, or to the linguistic philosophies and the philosophies of analysis originating in Britain. Anthony Quinton has given a brief resume of the latter development in an article which appeared in the *Times Literary Supplement* of June 13, 1975.

American thinkers began their engagement with the philosophy of existence through the study of Kierkegaard almost a half century ago, and in the intervening years many have followed the pursuit of *Existenz* through the numerous writings of Heidegger, Sartre, Camus, Marcel, Unamuno and others. Consider that, before the position could be understood and appropriated, translations of the principal works had to be prepared involving several foreign languages, unfamiliar styles of thought, and obscurities so formidable that even our best translations of the major works are still interlaced with words and phrases from the original languages. *Existenz* and *Dasein*, for example, are by no means adequately represented in their meaning by the English term "existence" and consequently we have had to add them to the language. With the texts themselves in hand, commentaries and interpretation were forthcoming, and in the end the various forms of existential philosophy came to exert a powerful influence not only upon philosophy itself, but upon psychiatry, literature and theology on the American scene. Neither mere curiosity nor casual interest will explain the persistent and laborious thought and scholarship which have been expended in the attempt to understand and come to terms with the complex issues—being, freedom, thought, time, anxiety, death—forming the substance of the existential outlook. I cannot attempt to explain the many motives behind the reception of this type of philosophy in America; obviously there were cultural, psychological, and religious factors at work along with philosophical considerations in the entire development. In my view, the underlying directive force, however, in the appropriation of existentialism was the attitude of receptivity the openness to fresh experience and novel ideas rooted in the sense that no one standpoint encompasses everything and therefore that intellectual life and growth demand a willingness to penetrate the thought and experience of others no matter how strange and discontinuous they may be in relation to familiar patterns of thought.

The receptivity here manifested stands in sharp contrast to the insularity frequently displayed by philosophers in foreign parts in the face of American pragmatism. Let us take note of the fact that this position had its beginnings roughly a century ago in Peirce's papers of the 1870's and in James's essay "Philosophical Conceptions and Practical Results" of almost eighty years ago, and that it developed continuously in a voluminous literature through at least the fourth decade of this century. Exactly twenty years ago, Sidney Hook, in *American Philosophers at Work*, complained that America has remained a largely undiscovered country on its intellectual side, especially its pragmatic philosophy. The striking fact is that, until recently, the situation had not changed much both on the Continent and in Britain. With a few exceptions, there has not been a major concern to understand pragmatism in its basic doctrines and motives after the fashion of the concern of American philosophers to plumb the depths of existentialism (and one could of course add the philosophies of analysis and the types of phenomenology as well). And the attention which pragmatism is now beginning to receive abroad shows not so much an interst in coming to grips with the basic ideas of the pragmatists as an attempt to accommodate them for other purposes. Thus Ayer, in *The Origins of American Pragmatism*, disregards, for the most part, the pragmatists' critique of classical British empiricism and the primacy of epistemology, and treats these thinkers as if they were seeking to answer all the questions about perception and the external world associated with British philosophy since Hume. Current interest in Peirce on the Continent, moreover, tends, in accordance with familiar trends, to focus almost entirely on his logic to the exclusion of those more adventurous features of his thought represented by tychism, synechism, scholastic realism and panpsychism. Such selective or differential interest is *something less* than what I have been describing as receptivity.

I cannot leave this topic without mentioning two more immediate indications of receptivity as a hallmark of the American habit of mind in contrast to what is characteristic in other philosophical quarters. Not long ago news was received of the death of Professor Michael Polanyi, a scientist and philosopher whose roots were firmly established in the European tradition of thought. I find it highly significant and illustrative of the point I am making that there appeared in the obituary published by the *New York Times* the following sentence: "Professor Polanyi was a visiting professor at 14 universities, and his work as a chemist and his philosophic writings *were perhaps better known in the United States than in Europe.*" This judgment is undoubtedly true and the reason for it is not difficult to find. Abroad he was earmarked as a scientist and not as a philosopher but in this country, regardless of labels, many philosophers were interested in and receptive to his attempts, admittedly dark in places and sometimes out of focus, to describe the role played by the scientist himself and his assumptions in the conduct of actual inquiry. His conception of tacit knowing evoked interest among us and, without allowing the fact that he was not ticketed as a professional philosopher to stand in the way, we were anxious to give him a hearing and to understand what he had to say about the logic of the scientific enterprise and the place of science in human society.

My final comment on receptivity takes the form of a personal anecdote. Some twenty years ago I was invited as a guest of the *Philosophisches Seminar* at the University of Heidelberg and in the course of my stay it was suggested that I might give a talk or two there and at the neighboring University of Mainz. I soon divined, however, that there was little interest in my speaking about Dewey or Royce or the then current situation in American philosophy; instead I ended by giving some talks, in German, on "*Der Raumbegriff bei Kant*"! I remember thinking at the time that whereas I might have delivered some fresh ore, I was condemned to carrying coals to Newcastle.

II. *Change*

In citing the basic fact of *change* as a matter of special concern to American philosophers, I want to begin by calling attention to a difficult problem which first made its appearance with the doctrine of evolution in the last century and has made itself felt in every domain of life since that time. In considering the influence of Darwinism on philosophy, Dewey laid the greatest emphasis on change and development as ultimate facts and generic traits of existence. Peirce, James, Whitehead and countless others were to reinforce this emphasis, reminding us that we must, as the phrase goes, "take time seriously." That this is no simple injunction or one that is easy to follow can be readily seen. For two millennia the great majority of philosophers of the Western tradition sought to explain whatever change and temporality they acknowledged in terms of reality which is essentially timeless and does not change. The results were invariably the same; either time and change were demoted to the sphere of appearance, or basic and pervasive facts about each were ignored or distorted in the interest of preserving the explanatory scheme. The revolution in thought which took place in connection with the introduction of the evolutionary viewpoint in the last century may be seen as the exact reversal of a pattern of thinking which is as old as the paradoxes of Zeno. Whatever the fundamental purpose of these paradoxes was, they make abundantly clear that certain static or fixed elements were thought adequate for representing ultimate fact with the result that motion and change become impossible, unintelligible or both. The evolutionary conceptions of the past century precisely reversed this relationship; change, growth and development in time were established as the ultimate facts and the fixed or unchanging was seen as either a limiting case or totally abstract in character.

The critical point at which the fact of change became a major philosophical issue was in connection with the theory of truth and knowledge and consequently with the interpretation of science. Truth, it had long been argued, must have a timeless character and have a tenure which transcends change. Consequently, knowledge, if it is to be knowledge of such truth, must itself share in a similar superiority to both time and change, which is the principal reason for the frequent identification of knowledge with certainty in a large segment of modern philosophy. The curious fact, however, is that while many philosophers were developing theories of truth entailing its timeless and certain character, natural scientists were emphasizing the tentativeness, the fallibility, and the contingency of their own conclusions; they were emphasizing the fact that the warrant for their assertions is limited to the available evidence and therefore that the possibility of revision in the future cannot be ruled out in advance. The situation, however, was highly ambiguous because many of the philosophers who conceived of truth and knowledge in terms essentially timeless were simultaneously assuming that the sciences represent the most reliable knowledge we have. The discrepancy, moreover, is not removed merely by insisting on the distinction between a theory of the nature of truth and a specification of the tests of truth, because the two cannot remain unrelated and if the former is understood as a timeless affair we are faced with the same problem all over again because the tests of truth will necessarily be involved in contingency and fallibility.

American philosophers since the days of Peirce have been wrestling with this perplexing problem of bringing philosophical thinking into accord with the facts of an historically conditioned and self-corrective inquiry. How is it possible to take seriously the facts of change and fallibility in the knowing situation and at the same time avoid a relativism which suggests that in essence we have no knowledge at all? Russell laid hold of the issue many years ago when he deplored the fact that in the Index to Dewey's *Logic* he could find no entry under "Truth," but only the directive to consult "Warranted Assertibility." As a believer in the thesis that present and given fact is the causal and commanding condition for the truth of the proposition which asserts it, Russell was totally dissatisfied with Dewey's approach and placed it at once in that suspect category of "Transatlantic Truth" through which he had wittily described James's theory of truth as set forth in *Pragmatism*. That the central issue is not an idle one can be seen from a number of developments on the contempary scene; the discussion about foundationalism in knowledge, the argument about observation and the theory-dependent character of observational, descriptive terms, and the many-sided controversy about the proper interpretation of the course of the development of scientific knowledge. It would be fair to say that all these discussions find essential roots in the recognition of the facts of time and change and the need to incorporate them consistently into a theory of human knowing.

It is important to notice that the classical pragmatists, each in his own way, addressed the problems posed by the need to take time and change seriously into account with respect to existence generally, but especially in connection with knowledge, and it it is not without significance that some of their ideas on this head are being revived on the current scene. In view of this fact, it is pertinent to recall some central points. I shall mention three; first, the focus on inquiry as an actual process aimed at the finding of critical conclusions; second, the thesis that the warrant for these conclusions is a combined function of evidence and of the normative structure controlling the critical or experimental process by which they were reached; and third, the belief that knowing is the answering of questions under existential conditions and that every warranted answer represents a community of agreement among those qualified to judge unaccompanied by actual grounds for doubting the answer within the confines of the evidence available at a given time. It is, of course, obvious that no critical account of these notions can be attempted here, but a brief resume of each will serve the purpose at hand which in this case is to illustrate the grappling with the problem of change as a hallmark of philosophical thinking in America.

As regards the first topic, Peirce, James, Dewey and Royce each in a different vein were at one in approaching the nature of knowing via analyses of actual inquiry , including both particular techniques appropriate to particular subject matters and the logical structure of inquiry as such. In each case an attempt was made to determine, in the words of James, "what knowing is known as" and thus to avoid purely dialectical conceptions with little or no foundation in the facts about actual inquiry. Accordingly, Peirce developed the theory of the three types of reasoning in inquiry— abduction, deduction and induction—showing how the first initiates the process in the proposal of hypotheses, how the second functions in the derivation of consequences, and how the third figures in testing through sampling and other experimental procedures. James called attention to the process whereby new fact—the discovery, for example, of radioactivity—is married to old truth and broadly based theory so as to preserve a maximum of continuity and a minimum of dislocation. Royce taught for many years a seminar on methods in the sciences and sought to elucidate the distinctive roles of the mechanical, historical and statistical models in scientific research. And Dewey in his *Logic, The Theory of Inquiry* aimed at producing a comprehensive account of empirical method exhibiting the functional role of logical forms in the directed process of reaching warranted assertions. The important point in all this is that decades before the revolutionary impact of introducing the history of science into the philosophical discussion, all these thinkers had acknowledged the crucial fact that inquiry is a temporal process taking place under historical conditions and that no account of it is adequate which ignores these facts and concentrates exclusively on the supposedly atemporal or purely logical features in it. As recent discussion makes plain, this lesson has now been learned, if not so well learned that the impact of change, as perceived by some interpreters, becomes overwhelming and threatens both the objectivity and continuity of scientific thought. But that is another topic.

The second sign previously mentioned which points to the willingness to acknowledge the facts of temporality and change and to deal directly with the ensuing problems is found in the thesis that knowledge is an outcome of a temporally conditioned process and that the warrant for this outcome resides in the self-correcting, critical method through which it was reached. This claim, as Peirce and Dewey well understood, raises serious questions concerning the validity of the thesis, maintained in modern thought by rationalists and empiricists alike, that knowledge must have "foundations"—to use the current term—in the sense of being rooted ultimately in some *incorrigible* item—clear ideas, ultimate data of sense, ultimate premises—which provides a guarantee for whatever further claims to knowledge may be built on that foundation. Peirce, it will be recalled, specifically objected to this thesis as based on an "exploded" conception of logic going all the way back to Aristotle's belief that if man is to have knowledge at all there must be first premises which are prior and better known than any propositions derived from them. The attempts of Peirce and Dewey to replace this view by a logic of inquiry which rests not on the incorrigible but on what is not actually doubtful *in situ* and on the condition of the available knowledge at the time subject to the critical control of empirical test, are, of course, well known.

The problems they envisaged and sought to resolve are being discussed at present under the rubric of foundationalism and anti foundationalism. The central issue can be expressed by means of a familiar figure which, though like all such devices it breaks down in the end, is nevertheless illuminating. For the foundationalists the ship of knowledge, though it sails the seas of inquiry, has an anchor which is in some sense always taking hold on all its voyages—even if the anchor chain is of an infinite length—and the ship arrives at no destinations beyond the reach of the anchor and its chain. The opposing view holds that the ship of knowledge has no anchor but it does sail in the sea of inquiry and whenever it arrives at a destination it does so as the explicit result of having been guided by sound navigational principles and operations. I am not, of course, suggesting that the situation is anything like this simple; I am merely attempting to call attention to the recognition by the non-foundationalists of the temporal character of the knowledge process and its control by the logic of inquiry in comparison with conceptions of truth which abstract from the process through which it is gained in order to uphold some form of incorrigibility.

Closely related to the foregoing, and a third sign of the sensitivity of American philosophers to the fact of change and its consequences, is the idea, again proposed by Peirce and much in evidence at present, of knowledge being a function of a critical community of investigators whose activity results, at least on some occasions, in a convergence of opinion which represents the answer to some question under investigation by many inquirers. This conception of a funded result of inquiry was, of course, a direct response to the problem posed by the development of knowledge under historical conditions and the need to revise or even discard to some degree previous conclusions as erroneous. Certain facts about asymmetries in nature—for example, the existence of incongruous counterparts—have long been known, but for a long time it was assumed that this fact had no empirical consequences. At the present time, it is known, in contrast to earlier opinion, that these differences in spatial orientation are not vacuous, but are the source of different behavior patterns in both physical and organic systems. In order to avoid having to say that previous generations of scientists "knew" what later turned out to be either false or only partly true the proposal was to interpret the intersubjectively corroborated results of research as *convergent opinion* which represents coming as near the truth as actual inquiry has been able to come *at a given time*. That such an opinion may be in need of modification, correction or even replacement *at some subsequent time* is a presupposition of the entire process of inquiry. In not calling the opinion which has turned out to be either false or in some degree incorrect by the name of "knowledge" taken in some simple and unqualified sense, we at the very least avoid the paradox wherein it turns out that large numbers of people "knew" what was not true.

The view of scientific knowledge as a convergence of opinion within a determinate community of inquirers has not been without its critics, but whatever difficulties it presents I feel constrained to point out two criticisms which seem to me invalid. Years ago Russell raised the critical query as to why Peirce thought there is an "ideal limit" to which scientific belief tends, and more recently others have followed this up, claiming that Peirce never showed that there *must be* a convergence. But such criticism misses the point by ignoring the empirical context of Peirce's view. If one attends to Peirce's many illustrations from the history of science, one sees that he was basing the theory on the evidence of what actually happens when there is general agreement on the answer to some question. What Peirce had in mind is nicely illustrated by Polanyi's example of the periodic table. The general acceptance of the validity of that arrangement of the elements and the theory on which it is based is set in high relief by the anomalies in it. As Polanyi points out, these anomalies led no one to reject the table but rather to seek further explanation of the discrepancies. To ask for a *must be* proof of such agreement is to ask for the very foundationalism Peirce was rejecting and at the same time to betray the fact that one is not much of an empiricist after all. Whatever "must be" there is about Peirce's ideal limit is more like the assertion that a thrown die *must* come up 6 at some time or other than it is like the proposition that every prime number *must* have some successor which is prime.

The criticism which says that the community-of-inquirers-seeking-convergence conception cannot provide a guarantee against conventionalism or a large-scale conspiratorial hoax is based on a misunderstanding of what is involved. The convergence is far from being some sort of democratic referendum because the requisite opinions are under the constraint of public evidence together with logical and experimental canons of inquiry. In comparing the situation with that of an insurance company, Peirce argued that just as no company can accept a single risk where failure would bankrupt the entire operation, the scientific community cannot accept the opinion of any investigator whose personal interest in the outcome of the inquiry exceeds his commitment to finding the truth.

III. *Relevance*

In coming to my final hallmark of philosophical thinking in America, a word of caution is in order. By "relevance," I do not mean concern for some short-run utility in thought or the demand that thinking be under the constraint of an immediate program for action; I mean something closer to what Whitehead meant by "importance," what James meant by the idea that counts, or what

Susan Stebbing had in mind when she wrote that excellent little book entitled *Thinking to Some Purpose*. Running throughout American thought from one end to the other like a scarlet thread visible at every point in a fabric has been a persistent belief that thought must have an orientation in terms of purposes which serve as principles of selection for relevance. The idea is illustrated to the utmost in the conception of intelligence as problem-solving where the task is to discover not how much we know but precisely what items in our store of knowledge count or have relevance for dealing with the problem at hand. It seems clear that the characteristic American suspicion of conceiving of the aim of philosophy as that of arriving at one comprehensive system of reality wherein all parts are internally related to each other stems from the sense that under these conditions finite terms and situations would become difficult to define, and thinking would find itself lost because deprived of a principle of selection or limitation. Every determination makes a "difference" in the total mapping of the whole, but the remaining problem is what particular determinations count for the resolution of a particular problematic situation *within* the totality? It is precisely this consideration which James had in mind when he pointed to the encyclopedia on his book shelf as representative of a totality of knowledge and then asked, "When do I say these things?" What determines my judgment that a given item of knowledge is relevant whereas another may be ignored? The pragmatists may have been too sanguine in their belief that this question is answered in and through the demands imposed by a problematic situation, especially since we cannot suppose that all problems present themselves with the obviousness characteristic of such standard examples as those of finding my way out of a forest or of removing some physical obstacle which thwarts a habitual response. But underneath the belief in the selective function of the problematic lurks another belief, namely that if knowledge is ever to function in the resolution of human perplexities and especially in the meeting of human needs and the overcoming of obstacles to the advance of civilization, not only must there be a purpose or aim invoked, but it must be one which stands in addition to the purely theoretical purpose of mirroring the entire universe in thought. Relevance becomes a desideratum at the point where it is seen that while every single fact must stand related in myriad ways to an infinite environment which is, on the occasion of abstracting that fact, suppressed, nevertheless not all of these relations will count in the same way and to the same degree when our interest in and concern for that fact is something other than knowing it from a theoretical standpoint.

There are, to be sure, many facets to the entire topic of relevance; I am concentrating on but one, the feature of purposive selection in achieving an intellectual aim, and I would like to offer an example which is particularly well suited for making clear what is meant. Ornithology is a branch of knowledge which had rudimentary beginnings several millennia ago but, like numerous other sciences, it was developed on a sophisticated taxonomic basis only in the past three centuries. The bird population of the world, though not as numerous as the insect, is still staggering in its numbers and an accurate mapping of the many families and species plus their characteristics, distributions and relations to the environment has been the monumental task of scientists in many countries since the seventeenth century. A science of this sort naturally relies heavily on observation and at many levels and for different purposes. The most accurate descriptions of individual specimens will, of course, be possible only under conditions where, as the expression goes, the bird is in the hand. Under these conditions the anatomy, musculature, plumage, etc., of every known species can be exhaustively determined and recorded, resulting in the vast record which contains our scientific knowledge of these feathered creatures. Other features of the kingdom of the birds—their nesting, feeding, reproduction, migration, etc., habits—will have to be investigated by other and more laborious forms of observation involving patient cooperation with natural conditions beyond human control.

Now suppose the idea should occur to someone—as it did to Roger Tory Peterson—that it should be possible to construct a *field guide* to the birds of a geographical region which would enable a person with ordinary powers of observation and memory to make *identifications* of individual birds and flocks of birds perching, hopping and on the wing in fields, meadows and swamps with no equipment save binoculars. Notice that the conditions are definite, but quite different from those obtaining when a given bird is in the hand or when the behavior of pairs or groups of birds is being observed under such limited conditions of control as can be imposed when one studies the birds in their natural habitat. Only those identifying marks will be of service which can be seen or heard under field conditions and hence a principle of selective relevance is indicated. Obviously not everything known about the species likely to occur will be relevant. The size in centimeters of the lower mandible, the color of the roof of the mouth plus all the anatomical information about the bird no matter how accurate and detailed will be of no avail whatever for accomplishing the purpose at hand. What will be needed instead is a list of *identifying features* characteristic of the birds themselves and their known habits—wingbar colors, tail feather colors, bill and eye-ring colors plus characteristic songs, flight patterns discernible in the field, characteristic trees frequented by certain types of birds, etc.—plus a selection of *comparative features* enabling the observer to distinguish similar species from each other. From the available store of information making up the scientific record, there must be chosen the items which *count* or contribute to the purpose at hand. We have to be able to say, in the case before us, that, barring accidents and strays, such and such a species is the *only* one in the area which is larger than a robin and shows clearly a white rump patch when it takes to flight.

Although the foregoing illustration may seem to be far removed from more recondite philosophical topics, it represents quite precisely one aspect at least of that concern for selective relevance in thought which has ever been at the center of philosophical thinking in America. This concern has often been confused with the belief that all thought is for the sake of action, whereas the truth of the matter is otherwise. The essential contrast is not between thought and action but between our theoretical knowledge on the one side and the human purposes which should determine what items among that knowledge are relevant for these purposes and how that knowledge should be used. If this concern for the difference which thought and knowledge make in human life is being *practical*, then American philosophers have always exhibited the trait.

THE DISTINCTIVENESS OF
AMERICAN PHILOSOPHY

T. L. S. SPRIGGE

The University of Edinburgh, Scotland

1. When I was asked to talk on this topic I was told that acceptance would not imply belief that my title had a referent. Presumably, however, I should now consider such evidence as might help decide the point. But this is not really what I shall attempt to do. The task would be immense, for not only would one have to list properties widely distributed among American philosophers, throughout whatever period one might restrict the enquiry to, but one would have to show also that these properties were not found as widely distributed elsewhere. What I shall do rather is simply take this opportunity to point out some qualities, all of the virtues, which I have found to be possessed in a very strong degree by a group of philosophers who, for me, represent the high point as yet in the history of American philosophy, and which I believe make their place and time one of the noblest episodes of post-seventeenth century philosophy.

2. The place and time I have in mind are Harvard in the late nineteenth and early twentieth century taken together with the various philosophers elsewhere who took much of their inspiration from the great Harvard figures.

Before centering attention on this time and place, however, I would like to make in passing a comment on the American philosophical scene as it is at present. For someone from Britain there is great appeal in the pluralism of the situation. Whereas in Britain a very few major universities tend to set the tone of what is currently orthodox, or at least of what should be at the center of discussion, so that alternative views must define themselves by their relation to a certain dominant philosophic stance, it is no criticism of the best-known American universities to say that they do not, in the same way, set the tone as to what is currently considered worth discussion. *My* impression, at least, is that there is such a wide variety of centers of different sorts of philosophical activity, that there is scarcely a possible point of view which is not an orthodoxy for some department or philosophic society. The existence of so many orthodoxies leads, I believe, to a greater

199

openness of mind among American philosophers than is typically found in Britain (though more especially in England).

This feature is, of course, in great part a function of the size of your country, where a university like Harvard cannot play a role such as Oxford does in England, or as Harvard, and some few other universities, did in America at a time when Josiah Royce could bewail that he was the only philosopher in the whole of California. But I doubt if this is all there is to American pluralism, for it is similar in some ways to the character of American church going as it can be found within a single city, where the dominating ideal seems to be the desirability of a distinctive spiritual home, entitled to respect from others, for almost every type of human being.

This sort of ideal was expressed well, incidentally, by the man who brought Vedanta Hinduism to the U.S., Swami Vivekananda, when he said that the goal should be "Every man his own sect." This phrase exactly expresses, in fact, the guiding ideal of William James, whose pluralism, in this sense, may be one of his most distinctively American features. Certainly, James was utterly opposed to any orthodoxy, except such as is content to be the private possession of a minority fully aware of the merits of its rivals, and who, so far from attaching any particular credit to ideas because they came from an institution of proven academic respectability, looked, for his sources of wisdom, as much to the eccentric weight-lifter, Benjamin Paul Blood, and to the proponents of Mind Care as to the notables of the academic world. So I hope that a Jamesian recognition that no one type of philosophy can ever hope to command general assent, unless the human mind becomes completely atrophied, plays its part in producing the pluralism of the American scene, and I hope also that James will continue to remind us that it is not even Philosophy Departments in general which have a monopoly of philosophic wisdom.

The group of philosophers I shall be discussing certainly possess all the virtues of pluralism, but I shall try to show that they do, nonetheless, form a genuine unit which marks a very splendid episode in the history, not just of American, but of western philosophy. The Harvard philosophers of this period of most continuing significance were James, Josiah Royce, and George Santayana, and it should be borne in mind that Peirce also lectured there on some occasions. These philosophers, in particular the first three, in spite of their radically opposed doctrines and temperaments, still seem to me to have had a set of common conceptions and interests, and to have carried on discussions one with another, which made of them an intellectual unit with its own essence, an essence which has a subsequent American history not restricted to Harvard and which still has some actual, and I believe a considerably greater potential, life to it.

I do, in fact, believe that there is a distinctively American sort of philosophy which originated in Harvard at about the turn of the century, and which was carried on by such philosophers as the contributors to *New Realism* and *Critical Realism* and in such philosophers as C. A. Strong, Dickinson Miller, not to mention Dewey and his school. This sort of distinctively American philosophy seems to have come almost to an end by the cessation of World War II, by which time it was largely replaced, for reasons some of which are clear, but which I shall not discuss, by a philosophy much more like that for some time typical of Britain, though a certain flavor of it is still present in certain works, usually discussed much more in the context of Vienna and Oxford, e.g., C. L. Stevenson's "Ethics and Language."

3. There is, however, one particular thread still present in American philosophy, on which the choicest pearl is Charles Hartshorne, that stretching from a later Harvard philosopher, namely A. N. Whitehead. To regard Whitehead as an American philosopher is questionable, from the point of view of legal and party nationality, but not only did Whitehead have to come to America to burgeon as a philosopher and found a school, but his philosophy is more endued with the special virtues present in the work of James, Royce and Santayana than that of any other philosopher whose influence flourished subsequent to theirs.

4. So I shall now consider what I think the peculiar excellences of these three American philosphers and why I think their work, together with that of some other American philosophers whom I shall not discuss, constitutes an intellectual unit, in the sense in which say the systems of Spinoza and Leibniz jointly do, while, of course, being the very contrary of a school.

Since I have touched on the American-ness of Whitehead, I should doubtless puzzle you over that of Santayana as well. However, it seems sufficient to remark that, whatever he may sometimes have said, Santayana's style of philosophizing and the problems he faced, were very much in response to American thinkers, that he left Spain for America when he was nine and lived there until he was almost fifty, that his departure for and criticism of America are in the same broad category as those of

Henry James and Ezra Pound, and that his main philosophical contacts and influence were always decidedly American, all of which I will clinch in his own direct statement in old age: "it is as an American philospher that I shall be counted, if I am counted at all."

5. What then are some of these features which are distinctive of that group of philosophers of whom James, Royce and Santayana are the chief figures? I shall plunge straightaway into something fairly technical. The first point which is characteristic of these philosophers is the crucial role which the doctrine or the concept of the specious present played in the philosophy of each. It is something of which each makes an individual use in developing his metaphysics. Here, one may as well say at once, is one of the main ways in which Whitehead is linked with them, for his notion of an actual occasion is really the metaphysical generalization of this initially psychological concept, a generalization in which he is particularly at one with Santayana.

James found the concept of the specious present in an obscure American writer, E. R. Clay.

What the theory came to in James's thought is expressible rather inadequately in two propositions:

1. No one experience anyone has is ever merely of an instantaneous present, it is always of a stretch of time in which some elements are experienced as past, others as present, and others as about to occur.

2. Although there is no such thing, truly speaking, as an instant of experience, there are ultimate temporal units of experience. As Perry puts it: "There are mental units of a sort in James's view, but they are total pulses or waves, each having an indivisible unity, a transitory existence, and a unique identity. And these units are neither simple themselves nor analyzable into simple constituents." (*Thought and Character in the U.S.*, II, p. 77).

There is no doubt that the way James makes use of this concept shows a phenomenological subtlety absent so far as I know in earlier psychologies and philosophies. The crucial point is that temporal relations are immediately given and that the terms between which these relations hold are abstractions from the totality of what is experienced rather than elements out of which it is composed. It is little wonder that James was Bradley's most insightful critic, a far more serious opponent of Oxford idealism than the likes of Russell and Moore, for he had at the center of his psychology the chief phenomenological fact which underlies Bradley's metaphysics.

There are many problems which arise about the specious present. For example, granted that what is presented as experienced content in a single basic moment of experience has temporal span and is not instantaneous in its character, does it follow that the moment itself has temporal span—or is it instantaneous? Moreover, what sort of series do these moments form from a mathematical point of view?

From the point of view of James's final metaphysics the content of an experience is identical with the character of that experience, so that the fundamental units of experience have the very temporal span of which they are an experience and continue on from one another as they are experienced as doing. As for the proper mathematical description of this continuity James came to think, largely under the influence of Bergson, that it was something which could not be described mathematically.

We can say, at any rate, that for James the concept of the specious present, in spite of its seeming to break up experience into discrete pulses, went hand in hand with a belief in its felt continuity from moment to moment. He was always anxious to insist that the flow of experience was not broken up into little bits either at the instant, in spatial fashion, or into instants over time. Thus, although he came to believe that there were fundamental moments or pulses of experience, his emphasis was always on the way each moment flowed into, and somehow overlapped, the next (so that there was no division between them), rather than upon their distinctness.

It is interesting that for Santayana this conception, which he presumably learnt from James, of consciousness as coming in drops, each of which contains a time span, a before and after, within it, was used in the demonstration of a very un-Jamesian proposition to the effect that we do not have and cannot have immediate awareness of a real temporal flux, and that the actual temporal passage of events is quite opaque to consciousness. For what Santayana argued was that the temporal relations within a moment of experience are fundamentally different from those which hold between moments of experience. The former were specious in a sense James did not acknowledge, for they were temporal relations between elements which in a sense co-existed, whereas a real temporal relation of precedence must be such that when and where the one event is the other is simply not. Thus the more intensely we experience time within the specious present the further we get from real time which is the utter giving way of one moment to another.

In dealing with the kind of problem this raises Santayana finds reason to claim that the relation of consciousness to time is such that consciousness cannot be regarded straightforwardly as a natural object. Thus we see how, setting out from the same point, James and Santayana came to sharply contrasting conclusions as to the immediacies of the involvement of consciousness in the temporal flux.

Much of Whitehead's philosophy can be seen as the advocacy of a solution to this problem on a basis which fully shares their common starting point. Moreover this common starting point continues to bring James's and Santayana's metaphysics together in spite of some antithetical deductions they draw from it.

The specious present plays an equally fundamental and more grandiose role in the metaphysics of Josiah Royce, as most definitively expressed in *The World and the Individual*. For here the fact that a single concrete experience is always of a stretch of time and that there is no logical limit to the duration which could, theoretically, be given as a single content of consciousness is used to solve the final mysteries of the relation between the organic, the inorganic and God. The inorganic is, in its essence, sentient but its sentience is of time spans so different from ours that we cannot communicate with it or recognize its teleological character. As for God or the Absolute, the whole of cosmic history is present to Him as a single specious present. This conception allows Royce to share the view of such as Bradley that all finite experience is a part of one eternal and unchanging experience, while insisting that time is real, because the world which God experiences all at once is a genuinely temporal world, in which there is genuine before and after and temporal evolution.

This crucial role which the specious present plays in the thought of these American philosophers seems a genuinely distinctive feature, marking them as a group, and one which gives a concrete richness and imaginability to what they are saying.

6. This doctrine or concept of the specious present is, however, simply the core of a more general distinctive quality of these philosophers, namely a peculiarly vivid sense of the character of consciousness, or experience, as it is felt by each of us from moment to moment, and a realization that we must continually come back and engross ourselves in the fleeting, but rich and

concrete, moments of experience if we are to have any worthwhile conception of reality. In his own distinct way, each of these philosophers held the view that if a philosopher would grasp reality in its concreteness, and arrive at a philosophic position adequate to such grasp, he must take the flow of his own experience as his paradigm example of the true pulse of existence, and continually check the results of his reasonings by reference back to it. Not that there is any hint of solipsism; it is only that here one hears the pulse of Being beat most directly, and gets one's sense of what one believes when one believes that anything is really going on, in the minds of others or in the physical world.

7. James was, of course, the strongest advocate and practitioner of this view, and it is largely from him that the others learnt it, but it is a feature present in many American philosophers of this period, and much less common, I think, in British and European philosophy, the case of Bergson apart. What Royce, Santayana and many others learnt from James in this regard, and what lies also at the center of Whitehead's metaphysics, is a lesson of which contemporary philosophers stand in sore need.

8. How can one formulate this lesson? It has, really, two parts. First, a way of grasping the character of conscious experience, and second, a way of using this grasp in philosophy.

I find it difficult to treat the first as a doctrine, it is rather a habit of directing one's attention at a certain reality, one's own total experience, and bearing the character of what one then notes vividly in mind whenever theorizing about mind or related matters. What one learns from this particular direction of the attention is not something statable in a stable formula, but something rather conveyable in a more essentially literary manner, such as James showed himself a master of in his famous chapter on "The Stream of Thought" and elsewhere in *The Principles of Psychology*.

Santayana has described particularly well what those who have fallen under the spell of such parts of *The Principles* learnt therefrom.

> ... what I learnt from him [he says] was perhaps chiefly things that he never taught, but which I imbibed from the spirit and background of his teaching. Chief of these, I should say, was a sense for the immediate: for the unadulterated, unexplained, instant fact of experience. Actual experience, for William James, however varied or rich its assault might be, was always and altogether of the nature of a sensation; it possessed a vital,

leaping globular unity which made the only fact, the flying fact, of our being.

(*The Philosophy of George Santayana* ed. P. A. Schilpp, p. 15)

Or again:

In its ostensible outlook it [*The Principles of Psychology*] is a treatise like any other, but what distinguishes it is the author's gift for evoking vividly the life of the mind. ... He saw that experience, as we endure it, is not a mosaic of different sensations, nor the expression of separate hostile faculties, such as reason and the passions, or sense and the categories; it is rather a flow of mental discourse, like a dream, in which all divisions and units are vague and shifting, and the whole is continually merging together and drifting apart. It fades gradually in the past, like the wake of a ship, and bites into the future, like the bow cutting the water.

(*Character and Opinion in the U.S.*, pp. 67–68)

The value of this sense for the immediate, which is a distinctive feature of those American philosophers much influenced by James, is something one appreciates most by seeing the damage done by its absence. As Dickinson Miller well argued, one who possessed it could not have come out with the more peculiar aspects of Ryle's *Concept of Mind* or, one may add, have formulated the sort of identity theory of mind and brain which treat consciousness as a theoretical entity invoked to explain certain sorts of behavior as in Armstrong and Putnam.

But it is not just a sense for the immediate but the particular thesis that our own experience as lived through and recalled, and that of others as imagined, is that which supplies us with our prime and perhaps only grasp of what a real thing is like in its fullness, which occupies a place in American philosophy sufficiently striking to be regarded as distinctive.

That James held this view hardly needs demonstrating. It is the key thesis of radical empiricism that finite experience is the sole reality and that if physical things are more than shared elements in the concrete experience of percipients that more must consist in the experience they have of themselves.

James's inclinations to panpsychism are matched by Royce's full commitment to it. This is developed both in *The Spirit of Modern Philosophy* and in *The World and the Individual*. The chapter in the former called "The World of Description and the World of Acquaintance" develops with particular clarity the one form of identity theory, as between mind and brain, namely a panpsychist one, which I believe, makes any sense. Whitehead and beyond him

Charles Hartshorne have carried on this strongly American tradition according to which most ways of conceiving the world treat things as having a merely vacuous kind of actuality, so that nature can only be thought of as really real if its inner essence is regarded as the same as that of one's own stream of consciousness.

In some respects Santayana stands rather aside from this. Certainly his famous remark that knowledge is a salute not an embrace was meant as a criticism of any view that one can only have knowledge of realities with which one can imagine oneself merging. But when one comes to the heart of it, Santayana is not greatly at variance with the others on this point. His own account of the literal character of physical reality, so far as we can approximate to any such thing, is found in his theory of natural moments, which are conceived on some sort of analogy with moments of consciousness, while, at another level, he continually urges that it is only of the mental that we have any extensive literal knowledge, and that our knowledge of the physical has to be, so far at least as all details go, symbolic.

Thus I claim it as a particularly, though not a uniquely, American view that the stream of consciousness of finite individuals is, for us, the paradigm case of a concrete reality.

9. I can think of few things which would be more beneficial to modern philosophers than a real attempt to grasp the force which this theory must have for anyone involved with the work of these American philosophers. I feel that any philosopher who seems to deny that there is, associated with each man, a reality which can be called his stream of consciousness, investigatable in its own right, and concerning whose locus in reality a direct answer must be given by any genuine philosophy, should be forced to read and comment on James's "The Stream of Thought" and tell us what, if anything, he thinks is therein described.

It is a sad fact that it is the work of a philosopher, namely Wittgenstein, who was familiar with James's *Principles*, which has played so large a part in turning people away from the kind of insight of which I have been talking. It may be said, and it may be true, that the private language argument is, from the point of view of the wiser of those who accept it, not an argument against the way in which these philosophers treated the stream of consciousness, but if so, it does not affect the fact that this argument is associated in practice with a turning away from that point of view. Moreover, if the private language argument is not intended as a condemnation of the setting of each individual's sense of his own stream of consciousness at the center of the philosophical stage, one wonders whether it has the kind of central importance which seems to be attached to it. It becomes merely a critique of such extremely minor eddies in the history of philosophy as Carnap's one time methodological solipsism.

10. There is an inclination today for English speaking philosophers who are tired of the aridities of physicalism to turn to phenomenology as an alternative philosophy which stays closer to the experienced facts of human life. To those who are so inclined I would suggest that they might find something more valuable in this respect in the work of James and Santayana than in that of Husserl. For I suggest that Husserl, like the Austrian mental act school and the Bergmannites who, to some extent, follow them in America, accepts far too readily the docketings of the sorts of mental act there are, which are implied by our usual vocabulary and grammar, and lacks that sense of the arbitrariness of all boundaries between different sorts of mental activity which I have quoted Santayana as praising James for. But there is another still more fundamental respect in which I think philosophers such as James, Royce and Santayana offer a better alternative to the dominant philosophical trends in the English-speaking world than do the phenomenologists, namely in the far more serious metaphysical use to which they put their phenomenological insights and in their determination not to shelve the problem of the relation between mind or consciousness and its material conditions, or determinants, by some facile idealism regarding the status of the latter.

11. And this leads me to another, closely related, unifying factor present in James, Royce, Santayana and the lesser luminaries of new and critical realism, and that is the particular way in which they approached, as differently as they solved, the problem of mind's relation to those objects which it thinks about without actually having present as contents of consciousness.

12. Here it was Royce's writing which focussed attention on the issue. Both James and Santayana developed their particular views of mind's intending of its objects as attempts to avoid Royce's argument, developed in *The Religious Aspect of Philosophy*, that an absolute all-containing consciousness must be postulated to explain how this is possible.

Royce held that we can only understand what it is to be thinking about something on the lines of the case exemplified where both the thought and its object are present in one consciousness and the *aboutness* is an experienced relation, as when I think about my headache. That granted, it follows that I can only think about, say, George Washington, as opposed to about my image of him, because the Absolute experiences the aboutness which relates us. Expressed so elliptically the argument may sound trivial but it was enough to puzzle James for many years, and I believe rightly so. The upshot of his attempt to find a non-absolutistic theory of *aboutness* was a thesis which can be put, very roughly, thus: that my mental processes are thoughts about an object X if they are instruments of my adaptation to the presence of X in the world, with its corollary that these processes are *true* ideas of X to the extent that the adaptation is successful. This is, of course, one of the essential roots of pragmatism, as propagated by James, a doctrine which I might be expected to have announced, ere now, as *the* distinctive factor in American philosophy. Incidentally, when once this source of pragmatism is recognized, it should become clear why James thought it so odd that his critics thought of pragmatism as implying that objects were there because it felt good to postulate them, when his basic point was that thought was good because it represented an adaptation to their objective thereness.

13. Before turning to pragmatism, I would like to emphasize my opinion that these philosophers got down to real brass tacks with what I conceive to be the basic problem of intentionality, namely as to how thoughts, understood as actual dated events in our mind, transcend themselves and refer to objects which they do not include, in a way which one finds in few modern discussions. When intentionality is discussed today, the treatment tends to be thoroughly linguo-centric, either in the sense that it is the logic of certain linguistic forms which is the direct object of study or in the sense that what is said about mental acts and their relations to their objects is a mere unrolling of the implications of standard speech, something typical, I have suggested, of work in the mental act tradition. The result is an immense amount of detailed work on the relations between different linguisitic forms in which the central puzzle of the self-transcendence of the mental is lost sight of, or alternatively it is solved by the use of idioms which already presuppose its solution. All this seems to stand in the way of that direct confrontation with the basic puzzle which I find in these American philosophers.

14. It is time now to say a word about pragmatism, so often

thought of as the American philosophy *par excellence*. It is clearly time also for me to say something about Peirce.

I think it is fairly clear that if the question is raised of Peirce's influence on American philosophy, or philosophy elsewhere, until quite lately it was not really so very great, except via James's pragmatism, to whatever extent that really is a case of it. Thus, I do not think Peirce is so relevant in terms of the general drift of ideas during the decades of my concern, as are those philosophers I have discussed.

This has no bearings on the question of his greatness as a philosopher for the best of things may have sadly little influence. However, without any wish to deny his enormous significance as a logician and his great merits as a philosopher, I would justify my own neglect of him in this talk so far on the grounds that he does not seem to exhibit in any great degree those special merits which I find distinctive of those philosophers which make me think that American philosophers today have too little appreciation of their great inheritance. For example, his sense for the immediate seems to me a little bit cloudy compared with that of these others, as exhibited in the way he talks of firstness, etc., and he lacks the literary panache of which I shall talk shortly. And I would also say that James and the others seem to stand for things lost sight of in philosophy today, and to stand for them in a peculiarly excellent way. Peirce is admired, on the contrary, because of the elements of today's philosophy which he reinforces, rather than as supplying a forgotten insight—and, as for his more wildly metaphysical side, this is largely ignored and perhaps with more justice than is the metaphysics of the thinkers I have been discussing.

15. However this may be, the set of tendencies represented by the word "pragmatism," when used with any approach to accuracy, is, of course, a thing peculiarly typical of American philosophy in the early twentieth century—James and Dewey being the chief names here

As far as James's pragmatism goes, Peirce is clearly a strong influence but it is quite wrong to regard James as merely presenting a theory of Peirce's he had not quite grasped, as is so often done. It is an independent doctrine arrived at by James as much in reaction to Royce's thought, and possibly Renouvier's, as to Peirce's, and one in which his closest major ally was rather Bergson than anyone else.

What I myself value in pragmatism is, on the one hand, the

theory of reference or intending which it incorporates, a theory incidentally almost identical in broad tendency with that of Santayana, usually considered pragmatism's great foe, and the insistence that ways of thinking cannot be properly understood or evaluated without reference to the biological, emotional and social needs they subserve. As regards social needs, it must be said that James, the inveterate individualist, had fairly little to say about them and that this is an aspect of the theory which is only developed in such thinkers as Dewey and Mead. James's individualism and his absorption in lived experience, provides, however, a necessary complement to those strains of pragmatism which are most dominant in modern thought. I am thinking of the current stress on the determination of linguistic meanings by social context rather than by the language user's own states of consciousness.

16. I must deal more briefly with the other distinctive excellences I shall mention of our group of Harvard philosophers.

The fact that each of them was such a splendid wielder of the English language, so that their works are mostly gems of English prose, is for me a considerable merit. Both in this and other respects, their works shine forth as the products of men of great literary culture.

17. Royce must be the most lucid and readable exponent of absolute idealism of all time. For breathtaking purple passages he is no match, of course, for F. H. Bradley, someone only outstripped by Santayana in this regard. However, Bradley is almost as obscure at times as Kant, something which could never be said of Royce, whose apparently effortless flow of lucid exposition has a special sort of ponderous grace. No considerable thinker has ever presented the dilemma as between a naturalistic and a non-naturalistic ethic in so easy but accurate a form as it is presented in the first book of *The Religious Aspect*.

18. Santayana is, surely, the great philosophical stylist of the twentieth century, and has suffered for it. As for William James, who begged brother Henry to model his narrative style more upon that of R. L. Stevenson, one can say of him that he is the only man to have written major philosophy in a style with the raciness of *Kidnapped*. The presence of three such great literary craftsmen in one Philosophy Department must surely be something unique.

19. I wonder how much the chances of any real style or panache to philosophical writing today are reduced by the passion for the use of formal symbols, which save a little paper, but few people's

time, and in most cases offer no accuracy not obtainable more gracefully.

In discussions of philosophers who did not write quite recently, it is often implied that there is far greater accuracy of expression today, and therefore less slipshod thinking. If there is a little truth in this, I think it is much exaggerated. It is very doubtful to me whether the stylishness of the philosophers I have been discussing was associated with inexactitude. Certainly one may sometimes think their arguments fallacious and their distinctions unclear, but of how many contemporary philosophers will their critics now and to come not think this?

What really matters is that things should be thought out thoroughly and deeply, not that they should be expressed, like a legal document, in such a way as to prevent ill wishers from putting an unintended interpretation upon them. I do not believe that the readability of these American philosophers was connected with any particular looseness of thought.

20. The aspects of the thought of my chosen American philosophers on which I have dwelt so far have been fairly technical, but it is also fair to say that they each had a striking power to make philosophy relevant to the concerns of a much wider audience than technical philosophy tended to appeal to in Britain at that time or than it does anywhere in the English-speaking world today.

Royce, James and Santayana, in their different ways, surely had more influence on extra-academic thought and culture than, say, did Bradley, Bosanquet or Green, in respect of the actual content of their philosophies, as opposed to the rather generalized moral influence of the British idealists.

In the case of James a main factor here was his championship of a rather unintellectualized religious commitment as against the threats of scientific materialism. In this connection I would urge that James, Royce and Santayana make a fascinating trio for anyone interested in religious issues. Although they can all be characterised as in some sense favorably disposed to religion, and opposed to the claims of a scientific philosophy to dispose of it, there is virtually no agreement among them here. The interest lies in the way in which such extraordinarily different points of view are expressed by the three great figures of one department.

21. If, however, we turn to ethical theory there is a closeness in fundamentals which I think is not often noted. They are united in the advocacy of certain positions, at least some of which are

fundamental for Dewey too, which color also the ethics of Peirce and Stevenson.

First, there is the insistence that the basis of all value and obligation is felt value and felt demand. According to this view, the fact that something is felt to be good is the sole and sufficient reason why it is good. Thus feelings of value create a universe of value.

And then there is the claim, very significant for the whole question of ethical relativity if correct, that one cannot truly grasp the fact that something is a value for someone else without its becoming something of a value for oneself. Such grasp coincides with an imaginative reproduction of the way things look to the other, and this necessarily brings with it the associated conations.

From this it follows that the more one grasps the ideal colors in which things look to others the more one will take as one's aim the joint realization of as many of these values as possible in a single harmony. The essential point is that nothing anyone values is condemned as such, only, at most, as the realization of other values.

An ethical doctrine along these lines is found in Royce's *The Religious Aspect of Philosophy*, in James's "The Moral Philosopher and the Moral Life," and in many of Santayana's writings, particularly in *The Life of Reason*. Several features of such a point of view may be noted. First there is the insistent naturalism (present even in Royce), the claim that it is facts about human experience which underlie all truths about value. Second, there is the rejection of the possibility of any quantitative summing of different values in utilitarian fashion. Thirdly, there is the pluralism, the insistence on the existence and rights of different sorts of moral consciousness, and fourthly there is the view that a harmony of different values is a significant over-all aim, the necessary upshot of an initial openness to variety. There is a strong strand of common teaching here, turning (I think) on an agreement on many issues of psychology, however much associated with metaphysical and religious disagreement. This interest theory of values, with it specific affinities to and contrasts with utilitarianism, is still present in Perry and in a way even in Stevenson. I shall not attempt to evaluate this ethical doctrine or to see if it can be freed of certain *prima facie* logical difficulties. In fact, I think it possesses great significance and potential for development.

22. I would like just to say a word on a subject which Bruce Kucklick is much concerned with. Both Royce and James believed

that philosophical thinking should have an upshot in action, including presumably social and political action, but one may doubt whether their work had much impact here. Dewey would seem to be in a different case, but even here there is rather a gap, I should say, between rhetoric and achievement. I would be inclined to grant that, in spite of the deep human relevance of these philosophers, they were somewhat thin and abstract in their treatment of social issues.

But this does not mean that the relevance of their philosophy to concrete living is a mere pretence, for there are individual life problems, and different degrees of success which people can make of their lives within any sort of social structure. It would be interesting to know how much impact exposure to the teachings of any of these philosophers had on their students and readers, but I would guess that it was quite a significant part of their lives for many people.

23. I don't know whether I have cast much light on the distinctiveness of American philosophy, but I hope I have said something to suggest that America has produced a set of philosophers of major importance, from whose work there is still much more to be learnt, and, so far as universities in this country and elsewhere go, who should be allotted a far greater amount of attention than is usual at present.

THE CONTEMPORARY AMERICAN SYNTHESIS

A. C. GENOVA

The University of Kansas, Lawrence, Kansas

On matters pertaining to one's reputation, it is prudent to defer to the judgment of others. However, on very special occasions, e.g., the American bicentennial, it is hoped that our foreign colleagues will look benevolently on the prospect of American philosophy engaged in self-evaluation. After all, bicentennials are for that sort of thing.

Accordingly, I want to consider the question "What has America contributed to philosophy?" But I do not take this to be an invitation to provide a sweeping historical survey of philosophical activity in America. That has already been done— perhaps overdone. Nor do I take this to be a call for the significant contributions which American philosophers have made to already established, ongoing philosophical movements that owe their origin to other shores. That too is old hat. For me, the interesting version of the question concerns whether or not America is the home of any original philosophical movements or schools which can, without serious challenge, claim to be significant landmarks on the philosophical landscape. In short, I shall argue that in these terms America has not fared so well, but the landscape is changing before our very eyes. More specifically, there has been only one universally acknowledged, home-grown, major philosophical innovation in America and that is pragmatism; but there is another one currently in progress which has not received sufficient attention in the philosophical community.

In this connection, I want to do two things: (1) briefly present the outline of a thesis about what constitutes originality, profundity and significance in philosophy, and (2) take account of and develop some recent insights into what is unique about contemporary American philosophy. Perhaps, as a serendipitous result of this discussion, we can put to rest, once and for all, two fairly persistent views about American philosophy: the first being the view that there was (or is) such a thing as "early American philosophy," i.e., genuine philosophy in America from, say, the late seventeenth century and extending roughly to the nineteenth century; the second being the more or less contrary view that

215

American philosophy, with the possible exception of pragmatism, has always been and remains essentially derivative, eclectic and systematically out-of-date. Proponents of the first view are inclined to cite Jonathan Edwards as the "first major American philosopher" Advocates of the second tend to agree with the notorious remark attributed to C. D. Broad to the effect that old philosophies never die—they just go to America and begin a new life.

First then, what reasonably constitutes an adequate standard for assessing the importance or originality of what purports to be an instance of philosophical activity? Above all, I suppose one must be especially open-minded in providing an answer to such a question. We all have our philosophical favorites. I would think that what is needed are criteria which are both general enough to accommodate radically divergent philosophical points of view and specific enough to exclude certain obvious surrogates which occasionally pose as genuine instances of philosophy. I want to be able to identify major cases of philosophical originality while avoiding what can be more reasonably classified as important advances in science, religion, literature or whatever.

I submit that the mark of an original philosophical movement is either (a) a unique intellectual synthesis which resolves a major opposition between previously well-established traditions or major philosophies by mediating between apparently incompatible philosophical alternatives, or (b) the formulation of a radically new orientation in the style of philosophical inquiry which thereby restates traditional problems and engenders new problems of its own for future research. These two categories of synthesis and reorientation are not entirely independent. Indeed, the notion of radical reorientation is itself a kind of synthesis because in any such overall reorientation, the major philosophical positions of predecessors typically reappear as novel reconstructions respective combinations of old points of view with the new orientation. Thus, compare the materialistic atomism of Democritus with the psychological atomism of Hume with the logical atomism of the early Russell. A very prominent example—indeed a paradigm case—is the thought of Kant because he satisfied both of these criteria. On the one hand, his Critical Philosophy provided a compatible synthesis of the traditions of radical empiricism and dogmatic rationalism; on the other hand, his so-called "Copernican revolution" culminated a monumental reorientation which required that epistemological questions about the conditions and limitations of knowledge be logically prior to ontological questions about the character of the objects known. Although this epistemological reorientation is most associated with Kant, it is clear that it is (in somewhat different ways and to different degrees) a common presupposition of most of the philosophers of the modern period—"rationalists" like Descartes, Spinoza and Leibniz as well as "empiricists" like Hobbes, Locke, Hume and Berkeley. Moreover, I think it can be shown that these major philosophers (again, each in his own way) also bear the stamp of originality in virtue of significant syntheses of opposing philosophical theses of contemporaries, i.e., the first kind of synthesis listed above. The same is true for the classical philosophies of Greece. In the ontological setting of ancient philosophy, the Platonists and Atomists can be profitably read as alternative attempts to accommodate the contrary insights of the Eleatics and the Milesian materialists (or more narrowly, the ontologies of Parmenides and Heraclitus)— attempts to reconcile, in a single philosophy, unity and plurality, permanence and change, necessity and contingency; and Aristotle in turn believed that his analysis of cause provided a harmonious synthesis of Platonic and Atomistic doctrines. Similarly, much of the significance of medieval philosophy is lost unless we appreciate the "medieval synthesis" as an ingenious blend of ancient philosophical theory with theological and religious content, resulting in a novel interpretation of philosophical inquiry.

Now what I have said is simply a sketch designed to promote the feasibility of my claim that philosophical synthesis, in the senses delineated, is the predominant mark of philosophical originality. If this is essentially correct, then it is in these terms that American philosophy must be judged. Have we had anything like this in American philosophy?

Well, in respect to pre-twentieth century philosophy, I doubt it. I even find it difficult to support the lesser thesis that there were a significant number of professional *philosophers* in pre-twentieth century America, not to speak of original philosophical movements. At least this seems to be the case if we hold steadfastly to the proposed criteria. Although I doubt that Dagobert Runes (*Pictorial History of Philosophy* [New Jersey, 1963]) would have agreed with this thesis, still, even a cursory review of his account of early American philosophy seems to establish it: There was William Penn (1644–1718), the converted Quaker who is best known for his "holy experiment" of founding a "theocratic democracy" in Pennsylvania; there was Jonathan Edwards (1703–1758), an ordained minister who produced a variety of public sermons and theological treatises on the interests of "the Great Awakening" and his "consistent Calvinism"; there was James Bowdoin (1726–1790), dedicated to the idea of liberty and the promulgation of Christian principles; there was Benjamin Rush (1745–1813), a Surgeon General of the Revolutionary War who was fascinated with the relation between medicine and psychiatry, devoted to popular government, philanthropy and many other good things—just so long as they were conformable to the canons of Christianity; and Amos Bronson Alcott (1799–1888), an unremarkable New England transcendentalist notorious for his secrecy and cryptic sayings; and Henry Ward Beecher (1813–1887), who professed independent Presbyterianism in honor of all living things, the beauty of nature and God. One can go on with many more names like this and reinforce the list with more famous names like Ralph Waldo Emerson, Walt Whitman and Henry Thoreau—and even Ethan Allen, Thomas Paine, Benjamin Franklin, John Adams, Thomas Jefferson and Abraham Lincoln. These men may have been seers, sages, divines, prophets, mystics, poets, healers, statesmen or literary greats, but significant philosphers they were not.

Of course, with respect to the strictly academic realm, I would concede that America gradually developed its own cadre of philosophical professionals either through the direct process of immigration or the indirect one of importing philosophical ideas from abroad. Even as the early transcendentalists were offshoots of German idealism (with a helping hand from Coleridge), similarly, the later nineteenth century became dominated by the Scottish common-sensism of Reid in the east and the Hegelianism of the St. Louis group in the west. Moreover, this process of philosophical immigration and importation (with a few singular exceptions like Whitehead and Santayana whose identification as strictly American philosophers is certainly debatable) continued in the twentieth century and culminated in the philosophical hegemony of logical positivism and ordinary language philosophy in America. So to be sure, the Americans had their philosophical professionals. But this doesn't help much, because in this context, the sentiments of Broad take on an authentic ring.

I have been defending what I am sure is an unpopular thesis to the majority of American historians of ideas and experts in American philosophy. Consequently, I feel the urge to become more constructive, and fortunately, there is the major exception to which I already referred, viz., the "golden age" of American philosophy: pragmatism. I think that the pragmatic movement in America (1880–1920) can be reasonably said to be a component of what we call "recent philosophy." As such, it should exhibit one of the universal features of most recent philosophy, viz., a reorientation analogous to but different from the revolution in modern philosophy already discussed. It is generally acknowledged that just as modern philosophy argued or presupposed that since the objects of cognition are conditioned by the mode of cognition, questions about the latter had philosophical priority, analogously, recent philosophy argues or presupposes that since the mode of cognition is conditioned by the modes of expression, an analysis of the modes of expression (language, action, feeling) has philosophical priority to questions about the mode of cognition, and *a fortiori*, to questions about the objects of cognition. Its more familiar version, at least from the point of view of so-called analytic philosophy, is captured in the notion of the "linguistic turn," i.e., since our conceptual framework is directly dependent upon the mode by which concepts are expressed, an analysis of the primary vehicle of expression (language) is presupposed for any meaningful talk about concepts or reality. Pragmatism, in its emphasis on a theory of signs and the analysis of action, is an early representative of this recent revolution in philosophy. It is fundamentally through actions—"things done"—that concepts are expressed; and indeed, the very criterion of meaningfulness for concepts or linguistic signs is defined in terms of pragmatic content or practical effects. But there is more. Recent scholars of pragmatism have increasingly recognized that this philosophy can be construed as a complex synthesis containing essential ingredients from its major contemporaneous alternatives—especially from the German idealist tradition and the early positivist tradition, and I think, from the roots of phenomenology in thinkers like Brentano, Stumpf and Husserl. These features, in interestingly varying ways, are identifiable in the doctrines of Peirce, James, Dewey, Morris, C. I. Lewis and related thinkers. This is the reason, I suggest, that pragmatism meets the standard of philosophical originality I have been talking about. Pragmatism was not an old philosophy reborn in the land of opportunity, but a home-grown philosophy of America.

Let us now focus on contemporary American philosophy and its relation to post-pragmatic philosophy in America. One of the recent insights I alluded to at the beginning of this paper was, ironically enough, most clearly expressed (to my knowledge) by the

English philosopher, Anthony Quinton, in his "Philosophy in America" (*Times Literary Supplement*, June 13, 1975). But in Quinton's excellent essay, it occurs in an undeveloped and almost incidental way in one or two paragraphs near the end of his discussion. Quinton's central interests, it seems to me, are primarily historical, geographical and somewhat polemical in the best sense of that term. He offers us a lucid survey of the history of American philosophy, an account of its foreign influences, an identification of what he considers to be examples of original American philosophy, and a very charitable defense of America's philosophical autonomy in response to Broad's rather patronizing remark. The upshot is his contention that the center of philosophical activity has recently shifted from Oxford-Cambridge to the U.S.A. His conjecture is that the reason for the shift is the growing interest in such issues of American origin as Kripke's causal theory of reference, the application of the mathematical refinements of game theory to political philosophy as set forth by philosophers like Rawls and Nozick, the philosophical applications of modal logic by thinkers like David Lewis, Hintikka, Kripke and Plantinga, and the exact formalization of natural languages by Davidson, Chomsky, Montague, *et al.* In sum, it is the recent use of formalistic techniques that has been primarily responsible for this new-founded philosophical significance. But more importantly, it is the *way* these philosophers employ these techniques that is crucial.

Consider what is involved here in light of my earlier comments about philosophical synthesis. In the post-pragmatic period in America, the stage was set for another major philosophical synthesis. One pole of the imminent synthesis was provided by the remarkable influx of first-rank logical positivists and logicians, who, with their fellow travelers and enthusiastic American converts, made positivism (which quickly assimilated the more scientific aspects of pragmatism) tantamount to an American orthodoxy. The other pole, emerging somewhat belatedly and more by way of the importation of ideas than the immigration of philosophers in the flesh, was of course provided by the practitioners of ordinary language philosophy, who, again with the succor of impressionable Americans, made it seem as if philosophy itself was something like a category mistake, and who also reflected pragmatic influences via their notion of "use" coupled with their tendency to substitute behavioral descriptions for linguistic meaning. Now both the similarities and the differences between these two developments are important. Both shared the orientation of the "linguistic turn" in their desire to identify, clarify and resolve genuine philosophical problems (if indeed there were any) by determining the structure, limitations and organizing principles of our conceptual knowledge through an analysis of the language in which such knowledge was expressed. Both manifested a strong anti-metaphysical bias. They agreed that philosophical inquiry was essentially logical-linguistic analysis. And most relevant to my present concern, both believed that natural language was replete with ambiguity, vagueness, instability and indeterminacy—in short, was not capable of being systematically formalized by exact methods. Now Jerrold Katz (in his timely discussion in Chapter 2 in *The Philosophy of Language* [New York, 1966]) develops this comparison in detail and points out that it is precisely in their respective solutions to the common problem engendered by this last-mentioned similarity that their greatest difference is revealed. Katz, operating in the relatively narrow context of defending and developing his theory of generative and transformational grammar, does not argue for any thesis about the originality of current American philosophy. Rather, he represents a philosopher in action as it were one major instantiation of the thesis I am trying to develop. Nevertheless, his analysis of the two components of the synthesis and the way in which generative grammar functions as one mode or example of the synthesis, is illuminating.

It amounts to this: The positivists (I prefer to call them "logical analysts"), in reaction to the shortcomings of natural language, attempted to construct an ideal, artificial language which possessed all the virtues that ordinary discourse lacked. It was the technical apparatus and analytical tools of modern symbolic logic which were supposed to provide the formal precision for their verification principle, an exact formalization of the language of empirical science, and the logical criteria for distinguishing purely syntactical sentences from genuine empirical sentences, and for translating certain pseudo-object sentences into syntactical sentences while excluding the non-translatable ones as metaphysical nonsense. The upshot was that only an artificial language would admit of the required canonical regimentation; and that part of natural language which was recalcitrant to any translation into the ideal language could then be dismissed as cognitively meaningless. I do not say that this program failed, but the well-known difficulties it confronted were enormous. As for the ordinary language advocates

(I prefer "linguistic analysts"), they turned this whole approach upside down. The very "shortcomings" of natural language became its virtues. It was precisely because ordinary discourse contained the possibility of ambiguity, vagueness, and the variability of contextual dependence, that it was able to function effectively. Not only was it impervious to any logically precise systematic formalization, but any such artificial construction itself presupposed a natural language. Hence, the model of the technical language of mathematics or science, with its definitional rigor and formal axiomatization, was irrelevant and vacuous for the aim of linguistic analysis which, in its most radical Wittgensteinian form, was the program of piecemeal linguistic description yielding "reminders for a particular purpose" grounded on an examination of the linguistic behavior of fluent speakers with linguistic competence. Philosophical problems were not genuine issues clothed in the obscurity of natural language which achieved clarification and legitimacy by means of formal techniques; rather they were pseudo-problems whose obscurity and very existence dissolved by means of the processes of linguistic therapy and rehabilitation. The upshot was that the organizing principles of natural discourse were not abstract, specifiable and fixed formal rules but, rather, operational patterns dependent upon the indefinite occasions and circumstances of actual usage.

Well, what about the "contemporary American synthesis" and its relation to the new formal techniques of American philosophy cited by Quinton? Quinton says that "there is no accessible account in English" of these developments. I think that is essentially true, but if we restrict our attention to just one area— philosophy of language—and take account of what some representative philosophers involved in the new synthesis actually say, the picture begins to become clear. I have neither the competence nor the space to outline the correlative versions of the synthesis which my colleagues assure me also occur respectively in recent philosophy of science, possible worlds semantics, the theory of truth, political philosophy and other quarters. Besides, it is very difficult in philosophy to say exactly what is going on while it is going on. But I do think that recent philosophy of language reveals the clearest instances of the synthesis as I see it, viz., in the work of philosophers like Chomsky, Fodor, Katz, Davidson, Harman, Montague, Hintikka, Kripke, Searle, David Lewis and others in their recent development of theories of natural language. For what this comes to is a reconciliation between ordinary language and systematic formalization in virtue of an interpretation of linguistic activity in which purely formal rules have the status of essential organizing principles of natural discourse. In contrast to the logical analysts, this is not a conventional program of imposing independent abstract forms on the body of language; and in contrast to the linguistic analysts, it is not a process of generating indefinite regularities from the piecemeal description of the interaction between word usage and the context and circumstances of utterance. Instead, it rests on the basis of treating language as a substantial whole in its own right, as a rule-governed intentional activity wherein the rules are natural forms constitutive of their content and the activity is linguisitic performance in accordance with the rules. The previous discrepancy between the "amorphous discourse" of everyday life and the "pristine language" of an idealized canonical notation is mediated by means of a new interpretation of language as a seamless whole—one in which formal and material aspects stand in a natural relation of reciprocity and thereby manifest a synthesis of systematic form with linguistic elements. Now my characterization of this synthesis is necessarily very general and it is not meant to overlook or underplay the fact that the philosophers I have mentioned exhibit a great deal of diversity and disagreement among themselves. It was similar with the positivist and ordinary language traditions. Indeed some would no doubt disagree with my general interpretation or perhaps not recognize the philosophical significance of their own work on this general historical level.

Let us briefly look at the situation from a slightly different angle. In respect to the recent interpretations of *natural* language, one should not begin in the vacuum of a priori presuppositions about what constitutes an acceptable formal system based on preferred formal models taken from logic or mathematics; nor should one begin in the plenum of language usage as it is contingently modified on all sides by its complex interrelationship with externalized variables and the subjective peculiarities of language-users. Natural language does not find its principles in pre-established conventions that formally guarantee preferred modes of successful performance for a special class of speakers, all of this accomplished in abstraction from the actual activity of language-speaking. Nor does it find its principles in behavioral regularities relativized to individualized contexts and particular purposes, now in abstraction from the constitutive rules which govern the function of what is subsequently used. To do the former is to assimilate natural language to something like logic or mathematics; to do the latter is to assimilate it to something like psychology or perhaps rhetoric. Now none of what I have said should be construed as an unqualified rejection of logical positivism or ordinary language philosophy. Carnap's program for the logical syntax of language was and is an invaluable contribution to the formal science concerned with the construction of ideal languages. Similarly with Wittgenstein. His program of linguistic description excavated a plethora of particular truths about the instrumentality of language in relation to the world. Both of these approaches treat of a genuine philosophical subject matter and set forth appropriate principles. Carnap and others were concerned with language as an ideal symbolization for the characterization of purely formal truth and the verifiable statements of theoretic science, while Wittgenstein focused on the resultant character of language as an instrumentality in the world designed to get things done in accordance with contextual game plans. But the principles of natural discourse, construed now as an autonomous whole whose principles are self-contained, are not found in formal constructions or language games. So when formal semanticists like Katz argue that the positivists and natural language philosophers were both in error, paradoxically enough, on the crucial thesis which they both supported, viz., that the irregular character of natural language excluded in principle the possibility of systematic formalization, this could be misleading. I mean given their respective conceptions of the subject matter at hand, their methodologies and conclusions were in order. I think that this way of looking at it is important because it suggests the *reasons* why neither of these opposing movements pursued the possibility of natural principles of ordinary discourse which have the requisite degree of systematic form.

In Katz's formulation the principles of this synthetic interpretation of natural language have the status of linguistic universals (syntactical, phonological and semantical rules) arrived at by empirical generalization and extrapolation from successive levels of linguistic phenomena. On the basis of the linguistic evidence, descriptions of particular languages are formulated, followed by empirical generalizations which ultimately provide the basis for the construction of a theory of language in general. The formal semanticists using this approach point out that its primary advantage rests on the fact that such theories, at all levels, are substantive hypotheses resulting in predictions which admit of straightforward empirical confirmation and falsification by appeal to the relevant linguistic phenomena (as well as the intuitions of native speakers). Now the philosophical significance of this approach becomes manifest when we recall the basic presupposition of the linguistic revolution of recent philosophy. For if the nature and structure of our conceptual knowledge are logically dependent upon the correlative features of the language through which conceptual knowledge is expressed and communicated, then the universal rules which organize our linguistic framework will serve as the clue to the universal truths which characterize our conceptual framework. Hence, the identification, clarification, evaluation and resolution of philosophical problems becomes directly dependent upon the universal features of the theory of natural language. Philosophy concerns the analysis of conceptual frameworks, and metaphysics consists in the discovery of their fundamental principles. The only question which arises in this approach (as far as I am concerned) turns on the empirical motivation of most American semanticists and the consequent status of the "linguistic universals" as empirically dependent hypotheses. As such, the latter function like hypothetical imperatives. The question naturally arises as to whether or not there are any *categorical* principles of natural language which might be identified by means of a reflexive analysis as the logical presuppositions for the rational activity of speaking a language. If there are such categorical canons constitutive of linguistic performance, then the metaphysics of the "linguistic turn" would be a "descriptive metaphysics" which delineated the categorical principles of our conceptual system. It is only appropriate that we mention this point because the reader will be reminded of P. F. Strawson's *Individuals* in which he uses a mode of transcendental argument in order to justify principles which come very close to having just this categorical character—a timely reminder that the "American synthesis," at least in this connection, may not be exclusively American after all.

I have just scratched the philosophical surface of the recent philosophical synthesis which is currently being emphasized in American circles. I have restricted my discussion to philosophy of language—and even at that, to one relatively narrow context. For example, I think the whole case can be restated in terms of the recent work on speech act theory as developed by philosophers like John Searle; and moreover, I would argue that speech act theory, more than any other view, recognizes the need to construe language as an intentional rule-governed activity and deals with the problem of meaning (i.e., how it is possible that speakers can utter sounds, say what they mean and mean what they say, and hearers can both comprehend this and respond in kind) in terms of the dynamic context of communication. Speech act theory incorporates the concept of intentional meaning into the concept of linguistic activity, resulting in an interpretation of language as a mode of *communication* which requires an account of the purpose and function of language over and above that given by the purely formal structures of syntax and semantics established by the generative and transformational grammarians (see Searle's "Chomsky's Revolution in Linguistics," *The New York Review of Books* [special supplement, June, 1972]). If so, then the formal rules constitutive of the activity of language speaking will not be sufficiently identified by empirical generalizations over linguistic utterances or necessary presuppositions required to account for language behavior, but will require modifications or additions determined by the goals of communication and the intentions of speakers. What an utterance *means* must take account not merely of the lexical product of the meanings of its syntactical elements as those are assigned by formal semantic rules, but also of what a speaker is doing *in* uttering the sentence he utters, i.e., the speech act.

In sum then, advances in developing a formal semantics of natural language have recently been approached from at least three different directions which have intersected at various points, reflecting a shared orientation concerning the relation between natural discourse and formal structures, and a common focus on a whole host of interrelated problems (see the Davidson and Harman edition of *Semantics of Natural Language*, and the Hintikka, Moravcsik and Suppes edition of *Approaches to Natural Language* [D. Reidel Publishing Co., 1972 and 1973]). Logicians, concentrating on modal, intensional, deontic and pragmatic logics, have been increasingly applying formal methods to linguistic contexts which closely resemble those of natural languages. Theoretical linguists, from an independent basis and employing different methodologies, have abstracted formal syntactic and semantic systems of rules which apply to ordinary discourse. And some philosophers, like Searle, have approached the same problem from the perspective of action theory. The central feature common to these diverse approaches is the belief that natural discourse contains underlying formal structures which are sufficient to guarantee its clarity and precision—the distinctive trait of the new American synthesis.

At any rate, I shall close the discussion by going out on a philosophical limb. In terms of my earlier talk about the historical reorientations in philosophy, I would predict that the much belabored philosophical synthesis I have been trying to clarify— after it has been fully exhausted at all levels and in all quarters (as is typical for philosophical movements)—will culminate and bring an end to the linguistic orientation of recent philosophy. Where we go from there is anyone's guess.

GENTEEL SYNTHESES, PROFESSIONAL ANALYSES, TRANSCENDENTALIST CULTURE

RICHARD RORTY

Princeton University, Princeton, New Jersey

Santayana's reflections on philosophy in the new world have two singular merits. First, he was able to laugh at us without despising us—a feat often too intricate for the native-born. Second, he was entirely free of the instinctive American conviction that the westering of the spirit ends here —that whatever the ages have labored to bring forth will emerge between Massachusetts and California, that our philosophers have only to express our national genius for the human spirit to fulfill itself. Santayana saw us as one more great empire in the long parade. His genial hope was that we might enjoy the imperium while we held it. In a famous essay of 1913 on American philosophy, he suggested that we were still spoiling our own fun. We wanted to retain, he said, "agonized conscience" of our Calvinist ancestors while keeping, simultaneously if illogically, the idealistic metaphysics of their transcendentalist successors. This metaphysics embodied what he called the "conceited notion that man, or human reason, or the human distinction between good and evil, is the centre and pivot of the universe."[1] The combination of Calvinist guilt and metaphysical egoism he called "The Genteel Tradition in American Philosophy". He opposed to it what he called "America's ruling passion, the love of business"—"joy in business itself and in its further operation, in making it greater and better organized and a mightier engine in the general life."[2] "The American Will", he said, "inhabits the sky-scraper; the American Intellect inhabits the colonial mansion. The one is the sphere of the American man; the other, at least predominantly, of the American woman. The one is all aggressive emphasis; the other is all genteel tradition."[3] The academic mind of 1913, he thought, counted as feminine in this respect: "The genteel tradition has subsisted in the academic mind for want of anything equally academic to take its place."[4]

We can afford to smile at all this, as we look about at the manly, aggressive and business-like academics of our own time. The American academic mind has long since discovered the joy of making its own special enterprise "greater and better organized and a mightier engine in the general life". The well-funded professor, jetting home after a day spent advising men of power, is the envy of the provincial tycoon in the adjacent seat. If there is still something like a genteel tradition in American life, it cannot be identified with "the academic mind". Most academies now teach in skyscrapers. The public no longer associates our profession with epicene delicacy, but either with political violence and sexual license or with hard-nosed Presidential advisors. If there is anything remotely analogous to what Santayana spoke of, it is the specifically highbrow culture—the culture which produces poems, plays and novels, literary criticism and what, for want of a better term, we can call "culture criticism". Some highbrows inhabit the academy, mostly in literature departments, but they are not academic entrepreneurs. They do not get grants; they have disciplines rather than research teams; they inhabit whatever mansions may still be tucked away among the academic skyscrapers. Their more business-like colleagues treat them alternately with the deference due from tradesmen towards the clergy, and the contempt the successful feel for the shabby genteel.

Where, in the busy modern academy, do we find the philosophy professors? To treat this question properly we need to look at what has been going on in philosophy since Santayana wrote, and to divide it into two periods. The period between the World Wars was one of prophecy and moral leadership—the heroic period of Deweyan pragmatism, during which philosophy played the sort of role in the country's life which Santayana could admire. The period since the Second World War has been one of pro-fessionalization, in which philosophers have quite deliberately and self-consciously abdicated such a role. In the pre-World War I period which Santayana described, philosophy defined itself by its relation to religion. In the Deweyan period, it defined itself by its relation to the social sciences. At the beginning of the pro-fessionalizing period, philosophers attempted half-heartedly to define their activity in relation to mathematics and the natural sciences. In fact, however, this period has been marked by a withdrawal from the rest of the academy and from culture—an insistence on philosophy's autonomy.

The claim that philosophy is and ought to be a technical subject, that this recent professionalization is an important good, is usually not defended directly by pointing with pride to the importance of the issues philosophers discuss or to paradigms of successful philosophical inquiry. Rather, it is defended indirectly, by pointing with scorn to the low level of argumentative rigor among the competition—in the Deweyan philosophy of the 30's, in contemporary Continental philosophy, and in the culture criticism of the highbrows. Even philosophers who would like to break out of their professional isolation tend to insist that their special contribution will be in argumentative skill. It is not, they say, that philosophers know more about anything in particular, but that they have a kind of sensitivity to distinctions and presuppositions which is peculiarly their own.

Since the highbrow culture critic has usurped many of the functions which traditional philosophers had fulfilled in the past, while remaining oblivious to what contemporary academic philosophers are actually doing, highbrows try to dismiss American philosophy with journalistic sneers about "irrelevance" or "scholasticism". Philosophers, in turn, try to dismiss the highbrow literary culture in the same way as Santayana dismissed the genteel tradition. They see this culture as palliating cranky hypersensitivity with aesthetic comfort, just as Santayana saw Royce and Palmer as palming the agonized conscience off with metaphysical comfort. Accusations of softness and sloppiness are exchanged for accusations of pedantry and narrowness.

When these accusations become self-conscious and explicit, they are usually offered as views about "the essence of philosophy", as if a niche in a permanent a historical schema of possible human activities were in danger of vacancy or of usurpation. I think that such disputes are pointless, since philosophy does not have an essence, any more than do literature or politics. Each is what brilliant men are presently making them. There is no common standard by which to compare Royce, Dewey, Heidegger, Tarski, Carnap, and Derrida in point of "being a *real* philosopher". But although philosophy has no essence, it does have a history. Although philosophical movements cannot be seen as departures from, or returns to, True Philosophy, and although their successes are as difficult to assess as those of literary or political movements, one can sometimes say something about their grosser sociological consequences. In what follows, I want to sketch some of the things that have happened in American philosophy since Santayana wrote, and to make some predictions about the consequences of professionalization.

* * * *

Santayana noted that William James had already "turned the

flank" of the genteel tradition. A decade after Santayana's essay, it became clear that Dewey had consolidated James' gains and succeeded in doing what Santayana had described as "finding something equally academic to take the place of that [genteel] tradition". Dewey made the American learned world safer for the social sciences. In the 1920's the academy had to restructure itself to make room for half-a-dozen new departments, and for a new sort of academic who came to inhabit them. The American academy became the privileged sanctuary of attempts to reconstruct the American social order, and American philosophy became a call for such reconstruction. The Deweyan claim that moral philosophy was not the formulation of general principles to serve as a surrogate for divine commands, but rather the application of intelligence to social problems, gave the youth a new way of looking at the point of their education and their lives. With the New Deal, the social scientist emerged as the representative of the academy to the public, embodying the Deweyan promise. When, during the Depression, Stalinism recruited whole battalions of highbrows, a small circle around Sidney Hook—Dewey's chief disciple—kept political morality alive among intellectuals. Philosophers like Max Otto, Alexander Meiklejohn, and Horace Kallen offered their students the possibility that "America's ruling passion, the love of business", might be transformed into a love of social reconstruction. Having sat at their feet, a whole generation grew up confident that America would show the world how to escape both Gradgrind capitalism and revolutionary bloodshed. In the years between the wars, American philosophy not only escaped from the genteel tradition, but provided moral leadership for the country. For the first time, American philosophy professors played the sort of role which Fichte and Hegel had once played in Germany.

By the end of the Second World War, however, the great days of Deweyan philosophy and social sciences were over. The strenuous reformist attitude which succeeded the genteel tradition was in turn succeeded by an urge to be scientific and rigorous. Both social scientists and philosophers wanted to stop striking public attitudes and start showing that they could be as thoroughly and exclusively professional, and preferably as mathematical, as the natural scientists. American sociology, whose early stages had been satirized as the expenditure of a five thousand dollar grant to discover the address of a whorehouse, came to be satirized as the expenditure of a five million dollar grant to plot the addresses of a thousand whorehouses against a multi-dimensional array of socio-economic variables. American philosophy students realized that the previous generation—Dewey's pupils—had exhausted the market for celebrations of American democracy, naturalism, and social reconstruction. Nobody could remember what an idealist, a subectivist, a transcendentalist, or even an orthodox theist looked like, so nobody was interested in hearing them criticized. New heroes were needed, and they were found among that extraordinary body of men, the emigré scholars. A young American philosopher learning phenomenology from Gurwitsch or Schuetz, or logical empiricism from Carnap or Reichenbach, was trained to think of philosophy as a rigorous discipline, a matter of cooperation in joint inquiry and the production of agreed-upon results. By the mid-50's, the victory which the pragmatists had won on native ground over the genteel tradition seemed as remote as Emerson's victory over the Calvinists.

With exacting work to be done on the structure of visual awareness or on extensional criteria of nomologicality, there seemed no time and no need to ask what had happened in philosophy before Husserl or before Russell. As logical empiricism metamorphosed into analytic philosophy, and succeeded in driving phenomenology out into the academic shadows, American philosophers' disinterest in moral and social questions became almost total. Courses in moral philosophy were, for a time, little more than elaborate epistemological sneers at the common moral consciousness. Philosophers' contact with colleagues in the social sciences became as minimal and incidental as their contacts with colleagues in literature. Dewey had predicted that philosophy would turn away from the seventeenth-century tension between mathematical physics and the world of common sense, and would take up now new problems arising from the social sciences and arts. But this prediction was completely off target. On the contrary, all the good old Cartesian problems which Dewey thought he had disposed of were brought back, restated in the formal mode of speech and surrounded by new difficulties generated by the formalism.

What Dewey had predicted for American philosophy did, however, happen elsewhere: both in Continental philosophy and in the American highbrow literary culture. Attention to interpretation rather than verification—to what the arts and the "sciences of men" have in common—was the mark of the literary intellectual. One result of this—the most important result for my present purposes—was that the history of philosophy began to be taken over by the highbrows. Whereas professionalized philosophers insisted on treating the great dead philosophers as sources of hypotheses or instructive examples of conceptual confusion, the highbrows still treated them in the old-fashioned way, as heroes or villains. Dewey had still attempted to tell a great sweeping story about philosophy from Plato to himself, but philosophers in the professionalizing period distrusted such stories as "unscientific" and "unscholarly". So they are, but they also form a *genre* of writing which is quite indispensable. Besides the need to ask whether certain propositions asserted by Aristotle or Locke or Kant or Kierkegaard are true or were validly inferred, there is also the need to adopt an attitude towards such men, just as one must adopt an attitude towards Alcibiades and Euripides, Cromwell and Milton, Proust and Lenin. Because the writings of the great dead philosophers form a bundle of intertwined dialectical sequences, one has to have attitudes towards many of them to justify one's attitude towards the others. Nor can one's attitude towards Kant be independent of one's attitude towards Wordsworth and Napoleon. Developing attitudes towards the mighty dead and their living rivals—dividing the pantheon into the divine and the daemonic—is the whole point of highbrow culture. The kind of namedropping, rapid shifting of context, and unwillingness to stay for an answer which this culture encourages runs counter to everything that a professionalized academic discipline stands for. Normally, the conflict between the academy and this culture can remain implicit. But in the case of philosophy, it is bound to be expressed, if only because not even the most professionalized philosopher can stop seeing himself, if not as the contemporary counterpart of Plato and Kant, as at least their authorized commentator. So we have the conflict I described at the beginning of this paper—the highbrow and the academic philosopher viewing each other with equal suspicion, each harping on the vices of each other's virtues.

I want to claim that this is not a conflict which we need view with any great concern nor try to resolve. If we understand its historical background we can live with its probable consequence— that philosophy as a technical academic subject will remain as remote from highbrow culture as is paleontology or classical philology. To defend this attitude, I want to go on to say why I think that the mode of treating the great philosophers characteristic of highbrow culture *is* indispensable, and also why one should not confuse this culture with the genteel tradition of which Santayana was complaining. I shall try to do this by sketching the history of the emergence of highbrow culture, which seems to me as distinctively a nineteenth-century phenomenon as the New Science (and the philosophical problematic which it created) were seventeenth-century phenomena.

Beginning in the days of Goethe and Macaulay and Carlyle and Emerson, a kind of writing has developed which is neither the evaluation of the relative merits of literary productions, nor intellectual history, nor moral philosophy, nor epistemology, nor social prophecy, but all these things mingled together into a new genre.[5] This genre is often still called "literary criticism", however, for an excellent reason. The reason is that in the course of the nineteenth century imaginative literature took the place of both religion and philosophy in forming and solacing the agonized conscience of the young. Novels and poems are now the principal means by which a bright youth gains a self-image. Criticism of novels is the principal form in which the acquisition of a moral character is made articulate. We live in a culture in which putting one's moral sensitivity into words is not clearly distinguishable from exhibiting one's literary sensibilities. Episodes from the history of religion and from the history of philosophy are seen as instantiating literary paradigms, rather than serving as sources of literary inspiration. The creed or the philosophical doctrine becomes the emblem of the novelist's character or the poet's image, rather than conversely. Philosophy is treated as a parallel genre to the drama or the novel or the poem, so that we speak of the epistemology common to Vaihinger and Valéry, the rhetoric common to Marlowe and Hobbes, the ethics common to E. M. Forster and G. E. Moore. What culture criticism does *not* do is to ask whether Valéry wrote more beautiful lines than Marlowe, or whether Hobbes or Moore told more truths about the good. In the form of life, the true and the good and the beautiful drop out. The aim is to understand, not to judge. The hope is that if one understands enough poems, enough religions, enough societies, enough philosophies, one will have made oneself into something worth one's own understanding.

To understand the relations between the genteel tradition of our forebears and the highbrow culture criticism of the present, it helps to look more closely at the good and bad senses of the term "transcendentalism" which Santayana distinguished. He contrasted transcendentalist metaphysical systems, which he deplored as egotistical, with what he called "transcendentalism proper". This, he said,

> like romanticism, is not any particular set of dogmas about what things exist; it is not a system of the universe regarded as a fact. ... It is a method, a point of view, from which any work, no matter what it might contain, could be approached by a self-conscious observer. ... It is the chief contribution made in modern times to speculation.[6]

This transcendentalist point of view is the mark of the highbrow. It is the attitude that there is no point in raising questions of truth, goodness, or beauty, because between ourselves and the thing judged there always intervenes mind, language, a perspective chosen among dozens, one description chosen out of thousands. On one side, it is the lack of seriousness which Plato attributed to poets, the "negative capability" for which Keats praised Shakespeare. On another, it is the Sartrean sense of absurdity which Arthur Danto suggests may befall us when we give up the picture theory of language and the Platonic conception of truth as accuracy of representation. In the later Wittgenstein, it was the wry admission that anything has a sense if you give it a sense. In Heidegger, who hated it, it was the charter of the modern—of what he called "the age of the world-view". In Derrida, it is the renunciation of "the myth of the purely maternal or paternal language belonging to the lost fatherland of thought".[7] It is crystallized in Foucault's claim that he "writes in order to have no face".[8]

Transcendentalism, in this sense, is the justification of the intellectual who has no wish to be a scientific or a professional, who does not think that intellectual honesty requires what Kuhn calls a "disciplinary matrix". It is what permits the attitude of the literary intellectual towards science which scandalizes C. P. Snow: the view of, say, quantum mechanics as a notoriously great, but quite untranslatable, poem written in a lamentably obscure language. Transcendentalism is what gives sense to the very notion of the "highbrow"—a notion which is post-Romantic and post-Kantian. In the eighteenth century there were witty men and learned men and pious men, but there were no highbrows. Not until the Romantics did books become so various as to create readers who see what has been written as having no containing framework, no points of reference save the books one loves today but which may betray one tomorrow. Not until Kant did philosophy destroy science and theology to make room for moral faith, and not until Hegel did it seem possible that the room cleared for morality could be occupied by art. When Santayana traced "transcendentalism" (in the good sense) back to Kant, his point was that Kant's treatment of scientific truth makes science just one cultural manifestation among others. But since scientific truth has been, since the seventeenth century, the model for philosophical truth, Kant's treatment of scientific truth leads to Santayana's own aesthetic attitude towards philosophical vision. It was this sense of relativity and open possibility which Santayana thought we should admire in Emerson—the side of Emerson which resembled Whitman rather than the side which resembled Royce. It was precisely the inability to maintain the splendidly aristocratic posture which made the genteel tradition merely genteel. This tradition claimed that one could take both scientific truth and religious truth with full seriousness and weave them together into something new—transcendental philosophy—which was higher than science, purer than religion and truer than both. This claim was what Dewey, Russell, and Husserl were all reacting against: Dewey by social concern, and Russell and Husserl by inventing something scientific and rigorous and difficult for philosophy to become. By picking these three men as heroes, three major movements in American philosophy became obsessed with the dangers of a form of cultural life which no longer existed. American philosophers thought of themselves as guarding against idealistic speculations long after such speculations ceased to be written. They called "idealist" anything they didn't like—anything outside their own discipline which breathed the faintest trust in a larger hope.

The result was that culture criticism—the sort of writing done by T. S. Eliot and Edmund Wilson, by Lionel Trilling and Paul Goodman—was hardly visible to philosophers, though little else was visible to the best of the students they were teaching. When the Deweyan period ended, the moral sense of American intellectuals began to be formed without the intervention of the philosophy professors, who assumed that any decent kid would grow up to be the same sort of pragmatic liberal as themselves. As Harold Bloom writes,

> "The teacher of literature now in America, far more than the teacher of history or philosophy or religion, is condemned to teach the presentness of the past, because history, philosophy and religion have withdrawn as agents from the Scene of Instruction. ..."[9]

Whatever species of professor takes on the task of teaching the presentness of the great dead philosophers, those philosophers will be present at the Scene of Instruction as long as we have libraries. There will be a Scene of Instruction as long as there is an agonized conscience in the young. This conscience is not something which was left behind with Calvinism in the eighteenth century nor with religion generally in the nineteenth. If this conscience is not induced by one's early betrayals of one's early loves, it will nevertheless be ensured, for example, by the well-funded American academic's realization that his colleagues in Chile and Russia are presently enduring humiliation and pain to amuse the guards at their prisons. Though Santayana hoped that American culture would stop trying to solace the agonized conscience with metaphysical comfort, he did not think that it would go away. But American philosophers came to fear that anything which even touched upon the agonized conscience might be construed as metaphysical comfort. They reacted either by ignoring the great dead philosophers or by reinterpreting them so that they would be seen as addressing properly professional issues. The result of such reinterpretation was to obscure the presentness of the past and to separate the philosophy professors from their students and from transcendentalist culture. Whether the sort of links between transcendentalist culture and academic departments of literature which presently exist will someday be paralleled by links with philosophy departments is not terribly important. It may be that American philosophy will continue to be more concerned with developing a disciplinary matrix than with its antecedents or its cultural role. No harm will be done by this, and possibly much good. The dialectical dramas which began with Plato will continue. They will be enacted, if not by people paid to teach Plato, then by others. These others may not be called "philosophers" but something else, possibly "critics". Possibly they will be given a name which would seem as odd to us as our use of "critic" would have seemed to Dr. Johnson, or our use of "philosopher" to Socrates.

This is the conclusion I wish to draw from my survey of what has happened in American philosophy since Santayana wrote. It amounts to saying that professionalized philosophy may or may not join transcendentalist culture, but that it should not try to beat it. I shall end by turning back to Santayana once again, and commending the second of the two virtues I initially attributed to him. This was his ability to avoid the conviction that America is what history has been leading up to, and thus that it is up to American philosophy to express the American genius, to describe a virtue as uniquely ours as our redwoods and our rattlesnakes. This mild chauvinism was in vogue during the Deweyan period, and occasionally we still feel a nostalgia for it. But, *pace* Niebuhr, Deweyan philosophy did not start from the assumption that the American and Industrial Revolutions had, between them, rendered the agonized conscience obsolete. Nor, despite a certain amount of hopeful rhetoric from Dewey and his disciples, did it really teach that the combination of American institutions and the scientific method would produce the Good Life for Men. Its attitude was best expressed by Sidney Hook in an essay called "Pragmatism and the Tragic Sense of Life", which closes by saying

> Pragmatism ... is the theory and practice of enlarging human freedom in a precarious and tragic world by the arts of intelligent social control. It may be a lost cause. I do not know of a better one.[10]

There is indeed no better cause, and the nostalgia which philosophers in the professionalizing period have felt for the prophetic Deweyan period comes from their sense that they are not doing as much for this cause as they would like. But the defense of this cause is only incidentally a matter of formulating moral principles, and moral education is only incidentally a matter of choosing and defending a cause. Further, although America will go down in history as having done more for this cause than any of the great empires so far, there is no particular reason why a nation's philosophers, or indeed its intellectuals, need be identified in the eyes of history with the same virtues as its political and social institutions. There is no reason to think that the promise of American democracy will find its final fulfillment in America, any more than Roman law reached its fulfillment in the Roman Empire or literary culture its fulfillment in Alexandria. Nor is there much reason to think that the highbrow culture of whatever empire does achieve that fulfillment will resemble our own, or that the professors of moral philosophy then will build on principles being formulated now. Even if, through some unbelievable stroke of fortune, America survives with its freedoms intact and becomes a rallying point for the nations, the high culture of an unfragmented world need not center around anything specifically American. It may not, indeed, *center* around anything more than anything else: neither poetry, nor social institutions, nor mysticism, nor depth psychology, nor novels, nor philosophy, nor physical science. It may be a culture which is transcendentalist through and through, whose center is everywhere and its circumference nowhere. In such a culture, Jonathan Edwards and Thomas Jefferson, Henry and William James, John Dewey and Wallace Stevens, Charles Peirce and Thorstein Veblen will all be present. No one will be asking which ones are the Americans, nor even, perhaps, which ones are the philosophers.

NOTES

1. George Santayana, "The Genteel Tradition in American Philosophy", reprinted in *Santayana on America*, ed. R. C. Lyon (New York, 1968), p. 55.
2. Santayana, "Tradition and Practice", reprinted in Lyon, *op. cit.*, p. 31.
3. "The Genteel Tradition", pp. 37–38.
4. "The Genteel Tradition", p. 54.
5. In Martin Green's words, "Since Weimar, the culture critic has been the man with the big cigar".
6. "The Genteel Tradition", pp. 41–42.
7. Jacques Derrida, "Difference", in *Speech and Phenomena*, trans. D. Allison (Evanston, 1974), p. 159.
8. Michel Foucault, *The Archaeology of Knowledge*, trans. A. M. S. Smith (New York, 1972), p. 17.
9. Harold Bloom, *A Map of Misreading* (New York, 1975), p. 39.
10. Sidney Hook, *Pragmatism and the Tragic Sense of Life* (New York, 1974), p. 25.

PHILOSOPHICAL PROSPECTS
FOR A NEW WORLD

JOHN J. McDERMOTT

*Queens College of The City University of New York,
Flushing, New York*

INTRODUCTION

I concern myself here with two themes. First, the meaning of America as a "New World" and second, the implication of American experience for a "global New World." Put differently, if I were a global New World person, what could I learn from the American experience, or, in the phrase of Cotton Mather, from the "American Strand."

Following the Puritans in style, although not in content, I take as my text a passage from de Tocqueville, who describes the last sheerly geographical hope for human liberation.

> Thus the European leaves his cottage for the transatlantic shores, and the American, who is born on that very coast, plunges in his turn into the wilds of central America. This double emigration is incessant! It begins in the middle of Europe, it crosses the Atlantic Ocean, and it advances over the solitudes of the New World. Millions of men are marching at once towards the same horizon; their language, their religion their manners differ; their object is the same. Fortune has been promised to them somewhere in the West, and to the West they go to find it.

I could, of course, choose a countervailing text from the experience of those who knew this journey from its outcome rather than from its prophecy. In *Men of Old Catawba*, Thomas Wolfe writes:

> For it is the wilderness that is the mother of that nation, it was in the wilderness that the strange and lonely people who have not yet spoken but who inhabit that immense and terrible land from East to West, first knew themselves, it was in the living wilderness that they faced one another at ten paces and shot one another down, and it is in the wilderness that they still live.

PHILOSOPHICAL PROSPECTS FOR A NEW WORLD

I. In 1507, the *Cosmographiae Introductio* was published. It contained the Waldseemüller map which illustrated for the first time a fourth "land" of the earth. Named after Amerigo Vespucci, it was later given a feminine ending, America, to match the other three "lands," Africa, Europa and Asia. And so, it came to be called America, although it had still another name, *Mundus Novus*, a New World. We cannot overestimate the significance of this appellation, for the development of modern culture. Given the geographical and cosmological parameters of pre-Copernican culture, the term "new world" was equivalent to a new but accessible planet; nay, to a new but accessible galaxy.

The ramifications of the "coming into being" of a new world were far-reaching in both physical and psychological terms. The existence of a new world instantaneously created the fact of an old world. Where there are two, there are relations and the interrelations of the two worlds replayed in modern times those antique themes which recur in the evolution of human culture. In a short time, a set of invidious comparisons began to be set up, some from the side of the old, some from the side of the new. As the old world perceived itself to be civilized, so the new world was perceived to be barbaric. The old was a parent, indeed, a mother, whereas the new was a child, allegedly innocent. By contrast, the new world saw itself as fresh, a creature of nature, and looked back on the old world as desiccated, "urban." The new world was taken by openness and by the implicit cognitive richness of the novelties of experience, thereby casting a suspicious and sceptical eye towards the old traditions of formal learning. As late as the nineteenth century, Whitman can write:

> Creeds and schools in abeyance
> Retiring back a while sufficed at what they are, but never forgotten
> I harbor for good or bad, I permit to speak at every hazard,
> Nature without check with original energy.[1]

Nonetheless, despite the stentorian rhetoric of many Americans from the Puritans forward, it remained that at a deep level America was in fact a creature of European imagination and expectation. This was distinctively so with regard to the reflective life, especially in its public form, where America seemed doomed to a perpetual second-handedness. Witness Emerson, who chided us for our long intellectual apprenticeship and who yearned for the time "when the sluggard intellect of this continent will look from under its iron lids and fill the postponed expectation of the world

with something better than the exertions of mechanical skill."[2]
Yet, it was the same Emerson who plaintively asked:

> Why should not we also enjoy an original relation to the
> universe? Why should not we have a poetry and philosophy of
> insight and not of tradition, and a religion by revelation to us,
> and not a history of theirs? [3]

The dialectic between the realization of others' expectations and
the originating response to experience is at the heart of the
American journey. And journey it was, both actually and
mythically, for the trek "west" has been at the center of modern
culture at least since the explorations of the late Renaissance.
Inadvertently, America turned out to be the great discovery of that
journey west. In our time, however, it has turned out to be the end.
The Thoreau who wrote that when he walks, he walks west so as to
be free, for to walk east is to be trapped, is now out of date. The
Whitman who offered us a song of the open road must now be put
against the poem of Louis Simpson, "At the End of the Open
Road."[4] California is the end of the trek and the end of the
American physical journey. California is America turned back on
itself, introverted and bewildered, for open space, horizontal and
accessible, no longer stretches before us. Visually, California
announces China and reflectively, it forces us back onto our own
intellectual traditions, beginning with John Winthrop and in turn,
back further to the wisdom of antiquity. In a word, California
announces a new world, a global world, a world in which the trek
has doubled back on itself. And that shattering event of our own
time makes of America an old world. Can we learn to live with
that; more, can we make of it a creative contribution to a global
new world?

II.   From the perspective of a philosophy of culture, the burning
question has to do with our bequest to the new world of global
culture. Which side of the aforementioned dialectic are we to offer
a new world? Are we to repeat, inversely, our earlier burden and
pose now as a parent? Is not there little difference in the earlier
term, "colony," from the more recent one, "underdeveloped
nation"? Does not the phrase "third world" connote an increased
maturity in global consciousness, dispensing as it does with the
simplistic distinction between old and new as well as with the
invidious comparisons attendant on that distinction? Some of us
worry that, despite changes in language, we have appropriated for
our own use a masked version of the older form of arrogant

mercantilism, be it economic or ideological. Do we, in fact, have anything to offer a new world?

One way to respond to these difficult questions is to monitor the role of America in matters of economic and political responsibility, asserting the need over and over again, for integrity, understanding, compassion and for a genuine sense of global rather than simply national consciousness. Without gainsaying these irreducibly necessary political and diplomatic approaches to world culture, we point to still another response, this a philosophical bequest from the American angle of vision.

Speaking out of historical honesty, we must acknowledge the considerable offenses perpetrated in the American name. Leaving only broken and rightfully contentious Indians to tell the story, we are, after all, the only modern culture to commit successful psychological, if not physical, genocide. Our racism is longstanding, systematic and globally infamous. Further, over against an embattled and ancient culture, the Vietnamese, we have only recently abandoned a violent bullying, seldom matched in the annals of world history. Yet, in keeping with all truly great cultures, our history is creative as well as destructive. What seems different about America is that commentary on its contributions to world culture seem inevitably to focus on the mechanical, the gigantic, the physical, the quantitative, the energy, the power and the confidence. Granted that this is no faint praise and taken together they constitute the signs of a vast and many-sided achievement in world history. They do not, however, constitute America at its depth or in its sadness. They do not reveal America as America is revealed to itself. These ostentatious signs reveal an America seen through other eyes than our own. More to the point of our present theme, the America so spoken of does not yield "Philosophical Prospects for a New World." I contend that America in its own experience harbors such prospects and they are to be found not only in our physical pilgrimage but also in our reflective and spiritual pilgrimage. Of this America, Sidney Mead wrote:

> Their great and obvious achievement was the mastery of a vast, stubborn, and ofttimes brutal continent. This is the "epic of America," written with cosmic quill dipped in the blood, sweat, and tears of innumerable nameless little men and women and a few half-real, half-legendary heroes. ... This is the mighty saga of the outward acts, told and retold until it has over-shadowed and suppressed the equally vital, but more somber, story of the

inner experience. Americans have so presented to view and celebrated the external and material side of their pilgrims' progress that they have tended to conceal even from themselves the inner, spiritual pilgrimage, with its more subtle dimensions and profound depths.[5]

We make an effort now to isolate some of those assumptions in the American reflective tradition, which I regard as salutary in the formulation of a new world consciousness. In historical and philosophical terms, of most importance has been the long-standing priority given to the notion of experience in the development of an American reflective tradition, a tradition emergent through continuous geographical shifts and constantly infused with the presence of generation after generation of new people from old lands. The literature of early America—John Smith, the Puritans, and subsequent commentaries on the continuing waves of settlement of "free land"—attests to this re-formation and ultimately re-formulation of basic value structures under the press of a new setting. The realization of this new setting was the dominant theme of the second-generation Puritans, of whom Perry Miller said: "Having failed to rivet the eyes of the world upon their city on a hill, they were left alone with America."[6] The stage was set for a long series of transactions between theoretical structures and a primitive but malleable environment.

What is crucial here, from the philosophical side, is that the press of environment as a decisive formulator of thought about the basic structures of the world became the outstanding characteristic of the American temperament. Nineteenth century pragmatism, so often regarded as the typically American philosophical product, is but a pale reflection of an ingrained attitude affirming the supremacy of experience over thought. It should be emphasized that this sense of the ineptness of a priori and defining concepts for managing experience was not only paramount in the early colonial period but was characteristic of the growth of American culture until the end of the nineteenth century. This is true not only for those who lived at the behest of daily experience, but also for those whose responsibility involved an articulation of general responses to the life-situation. The tension between beliefs held and experiences generated by incessantly novel circumstances, often of a physical kind, is a central theme in the thought of John Winthrop, Jonathan Edwards, Horace Bushnell, Emerson, Whitman, and, of course, James and Dewey, to say nothing of the major lines of political literature. For the most part, that tradition of American *thought* which we now regard as seminal and even patriarchal, clearly sides with experience over reflection as the primary resource in formulating beliefs.

The message here is that in a very real sense each generation is faced with using the method of experience to develop a language that is consonant with the events and potentialities of its own situation. Such a transformation of the meaning of experience was accomplished by American philosophy at the end of the nineteenth century. Not only did this tradition, beginning with Chauncey Wright, effect a reworking of the properly philosophical meaning of experience, but it also provided an extensive set of metaphors, capable of being utilized in the reworking of social and political consciousness. By comparison with any other version of western culture this deeply felt American attitude forces theoretical statements to respond more to the language of events than to its own mode of discourse. What must not be forgotten is the primal fact that the American tradition of which we speak, due to its aversion to any separate mode of discourse, cannot be adequately confronted simply by an epistemological critique of its shortcomings. Historically considered, this tradition was faced with an ever-shifting scene, characterized by widespread geographical, political and spiritual upheavals. These crises were built into the very continuity of the culture, and it was thereby fitting that basic and even fundamental categories of understanding were transformed. Indeed, this transformation had its basis in the willingness of the culture, over a sustained period of time, to listen to the informing character of experience. This was a culture which knew what learning meant and, significantly, was heir to a great tradition of learning. Yet, it was also able to accept the press of experience without necessarily submitting such a transaction to the judgment of a conceptual framework. Although our openness to experience has been well documented in terms of the development of our political institutions, it has not been adequately understood as a broader doctrine of inquiry. Efforts in this latter direction have too often separated the concern for experience from the reflective attitude, thereby failing to realize that in the American context reflection is not necessarily the bearer of traditional intellectual values.

It is, therefore, not unimportant that, in a general way, the American tradition involves a crucial shift in the method for ascertaining the major focus of inquiry. Because of the pre-eminence of the experience of nature as open and as subject to reconstruction, the prime analogates for inquiry have centered on life metaphors. From the very outset, the notions of growth, experiment, liberty, and amelioration have characterized inquiry in American life. This holds not only for those endeavors traditionally directed to so-called practical concerns; these notions equally constituted the very fibre of religious thought. Indeed, more revealing, such concerns are at the center of the American philosophical tradition, when it finally emerges in the nineteenth century. With Emerson and again with Dewey, we have a philosophical approach which uses the language of ordinary experience. In a word, the *problematic* assumes the primary role, reserved elsewhere in philosophy for the ineffable, the good, or the language of being. In such a worldview, the most profound recesses of reflection are themselves burdened by the obligation to reconstruct experience so as to aid in the resolution of those difficulties seen to hinder growth. The passion for amelioration of the human plight, so carefully nurtured by the French *philosophes*, becomes almost a total cast of mind within the American tradition. Such a view is clearly put by Dewey, when he states that "Philosophy recovers itself when it ceases to be a device for dealing with the problems of philosophers and becomes a method cultivated by philosophers, for dealing with the problems of men."[7] Or again by James, who tells us that "Knowledge about life is one thing; effective occupation of a place in life, with its dynamic currents passing through your being, is another."[8] Thus, American classical philosophy comprises a highly original effort to maintain a genuinely metaphysical concern with the finite limits of time and nature. This endeavor is most obviously characterized by the refusal to separate the efforts of intellectual life, including those of philosophy, from the burden of confronting concrete problems. And in so doing, this approach affirms the seminal character of the things and affairs of ordinary experience. Dewey, for one, warns us of the dangers inherent in a downplay of the ordinary. "To waste of time and energy, to disillusionment with life that attends every deviation from concrete experience must be added the tragic failure to realize the value that intelligent search could reveal and mature among the things of ordinary experience."[9]

The American literary and philosophical tradition at its richest is characterized by such a celebration of the things and affairs of ordinary experience. It is also characterized by an aesthetic rendering of vernacularity; long before modern art and existential thought, the American reflective tradition stressed the riches and dangers of temporality, while warning against over-beliefs and assorted premises of salvation. We are a people aware that the sacred and the accursed, the precarious and the stable, are alternating realizations of the same thing, the same event, the same situation. Despite our vast powers, we are a people whose journey through modern history has been striated with blocked expectations, surprises, disasters, bypasses and only periodic realizations, relative to our hopes. Surely, the new global world cannot afford to be innocent of such a history. Active also in the American tradition is the assumption that the most perilous threat to a creative human life and culture is second-handedness, by which we live out the bequest of others, especially those who dispense already programmed possibilities. One bequest, then, of America to the new world is to be wary of all bequests, even those noble in intention, for it is the quality of experience as actually undergone by the culture that proves decisive for viability and a creative future.

The question confronting us is not so much the prospect of philosophy in the new world, nor is it the prospect of America in the new world. Rather we should focus on those philosophical dimensions of American culture which deserve to become operative factors in the formulation of a new world culture. Worthy of detailed analysis, these warranted assumptions of our cultural history are presented here on behalf of further scrutiny so as to assess their future viability. Taking them *seriatim*, I would single out the following commitments:

1. *Pluralism* as a positive and non-lamentable characteristic of the human condition. Pluralism is not a fall from grace or a style biding time for a future unity. Ethnic, religious, racial, social and aesthetic pluralism is a fundamental and fecund characteristic of the human condition. Patterns of unity, however intellectually desirable, are inevitably imposed, usually in a procrustean manner. Pluralism lacks neatness but unity lacks compassion and, being stingy, often misses the potentialities of loose ends.

2. *Provincialism* has a positive side. Surely we know in our time that to think only in terms of ourselves, our race, our nation, is to be cut off from insight and nutrition. Yet, if we do not feel and think deeply about our intimate experiences, what chance do we have of global experience? As twentieth century America has learned, to its chagrin, bigger is not better. Put

simply, neighborhoods are sacred and so too are all the provincial experiences of all the people in global culture.

3. For every step forward, there is one sideward, if not backward. Life is not lived in lineal jumps, but rather in a complex of relations. Modern America, devoted as it is to science and technology, is slowly learning that even majestic breakthroughs often hide time-bombs, set to go off generations hence. The miracle drug of one decade is the uterine cancer of a subsequent decade. One generation's pesticidal success is another's silent spring. As the Greeks knew long ago mythologically, and Anericans now discover scientifically: time extracts a price. The wisdom yielded is that we should not think simply in terms of objects and goals, but also in terms of implications and relations.

4. Finally, the most important operative contention of American cultural history has to do with the ultimate meaning of history, or rather, with the absence of such finality. American culture is chary of ideology, particularly that of an eschatological cast. Calvinist in origin and, therefore, indebted more to the Hebrew than to the Christian scriptures, America has more interest in saving experiences than in salvation outside of time. We are a people deeply sceptical of final solutions and philosophies of history that provide principles of total accountability. Although we tarry and dally with salvation cults of every kind, none seems able to ever get the upper hand. Indeed, in keeping with our pluralism, we have set one nostrum against another, in effect trimming the claim of each by the indulgence of many. Saying it front out, we believe in healing and amelioration, while persistently doubting the presence of any ultimate resolution. It may very well be that we have stumbled on the only viable philosophy of history for a pluralistic world culture.

Coming full circle, the land is one but the people are many. What is the new world to make of itself? A self-conscious planet in an infinite abyss, we alternate between self-preening centrality and cosmic triviality. Perhaps our best strategy, prospect, if you will, is to trim our sails and think in earth terms, albeit with cosmic horizons. The American Thoreau prophesied our collective future:

> All things invite this earth's inhabitants
> To rear their lives to an unheard of height
> And meet the expectation of the land.

In so meeting the expectation of the land, however, we should not forget the American experience and expect too much. Even the world-renowned poet T. S. Eliot, while searching for English origins, reflects rather his childhood in a border state, Missouri—smack in the middle of America. The new world should listen carefully to these American lines of Eliot's:

> There is only the fight to recover
> what has been lost
> And found and lost again and again;
> and now, under conditions
> That seem unpropitious. But perhaps
> neither gain nor loss.[10]

For us there is only the trying. The rest is not our business. What is our business, however, is that we give ourselves over to the problems of the new global world, for this world is not to be discovered. It must be built by all for all.

NOTES

1. Walt Whitman, *Leaves of Grass* (New York: The Modern Library, 1921) p. 24.

2. Ralph Waldo Emerson, "The American Scholar", *Works* (Boston: Houghton, Mifflin and Co., 1904) I, p. 81.

3. Ralph Waldo Emerson, "Nature", *Works*, I, p. 3.

4. Cf. Louis Simpson, "In California", *At the End of the Open Road* (Middletown: Wesleyan University Press, 1963) p. 11.

> Lie back, Walt Whitman,
> There, on the fabulous raft with the King and the Duke!
> For the white row of the Marina
> Faces the Rock. Turn round the wagons here.

5. Sidney E. Mead, "The American People: Their Space, Time and Religion", *The Lively Experiment* (New York: Harper and Row, 1963) pp. 7–8.

6. Perry Miller, *Errand Into the Wilderness* (Cambridge: Harvard University Press, 1956) p. 15.

7. John Dewey, "The Need for a Recovery of Philosophy" in John J. McDermott, ed., *The Philosophy of John Dewey* (New York: G. P. Putnam's Sons, 1973) p. 95.

8. William James, *The Varieties of Religious Experience* (New York: Longmans, Green and Co., 1902) p. 489.

9. John Dewey, *Experience and Nature*, 2nd ed. (La Salle: Open Court, 1929) p. 35.

10. T. S. Eliot, "East Coker", *Four Quartets* (London: Faber and Faber, 1949) p. 31.

PART IV: PUBLIC ISSUES

A. POLITICAL

LIBERALISM

RONALD DWORKIN

Professor of Jurisprudence, Oxford University,
Oxford, England

I

In this essay I shall propose a theory about what liberalism is; but I face an immediate problem. My project supposes that there is such a thing as liberalism, and the opinion is suddenly popular that there is not. Relatively recently—sometimes before the Vietnam War—politicians who called themselves "liberals" held certain positions that could be identified as a group. Liberals were for greater economic equality, for internationalism, for freedom of speech against censorship, for greater equality between the races and against segregation, for a sharp separation of church and state, for greater procedural protection for accused criminals, for decriminalization of "morals" offenses, particularly drug offenses and consensual sexual offenses involving only adults, and for an aggressive use of central government power to achieve all these goals. These were, in the familiar phrase, liberal "causes," and those who promoted these causes could be distinguished from another large party of political opinion that could usefully be called conservative. Conservatives tended to hold the contrary position to each of the classical liberal causes.

But a series of developments have called into question whether liberalism is in fact a distinct political theory. One of these was the war. Kennedy and his men called themselves liberals; so did Johnson, who retained the Kennedy men and added liberals of his own. But the war was inhumane, and discredited the idea that liberalism was the party of humanity. It would have been possible to argue, of course, that the Bundys and Mac Namaras and Rostows were false liberals, who sacrificed liberal principles for the sake of personal power, or incompetent liberals, who did not understand that liberal principles prohibited what they did. But many critics drew the different conclusion that the war had exposed hidden connections between liberalism and exploitation. Once these supposed connections were exposed, they were seen to

253

include domestic as well as external exploitation, and the line between liberalism and conservatism was then thought to be sham.

Second, politics began to produce issues that seemed no longer to divide into liberal and conservative positions. It is not clear, for example, whether concern for protecting the environment from pollution, even at the cost of economic growth that might reduce unemployment, is a liberal cause or not. Consumer protection appeals equally to consumers who call themselves liberal and those who say they are conservative. Many different groups—not only environmentalists and consumer protectionists—now oppose what is called the growth mentality, that is, the assumption that it should be an important aim of government to improve the total wealth or product of the country. It is also fashionable to ask for more local control by small groups over political decisions, not so much because decisions made locally are likely to be better, but because personal political relationships of mutual respect and cooperation, generated by local decisions, are desirable for their own sake. Opposition to growth for its own sake, and opposition to the concentration of power, seem liberal in spirit because liberals traditionally opposed the growth of big business and traditionally supported political equality. But they nevertheless condemn the strategies of central economic and political organization that have, certainly since the New Deal, been thought to be distinctly liberal strategies.

Third, and in consequence, politicians are less likely than before to identify themselves as "liberal" or "conservative," and more likely to combine political positions formerly thought liberal with those formerly thought conservative. President Carter, for example, professes what seem to be "liberal" positions on human rights with "conservative" positions on the importance of balancing the national budget even at the expense of improved welfare programs, and many commentators attribute his unanticipated success to his ability to break through political categories in this way. In Britain as well new combinations of old positions have appeared: the recent Labor government seemed no more "liberal" than the Tories on matters of censorship, for example, and scarcely more liberal on matters of immigration or police procedures. Citizens, too, seem to have switched positions while retaining labels. Many who now call themselves "liberal" support causes that used to be conservative: it is now self-identified "liberals" who want to curtail the regulatory power of the national executive. Politicians and analysts, it is true, continue to use the old categories: they debate, for example, whether Carter is "really" a liberal, and some of them (like George McGovern at a recent meeting of Americans for Democratic Action) still propose to speak for American "liberals." But the categories seem to many much more artificial than they did.

I want to argue that a certain conception of equality, which I shall call the liberal conception of equality, is the nerve of liberalism. But that supposes that liberalism is an authentic and coherent political morality, so that it can make sense to speak of "its" central principle, and these developments may be taken to suggest that that is not so. They may seem to support the following sceptical thesis instead: "The word 'liberalism' has been used, since the eighteenth century, to describe various distinct clusters of political positions, but with no important similarity of principle among the different clusters called 'liberal' at different times. The explanation of why different clusters formed in various cir- cumstances, or why they were called 'liberal,' cannot be found by searching for any such principle. It must be found instead in complicated accidents of history, in which the self-interest of certain groups, the prevalence of certain political rhetoric, and many other discrete factors play different parts. One such cluster was formed, for such reasons, in the period of the New Deal: it combined an emphasis on less inequality and greater economic stability with more abundant political and civil liberty for the groups then campaigning for these goals. Our contemporary notion of 'liberal' is formed from that particular package of political aims.

"But the forces that formed and held together that package have now been altered in various ways. Businessmen, for example, have now come to see that various elements in the package— particularly those promoting economic stability—work very much in their favor. White working men have come to see that certain sorts of economic and social equality for racial minorities threaten their own interests. Political liberties have been used, not merely or even mainly by those anxious to achieve the limited economic equality of the New Deal, but also by social rebels who threaten ideals of social order and public decency that the old liberal did not question. The question of Israel, and Soviet violations of the rights of intellectuals, have led the old liberal to withdraw his former tolerance for the Soviet Union and the expansion of its power. So New Deal 'liberalism,' as a package of political positions, is no longer an important political force. Perhaps a new cluster of positions will form which will be called 'liberal' by its supporters and critics. Perhaps not. It does not much matter, because the new cluster, whether it is called liberalism or not, will bear no important connections of principle to the old liberalism. The idea of liberalism as a fundamental political theory that produced the package of liberal causes, is a myth with no explantory power whatsoever."

That is the sceptic's account. There is, however, an alternative account of the break-up of the liberal package of ideas. In any coherent political program, there are two elements: constitutive political positions, that are valued for their own sake, and derivative positions that are valued as strategies, as means of achieving the constitutive positions.[1] The sceptic believes that the liberal package of ideas had no constitutive political morality at all; it was a package formed by accident and held together by self-interest. The alternate account argues that the package had a constitutive morality, and has come apart, to the extent it has, because it has become less clear which derivative positions best serve that constitutive morality.

On this account, the break-up of New Deal liberalism was the consequence, not of any sudden disenchantment with that fundamental political morality, but rather of changes in opinion and circumstance that made it doubtful whether the old strategies for enforcing that morality were right. If this alternate account is right, then the idea of liberalism as a fundamental political morality is not only not a myth, but is an idea necessary to any adequate account of modern political history, and to any adequate analysis of contemporary political debate. That conclusion will, of course, appeal to those who continue to think of themselves as liberals. But it must also be the thesis of critics of liberalism; at least of those who suppose that liberalism, in its very nature, is exploitative, or destructive of important values of community, or in some other way malign. For these comprehensive critics, no less than partisans, must deny that the New Deal liberal settlement was a merely accidental coincidence of political positions.

But of course we cannot decide whether the sceptical account or this alternative account is superior until we provide, for the latter, some theory about which elements of the liberal package are to be taken as constitutive and which derivative. Unfortunately liberals and their critics disagree, both between and within the two groups, about that very issue. Critics often say, for example, that liberals are committed to economic growth, to the bureaucratic apparatus of government and industry necessary for economic growth, and to the form of life in which growth is pursued for its own sake, a form of life that emphasizes competition, individualism and material satisfactions. It is certainly true that politicians often considered paradigmatic liberals, like Hubert Humphrey and Roy Jenkins, have emphasized the need for economic growth. But is this emphasis on growth a matter of constitutive principle because liberalism is tied to some form of utilitarianism that makes overall prosperity a good in itself? If so, then the disenchantment of many liberals with the idea of growth argues for the sceptical view that liberalism was a temporary alliance of unrelated political positions that has now been abandoned. Or is it a matter of derivative strategy within liberal theory—a debatable strategy for reducing economic inequality, for example—and therefore a matter on which liberals might disagree without deep schism or crisis? This question cannot be answered simply by pointing to the conceded fact that many who call themselves liberals once supported economic development more enthusiastically than they do now, any more than it can be shown that there is a connection of principle between imperialism and liberalism simply by naming men who call themselves liberals and were among those responsible for Vietnam. The vital questions here are questions of theoretical connection, and simply pointing at history, without at least some hypothesis about the nature of those connections, is useless.

The same question must be raised about the more general issue of the connection between liberalism and capitalism. It is certainly true that most of those who have called themselves liberals, both in America and Britain, have been anxious to make the market economy more fair in its workings and results, or to mix a market and collective economy, rather than to replace the market economy altogether with a plainly socialist system. That is the basis for the familiar charge that there is no genuine difference, within the context of western politics, between liberals and conservatives. But once again different views about the connection between capitalism and liberalism are possible. It may be that the constitutive positions of New Deal liberalism must include the principle of free enterprise itself, or principles about liberty that can only be satisfied by a market economy for conceptual reasons. If so, then any constraints on the market the liberal might accept, through redistribution or regulation or a mixed economy, would be a compromise with basic liberal principles, perhaps embraced out of practical necessity in order to protect the basic structure from revolution. The charge, that the ideological differences between liberalism and conservatism are relatively unimportant, would be supported by that discovery. If someone was persuaded to abandon capitalism altogether, he would no longer be a liberal; if many former liberals did so, then liberalism would be crippled as a political force. But perhaps, on the contrary, capitalism is not constitutive but derivative in New Deal liberalism. It might have been popular among liberals because it seemed (rightly or wrongly) the best means of achieving different and more fundamental liberal goals. In that case, liberals can disagree about whether free enterprise is worth preserving under new circumstances, again without theoretical crisis or schism, and the important ideological difference from conservatives may still be preserved. Once again, we must give attention to the theoretical question in order to frame hypotheses with which to confront the political facts.

These two issues—the connection of liberalism with economic growth and capitalism—are especially controversial, but we can locate similar problems of distinguishing what is fundamental from what is strategic in almost every corner of the New Deal liberal settlement. The liberal favors free speech. But is free speech a fundamental value, or is it only a means to some other goal like the discovery of truth (as Mill argued) or the efficient functioning of democracy (as Meiklejohn suggested)? The liberal disapproves of enforcing morality through the criminal law. Does this suggest that liberalism opposes the formation of a shared community sense of decency? Or is liberalism hostile only to using the criminal law to secure that shared community sense? I must say, perhaps out of unnecessary caution, that these questions cannot be answered, at the end of the day, apart from history and developed social theory; but it does not contradict that truism to insist that philosophical analysis of the idea of liberalism is an essential part of that very process.

So my original question—what is liberalism?—turns out to be a question that must be answered, at least tentatively, before the more clearly historical questions posed by the sceptical thesis can be confronted. For my question is just the question of what morality is constitutive in particular liberal settlements like the New Deal package.

My project does take a certain view of the role of political theory in politics. It supposes that liberalism consists in some constitutive political morality that has remained roughly the same over some time, and that continues to be influential in politics. It supposes that distinct liberal settlements are formed when, for one reason or another, those moved by that constitutive morality settle on a particular scheme of derivative positions as appropriate to complete a practical liberal political theory, and others, for their own reasons, become allies in promoting that scheme. Such settlements break up, and liberalism is accordingly fragmented, when these derivative positions are discovered to be ineffective, or when economic or social circumstances change so as to make them ineffective, or when the allies necessary to make an effective political force are no longer drawn to the scheme. I do not mean that the constitutive morality of liberalism is the only force at work in forming liberal settlements, or even that it is the most powerful, but only that it is sufficiently distinct and influential to give sense to the idea, shared by liberals and their critics, that liberalism exists, and to give sense to the popular practice of arguing about what it is.

But the argument so far has shown that the claim that a particular position is constitutive rather than derivative in a political theory will be both controversial and complex. How shall I proceed? Any satisfactory description of the constitutive morality of liberalism must meet the following catalogue of conditions. (a) It must state positions that it makes sense to suppose might be constitutive of political programs for people in our culture. I do not claim simply that some set of constitutive principles could explain liberal settlements if people held those principles, but that a particular set does help to explain liberal settlements because people actually have held those principles. (b) It must be sufficiently well tied to the last clear liberal settlement—the political positions I described at the outset as acknowledged liberal "causes"—so that it can be seen to be constitutive for that entire scheme; so that the remaining positions in the scheme can be seen, that is, to be derivative given that constitutive morality. (c) It must state constitutive principles in sufficient detail so as to discriminate a liberal political morality from other, competing political moralities. If, for example, I say simply that it is constitutive of liberalism that the government must treat its citizens with respect, I have not stated a constitutive principle in sufficient detail, because, although liberals might agree that all their political schemes follow from that principle, conservatives, Marxists and perhaps even fascists would make the same claim for their theories. (d) Once these requirements of authenticity, completeness and distinction are satisfied, then a more comprehensive and frugal statement of constitutive principles meeting these requirements is to be preferred to a less comprehensive and frugal scheme, because the former will have greater explanatory power, and provide a fairer test of the thesis that these constitutive principles both precede and survive particular settlements.

The second of these four conditions provides a starting point. I must therefore repeat the list of what I take to be the political positions of the last liberal settlement, and I shall, for convenience, speak of "liberals" as these who support those positions. In economic policy, liberals demand that inequalities of wealth be reduced through welfare and other forms of redistribution financed by progressive taxes. They believe that government should intervene in the economy to promote economic stability, to control inflation, to reduce unemployment, and to provide services that would not otherwise be provided, but they favor a pragmatic and selective intervention over a dramatic change from free enterprise to wholly collective decisions about investment, production, price and wage. They support racial equality, and approve government intervention to secure it, through constraints on both public and private discrimination in education, housing and employment. But they oppose other forms of collective regulation of individual decision: they oppose regulation of the content of political speech, even when such regulation might secure greater social order, and they oppose regulation of sexual literature and conduct even when such regulation has considerable majoritarian support. They are suspicious of the criminal law and anxious to reduce the extension of its provisions to behavior whose morality is controversial, and they support procedural constraints and devices, like rules against the admissibility of confessions, that make it more difficult to secure criminal convictions.

I do not mean that everyone who holds any of these positions will or did hold them all. Some people who *call* themselves liberal do not support several elements of this package; some who call themselves conservative support most of them. But these are the positions that we use as a meter bar when we ask how liberal or conservative someone is; and indeed on which we now rely when we say that the line between liberals and conservatives is more blurred than once it was. I have omitted those positions that are only debatably elements of the liberal package, like support for military intervention in Vietnam, or the present campaign in support of human rights in communist countries, or concern for more local participation in government or for consumer protection against manufacturers, or for the environment. I have also omitted debatable extension of liberal doctrines, like busing and quotas that discriminate in favor of minorities in education and employment. I shall assume that the positions that are uncontroversially liberal positions are the core of the liberal settlement. If my claim is right, that a particular conception of equality can be shown to be constitutive for that core of positions, we shall have, in that conception, a device for stating and testing the claim that some debatable position is also "really" liberal.

II

Is there a thread of principle that runs through the core liberal positions, and that distinguishes these from the corresponding conservative positions? There is a familiar answer to this question that is mistaken, but mistaken in an illuminating way. The politics of democracies, according to this answer, recognizes several independent constitutive political ideals, the most important of which are the ideals of liberty and equality. Unfortunately, liberty and equality often conflict: sometimes the only effective means to promote equality require some limitation of liberty, and sometimes the consequences of promoting good government consists in the best compromise between the competing ideals, but different politicians and citizens will make that compromise differently. Liberals tend relatively to favor equality more and liberty less than conservatives do, and the core set of liberal positions I described is the result of striking the balance that way.

This account offers a theory about what liberalism is. Liberalism shares the same constitutive principles with many other political theories, including conservatism, but is distinguished from these by attaching different relative importance to different principles. The theory therefore leaves room, on the spectrum it describes, for the radical who cares even more for equality and less for liberty than the liberal, and therefore stands even further away from the extreme conservative. The liberal becomes the man in the middle, which explains why liberalism is so often now considered wishy-washy, an untenable compromise between two more forthright positions.

No doubt this description of American politics could be made more sophisticated. It might make room for other independent constitutive ideals shared by liberalism and its opponents, like stability or security, so that the compromises involved in particular decisions are made out to be more complex. But if the nerve of the theory remains the competition between liberty and equality as constitutive ideals, then the theory cannot succeed. In the first place, it does not satisfy condition (b) in the catalogue of conditions I set out. It seems to apply, at best, to only a limited number of the political controversies it tries to explain. It is designed for economic controversies, but is either irrelevant or misleading in the case of censorship and pornography, and indeed, in the criminal law generally.

But there is a much more important defect in this explanation. It assumes that liberty is measurable so that, if two political decisions each invade the liberty of a citizen, we can sensibly say that one decision takes more liberty away from him than the other. That assumption is necessary, because otherwise the postulate, that liberty is a constitutive ideal of both the liberal and conservative political structures, cannot be maintained. Even firm conservatives are content that their liberty to drive as they wish (for example to drive uptown on Lexington Avenue) may be invaded for the sake, not of some important competing political ideal, but only for marginal gains in convenience or orderly traffic patterns. But since traffic regulation plainly involves some loss of liberty, the conservative cannot be said to value liberty as such unless he is able to show that, for some reason, less liberty is lost by traffic regulation than by restrictions on, for example, free speech, or the liberty to sell for prices others are willing to pay, or whatever other liberty he takes to be fundamental.

But that is precisely what he cannot show, because we do not have a concept of liberty that is quantifiable in the way that demonstration would require. He cannot say, for example, that traffic regulations interfere less with what most men and women want to do than would a law forbidding them to speak out in favor of communism, or a law requiring them not to fix their prices as they think best. Most people care more about driving than speaking for communism, and have no occasion to fix prices even if they want to. I do not mean that we can make no sense of the idea of fundamental liberties, like freedom of speech. But we cannot argue in their favor by showing that they protect more liberty, taken to be an even roughly measurable commodity, than does the right to drive as we wish; the fundamental liberties are important because we value something else that they protect. But if that is so, then we cannot explain the difference between liberal and conservative political positions by supposing that the latter protect the commodity of liberty, valued for its own sake, more effectively than the former.[2]

It might now be said, however, that the other half of the liberty-equality explanation may be salvaged. Even if we cannot say that conservatives value liberty, as such, more than liberals, we can still say that they value equality less, and that the different political positions may be explained in that way. Conservatives tend to discount the importance of equality when set beside other goals, like general prosperity or even security; while liberals, in contrast, value equality relatively more, and radicals more still. Once again, it is apparent that this explanation is tailored to the economic controversies, and fits poorly with the non-economic controversies. Once again, however, its defects are more general and more important. We must identify more clearly the sense in which equality could be a constitutive ideal for either liberals or conservatives. Once we do so we shall see that it is misleading to say that the conservative values equality, in that sense, less than the liberal. We shall want to say, instead, that he has a different conception of what equality requires.

We must distinguish between two different principles that take equality to be a political ideal.[3] The first requires that the government treat all those in its charge *as equals*, that is, as entitled to its equal concern and respect. That is not an empty requirement: most of us do not suppose that we must, as individuals, treat our neighbor's children with the same concern as our own, or treat everyone we meet with the same respect. It is nevertheless plausible to think that any government should treat all its citizens as equals in that way. The second principle requires that the government treat all those in its charge *equally* in the distribution of some resource or opportunity, or at least work to secure the state of affairs in which they all are equal or more nearly equal in that respect. It is, of course, conceded by everyone that the government cannot make everyone equal in every respect, but people do disagree about how far government should try to secure equality in some particular resource; for example, in monetary wealth.

If we look only at the economic political controversies, then we might well be justified in saying that liberals want more equality in the sense of the second principle than conservatives do. But it would be a mistake to conclude that they value equality in the sense of the first and more fundamental principle any more highly. I say that the first principle is more fundamental because I assume that, for both liberals and conservatives, the first is constitutive and the second derivative. Sometimes treating people equally is the only way to treat them as equals; but sometimes not. Suppose a limited amount of emergency relief is available for two equally populous areas injured by floods; treating the citizens of both areas as equals requires giving more aid to the more seriously devastated area rather than splitting the available funds equally. The conservative believes that in many other, less apparent, cases treating citizens equally amounts to not treating them as equals. He might concede, for example, that positive discrimination in university admissions will work to make the two races more nearly equal in wealth, but nevertheless maintain that such programs do not treat black and white university applicants as equals. If he is a utilitarian he will have a similar, though much more general, argument against any redistribution of wealth that reduces economic efficiency. He will say that the only way to treat people as equals is to maximize the average welfare of all members of the community, counting gains and losses to all in the same scales, and that a free market is the only, or best, instrument for achieving that goal. This is not (I think) a good argument, but if the conservative who makes it is sincere he cannot be said to have discounted the importance of treating all citizens as equals.

So we must reject the simple idea that liberalism consists in a distinctive weighting between constitutive principles of equality and liberty. But our discussion of the idea of equality suggests a more fruitful line. I assume (as I said) that there is broad agreement within modern politics that the government must treat all its citizens with equal concern and respect. I do not mean to deny the great power of prejudice in, for example, American politics. But few citizens, and even fewer politicians, would now admit to political convictions that contradict the abstract principle of equal concern and respect. Different people hold, however, as our discussion made plain, very different conceptions of what that abstract principle requires in particular cases.

III

What does it mean for the government to treat its citizens as equals? That is, I think, the same question as the question of what it means for the government to treat all its citizens as free, or as independent, or with equal dignity. In any case, it is a question that has been central to political theory at least since Kant.

It may be answered in two fundamentally different ways. The first supposes that government must be neutral on what might be called the question of the good life. The second supposes that government cannot be neutral on that question, because it cannot treat its citizens as equal human beings without a theory of what human beings ought to be. I must explain that distinction further. Each person follows a more-or-less articulate conception of what gives value to life. The scholar who values a life of contemplation has such a conception; so does the television-watching, beer-drinking citizen who is fond of saying "This is the life," though of course he has thought less about the issue and is less able to describe or defend his conception.

The first theory of equality supposes that political decisions must be, so far as is possible, independent of any particular conception of the good life, or of what gives value to life. Since the citizens of a society differ in their conceptions, the government does not treat them as equals if it prefers one conception to another, either because the officials believe that one is intrinsically superior, or because one is held by the more numerous or more powerful group. The second theory argues, on the contrary, that the content of equal treatment cannot be independent of some theory about the good for man or the good of life, because treating a person as an equal means treating him the way the good or truly wise person would wish to be treated. Good government consists in fostering or at least recognizing good lives: treatment as an equal consists in treating each person as if he were desirous of leading the life that is in fact good, at least so far as this is possible.

This distinction is very abstract, but it is also very important. I shall now argue that liberalism takes, as its constitutive political morality, the first conception of equality. I shall try to support that claim in this way. In the next section of this essay I shall show how it is plausible, and even likely, that a thoughtful person who accepted the first conception of equality would, given the economic and political circumstances of America in the last several decades, reach the positions I identified as the familiar core of liberal positions. If so, then the hypothesis satisfies the second of the conditions I described for a successful theory. In the following section I shall try to satisfy the third condition by showing how it is plausible and even likely that someone who held a particular version of the second theory of equality would reach what are normally regarded as the core of American conservative positions. I say "a particular version of" because American conservatism does not follow automatically from rejecting the liberal theory of equality. The second (or non-liberal) theory of equality holds merely that the treatment government owes citizens is at least partly determined by some conception of the good life. Many political theories share that thesis, including theories as far apart as, for example, American conservatism and various forms of socialism or Marxism, though these will of course differ in the conception of the good life they adopt, and hence in the political institutions and decisions they endorse. In this respect, liberalism is decidedly not some compromise or half-way house between more forceful positions, but stands on one side of an important line that distinguishes it from all competitors taken as a group.

I shall not provide arguments in this essay that my theory of liberalism meets the first condition I described—that the theory must provide a political morality that it makes sense to suppose people in our culture hold—though I think it plain that the theory does meet this condition. The fourth condition requires that a theory be as abstract and general as the first three conditions allow. I doubt there will be objections to my theory on that account.

IV

I now define a liberal as someone who holds the first, or liberal, theory of what equality requires. Suppose that a liberal is asked to found a new state. He is required to dictate its constitution and fundamental institutions. He must propose a general theory of political distribution, that is, a theory of how whatever the community has to assign, by way of goods or resources or opportunities, should be assigned. He will arrive initially at something like this principle of rough equality: resources and opportunities should be distributed, so far as possible, equally, so that roughly the same share of whatever is available is devoted to satisfying the ambitions of each. Any other general aim of distribution will assume either that the fate of some people should be of greater concern than that of others, or that the ambitions or talents of some are more worthy, and should be supported more generously on that account.

Someone may object that his principle of rough equality is unfair because it ignores the fact that people have different tastes, and that some of these are more expensive to satisfy that others, so that, for example, the man who prefers champagne will need more funds if he is not to be frustrated than the man satisfied with beer. But, the liberal may reply, tastes as to which people differ are, by and large, not afflictions, like diseases, but are rather cultivated, in accordance with each person's theory of what his life should be like.[4] The most effective neutrality, therefore, requires that the same share be devoted to each, so that the choice between expensive and less expensive tastes can be made by each person for himself, with no sense that his overall share will be enlarged by choosing a more expensive life, or that, whatever he chooses, his choice will subsidize those who have chosen more expensively.[5]

But what does the principle of rough equality of distribution require in practice? If all resources were distributed directly by the government through grants of food, housing, and so forth; if every opportunity citizens have were provided directly by the government through the provisions of civil and criminal law; if every citizen had exactly the same talents; if every citizen started his life with no more than what any other citizen had at the start; and if every citizen had exactly the same theory of the good life and hence exactly the same scheme of preferences as every other citizen, including preferences between productive activity of different forms and leisure, then the principle of rough equality of treatment could be satisfied simply by equal distributions of everything to be distributed and by civil and criminal laws of universal application. Government would arrange for production that maximized the mix of goods, including jobs and leisure, that everyone favored, distributing the product equally.

Of course, none of these conditions of similarity holds. But the moral relevance of different sorts of diversity are very different, as may be shown by the following exercise. Suppose all the conditions of similarity I mentioned did hold except the last: citizens have different theories of the good and hence different preferences. They therefore disagree about what product the raw materials and labor and savings of the community should be used to produce, and about which activities should be prohibited or regulated so as to make others possible or easier. The liberal, as lawgiver, now needs mechanisms to satisfy the principles of equal treatment in spite of these disagreements. He will decide that there are no better mechanisms available, as general political institutions, than the two main institutions of our own political economy: the economic market, for decisions about what goods shall be produced and how they shall be distributed, and representative democracy, for collective decisions about what conduct shall be prohibited or regulated so that other conduct might be made possible or convenient. Each of these familiar institutions may be expected to provide a more egalitarian division than any other general arrangement. The market, if it can be made to function efficiently, will determine for each product a price that reflects the cost in resources of material, labor and capital that might have been applied to produce something different that someone else wants. That cost determines, for anyone who consumes that product, how much his account should be charged in computing the egalitarian division of social resources. It provides a measure of how much more his account should be charged for a house than a book, and for one book rather than another. The market will also provide, for the laborer, a measure of how much should be credited to his account for his choice of productive activity over leisure, and for one activity rather than another. It will tell us, through the price it puts on his labor, how much he should gain or lose by his decision to pursue one career rather than another. These measurements make a citizen's own distribution a function of the personal preferences of others as well as of his own, and it is the sum of these personal preferences that fixes the true cost to the community of meeting his own preferences for goods and activities. The egalitarian distribution, which requires that the cost of satisfying one person's preferences should as far as is possible be equal to the cost of satisfying another's, cannot be enforced unless those measurements are made.

We are familiar with the anti-egalitarian consequences of free enterprise in practice; it may therefore seem paradoxical that the liberal as lawgiver should choose a market economy for reasons of equality rather than efficiency. But, under the special condition that people differ only in preferences for goods and activities, the market is more egalitarian than any alternative of comparable generality. The most plausible alternative would be to allow decisions of production, investment, price and wage to be made by elected officials in a socialist economy. But what principles should officials use in making those decisions? The liberal might tell them to mimic the decisions that a market would make if it was working efficiently under proper competition and full knowledge. This mimicry would be, in practice, much less efficient than an actual market would be. In any case, unless the liberal had reason to think it would be much more efficient, he would have good reason to reject it. Any minimally efficient mimicking of an hypothetical market would require invasions of privacy to determine what decisions individuals would make if forced actually to pay for their investment, consumption and employment decisions at market rates, and this information gathering would be, in many other ways, much more expensive than an actual market. Inevitably, moreover, the assumptions officials make about how people would behave in a hypothetical market reflect the officials' own beliefs about how people should behave. So there would be, for the liberal, little to gain and much to lose in a socialist economy in which officials were asked to mimic a hypothetical market.

But any other instructions would be a direct violation of the liberal theory of what equality requires, because if a decision is made to produce and sell goods at a price below the price a market would fix, then those who prefer those goods are, *pro tanto*, receiving more than an equal share of the community at the expense of those who would prefer some other use of the resources. Suppose the limited demand for books, matched against the demand for competing uses for wood-pulp, would fix the price of books at a point higher than the socialist managers of the economy will charge; those who want books are having less charged to their account than the egalitarian principle would require. It might be said that in a socialist economy books are simply valued more, because they are inherently more worthy uses of social resources, quite part from the popular demand for books. But the liberal theory of equality rules out that appeal to the inherent value of one theory of what is good in life.

In a society in which people differed only in preferences, then, a market would be favored for its egalitarian consequences. Inequality of monetary wealth would be the consequence only of the fact that some preferences are more expensive than others, including the preference for leisure time rather than the most lucrative productive activity. But we must now return to the real world. In the actual society for which the liberal must construct political institutions, there are all the other differences. Talents are not distributed equally, so the decision of one person to work in a factory rather than a law firm, or not to work at all, will be governed in large part by his abilities rather than his preferences for work or between work and leisure. The institutions of wealth, which allow people to dispose of what they receive by gift, mean that children of the successful will start with more wealth than the children of the unsuccessful. Some people have special needs, because they are handicapped; their handicap will not only disable them from the most productive and lucrative employment, but will incapacitate them from using the proceeds of whatever employment they find as efficiently, so that they will need more than those who are not handicapped to satisfy identical ambitions.

These inequalities will have great, often catastrophic, effects on the distribution that a market economy will provide. But, unlike differences in preferences, the differences these inequalities make are indefensible according to the liberal conception of equality. It is obviously obnoxious to the liberal conception, for example, that someone should have more of what the community as a whole has to distribute because he or his father had superior skill or luck. The liberal lawgiver therefore faces a difficult task. His conception of equality requires an economic system that produces certain inequalities (those that reflect the true differential costs of goods and opportunities) but not others (those that follow from differences in ability, inheritance, etc.). The market produces both the required and the forbidden inequalities, and there is no alternative system that can be relied upon to produce the former without the latter.

The liberal must be tempted, therefore, to a reform of the market through a scheme of redistribution that leaves its pricing system relatively intact but sharply limits, at least, the inequalities in welfare that his initial principle prohibits. No solution will seem perfect. The liberal may find the best answer in a scheme of welfare rights financed through redistributive income and inheritance taxes of the conventional sort, which redistributes just to the Rawlsian point, that is, to the point at which the worst-off group would be harmed rather than benefited by further transfers. In that case, he will remain a reluctant capitalist, believing that a market economy so reformed is superior, from the standpoint of his conception of equality, to any practical socialist alternative. Or he may believe that the redistribution that is possible in a capitalist economy will be so inadequate, or will be purchased at the cost of such inefficiency, that it is better to proceed in a more radical way, by substituting socialist for market decisions over a large part of the economy, and then relying on the political process to insure that prices are set in a manner at least roughly consistent with his conception of equality. In that case he will be a reluctant socialist, who acknowledges the egalitarian defects of socialism but counts them as less severe than the practical alternatives. In either case, he chooses a mixed economic system—either redistributive capitalism or limited socialism—not in order to compromise antagonistic ideals of efficiency and equality, but to achieve the best practical realization of the demands of equality itself.

Let us assume that in this manner the liberal either refines or partially retracts his original selection of a market economy. He must now consider the second of the two familiar institutions he first selected, which is representative democracy. Democracy is justified because it enforces the right of each person to respect and concern as an individual; but in practice the decisions of a democratic majority may often violate that right, according to the liberal theory of what the right requires. Suppose a legislature elected by a majority decides to make some act criminal (like speaking in favor of an unpopular political position, or participating in eccentric sexual practices) not because the act deprives others of opportunities they want, but because the majority disapproves of those views or that sexual morality. The political decision, in other words, reflects not simply some accommodation of the *personal* preferences of everyone, in such a way as to make the opportunities of all as nearly equal as may be, but the domination of one set of *external* preferences, that is, preferences people have about what others shall do or have.[6] The decision invades rather than enforces the right of citizens to be treated as equals.

How can the liberal protect citizens against that sort of violation of their fundamental right? It will not do for the liberal simply to instruct legislators, in some constitutional exhortation, to disregard the external preferences of their constituents. Citizens will vote these preferences in electing their representatives, and a legislator who chooses to ignore them will not survive. In any case, it is sometimes impossible to distinguish, even by introspection, the external and personal components of a political position: this is the case, for example, with associational preferences, which are the preferences some people have for opportunities, like the opportunity to attend public schools, but only with others of the same "background."

The liberal, therefore, needs a scheme of civil rights, whose effect will be to determine those political decisions that are antecedently likely to reflect strong external preferences, and to remove those decisions from majoritarian political institutions altogether. Of course, the scheme of rights necessary to do this will depend on general facts about the prejudices and other external preferences of the majority at any given time, and different liberals will disagree about what is needed at any particular time.[7] But the rights encoded in the Bill of Rights of the United States Constitution, as interpreted (on the whole) by the Supreme Court, are those that a substantial number of liberals would think reasonably well suited to what the United States now requires (though most would think that the protection of the individual from external preferences in the matter of sexual publication and practice are much too weak).

The main parts of the criminal law, however, present a special problem not easily met by a scheme of civil rights that disable the legislature from taking certain political decisions. The liberal knows that many of the most important decisions required by an effective criminal law are not made by legislators at all, but by prosecutors deciding whom to prosecute for what crime, and by juries and judges deciding whom to convict and what sentences to impose. He also knows that these decisions are antecedently very likely to be corrupted by the external preferences of those who make these decisions because those they judge, typically, have attitudes and ways of life very different from their own. The liberal does not have available, as protection against these decisions, any strategy comparable to the strategy of civil rights that simply remove a decision from an institution. Decisions to prosecute, convict and sentence must be made by someone. But he has available, in the notion of procedural rights, a different device to protect equality in a different way. He will insist that criminal procedure be structured to achieve a margin of safety in decisions, so that the process is biased strongly against the conviction of the innocent. It would be a mistake to suppose that the liberal thinks that these procedural rights will improve the *accuracy* of the criminal process, that is, the probability that any particular decision about guilt or innocence will be the right one. Procedural rights intervene in the process, even at the cost of inaccuracy, to compensate in a rough way for the antecedent risk that a criminal process, especially if it is largely administered by one class against another, will be corrupted by the impact of external preferences that cannot be eliminated directly. This is, of course, only the briefest sketch of how various substantive and procedural civil rights follow from the liberal's initial conception of equality; it is meant to suggest, rather than demonstrate, the more precise argument that would be available for more particular rights.

So the liberal, drawn to the economic market and to political democracy for distinctly egalitarian reasons, finds that these institutions will produce inegalitarian results unless he adds to his scheme different sorts of individual rights. These rights will function as trump cards held by individuals; they will enable individuals to resist particular decisions in spite of the fact that these decisions are or would be reached through the normal workings of general institutions that are not themselves challenged. The ultimate justification for these rights is that they are necessary to protect equal concern and respect; but they are not to be understood as representing equality in contrast to some other goal or principle served by democracy or the economic market. The familiar idea, for example, that rights of redistribution are justified by an ideal of equality that overrides the efficiency ideals of the market in certain cases, has no place in liberal theory. For the liberal, rights are justified, not by some principle in competition with an independent justification of the political and economic institutions they qualify, but in order to make more perfect the only justification on which these other institutions may themselves rely. If the liberal arguments for a particular right are sound, then the right is an unqualified improvement in political morality, not a necessary but regrettable compromise of some other independent goal, like economic efficiency.

V

I said that the conservative holds one among a number of possible alternatives to the liberal conception of equality. Each of these alternatives shares the opinion that treating a person with respect requires treating him as the good man would wish to be treated. The conservative supposes that the good man would wish to be treated in accordance with the principles of a special sort of society, which I shall call the virtuous society. A virtuous society has these general features. Its members share a sound conception of virtue, that is, of the qualities and dispositions people should strive to have and exhibit. They share this conception of virtue not only privately, as individuals, but publicly. They believe their community, in its social and political activity, exhibits virtues, and that they have a responsibility, as citizens, to promote these virtues. In that sense they treat the lives of other members of their community as part of their own lives. The conservative position is not the only position that relies on this ideal of the virtuous society (some forms of socialism rely on it as well). But the conservative is distinct in believing that his own society, with its present institutions, is a virtuous society for the special reason that its history and common experience are better guides to sound virtue than any non-historical and therefore abstract deduction of virtue from first principles could provide.

Suppose a conservative is asked to draft a constitution for a society generally like ours, which he believes to be virtuous. Like the liberal, he will see great merit in the familiar institutions of political democracy and an economic market. The appeal of these institutions will be very different for the conservative, however. The economic market, in practice, assigns greater rewards to those who, because they have the virtues of talent and industry, supply more of what is wanted by the other members of the virtuous society; and that is, for the conservative, the paradigm of fairness in distribution. Political democracy distributes opportunities, through the provisions of the civil and criminal law, as the citizens of a virtuous society wish them to be distributed, and that process will provide more scope for virtuous activity and less for vice than any less democratic technique. Democracy has a further advantage, moreover, that no other technique could have. It allows the community to use the processes of legislation to reaffirm, as a community, its public conception of virtue.

The appeal of the familiar institutions to the conservative is, therefore, very different from their appeal to the liberal. Since the conservative and the liberal both find the familiar institutions useful, though for different reasons, the existence of these institutions, as institutions, will not necessarily be a point of controversy between them. But they will disagree sharply over which corrective devices, in the form of individual rights, are necessary in order to maintain justice, and the disagreement will not be a matter of degree. The liberal, as I said, finds the market defective principally because it allows morally irrelevant differences, like differences in talent, to affect distribution, and he therefore considers that those who have less talent, as the market judges talent, have a right to some form of redistribution in the name of justice. But the conservative prizes just the feature of the market that puts a premium on talents prized in the community, because these are, in a virtuous community, virtues. So he will find no genuine merit, but only expediency, in the idea of redistribution. He will allow room, of course, for the virtue of charity, for it is a virtue that is part of the public catalogue; but he will prefer private charity to public, because it is a purer expression of that virtue. He may accept public charity as well, particularly when it seems necessary to retain the political allegiance of those who would otherwise suffer too much to tolerate a capitalist society at all. But public charity, justified either on grounds of virtue or expediency, will seem to the conservative a compromise with the primary justification of the market, rather than, as redistribution seems to the liberal, an improvement in that primary justification.

Nor will the conservative find the same defects in representative democracy that the liberal finds there. The conservative will not aim to exclude moralistic or other external preferences from the democratic process by any scheme of civil rights; on the contrary, it is the pride of democracy, for him, that external preferences are legislated into a public morality. But the conservative will find different defects in democracy, and will contemplate a different scheme of rights to diminish the injustice they work.

The economic market distributes rewards for talents valued in the virtuous society, but since these talents are unequally distributed, wealth will be concentrated, and the wealthy will be at the mercy of an envious political majority anxious to take by law what it cannot take by talent. Justice requires some protection for the successful. The conservative will be (as historically he has been) anxious to hold some line against extensions of the vote to those groups most likely to be envious, but there is an apparent conflict between the ideals of abstract equality, even in the conservative conception, and disenfranchisement of large parts of the population. In any case, if conservatism is to be politically powerful, it must not threaten to exclude from political power those who would be asked to consent, formally or tacitly, to their own exclusion. The conservative will find more appeal in the different, and politically much more feasible, idea of rights to property.

These rights have the same force, though of course radically different content, as the liberal's civil rights. The liberal will, for his own purposes, accept some right to property, because he will count some sovereignty over a range of personal possessions essential to dignity. But the conservative will strive for rights to property of a very different order; he will want rights that protect, not some minimum dominion over a range of possessions independently shown to be desirable, but an unlimited dominion over whatever has been acquired through an institution that defines and rewards talent.

The conservative will not, of course, follow the liberal in the latter's concern for procedural rights in the criminal process. He will accept the basic institutions of criminal legislation and trial as proper; but he will see, in the possible acquittal of the guilty, not simply an inefficiency in the strategy of deterrence, but an affront to the basic principle that the censure of vice is indispensable to the honor of virtue. He will believe, therefore, that just criminal procedures are those that improve the antecedent probability that particular decisions of guilt or innocence will be accurate. He will support rights against interrogation or self-incrimination, for example, when such rights seem necessary to protect against torture or other means likely to elicit a confession from the innocent; but he will lose his concern for such rights when non-coercion can be guaranteed in other ways.

The fair-minded conservative will be concerned about racial discrimination, but his concern will differ from the concern of the liberal, and the remedies he will countenance will also be different. The distinction between equality of opportunity and equality of result is crucial to the conservative: the institutions of the economic market and representative democracy cannot achieve what he supposes they do unless each citizen has an equal opportunity to capitalize on his genuine talents and other virtues in the contests these institutions provide. But since the conservative knows that these virtues are unequally distributed, he also knows that equality of opportunity must have been denied if the outcome of the contest is equality of result.

The fair conservative must, therefore, attend to the charge that prejudice denies equality of opportunity between members of different races, and he must accept the justice of remedies designed to reinstate that equality, so far as this may be possible. But he will steadily oppose any form of "affirmative action" that offers special opportunities, like places in medical school or jobs, on criteria other than some proper conception of the virtue appropriate to the reward.

The issue of gun control, which I have thus far not mentioned, is an excellent illustration of the power of the conservative's constitutive political morality. He favors strict control of sexual publication and practice, but he opposes parallel control of the ownership or use of guns, though of course guns are more dangerous than sex. President Ford, in the second Carter-Ford debate, put the conservative position of gun control especially clearly. Sensible conservatives do not dispute that private and uncontrolled ownership of guns leads to violence, because it puts guns in circulation that bad men may use badly. But, as President Ford said, if we meet that problem by not allowing good men to have guns, we are punishing the wrong people. It is, of course, distinctive to the conservative's position to regard regulation as condemnation and hence as punishment. But he must regard regulation that way, because he believes that opportunities should be distributed, in a virtuous society, so as to promote virtuous acts at the expense of vicious ones.

VI

In place of a conclusion, I shall say something, though not much, about two of the many important questions raised by what I have said. The first is the question posed in the first section of the essay. Does the theory of liberalism I described answer the sceptical thesis? Does it explain our present uncertainty about what liberalism now requires, and whether it is a genuine and tenable political theory? A great part of that uncertainty can be traced, as I said, to doubts about the connections between liberalism and the suddenly unfashionable idea of economic growth. The opinion is popular that some form of utilitarianism, which does take growth to be a value in itself, is constitutive of liberalism; but my arguments, if successful, show that this opinion is a mistake. Economic growth, as conventionally measured, was a derivative element in New Deal liberalism. It seemed to play a useful role in achieving the complex egalitarian distribution of resources that liberalism requires. If it now appears that economic growth injures more than it aids the liberal conception of equality, then the liberal is free to reject or curtail growth as a strategy. If the effect of growth is debatable, as I believe it is, then liberals will be uncertain, and appear to straddle the issue.

But the matter is more complicated than that analysis makes it seem, because economic growth may be deplored for many different reasons, some of which are plainly not available to the liberal. There is a powerful sentiment that a simpler way of life is better, in itself, than the life of consumption most Americans have recently preferred; this simpler life requires living in harmony with nature, and is therefore disturbed when, for example, a beautiful mountainside is spoiled by strip mining for the coal that lies within it. Should the mountainside be saved, in order to protect a way of life that depends upon it, either by regulation that prohibits mining, or by acquisition with taxpayers' money for a national park? May a liberal support such policies, consistently with his constitutive political morality? If he believes that government intervention is necessary to achieve a fair distribution of resources, on the ground that the market does not fairly reflect the preferences of those who want a park against those who want what the coal will produce, then he has a standard, egalitarian reason for supporting intervention. But suppose he does not believe that, but rather believes that those who want the park have a superior conception of what a truly worthwhile life is. A non-liberal may support conservation on that theory; but a liberal may not.

Suppose, however, that the liberal holds a different, more complex, belief about the importance of preserving natural resources. He believes that the conquest of unspoilt terrain by the consumer economy is self-fueling and irreversible, and that this process will make a way of life that has been desired and found satisfying in the past unavailable to future generations, and indeed to the future of those who now seem unaware of its appeal. He fears that his way of life will become unknown, so that the process is not neutral amongst competing ideas of the good life, but in fact destructive of the very possibility of these. In that case the liberal has reasons for a program of conservation that are not only consistent with his constitutive morality, but in fact sponsored by it.

I raise these possible lines of argument, not to provide the liberal with an easier path to a popular political position, but to illustrate the complexity of the issues that the new politics has provided. Liberalism seems precise and powerful when it is relatively clear what practical political positions are derivative from its fundamental constitutive morality; on these occasions politics allows what I called a liberal settlement of political positions. But such a settlement is fragile, and when it dissolves liberals must regroup, first through study and analysis, which will encourage a fresh and deeper understanding of what liberalism is, and then through the formation of a new and contemporary program for liberals. The study and theory are not yet, and the new program is not yet tomorrow.

The second question I wish to mention, finally, is a question I have not touched at all. What is to be said in favor of liberalism? I do not suppose that I have made liberalism more attractive by arguing that its constitutive morality is a theory of equality that requires official neutrality amongst theories of what is valuable in life. That argument will provoke a variety of objections. It might be said that liberalism so conceived rests on scepticism about theories of the good, or that it is based on a mean view of human nature that assumes that human beings are atoms who can exist

and find self-fulfillment about from political community, or that it
is self-contradictory because liberalism must itself be a theory of
the good, or that it denies to political society its highest function
and ultimate justification, which is that society must help its
members to achieve what is in fact good. The first three of these
objections need not concern us for long, because they are based on
philosophical mistakes which I can quickly name if not refute.
Liberalism cannot be based on scepticism. Its constitutive morality
provides that human beings must be treated as equals by their
government, not because there is no right and wrong in political
morality, but because that is what is right. Liberalism does not rest
on any special theory of personality, nor does it deny that most
human beings will think that what is good for them is that they be
active in society. Liberalism is not self-contradictory: the liberal
conception of equality is a principle of political organization, is
required by justice, not a way of life for individuals; and liberals,
as such, are indifferent as to whether people choose to speak out on
political matters, or to lead eccentric lives, or otherwise to behave
as liberals are supposed to prefer.

But the fourth objection cannot so easily be set aside. There is
no easy way to demonstrate the proper role of institutions that have
a monopoly of power over the lives of others; reasonable and moral
men will disagree. The issue is at bottom the issue I identified:
what is the content of the respect that is necessary to dignity and
independence? That raises problems in moral philosophy and in the
philosophy of mind that are fundamental for political theory
though not discussed here; but this essay does bear on one issue
sometimes thought to be relevant. It is sometimes said that
liberalism must be wrong because it assumes that the opinions
people have about the sort of lives they want are self-generated,
whereas these opinions are in fact the products of the economic
system or other aspects of the society in which they live. That
would be an objection to liberalism if liberalism were based on
some form of preference-utilitarianism which argued that justice in
distribution consists in maximizing the extent to which people have
what they happen to want. It is useful to point out, against that
preference-utilitarianism, that since the preferences people have are
formed by the system of distribution already in place, these
preferences will tend to support that system, which is both circular
and unfair. But liberalism, as I have described it, does not make
the content of preferences the test of fairness in distribution. On
the contrary, it is anxious to protect individuals whose needs are

special or whose ambitions are eccentric from the fact that more popular preferences are institutionally and socially reinforced, for that is the effect and justification of the liberal's scheme of economic and political rights. Liberalism responds to the claim, that preferences are caused by systems of distribution, with the sensible answer that in that case it is all the more important that distribution be fair in itself, not as tested by the preferences it produces.

NOTES

1. I shall provide, in this footnote, a more detailed description of this distinction. A comprehensive political theory is a structure in which the elements are related more or less systematically, so that very concrete political positions (like the position that income taxes should now be raised or reduced) are the consequences of more abstract positions (like the position that large degrees of economic inequality should be eliminated) that are in turn the consequences of still more abstract positions (like the position that a community should be politically stable) that may be the consequences of more abstract positions still. It would be unrealistic to suppose that ordinary citizens and politicians, or even political commentators or theoreticians, organize their political convictions in that way; yet anyone who supposes himself to take political decisions out of principle would recognize that some such organization of his full position must be possible in principle.

We may therefore distinguish, for any full political theory, between constitutive and derivative political positions. A constitutive position is a political position valued for its own sake: a political position such that any failure fully to secure that position, or any decline in the degree to which it is secured, is *pro tanto* a loss in the value of the overall political arrangement.

A constitutive position is not necessarily absolute, within any theory, because a theory may contain different and to some degree antagonistic constitutive positions. Even though a theory holds, for example, that a loss in political equality is *pro tanto* a loss in the justice of a political arrangement, it may nevertheless justify that loss in order to improve prosperity, because overall economic prosperity is also a constitutive position within the theory. In that case, the theory might recommend a particular economic arrangement (say a mixed capitalistic and socialistic economy) as the best compromise between two constitutive political positions, neither of which may properly be ignored. Neither equality nor overall well-being would be absolute, but both would be constitutive, because the theory would insist that if some means *could* be found to reach the same level of prosperity without limiting equality, then that result would be an improvement in justice over the compromise that is, unfortunately, necessary. If, on the other hand, the theory recognized that free enterprise was on the whole the best means of securing economic prosperity, but stood ready to abandon free enterprise, with no sense of any compromise, on those few occasions when free enterprise is not efficient, then free enterprise would be, within that theory, a derivative position. The theory would not argue that if some other means of reaching the same prosperity could be found, without curtailing free enterprise, that other means would be superior; if free enterprise is only a derivative position, then the theory is indifferent whether free enterprise or some other derivative position is sacrificed to improve the overall state-of-affairs. We must be careful to distinguish the question of whether a particular position is constitutive within a theory from the different question of whether the theory insulates the position by arguing that it is wrong to re-examine the value of the position on particular occasions. A theory may provide that some derivative positions should be more or less insulated from sacrifice on specified occasions, even when officials think that such a sacrifice would better serve constitutive positions, in order better to protect these constitutive goals in the long run. Rule utilitarianism is a familiar example, but the constitutive goals to be protected need not be utilitarian. A fundamentally egalitarian political theory might take political equality (one man, one vote) as an insulated though derivative position, not allowing officials to rearrange voting power to reach what they take to be a more fundamental equality in the community, because a more fundamental equality will be jeopardizing rather than served by allowing tinkering with the franchise. Insulated derivative positions need not be absolute—a theory may provide that even an insulated position may be sacrificed, with no loss in overall justice even *pro tanto*, when the gain to constitutive positions is sufficiently apparent and pronounced. But insulated positions might be made absolute without losing their character as derivative.

2. See Dworkin, *Taking Rights Seriously*, London, Duckworth, 1977, chapter 12.

3. See *Taking Rights Seriously*.

4. T. M. Scanlon, "Preference and Urgency", *Journal of Philosophy*, 72 (1975), 655–669.

5. A very different objection calls attention to the fact that some people are afflicted with incapacities like blindness or mental disease, so that they require more resources to satisfy the *same* scheme of preferences. That is a more appealing objection to my principles of rough equality of treatment, but it calls, not for choosing a different basic principle of distribution, but for corrections in the application of the principle like those I consider later.

6. *Taking Rights Seriously*.

7. See Dworkin, "Social Sciences and Constitutional Rights," *The Educational Forum* XLI (March 1977) 271.

ON RONALD DWORKIN'S LIBERALISM AND CONSERVATISM*

VIRGINIA HELD

Hunter College and the Graduate School of the City University of New York, New York City

Professor Dworkin has been admirably unafraid to use labels we all find useful. Those who shun such labels too often shun the criticism their positions deserve and hide behind a screen of evasion. So I accept his use of the terms "liberal" and "conservative." I agree with him that the distinction between them cannot well be found in their differing valuations of liberty and equality, though I would formulate the lack of difference somewhat differently. Professor Dworkin argues that liberals value liberty as much as conservatives. It might be more accurate, I think, to say that liberals have as limited a conception of liberty as conservatives, and thereby invite similar avoidable conflicts between the claims of liberty and equality. Professor Dworkin argues, perhaps surprisingly, that conservatives value equality—in the sense of according all persons equal concern and respect—as much as liberals. It might be more accurate, I think, to say that liberals share with conservatives a conception of equality derived from the same tradition, and share its defects.

I think Professor Dworkin dismisses far too casually the connection between the conservative and liberal positions and the self-interest of the holders of these positions. I think a slight re-interpretation of the evidence would strengthen the case for such a connection. But I am willing to acknowledge that if one *searches* one *may* find conservatives and liberals who hold their positions on the basis of reasoned moral principles, not mere self-interest. And so, thinking of them in this way, I shall concentrate on what Professor Dworkin takes to be the major difference between the liberal and conservative positions, namely, their conflicting views on the right relation between morality and politics. The conservative, he says, thinks that government ought to be used to promote virtue in the society, the liberal thinks that it ought not.

As Professor Dworkin explains them, it may seem difficult to choose between the liberal and conservative outlooks, though he himself chooses the liberal. I shall try to explain why I find both of the positions he describes seriously inadequate.

282

And I will try to suggest a third position. The third position will share with the conservative one the view that a conception of the good society ought to be used in judging political activity, and ought to be reflected in our choice of political policies. It will reject the liberal view that morality has no place in public life beyond that which, on the basis of moral principles, can be incorporated into legal rights. But on questions of what virtue *is* and what has it, and on its stands towards the issues on Professor Dworkin's list, this third position would be much closer to the liberal one than to the conservative one.

I will label this third position the "not wrong" position. In terms of a political left and right, it is certainly not a position *on* the right. And it would be misleading to call it "not liberal" since on many issues it would be closer to the liberal position than to the conservative one. In depicting its relation to the conservative and liberal positions Professor Dworkin describes, I would suggest a triangular configuration, rather than a left-right spectrum one. The "not wrong" position would then occupy one corner of the triangle. If anyone wishes to label my position "radical," they can themselves take responsibility for doing so; since Professor Dworkin has told us that the radicals "do not count very much," and since I would not want to use up my limited time on what doesn't count, I shall limit myself here to the labels already specified.

I refrain, on purpose and for good reasons, from calling the third position a synthesis. And I welcome the fact that none of the three positions is shrouded behind a veil of ignorance. All begin with *where we are now* and consider what we, and government, ought to do.

A social theory which will adequately indicate what government ought or ought not to do to seek virtue must be more than a theory about what *government* ought to do. It must also be a theory about what persons ought to do in seeking virtue, especially when government fails. So I will include this question in my discussion, and consider the question to be one concerning the proper relation between politics and morality. This will be a different question from one concerning the proper relation between law and morality. Professor Dworkin distinguishes the area of individual rights, to be determined by principles of fairness, from the area of collective policies, or goals which a society may seek. I do not share his view that rights are always individual and the goals of policies always collective. If actions taken against those who seek to overthrow a state are justified, they are justified in terms of the right of the state to protect its existence, and this must be a collective right. On the other side, the goals of even policies may often be the serving of partial political interests, as when an administration's policy of appointing more persons associated with labor and fewer with business to certain agencies may reflect a policy of responding to labor interests. And the interests pursued by most groups and by individuals are individual interests. But these disagreements are not central to our discussion here.

A more serious one has to do with our conceptions of "politics." In discussing theories of government and of society, Professor Dworkin considers the roles of judges and legislators. But he speaks rather little of political agents who are neither judges nor legislators, namely presidents, cabinet members, agency officials, bureaucrats, lobbyists, voters, political activists, etc. He seldom considers those political acts which are best understood as *neither* components of political policies *nor* based on legal principles. To think of many actions in politics as reflecting choices of policy is to use "policy" so loosely as to undermine its meaning. However, such acts ought still to be judged on moral grounds. I suspect Professor Dworkin's conception of politics to be unduly restricted and formalistic. Accordingly, when I speak of the relation between morality and politics, I will understand "politics" in a sense much wider than as the activity of those who legislate, and, at the same time, as distinct from the activity of those who adjudicate. As I have elsewhere explained, the political system and the legal system seem to me distinct, though overlapping.[1]

In recent decades a solution to the question of the proper relations between morality and politics has been sought in adherence to law. Professor Dworkin's liberal position seems to present a more sophisticated version of this view. It has been suggested that in a pluralistic society such as ours, with different groups holding a wide range of different moral views, and pressing them as political interests, the best, or only possible, resolution of such differences is to be found in the courts, or in legislation concerned with what Professor Dworkin calls fairness. Civil rights issues, the controversies over busing, and abortion, are offered as examples of the plausibility of this position. I would like to argue that it is deficient for two reasons.

First, it assumes that the decisions of what can be described as the legal system will be morally superior to those of what can be described as the political system, and this assumption may be false. Over any extended period of time, mistakes seem well distributed.

Second, it assumes that law and the courts will be able to perform functions which they are not capable of performing.

In the wake of Watergate there has been much loose talk to the effect that morality always requires strict obedience to the law. Anthony Lewis, for instance, has preached in column after column, that no one must ever put himself above the law. We must have, he and others have repeated, "a government of laws, not men" (unfortunately there is little danger of our having—soon—a government of women). We are told that when men in power think of themselves as unbound by the laws that restrict others, *that* is when they become capable of the terrible abuses of power of which the Nixon administration provided such memorable examples.

I think this response to Watergate is misleading. The problem was not simply that the crooks of the White House put themselves above the law, but that the grounds on which they did so were immoral rather than morally justifiable. Of course to put oneself above the law for the sake of excessive personal gain or because of an outrageous lust for power is wrong; but to pursue power for its own sake *within* the law—which can very well be done—is wrong as well. And morality *may* require—in special circumstances— putting oneself outside (a more appropriate term than above) the law. Obedience to law as such, or even to law as *law* ought to be, should never be imagined to be synonymous with morality, nor, I shall argue against Professor Dworkin's liberal, with political morality.

Civil disobedience is by definition a violation of law on grounds of conscience. It may well be morally justifiable in the single acts of individuals who refuse on moral grounds to accept an immoral law or policy. During the Vietnam war, protests against our government's moral crimes were often not hard to justify, though they required citizens to put themselves outside the law. Or, such violations of law may be justifiable in some collective actions such as strikes. We should not forget that the history of the labor movement is replete with actions such as "illegal picketing," "illegal restraint of trade," "illegal interference"—actions which by now are a perfectly standard part of the political-economic workings of the United States and are fully protected as rights in our most basic labor laws. Still, they once required the persons performing them to put themselves "outside the law," though we can now judge such persons to have been acting in ways that were morally justifiable.[2]

Nor need such violations of law on grounds of morality be

confined to plain citizens without official positions in government. Just as civilly disobedient citizens may have to suffer a penalty when the law they have violated is enforced and they are punished, so an official violating the requirements of his office may have to suffer the penalty of dismissal, and this may be in addition to any penalty he will suffer from having violated the same law as a mere citizen. His action may well be morally justifiable, as were the violations by various officials in Nazi Germany of laws pertaining to Jews, and as may have been the actions of some American officials in illegally giving to the press information that hastened the end of some of the worst government excesses in the conduct of the war in Vietnam.

In recent years much concern with the relation of politics and morality has been directed towards deception in high places—as in Watergate and with the CIA and FBI, and towards sexual lapses in low places—such as in the issues of pornography and homosexuality. Concern has been deflected far too successfully from a major area where it most clearly belongs, the area of *economic* immorality. A little attention to corporate bribery is no substitute for the gross inattention given to the lack of moral foundations for most *normal* corporate and economic activity in the United States. And the indifference of officials and electorates to the evils of massive poverty and unemployment ought surely to be judged on moral grounds.

Many things are immoral that the law plainly allows. Citizens may have *moral* rights to a decent minimum of what they need to live, but neither the courts nor the legislatures in the United States have begun to recognize such rights as *legal* rights. For the next several years, although we will not have Nixon, we will have a Nixon Supreme Court. On lower levels and on up through the highest court, we can expect little progress in the recognition of basic economic and welfare rights. And what progress Congress may make is apt to be minimal.

Bringing about a recognition and realization of rights is, I think, a *political* matter in which the actions of agents should be judged on the basis of their consequences, and thus their virtue. Though a theory of rights may recognize *rights* to civil disobedience, it cannot tell us when and how we ought to exercise such rights.[3] Agents cannot look to *law* to answer such questions as when and how to press for the policies and programs and budget allocations that taking rights seriously would require. Such questions of political morality cannot be answered by turning to law but must be answered, directly by an appropriate part of morality. Doing so will tell us, I think, that modest violations of existing law may be justifiable when they contribute to bringing about political progress toward the recognition of rights. And doing so will tell us that persons with political power should respond to such pressures in the political terms of negotiation and settlement, not in the legal terms of either enforcement or nonenforcement. *Political* progress is not made by prosecutors looking the other way.[4] In short, judging the political actions taken to *bring about* a recognition of rights requires a theory of virtue in society, and assuring that rights *come to be* recognized requires much more than fairness.

The second reason we cannot solve the problem of the right relation between morality and politics by appealing to the law is that there are many things the law cannot do and ought not to try to do, even in the best of times, and even should the rights of all eventually be recognized. For even within the law and within the requirements of fairness, alternatives present themselves for choice. Whom should a president gather into his administration? The law cannot tell him. To whom and to what goals should virtuous citizens give their support? The law cannot tell them. On what basis then should the acts and policies of governments and citizens be decided?

Professor Dworkin considers what it would be like to interpret the conservative position that government ought to promote virtue as a utilitarian position. At this point I wondered: what *can* he be getting at? William Buckley a utilitarian? Irving Kristol a utilitarian? In the end Professor Dworkin concedes that of course the conservative position is *not* based on utilitarianism, even unbeknownst to its holders. But then, neither is the liberal position he describes based on utilitarianism, except insofar as utilitarianism might recommend the reflection in *law* of fairness in government. Professor Dworkin has thus left *no one* to argue for a utilitarian morality in politics.

I would like to suggest, as I have argued elsewhere, that although as a complete morality, utilitarianism is deficient, and although as a legal morality, utilitarianism is out of place, as a political morality, it has much to recommend it. It is a vast improvement over the mere reflection, in choosing actions and policies, of the opinions of electorates and pressures of interest groups. And it is better, I think, than the politically amoral liberalism for which Professor Dworkin has made a strong case. For government can, with fairness, bring about no good for anyone, and it can, with only fairness to guide it, further the unhappiness of all equally. And this would be true with *either* a conception of equal treatment or one of treatment as an equal.

For Professor Dworkin, there is a deep disparity between the level of morality appropriate in judicial decisions, and that appropriate in the choice of political policies. He has elsewhere advised judges deciding hard cases to be total moral agents, doing what is required by moral principles which take priority over existing precedents and practices, and he demands from the judicial system as complete a consistency as is humanly possible.[5] But from politicians and those who seek to influence the choice of policies, Professor Dworkin lifts the burden of morality almost completely. Once they have satisfied the requirements of fairness, political agents—whether in government or outside—need not, in Professor Dworkin's view, even *aim* at virtue, and they can throw consistency to the winds. In the folds of such a free-floating politics, I fear, lie the outlines of future Vietnams, future Watergates, of political influence for giant corporations, and malign neglect for those who suffer.

Adherents of the position I have labelled "not wrong" will, like conservatives, appeal to moral grounds to justify political decisions. But of course not all moral grounds are equally valid. Defenders of the third position will appeal to moral grounds with more consistency and plausibility than the patchwork composing conservative positions. For instance, the conservative thinks that conventional sexual morality is a good thing and government *ought* to be used to promote it, the conservative thinks that charity is a good thing but that government ought *not* to be used to promote it, yet the conservative is unable to account for this difference of approach. The conservative favors more governmental activity to apprehend and punish criminals, but less governmental activity to provide potential criminals an alternative means of obtaining necessities. The conservative thinks that government should not interfere with the activities of corporations, which he calls "private," but that it should interfere with what citizens do in bed, which he calls "not private." And this is to speak only of inconsistencies in the conservatives' position on the appropriate role of government. The conservative has, as well, other failings than mere inconsistency.

Conservatives are frequently not interested in evidence, and when the evidence in front of them is unpleasant, or in conflict with their theories, they deny that it should *count* as evidence.

They have refused, for instance, to see poverty as a real condition of suffering, calling it instead a function of our definitions, as we designate a certain proportion of lowest incomes "poor" no matter the absolute amount of these incomes. And at a time when the senior arts and sciences faculty at Harvard University consisted of 483 men and not one single woman, some conservatives asserted that there was no evidence that Harvard had ever discriminated against women in choosing its faculty.

And conservatives easily imagine that their privileges are based on merit and talent. It is a measure of the capacity of many conservatives for self-deception that they actually believe the privileges and powers of white males relative to blacks and females to be an accurate reflection of the superior merit and talent of white males. The conservative claims that he favors rewarding achievement—a defensible position—but he considers that to have got oneself born with certain characteristics is an achievement!

Is the liberal view outlined by Professor Dworkin then the answer? I hardly think so. Conservatives are wrong not because they bring moral objectives into politics but because they too often bring wrong and misconstrued moral objectives into politics. Of course we have to try to distinguish objectives we ought to pursue from those we ought not to pursue, we have to try to sort out good consequences from bad. Of course this is difficult, but any discussion of what the role of government and politics ought to be presupposes that we can at least try to make the relevant moral judgments. There is anyway no way to escape making them, somehow or other, through our actions and decisions. And I think it is unfair to suggest that conservatives have no theory of rights and *only* a theory of virtue.

According to the position I am calling "not wrong," the damage being done by the current political power of conservatives will not be corrected by a return to liberalism's banishment of morality from politics.

Let us not forget that it was liberals who gave us the imperialistic ventures of the Bay of Pigs and the original bombing of North Vietnam. Except when they were violating the law, the policies of the best and the brightest would, I fear, all too often have passed Professor Dworkin's tests for liberal acceptability. And let us not forget that the almost complete non-redistribution of income that has persisted in America unrelievedly for the last thirty years has persisted over years of liberal ascendency as well as in the years of Nixon and Ford.

A liberal politics that does not seek virtue may well be an improvement in some respects over a conservative politics that maintains or increases vice in its misguided search for virtue. But let us not build this temporary and unfortunate fact into a theory of what politics ought to be. What we need is not less moral concern in politics but a better understanding of what morality demands of conscientious political agents.

NOTES

* These comments refer to the version of Ronald Dworkin's paper that was delivered at the Bicentennial Symposium, not to the version in this volume. Many points in Dworkin's original paper have appeared in his "Liberalism," in *Public and Private Morality*, ed. Stuart Hampshire (London: Cambridge University Press, 1978).

1. See V. Held, "Justification: Legal and Political," *Ethics*, LXXXVI, no. 1 (October, 1975).

2. For further discussion see V. Held, "Civil Disobedience and Public Policy," in *Revolution and the Rule of Law*, ed. E. Kent (Englewood Cliffs, N. J., Prentice-Hall, 1971), and V. Held, "On Understanding Political Strikes," in *Philosophy and Political Action*, V. Held, K. Nielsen and C. Parsons, eds. (New York, Oxford University Press, 1972).

3. See R. Dworkin, "Taking Rights Seriously," *New York Review of Books*, December 17, 1970.

4. See R. Dworkin, "On Not Prosecuting Civil Disobedience," *New York Review of Books*, June 6, 1968.

5. See R. Dworkin, "Hard Cases," *Harvard Law Review*, LXXXVIII (1975) 1057.

TWO WAYS OF JUSTIFYING
CIVIL DISOBEDIENCE

REX MARTIN

The University of Kansas, Lawrence, Kansas

In the system of political thought to which Americans are heir (that found in Locke and in the *Declaration of Independence*) there is a deep ambivalence regarding disobedience to law. Locke believed that one was strictly obligated to keep the laws of a constitutionally authorized government, in particular if that state was more or less effective in protecting the rights of citizens. Of course, if the government forfeited its authorization by tampering with the constitution or if it invaded the rights of its subjects, then the obligation was altogether annulled. There was no middle ground: either governmental authority was joined with the citizens' strict obligation to obey the laws or there was a total absence of both authority and allegiance.

The ambivalence results from the fact that an important new way of looking at the citizens' obligation to law has evolved in the intervening years. This new way is conventionally called *civil disobedience*. Some of the things that would be included, definitionally, under this concept are relatively uncontroversial: that it involves a deliberate violation of public law (policy or code), that it is done out of protest and is meant to serve some vital social or moral purpose. After these points, however, we come to a significant divergence in the way the term "civil disobedience" is used.

Some people will say that a knowing or deliberate violation of public law is *civil* only if it is peaceably done (nonviolent) and the violator more or less willingly takes the penalty for his violation. In America we are familiar with this *sense* of "civil disobedience" from the practice and from the pen of Martin Luther King. This can be offered, then, as the crux of a general definition of the term in question: "civil disobedience is a public, nonviolent, submissive violation of law as a form of protest."[1] On the other hand, some people will say that a knowing or deliberate violation of public law is *civil* only if it is done in such a way as to indicate recognition that the laws in question are duly enacted or authoritative. Thus, John Rawls emphasizes that civil disobedience is within the "boundary of fidelity to law."[2] In his opinion, civil disobedience is

291

problematic principally because it is an act of disobedience by citizens who at the same time "recognize and accept the legitimacy of the constitution."[3] And, interestingly, Robert Paul Wolff attaches the notion of civil disobedience to that of the legitimacy of the state when he argues that the demise of the concept of legitimate political authority would completely undercut the very notion of *civil* disobedience.[4]

Now, of course, these two senses of civil disobedience can be blended together in a variety of ways. The important thing to note, though, is that we have two distinct *basic* ways for conceiving civil disobedience: the one way sees protesting and disobedient conduct as "civil" insofar as it is nonviolent and submissive; the other sees that conduct as "civil" insofar as it recognizes the authority of the lawmakers and the authoritativeness of the laws.

I want to suggest in this paper that the way one defines and, by extension, conceives civil disobedience has an important bearing on the way one would go about justifying it. More particularly, I want to show that each of these basic ways of conceiving civil disobedience marks out a distinctive way of relating moral standards to the practice of civil disobedience.

I think it obvious that moral judgment can provide a *reason* for protesting actions or policies of government and for disobeying laws. But when would it provide a good reason for *civil* disobedience? Or, to ask the question another way, when would a conscientious action also be a case of justified civil disobedience? Let us deal with this question by taking up the basic senses in turn.

We can suppose, first, the case of a person who feels constrained to keep his disobedience to law *civil* in the sense of nonviolent and open to reprisals and other actions by the government. Now, why would he require these restraints? The answer is, presumably, that he has moral or, perhaps, religious reasons for eschewing violence and for performing his actions publicly and thereby being open to penalty. Hence, it seems that the kind of reason that dictates his breaking the law in the first place is of the same sort as the reason which dictates that his disobedience be nonviolent and submissive. So the question for him becomes: when do *moral* reasons constitute good grounds both for breaking the law and for doing it in a nonviolent and public way? The answer is that they do so whenever *civil* disobedience, in the nonviolent sense, is morally justified.

In short, when the moral reasons for a certain line of conduct are consistent with or when they require civil disobedience, then we have the case where appeals to conscience can, or do, constitute *good* grounds for civil disobedience. For example, a man whose moral reasons for breaking the law included the belief that injury should not be done to other people would be constrained to the practice of civil disobedience in the nonviolent sense. On the other hand, if the agent's moral reasons for conscientious action did not themselves preclude violence or if he had no important restraint on violence in his other moral beliefs, then his conscientious actions justified civil disobedience; for him there would be no *justified* civil disobedience and hence no such limits.

The point, in each of these cases, is that conscientiousness can constitute good grounds only when civil disobedience is morally justified: that is, when it is morally justified both to break the law and to break it in a nonviolent, submissive manner. Here, then, we have provided a kind of answer to our question. The answer is that conscientious actions can only be limited by conscience itself (that is, by the moral rules themselves appropriately applied); nothing independent of conscience can properly serve as a limit. So, if an action is truly conscientious then it cannot properly be limited by mere *civic* standards. Surely, Thoreau thought this when he said, "The only obligation which I have a right to assume, is to do at any time what I think right." And Howard Zinn, when he said, "If the protest is morally justified (whether it breaks a law or not) it is morally justified to the very end, even past the point where a court has imposed a penalty."[5] And again, "If a specific act of civil disobedience is a morally justifiable act of protest, then the jailing of those engaged in that act is immoral and should be opposed, contested to the very end. The protester need be no more willing to accept the rule of punishment than to accept the rule he broke."[6]

Now let us turn to the other basic sense of civil disobedience, where *civil* has the sense of "recognizing authority." Can this notion of civil disobedience provide any sort of limitation on conscientious actions?

To answer this question, we can again suppose the case of a person engaged in conscientious lawbreaking who feels constrained to keep his disobedience to law *civil*, but this time because he recognizes the authority of the government to make laws and considers the relevant law to be duly enacted. He would appear to have *political* reasons for feeling this constraint. I say this because his categories of thought are political ones: the "authority of government" and "laws duly enacted." He conceives civil disobedience politically. The question for him becomes, when do *political* reasons constitute good grounds for civil disobedience?

The answer would be: when civil disobedience, in the authority-recognizing sense, is *politically* justified.

In short, when the political grounds that he has in such notions as "governmental authority" and "duly enacted laws" are compatible with disobedience to law, under certain conditions, or when they actually license some sorts of disobedience to law, as a feature of the political system that they establish, then we have the case where authority-recognizing disobedience to law is possible. It is only here that the political grounds cited could constitute *good* grounds for civil disobedience. For example, a man who believed a particular government's authority to be founded on the preservation of the citizens' rights to life, liberty, and estate would believe that sometimes disobeying a law is justifiable, or at least allowable, in a state where the protection of these rights is defective; disobedience might be justified, conceivably, when it was a way of protesting an evident defect within the system of rights. Hence, where we have a rights-producing state dedicated to the protection and preservation by law of life, liberty, and estate, then the individual citizen could disobey a rights-law, while at the same time recognizing the basic ground of authority; and that act of disobedience could be, by reference to that same basic ground, *justified.*

On the other hand, we could well imagine a state in which the grounds of authority precluded *civil* disobedience, a state in which its acknowledged character made it impossible both to accept that authority and to disobey the duly enacted laws. For instance, the character of authority of the Guardians in Plato's State (*Republic*, Books 3 and 4) is such that the decrees of the Rulers should not be disobeyed; indeed, we are explicitly told that the "virtue" of the citizen in such a state is simply to do what he is told by the Wise Rulers (see *Republic*, Book 10, the "Myth of Er"). Now, the citizen in that kind of state would have no concept of *justified* civil disobedience, where "civil" has the sense of authority-recognizing and where the justification, if it had existed, would have to rest on the basic political ideal itself. A person in that state could never, no matter what his conscience told him to do, be civilly disobedient; for any time he broke the law, his so acting might be morally conscientious but it could never be civilly justified. Hence, for him the possibility of *civil* disobedience is never available.

Thus, when we talk about civil disobedience in the authority-recognizing sense the discussion must take place *within* a given or determinate theoretic system of political concepts and the question whether *civil* disobedience is ever justified is decided by reference to the other concepts within that same theoretic system. The ground of civil disobedience—whether it is to be allowed or not—and the ground of authority within a system are the same. Hence, the kind of state, the exact nature of the theoretic system of political concepts for that particular state, becomes the crucial question.

We must then determine what conditions are required, in order for an act of disobedience to be civil, by the theoretic system of politics in which the disobedience occurs. These conditions would be the conditions of a justified civil disobedience—that is, if there is to be such a thing—for a given person in that particular state. We can view these conditions as a kind of bridge between that person's recognition of the authority of a government and its laws, on the one hand, and his disobeying of the law civilly, that is, while *still* recognizing that authority, on the other. One might say, then, that the ability to construct such a set of conditions is to state what would count as justified civil disobedience in that particular political system.

If we were to return to our original example of a state whose authority is grounded in its efforts to maintain the rights to life, liberty, and estate of those subject to its duly enacted laws, then we could see more clearly how these conditions are generated. For such a state the conditions would surely include the following two: (1) In disobeying the law, the citizen neither intends nor brings about, in a way that could reasonably be foreseen, a substantial violation of the rights of other citizens (including their right to property); for violation here would be incompatible with the basic goal of preserving the right to life and estate of those subject to that state's laws. (2) The citizen should disobey the law publicly and in willingness to take the legally prescribed penalty for breaking the law; for otherwise he sets himself above the laws and, by so doing, cannot be said to recognize their authority. There are, very likely, other conditions as well; I have specified these two in order to indicate the sort of thing I have in mind when I speak of conditions of a justified civil disobedience in a particular kind of state.

Concern for the preservation of rights (which overlaps considerably with what was earlier described as nonviolence) and willingness to accept penalty are here conceived as features, not of the *definition* of civil disobedience, but of its *justification*. This is one of the important differences between the "moral" sense of civil, in the definition of "civil disobedience," and the "political" sense, where *civil* has the force simply of authority-recognizing. But this is not the most important difference between the moral and the political sense of civil disobedience: the most important difference comes at the point of the relationship between civil disobedience and conscientious actions.

Consider here the mixed case in which a person lives in a state dedicated to protecting the right to "life, liberty, and property" and for whom conscience might provide reasons for disobeying the law. Such reasons might even be described as good *moral* reasons; nonetheless, this act of disobeying the law would count as justified civil disobedience, in the *political* sense, only when the person disobeying the law recognized the authority of the state and acted accordingly. In this event the agent, though acting in disobedience to law for reasons of conscience, would be acting in accordance with principles which underwrote the authority of the government, or at least could be shown to have acted that way; and the agent, in disobeying, would observe "bridge" conditions of the sort already indicated.

The important point is that the "bridge" conditions of civil disobedience (in the political sense)—such as not violating the rights of others and willingness to accept penalty—would impose certain limitations on a person's performance of conscientious actions, that is, they would where he accepted both moral rules and political authority. Or, to put the matter somewhat differently, conscientious actions, even where they are properly regarded as morally approved actions, can be constrained by limitations inherent in a concept of civil disobedience only where that concept has a political as distinct from a moral sense. Thus conscientious actions can be limited other than by conscience itself (that is, by moral rules and so on) only where the alternative standard goes significantly beyond these moral rules into another "domain," the political. Where justified civil disobedience is itself a political idea, it can provide significant limitations to conscientious actions in which laws are disobeyed.

If my analysis is sound there is an intermediate case between that of Lockean strict obligation and moralistic disobedience which is unrestrained politically; for we have the possibility both of recognizing authority in a government and of disobeying some of its laws. This possibility, except in the case of *religious* conscience, did not exist in the political theory of the seventeenth and eighteenth centuries. If it is allowed we have the foundation for a theory of political allegiance significantly different from the obligationist one which prevailed in the past—and one that gives greater scope to the initiative of individual citizens in the fashioning of the laws. This idea, then, of politically justified civil disobedience is perhaps one of the most important contributions of contemporary thought to the stock of traditional civil philosophy.[7]

NOTES

1. James Childress, *Civil Disobedience and Political Obligation* (New Haven, Yale University Press, 1971), p. 11.

2. John Rawls, *Theory of Justice* (Cambridge, Mass., Harvard University Press, 1971), p. 367.

3. *Ibid.*, p. 363.

4. Robert Paul Wolff, "On Violence," *Journal of Philosophy* LXVI (1969), 610 and esp. 611.

5. Howard Zinn, *Disobedience and Democracy* (New York, Random House [Vintage], 1968), p. 30.

6. *Ibid.*, pp. 120–21.

7. For extension and elaboration of my argument, with special reference to the Ellsberg case, see Rex Martin, "Conscientious Actions and the Concept of Civil Disobedience," in *Conscientious Actions: The Revelation of the Pentagon Papers*, ed. Peter A. French (Cambridge, Mass., Schenkman/General Learning Press, 1974), pp. 36–52.

CRITICAL PHILOSOPHY AND SOCIAL CHANGE

MIHAILO MARKOVIC

University of Belgrade, Belgrade, Yugoslavia

The subject that we are discussing today is not only extremely important, indeed fascinating, but also very appropriate to be discussed in this country. Why appropriate here? The least I could say is that during my eight visits to this country during the last fifteen years I have seen quite a lot of change. Every time I came I saw something new, not only quantitatively new, i.e., more, but also involving novelties in human relationships, in styles of life, in institutions. Further, while efforts are being made almost everywhere to create a new and better world, much that passes as new is nothing but all kinds of most bizarre mixtures of genuine novelty with elements of archaic tyranny, feudal obedience, most primitive forms of early capitalist abuse and human degradation.

Unfortunately, the lesson of history seems to be that we cannot fly too high from the ground and if the ground is low then the point that we reach is also not very high. And in this country the ground is already rather high: a high material potential for the satisfaction of basic human needs, a most radical democratic anti-feudal revolution which long ago and I hope for good wiped out certain despotic institutions and habits which will pester many nations for another century.

There is also a consciousness here of the individual as citizen and also a perception of the public official as a public servant, a critical attitude toward leaders. There is a democratic political culture which is a *conditio sine qua non* for any really new more just and free society. This opens great historical possibilities for non-violent progressive development and creation of a new more just and more free world. Whether these possibilities will be realized depends in a crucial way on theory in general, and especially on philosophy.

Unfortunately, philosophy is not always aware of this great historical responsibility. If present-day philosophy is to remain as relevant for human life as it was in the hands of our great predecessors, it must not only analyze, clarify and build up a more precise language of abstract thought, which is necessary and important and will always have to be done, but also must critically

298

examine human historical conditions and explore potentialities of that condition.

The term "philosophy of history" is very often taken to mean only one of the disciplines of philosophy, dealing with either methodology of historical research or the analysis of concepts used in the language of history, which is, as I said, important but too restrictive. The crucial problems are substantial rather than methodological. What happens to human beings in history? What is the nature of their relationships, their communities, quality of their life at a certain stage of historical development? To what extent do they manage to realize their basic capacities and needs under given historical conditions?

What are the essential limitations of their condition in the present? What are the optimal possibilities for the future? Asking such questions is perfectly legitimate and indeed indispensable for rational beings to have a chance of consciously making their own history. On the other hand, when such questions are neither asked nor answered, history becomes mindless, a playground of uncontrollable blind forces.

A critical theory of the present and a vision of the future might be but need not necessarily be Utopian. Even Utopian philosophy of history does not deserve to be brushed aside as a worthless marginal product of intellectual life. Utopian thought is a repository of genuine and universal human aspirations: justice, freedom, equality, communal solidarity, power over nature, creativity. While it is true that too often it gives birth to illusory expectations which end up in tragic frustration, it is also true that some of the most important breakthroughs in history would hardly have been possible without some Utopian illusions, without idealizations of great historical initiatives.

Great social energies necessary to bring about great historical changes and to clear the ground for freer and more rapid development can be set into motion sometimes just by great, exciting, passionately advocated, more or less Utopian ideas.

For all these reasons Utopian philosophy of history cannot simply be written off, but it can be transcended. Its basic theoretical limitations are excessive abstractness of its projections, absence of any mediation between a unique present historical situation and a universal vision of a distant future. And also, a great limitation is a very simplistic view of historical determination.

A critical theory of history will preserve the Utopian general tendency to go beyond the given historical reality, but, far from simply condemning the present and offering an essentially different vision of the future, it will embark on a concrete interdisciplinary study of the given historical situation, its crucial problems, its economic, political and cultural constraints, and actual and possible social forces. Such a critical theory will no longer be pure philosophy and yet its theoretical ground will be constituted by a philosophica study of human being, its basic capacities and needs, its potential for development.

Only a critical theory that is much richer and more concrete than the Utopian is able to mediate between the singular present situation and an optimal future horizon of the whole epoch. And of course this horizon, as we all know, is not the same at every place on earth.

It will be able to indicate specific types of transition and intermediary phases of the process. It will be able to point out the practical steps which are necessary in each phase in order to reach the envisaged objectives. But nothing is certain and nothing is guaranteed in the whole process. Various alternatives remain open all the time. Most Utopias assume a conception of historical determination which is quite obsolete nowadays. There is no linear logic or dialectic of history, no end, no *eschaton* which will inevitably be reached sooner or later.

On the other hand, the historical process is also not so open that one can completely disregard things that happened in the past, the way our ancestors molded their natural and social surroundings and themselves; habits and products of the past are very real constraints excluding many ideal conceivable possibilities, making only a limited set of them likely to occur.

But within this more or less limited framework, we are free to produce our future history and we are able to increase our freedom by raising the level of our knowledge, critically examining and transcending our past conduct, making bold choices, avoiding fruitless, wasteful frictions and coordinating the activity of all those who share some basic commitments.

The last point is of crucial importance for understanding how lonely, socially isolated philosophers can effectively contribute to the conscious making of history. They overcome their loneliness and isolation when they happen to raise precisely those general issues which translate into articulated, theoretical terms, actually experienced grievances, sufferings and needs of large actually or potentially powerful social groups. Philosophy begins to live when its universal ethical and political ideals become a practical standpoint for a vivid, forceful critique of the narrowness, irrationality and inhumanity of actual arrangements in one's *own* society. (It is easy to attack another society.)

The secret of the practical relevance of philosophy is in the meeting of vaguely felt, unarticulated popular needs, and elaborated theoretical projects derived from the immensely rich world of culture and ultimately from accumulated universal experience of hundreds of preceding generations. Without philosophically grounded theory, practical engagement remains shallow, short-lived, inspired only by the meager experience of one generation in one country or one part of the world during a brief interval of time.

Theory is necessary to mediate between this limited particular experience and the comprehensive universal experience of human-kind. The greater the crisis of society and the greater the urgency of radical global solution of existing problems, the greater the objective need for philosophical guidance.

Two clear examples of how philosophy can affect actual history by offering a general orientation to great social change are the American and Russian Revolutions. In both cases, there was a powerful preceding political philosophy which gave clarity, rational justification, durability and deep conviction to the vaguely felt needs of large social groups in a situation of social crisis. The roots of both are a whole humanist tradition since early Stoic philosophy. The root is in great aspirations to freedom, equality and human brotherhood which have been invariant, transcultural themes of human history.

The heart of great emancipatory movements has always been the group, or several groups, which directly suffer and which have the clearest perception of unjust social constraints. But the mind of the emancipation is philosophy. All genuine revolutions have indeed been born in the heads of philosophers. The crucial problem is not the ineffectiveness of philosophical thought but the loss of the original message, in the process of reinterpretation and adaptation to all kinds of historical conditions for which this original message was not meant.

It is in the very nature of philosophy that it cannot be simply applied. Each step in its practical application will be either its crea-tive transcendence or its dogmatic reformulation and vul-garization. The tragedy of revolutionary philosophical thought is that too often, in the hands of victors and carriers of a new political authority, it gets adapted and transformed into a new official ideology, into rationalization and an apology for a new social hierarchy. Neither liberalism nor Marxism was able to escape this destiny.

No theory is safeguarded against this specific form of alienation: loss of control over products of our own intellectual activity, the emergence of practical consequences that betray original intentions. And yet clear awareness of this problem is the starting point of its solution. Philosophy, and science in general, could begin to develop an articulated, critical perception of its own use and misuse, a kind of philosophical praxiology.

The general problem is this: if we treat action-oriented philosophy as a symbolic activity, which can be translated into overt practical activity according to some general principles, then how can we establish those principles in such a way as to minimize the possibilities of degenerate interpretations, and applications which betray the original purpose? Philosophical praxiology demands as much rationality, consistency, critical spirit, openness, clarity and transcultural solidarity in the practical use of theories as in their building. These are special cases of a universal rationality of human behavior. A philosophical praxiology that would demand as much rationality in the practical use of theories as in their building might alert us to the dangers of abuse and help to preserve the original purpose.

What are the prospects for a new world? Whatever deserves to be regarded truly as a new world will probably emerge in a plurality of shapes. There is nothing in the stars nor in the laws of history that strictly determines the outcome of human creativity. But the framework of possibilities among which to choose differs from country to country, depending on the already reached level of material and cultural development, and also depending on the specific objective habits of different social groups formed during preceding history. If we now ask about the future of liberal industrialized Western societies, provided that we are reasonably acquainted with the past and the present, we have first to consider several methods of social change. I have briefly mentioned one such method, namely Utopian projection. Another possible method is the gradual discovery and creation of the future by trial and error. This method could be improved if politics were enlightened by positive science.

Western liberal societies live today with a false dilemma. The only alternative seems to be on the one hand a Utopia of equality which can only be reached by violence and destruction, and which too often ends up in a bureaucratic despotism; and on the other hand an unjust, wasteful reality which nevertheless offers at least a reasonable level of stability, security and civil liberty. But a third alternative is historically possible and indeed optimal: a series of substantial reforms implemented in a non-violent, continuous way, but as a whole transcending the basic social framework of liberal capitalism and bringing to life a more just political and economic participatory democracy. The theoretical ground of such revolutionary reformism is a philosophical and scientific critique of the given society. The method of this critique is the opening and radical solution of its essential problems. Each essential problem is a certain incompatibility between defining structural characteristics of liberal capitalism and some basic universal needs of human beings to survive, to develop, to genuinely belong to a social community.

To solve such problems radically means to reorganize social institutions and structures and make them fit the needs. Five crucial problems deserve to be singled out: privatization, bureaucratization, material and spiritual poverty, alienated labor, and ecological degradation.

As to the first, one of the strongest human needs is to belong to a community, to share some common values with other members of a community, to live in solidarity with them and rationally coordinate individual activities of general social concern. These needs, I am afraid, cannot be fulfilled with existing forms of liberal capitalism. Its economic arrangements make permanent competition and conflict indispensable and push individuals toward increasing privatization. As a surrogate, illusory communities are formed on the basis of shared religious faith or national interest, ultimately on the basis of shared fear.

With the decline of religion, with a sense of growing crisis in social institutions, disintegrative forces tend to prevail over integrative ones. A drastic recent example is the actual or threatening economic breakdown of great American cities, which is unbelievable to many of us from Europe who come and visit America regularly, and the exodus from cities to suburbs which do not satisfy even the minimal conditions to be considered communities. The problem looks insoluble as long as it is believed that the only alternatives are corporate capitalism or state-owned and controlled economies. But there is a third alternative, and it has already been practically tested with very good results, even in the

United States. The solution is a policy of strong social support for public economic enterprises and associations owned and managed by the workers and employees themselves, independently of either corporate capital or the state. Only when aggressive competition, insecurity, envy and hatred are eliminated from the economic sphere can real communal life be brought into existence in the sphere of politics and culture. This is a necessary although not a sufficient condition.

Second, there is a universal human capacity and need to participate in social decision-making. This need is increasingly strong in all liberal Western countries, especially in Scandanavia and Western Europe, and it exists also in this country. This need cannot be fulfilled under the conditions of a mere representative democracy. It is true that in this initial form, democracy, civil liberties are better protected than in any other existing political structure. On the other hand, the increasing role of the state in economy and public welfare has resulted in a quickly growing bureaucracy, abuse of power and corruption. Just at a time when better material conditions of life, more leisure, better quality of education and a high level of political culture have enabled millions of citizens to meaningfully and rationally participate in social decision-making, this natural tendency of further democratization has been blocked by gigantic bureaucratic machinery in the state, the political parties and the enterprises.

The problem again looks insoluble as long as it is believed that the only three alternatives are first, an obsolete *laissez-faire* system where economic coordination and public welfare are completely outside the political sphere; second complete state control over all social processes; or third, bureaucratic control within the framework of a multiparty parliamentary system. But there is a fourth alternative, building up a network of self-governing bodies composed of elected, recallable, and rotatable non-professional delegates of the people, at all levels of social organization in the local communities and enterprises where people live and work, at the level of regions and whole branches of activity, and finally at the macro-level, at the level of the whole society.

These bodies, councils, and assemblies would assume responsiblity for policy-making and overall control in all those and only those functions where coordination and rational direction are indispensable. They would assign definite technical tasks to experts and administrators, but would retain full power over them and would remain supreme organs of public authority in their parti-

cular field of territory. The basic differences between representative and participatory democracy are first, an incomparably high
degree of active participation of an increasing number of citizens in
the latter and second, a profound change in the character and role
of the political parties. Parties, themselves hierarchical and more or
less bureaucratic organizations, appear in the role of mediators
between the people and the government in representative
democracy.

In the classical form of representative democracy in Great
Britain, less so in the United States, members of Parliament and of
the government, once elected, owe their loyalty to their party
rather than to the electorate. In participatory democracy, members
of self-governing bodies—whatever political organization they
might belong to—are directly responsible to those who delegated
their power to them. Parties are no longer ruling organizations but
at best political organizations that articulate programs, raise the
political consciousness of the people, try to mobilize them for
specific goals, help to select the best candidates. Under these
conditions, professional politics is no longer needed. Bureaucracy
loses its *raison d'etre*, and disappears as a ruling stratum, although
it retains technical functions.

Third, poverty, once a necessary consequence of the low
productivity of labor, becomes an anachronism in wealthy West
European and North American societies with $6-7000 average
national income per capita. It has for the first time in history
become possible to satisfy the elementary needs of each individual:
food, housing, basic education, health protection, etc. In some
northern American and European countries the problem has been
solved, but in other countries, there is still a considerable part of
the population that lives under conditions of both material and
spiritual misery: inadequately fed, in slums, permanently unemployed, without health protection, without satisfactory education,
with hardly any culture, and socially discriminated against,
especially when they belong to racial minorities.

The problem cannot be solved within classical *laissez-faire*
capitalism where business needs a segment of unemployed and poor
population in order to improve its bargaining position against
organized labor. The solution offered by the present American
variant of welfare capitalism is partial and inadequate; it involves
the humiliation of being unwanted and thrown out of any useful
work and out of social life, and it also involves wasteful and
corrupt bureaucratic treatment of welfare programs which then

generate considerable resistance to the very idea of social care for the weak, old and sick.

Fourth, there is a universal human capacity and need to act freely, spontaneously, imaginatively, to engage in praxis. But modern industrial production with its extreme specialization and mechanization at first destroyed every trace of creativity which there still was in the work of the artisan. Now, at a much higher level of productivity, it opens up new possibilities of freer organization of work, of beautification of the industrial milieu, of increasing participation of workers, and above all of substantially reducing obligatory working hours and creating a sufficient amount of leisure. With better education, this leisure could be used for creative activities, play, communal engagement, greater participation in the political process. But most of these possibilities are wasted. The system is geared toward expansion of output and increase of corporate power, not toward the improvement of the quality of each person's active life.

Consequently, the increase of productivity is used to increase consumption, not to liberate time and offer to each individual substantially more culture and more opportunity for praxis. This solution is irrational because, on the one hand, it leads to increasingly wasteful production, and on the other hand it blocks possible human development, both of those workers who must waste their lives in unnecessarily long hours of stupefying work, and of those who are thrown out of the production process and offered compensation for non-work.

And last, fifth, the system which rests on a need to constantly expand material output and encourage wasteful consumption is incompatible with an overriding necessity to use natural resources wisely and preserve balanced, healthy, natural surroundings. At a time when we know how scarce and irrevocably limited certain natural materials and energies are, a whole industry works hard to create artificial needs and to increase consumption of those very scarce natural resources. The only rational solution quite compatible with solutions of other problems seems to be to give to all individuals the chance to develop high-level needs which do not require the accumulation of material goods and thus to allow a natural transition from excessive comfort to culture, communal engagements and praxis. In different societies these problems will be solved in different order, in different degrees, with different speed, in more or less peaceful or violent ways, with more or less ingenuity and creativity. If these problems are not solved at all, the whole story, I am afraid, will be repeated once more. One more civilization might go down the drain forever.

Only philosophically grounded social theory can see beyond immediate practical problems and provide an epochal, critical consciousness that would both alert us to the dangers of degradation and direct us to look for creative and rational long-range solutions. Such a theory will not always reach the majority of people no matter how loudly it speaks. It will not always generate sufficient social energies to significantly accelerate historical progress and radically reshape existing social forms. But the least it can do is to exert pressure in a proper direction within an otherwise spontaneous development pushed by necessity.

There is always a more enlightened part of the ruling class which realizes that certain urgent problems have to be solved even at the price of sacrificing some existing institutions in order to preserve other more basic ones. And there is always a chance that a reform, meant to be partial, will generate new forces that will carry the process of social change beyond its initial limited intention. So we might conclude that reason is powerful even when it is not already an overwhelming immediate material force; in the struggle of existing material forces, it can always manage to give a rational direction.

PART IV: PUBLIC ISSUES

B. MORAL

PHILOSOPHY AND MORAL STANDARDS

WILLIAM F. FRANKENA

University of Michigan, Ann Arbor, Michigan

Ten score and zero years ago our fathers brought forth upon this continent a new nation, conceived in liberty and dedicated to certain ethical propositions. One score and six years ago, at mid-century, I wrote an essay seeking to describe and to influence the course of its moral philosophy as of that time,[1] and now I am commissioned to write another at the three-quarter mark, which is also the bi-centennial of that nation. My only comfort—or, rather, yours—is an assurance that, having lived through one-third of its history, I shall not live to write yet another in the year 2000.

My topic is listed simply as "Standards of Moral Behavior" but it was conceived by the founding fathers of this symposium as a discussion on the future role of philosophy in the life of our nation under the title "Philosophy and Standards of Moral Behavior." This essay will therefore not be a systematic piece of moral philosophy on the subject of moral standards but something more like a programmatic piece on moral philosophy in relation to the future moral standards of our society.

I

Back of the conception of this topic is a widespread concern about our moral standards, i.e., about the general moral norms, principles, rules, or values governing (or not governing) our behavior, a concern felt because of a number of facts about contemporary society. There are too many people who have no moral standards or disregard too often those they have. Many of them seem to be against having moral standards at all. Too many people are akratic, cynical, or wicked, a-moral, immoral, or non-moral. Even among those who are moral or mean to be, there is too much disagreement, pluralism, and variation in the moral standards they have. There is also a rather prevalent state of confusion, doubt, uncertainty, relativism, subjectivism, and scepticism, often described by quoting from John Donne.

'Tis all in pieces, all coherence gone;

311

All just supply, and all relation:
Prince, subject, father, son, are things forgot, ...

Both as a cause and as a result of all this, there has been a tragic inadequacy in our moral education; not enough of us are doing it, or even believing in it, and too many individuals and organizations are acting in ways that defeat or nullify it.

No doubt the picture generating this concern is somewhat one-sided, but it is also true as far as it goes. Our present situation in the matter of moral standards is deeply troubling, as almost every previous generation has said its situation was; and it may well be that ours is more so than any earlier one, if only because of our new levels of technology, population, and mutual involvement. Not least troubling for our purposes here is the thought that philosophy, even moral philosophy, may be partly responsible for our situation, along with psychology, the social sciences, historical events, and many other things. Whatever is true of that of earlier periods, I do not believe that the moral philosophy of today can be blamed on this score. In any case, it is not the past but the future that we are interested in here, and I believe, as I shall seek to show, that recent moral philosophy has been moving in a helpful direction. The question we must address is that of what to do about moral standards, assuming we can do something if we put our minds to it, and that we have some options from which to choose. Philosophy, social and moral, can at least discuss this question, hopefully not in the merely epiphenomenal way suggested by Hegel's remarks about the owl of Minerva. Perhaps it can not only tell us what our options are but also provide a theory to guide what we do, so that we need not leave matters to the politicians, the theologians, the heads of industry, the revolutionists, or to chance.

Looking back at our situation as earlier described, it seems to me that we should see as the most pressing current moral problem today that of the moral education of the members of society, and not those problems, bio-ethical and otherwise, which so many of us are now teaching and writing about, important as they are. I am all for moral philosophers discussing such "practical" normative problems, as I urged twenty-five years ago, but I think we are too much neglecting the most basic and urgent of them all and am therefore taking this occasion as an excuse for a plea for putting moral education at the top of our agenda. In effect, what we should be doing, as I now see it, is to think of ourselves as trying to work out the theory of moral education. As will appear, much recent

British and American moral philosophy is relevant to the development of such a theory, so that my proposal is a call, not so much for a reconstruction of its substance, as for a re-orientation of its purpose and a recasting of its form. But it is at least that.

If this slightly Copernican turn is well taken, our question about philosophy and the moral standards of society becomes a question about moral education. What, then, are we to do about this? One answer, or course, is: do nothing, let what will be be. Both optimists and pessimists can take this line, but I am assuming that we mean to be meliorists. Many, looking for "law and order," find another line tempting: do what is necessary to bring about a situation in society in which the condition described above does not obtain—in which there is a complete, or almost complete, acceptance, teaching of, and devotion in action to some set of standards, the same or nearly the same for everyone. One may wonder, however, whether it is possible thus to turn the clock back (assuming that such a situation did obtain in the past), or, if it is, whether it is desirable or right to use the means necessary for doing so. There would seem in the abstract to be three possible means: law, revolution, and education of an indoctrinating kind. In practice, however, they would probably all involve revolution. As R. M. Hare puts it, "... we have opted for a wholly different, pluralist, liberal society, and it would be impossible, short of some kind of totalitarian revolution of the right or the left, to alter this."[2] At best, a mass moral revivalism—which may be needed in any case—would be required, if only to get an educational program going. Even assuming that it could bring its goal about without revolution and totalitarianism, one can hardly regard the state of culture aimed at as a desideratum, even if one is not a moral philosopher. Whether it is desirable or not depends on the standards the resulting society would have; they must in some sense be sound or good standards—the right ones—in content and form. The problem is not just to secure a general acceptance of and devotion to some set of standards, but also to find the most defensible standards possible. And, if one is a moral philosopher, one will further object that reason and critical reflection are necessary to find such standards or to make the process of moral education self-correcting until they are found, and that, in any case, the unexamined life is not worthy of a human being—a dictum which is not true without any qualification but must in some sense be an article of philosophical faith.

Here we must notice a line of thought forcibly expressed by a trio of recent British philosophers, D. Z. Phillips, H. O. Mounce, and R. W. Beardsmore.[3] They think of a morality as a set of moral "concepts," "notions," or "practices" actually prevailing in a society (a nation, a church, etc.) in the form of rules of ethical grammar, e.g., honesty, truthfulness, generosity, etc. They do find some room for the members of a society to criticize or even reform its practices, but they insist that all such criticism must be rooted in those practices somehow, for there is no more basic, external, general, or transcendent ground or point of view from which it can begin or on which it can rest. Morality is just a lot of moralities, whose practices may overlap or resemble each other but may also be very largely different. On this view, I take it, we can do something, and it need not be simply a turning back of the clock; but, still, what we can do must be largely a renewed inculcation of and adherence to the moral notions of our society, plus perhaps some piecemeal revisions made mainly in their own spirit, possibly to deal with conflict cases, new situations, etc. One trouble is that it gives us very little to guide us in these revisions. Another is the fact that our society either has no such set of basic practices or has a plurality of them, and that this theory can neither help us to find one nor to choose between divergent ones.

II

As might be expected, then, most moral philosophers have not followed any of the above lines of thought, but have presented us with other kinds of pictures of morality and, by implication at least, of moral education. They have advocated a more thorough use of reflection and criticism and been more convinced of the necessity and possibility of discovering moral standards that are in some sense rationally justifiable. This is especially true of recent British and American moral philosophy, which I shall mainly have in mind in what follows. Even earlier, however, philosophers characteristically looked for something that could reasonably be taken as basic in morality—some principle, end, virtue, method, or point of view ("the moral point of view"), by reference to which it can be determined, either directly or indirectly, what it is morally right, rational, or good to do or be. They have looked for a rational method—let us say the Method—to use in moral reasoning and judging. Moreover, at least recently, they have generally given up any belief that it can begin with or even uncover moral knowledge that is either innate (in reason or conscience), self-evident or otherwise a priori—let alone revealed. It is true, as we shall see, that they have different conceptions of what the Method is and of the way in which it is to be applied—e.g., some are act-utilitarians, some are rule or principle utilitarians, and some are non-utilitarians—and also that many of them are non-methodological relativists, believing that, while there is, indeed, a rational Method for answering ethical questions, it is not such as enables us always to decide between conflicting views.

All such Methods obviously have to be described in abstract and general terms and my review of them must likewise be rather abstract and general; I hope, however, that it will be intelligible, without being too schematic to be helpful. In reviewing them, part of my purpose will be to bring out the conceptions of moral education they seem to imply, since, if I am right, this is what matters most for present purposes. For, as Oakeshott points out,

> Every form of the moral life ... depends upon education. And
> the character of each form is reflected in the kind of education
> required to nurture and maintain it.[4]

Today, some of these Methods still take as basic some end or principle, e.g., the general welfare, the amelioration of the human predicament, the law of love, or the principle of utility. Most of them, however, involve the idea of a basic "original position" or "moral point of view" by the taking of which the more substantive goals, principles, practices, and judgments of morality are to be arrived at and certified. In one way or another Kurt Baier, R. B. Brandt, J. N. Findlay, R. Firth, R. M. Hare, John Rawls, P. W. Taylor, and myself, espouse Methods of this type. These are of three main sorts: (a) benevolent or impartial spectator theories, (b) rational contractor theories, and (c) universal prescriptivist theories. The main difference between the three sorts lies in the way in which they define or characterize the "original position" (OP) or "moral point of view" (MPV), and theories of each sort may also describe them in somewhat different ways, e.g., some theories of the first kind say that the spectator is to be benevolent, others that he is to be impartial.

Obviously, for each view of the nature of the Method, there will be a related view of moral education, since, if there is such a Method, it must be a primary aim of moral education to teach all or some of us this Method and to foster in all of us a disposition to live by its conclusions. The ends and means of moral education may overlap or be similar for different Methods, but they will also differ in certain respects. However, whatever the Method may be (or almost whatever), it may still be applied in rather diverse ways, and much the same options about this are open under each Method. Most of them have been advocated by some recent moral philosopher or other, and each of them has implications for moral education. These options and their educational implications I shall now review, I fear rather sketchily. I shall ignore some important issues, e.g., those between an ethics of duty and an ethics of virtue or between a deontological Method and a teleological one.

III

Two other issues are more central in the present connection. Suppose that we are convinced that a certain Method is the one to use in an examined morality. Then the first question is whether we should regard this Method as a method for *individuals*, i.e., as the method by which an individual is to determine how he should act; as a method for *institutions*, i.e., as the method by which society is to determine what social institutions it should have or set up, including perhaps a socially sanctioned moral code (or "positive social morality" or PSM), the understanding being that individuals are to guide themselves, not by using the Method, but by the rules of these institutions; or both as a method for individuals and as a method for institutions. The second question, if we hold that our Method is for individuals, is whether it is to be used *directly* to determine what one should do in a particular situation, as it is, e.g., in act-agapism or act-utilitarianism, or *indirectly*, i.e., whether it is to be used to find what I shall call Gens (standards, principles, norms, rules, etc.) like "Treat people equally" or "Do not lie," by which one is then to determine what one should do in concrete cases. If a Method is to be used indirectly in this way, then moral reasoning is a two-story affair, as, e.g., in rule-utilitarianism, otherwise it is a single-story business. If a Method is to be taken as a method for institutions, then morality necessarily involves two stories, since institutions consist of Gens of a certain kind (i.e., rules), but the stories will be of a somewhat different sort. I shall, however, present the different types of answers to these two questions as if they formed a single spectrum.

At one end of this spectrum is an extreme form of what I shall call Actarianism. It is one of the many kinds of things so confusingly and confusedly called "situation ethics" (some of which are not ethics at all); but there is an even more extreme kind of situation ethics that denies there is any such Method as we are talking about, insisting that morality is or should be a matter of wholly unguided personal decision or intuition in particular cases. The present theory holds that there is a Method to guide particular judgments, and that it is a method for individuals, but it is like the more extreme view in holding also that no Gens, not even rules of thumb, are to intervene between the Method and the particular judgment; nothing is to intervene except the relevant facts relating to the case. Some of these may be general, but at any rate no intermediate *moral* Gen is to play a part in moral reasoning and deliberation, only the Method and the facts. Among the facts, of course, may be facts about the rules and institutions obtaining in society, perhaps even facts about a prevailing moral code consisting of Gens, and these facts may have to be taken into consideration along with others, but, even so, the Gens, rules, etc., are not themselves to be used as bases for determining what to do.

This view may be taken by an act-agapist or act-utilitarian who is willing to be that situational. For it, a Method is to be used only to reach particular conclusions and to do so directly. An action is right in a situation if and only if it is dictated directly by the Method plus the relevant facts, and an action is to be *judged* right only if it is seen as being so dictated. The view may, however, take two forms, both of which represent interesting options. According to the first, morality is a purely personal matter; one is not to praise, blame, or otherwise apply moral sanctions (as distinct from legal ones) to the actions of others. "Judge not, that ye be not judged." Many so-called new morality buffs seem to hold this position. On the other form of the view, acts of praising or blaming others, etc., are permissible, but one must *each time* decide whether or not to engage in such an act by looking to see if doing so is itself dictated by the Method plus the facts. One must distinguish between the rightness of an action and the rightness of praising or blaming it (or otherwise punishing or rewarding it) but in both cases the rightness is to be determined by a direct application of the Method in each particular situation; no Gens are to intervene in either case, not even rules of thumb.

It is important to notice here that, on the second form of this rather extreme actarian view, it might sometimes be right to praise or sanction action in accordance with a certain rule or Gen, even if this is stronger than a rule of thumb, e.g., a law or a social rule, or even to advocate such a rule or Gen, provided, of course, that in each case the act of praising, sanctioning, or advocating is directly dictated by the Method and the facts. Even on this view, then, it would be possible for individuals to support a system of laws or a positive social morality, though only in those particular situations in which an act of doing so is required by the Method espoused. An action would, however, never *be* morally right because it is required by the law or the moral code, but only because it is called for, or at least permitted, by the Method. It should not even be *judged* to be right simply because it is required or permitted by the law or social code.

As for moral education—it would on both forms of this theory consist in teaching the Method and a disposition to act according to its conclusions, together with a disposition to get the facts straight about the situations one is faced with. It would involve no teaching of any intermediate Gens telling us what is morally right or wrong, though it might sometimes (even often) be right to perform an act of teaching a Gen, law, or rule, viz., when and only when performing that act is right according to the Method.

It is, however, hard to see how morality and moral education can do without moral Gens of any kind, and, in fact, the view just described is too extreme even for Joseph Fletcher; he calls it anti-nominism as distinct from situationalism, which for him admits rules of thumb or "maxims" into the application of the law of love.[5] It is even harder to see how, in its second version, one can refrain from using the words "morally right" and "morally wrong" in any of the Gens one may, perhaps correctly, regard it as right to advocate, sanction, or teach, as the theory requires one to do. Rather more plausible, then, is a somewhat less extreme view, also actarian, one which allows us to formulate and act on Gens of a different sort, viz. rules of thumb, maxims, or what Rawls has called "summary rules." It also allows us to teach such Gens to others, especially to the young, for use when time is short or ignorance of fact irremediable. These Gens would be built up by inductive generalization from previous cases in which the Method has declared a certain action to be right or wrong; they would in effect say that, in situations of a certain sort, the Method has judged that one should or should not do so-and-so and probably will so judge next time.[6] Notice that, on this more modified form of actarianism, an action will still be right if and only if it is required or at least permitted by the method in the light of the facts, but it may sometimes be *judged* to be right, or rather probably right, even when it is not itself seen as called for or permitted by the Method. An action may also be overtly *said* to be right, even when it is not (and is judged not to be), if the act of saying so is called for by the Method on that occasion (or is suggested by a rule of thumb based on previous use of the Method). For on this kind of view, lying (or whatever) may sometimes be right, if found so by use of the Method; a rule of not lying can have only the force of a rule of thumb, even if it is sometimes right to treat it as if it were stronger. An action or its agent may, however, be judged to be *good*, whether it is right or not, if it is motivated by moral concern—and may be *said* to be good if saying so is right, whether the act or agent is actually good or not.

IV

Just as in moral theology there has been much criticism of Fletcher and situation ethics, so in philosophy there has been much criticism of these extreme actarian Methods, usually in the form of attacks on act-utilitarianism. Often the critics accept the basic Method (e.g., the principle of utility or the law of love), but disagree with this kind of theory about how it is to be applied. One thing that troubles them, of course, is the point just mentioned about lying. More generally, there is a conviction, not only that Gens are needed in the moral regulation of conduct and in moral education, but also that rules of thumb are not strong enough to do the job. It is not just that time is often too short for the Method to be applied directly, there is also the fact that not following a rule of thumb can hardly occasion a feeling of compunction, the fact that people are often under stress or temptation, the fact that they are often ignorant, stupid, or careless and irresponsible in their thinking, and the fact that, even when they are not, their thinking may go awry because of bias or self-deception, often unconscious, due to desire or self-interest. These facts lead many, myself included, to doubt the wisdom of views that leave an individual's judgments and decisions so entirely to his own application of a Method in each situation he is in, and to look for a form of morality in which there are Gens about what is right or wrong, which are stronger than rules of thumb and taught and perhaps even sanctioned as such, whether regarded as absolute or not.

Even if we take this anti-situationalist position, however, a number of options are still open to us. We have a choice between taking our Method, whatever it is, as a method for individuals and taking it as a method for institutions. We must also decide between the view that an action is right if and only if it is itself directly dictated by our Method plus the relevant facts and the view that it is right if or because it is required by our intermediate Gens. And we must decide whether morality is or should be a purely personal business *or* take, at least in part, the form of a socially sanctioned moral code or PSM. There is also the question whether intermediate Gens should be regarded as absolute or as prima facie in W. D. Ross's sense (though still more stringent than rules of thumb), but I shall leave it to one side except for one or two references. Depending on how we answer these questions, we will be espousing one or another of the following theories.

At the opposite end of our spectrum from the theories discussed in Section III, there are or may be a family of interesting views, which must be described here, though they are not very widely held today. For them morality is not a personal business at all; it is a matter of social codes and institutions. They are not only genarian as versus actarian,[7] they are social and institutional in a special sense. For them an action is right if and only if it conforms to the moral code and moral institutions of the society in question. In this respect such theories resemble that of Phillips, Mounce, and Beardsmore. They differ from it in holding that there is a single Method which in some sense underlies the evolution and variation of social codes and institutions. They even believe that the evolution of these codes and institutions involves a kind of reflective application of this Method, but they think of this reflection mainly as an activity of something like a general, social, or universal mind, and as being largely implicit and unconscious, at least until it is made explicit by some philosopher appearing rather late in the process; it may on occasion peak in the thinking and activity of some reformer serving as its instrument, but in general it is not of the conscious, individualistic sort usually favored by philosophers. The views of Hegel and his followers come readily to mind as examples; today the position of W. H. Walsh at least approximates to being a theory of this type.[8] But what is sometimes now called actual-rule-utilitarianism must also be listed here; it holds that individuals should conform to the institutions of society but believes that these tend to arise and change as they are seen by society to be or not to be conducive to the general welfare (Hegel thought they arise and change as they are seen by universal mind to be or not to be conducive to freedom or self-realization).

As for the moral education of the young, it will on such views consist largely in the teaching and internalization of the Gens incorporated in social codes and institutions. There will not be much explicit teaching of the Method, for individuals are not to use it to guide their actions, since they are to be guided by existing codes and institutions, nor are individuals given much room for themselves to use the Method to criticize and change these codes and institutions. They need not even spend much time trying to think out a blueprint for a reform of moral education, as I am proposing we do, since this is presumably taken care of by the ruminations of the social or universal mind. In practice, then, these last theories are very much like those which propose that we do nothing about "the present crisis" or at most work harder to pass on our present social norms—except that some of them tell us what the process is all about when it is effectively over, while others believe that a revolution may on occasion be called for by the dialectic of history. But, as I said to begin with, I am here assuming that such views are mistaken.

V

More common in British and American philosophy at present is a type of theory that is also genarian and, in a sense, institutional, but much more individualistic. The nicest example is a certain kind of ideal-rule-utilitarianism, perhaps best expounded by R. B. Brandt.[9] It takes the Method to be a method for determining what moral code and moral institutions a society should have, and contends that an action is right if and only if it conforms to the Gens institutionalized in those codes and institutions. However, unlike the preceding theory, it gives to the individual the job of using the Method to decide on the ideal set of rules for society to have (teach, sanction, etc.), with the understanding that *this* is what he is to live and judge by in practice (and not by a direct application of the Method in each situation), and that he is to do his bit to make it the code of his society—until he sees reason to revise it. The reflection involved is more conscious and individual, but its function is to work out and realize a set of social rules and institutions, not to determine directly what one should do. Like the previous theory this one takes the idea of a positive social morality as central, but it does not tell the individual to live by the prevailing one, or even to live by it except where he can "persuade" it to change (as Socrates held in the *Crito*), but rather to think out an ideal positive social morality and act according to it, while also acting to persuade his or her society to adopt it, applying sanctions in accordance with it, etc.

To my mind, this is the most satisfactory of the conceptions of morality so far reviewed. It says, roughly, that one should judge and act on the moral code which, using the Method (e.g., the principle of utility or some other Method), one perceives as ideal for one's society. Moral education will, then, have two aspects: one, the teaching of the Method to everyone, at least to those capable of grasping it and living by its conclusions, the other, the teaching of a code of moral rules seen as ideal through a use of the Method, plus a disposition to act according to them, feel compunction on violating them, disapprove of others violating them, etc.

There are, however, still other views to look at. They are of rather different sorts but we may think of them as occupying the middle portion of our spectrum, between the theories just discussed and the rather extreme actarian ones reviewed earlier. All of them take the Method to be a method for individuals, but they insist that morality must or should involve Gens that are stronger than rules of thumb, and that we are normally to act according to these Gens, rather than applying the Method directly. At the same time they maintain that the Gens must somehow be themselves justified by appeal to the Method, though not necessarily in the way rules of thumb are. The Gens one should normally act on are not necessarily those that prevail in society; they are, rather, those generated by an appeal to the Method in conjunction with the facts. But some of these theories hold that these Gens should be given the form of social rules (a PSM) while others do not, arguing that morality is a personal affair, and some of them allow that sometimes an individual may or must apply the Method directly in order to determine what to do. All of them agree that one may *judge* an action to be right or wrong by reference to some set of intermediate Gens and act accordingly; what they differ about is whether these Gens should be incorporated in a PSM, and especially whether an action *is* right if and only if it conforms to them. As for *saying* that it is right when it is not and is not judged to be right, most proponents of these views would regard this as violating a Gen telling us that lying is wrong.

One of them is best illustrated by the more recent papers of R. M. Hare, though it need not be so utilitarian as he seems inclined to be.[10] As a result of a difficult piece of argument, which I shall not try to recount (and do not find convincing), Hare thinks of the Method as equivalent to a kind of act-utilitarian reasoning that issues in particular moral judgments (or rather, since these must be universalizable, in principles of unlimited specificity) about what to do in a certain situation, and he maintains, as I understand him, that an action is right if and only if it is dictated by correct act-utilitarian thinking, whether it conforms to any of our usual moral Gens or not. This distinguishes his position from that of rule-utilitarians like Brandt, with whom Hare otherwise largely agrees, and makes Hare an actarian in my sense rather than a genarian. However, he also contends, for such reasons as were indicated earlier, that morality cannot be simply a matter of everyone's trying to apply the Method directly; we must try to generate, teach, and sanction a set of standards of limited specificity, such as we usually think of in morality. And normally we should simply live by these Gens, rather than try to apply the Method, though there may be occasions when we must resort to it, e.g., in new or in conflict situations, so that we must, if possible, have a grasp of the Method and an ability to use it. This set of Gens may not coincide with the prevailing ones, but they should be given the form of a socially sanctioned moral code, insofar at least as this is necessary and as we can agree about the Gens to be included. The Gens must, however, be selected and tested by the Method, i.e., for Hare, by act-utilitarian (not rule-utilitarian) reasoning; they must be those whose general acceptance in our lives will lead to the nearest possible approximation to the prescriptions of correct act-utilitarian thinking, since an action is right if and only if it is prescribed by the Method directly, i.e., by such thinking.

This is an actarian view, but one that entails a belief that morality should include a PSM and not be a purely personal matter, at least not while human beings are as they now are. As Hare thinks of it, it involves a kind of "double intellectual life" or two levels of moral thinking: Level I thinking, which is pretty much a matter of applying the rules one has been taught or taught oneself, feels compunction about violating, etc., and Level II thinking, which is a direct use of the Method (however this is conceived), and is to be used in selecting, testing, and revising these rules, in cases for which one has as yet no rules, and perhaps in a "cool hour," when one has the time and the necessary factual knowledge and is not under stress or in danger of self-deception. The task of moral education on such a view is to dispose and equip one—or everyone capable of it—for leading such a double moral life.

A very different kind of conception of morality is best illustrated by the view put forward not long ago G. J. Warnock.[11] This is a genarian but non-institutional conception. Like rule-utilitarianism, it says not only that an action may be *judged* right if it conforms to certain Gens, but that it *is* right if and only if it conforms to them. Like rule-utilitarianism too, it holds that these Gens must be justified by appeal to the Method, i.e., for Warnock, by a consideration of what is needed for "the amelioration of the human predicament." However, the view rejects the idea that morality should take the form of a positive social code of rules supported by moral sanctions, etc.; it thinks of its intermediate Gens, not as quasi-legal rules, but as simply "moral views" or "principles," though not as mere rules of thumb. In this sense, it regards morality as a personal affair of accepting and acting on one or more (Warnock thinks four) principles. These principles, however, are thought of as established by a procedure analogous to that of rule-utilitarianism, not, as in Hare's scheme, to that of act-utilitarianism. Moral education, then, will not involve the use of rules and social sanctions, but the fostering of a concern for the amelioration of the human predicament (or whatever, depending on how the method is conceived) and a kind of instruction in the use of certain Gens thought of as justified by the Method and hopefully actually so justifiable. As it were, on this view, morality and moral education are conceived in liberty and dedicated to the proposition that they should ameliorate the human predicament (or whatever).

Actarians will object that, like rule-utilitarianism, such a view entails a species of "rule-worship," or rather, Gen-worship, since it takes the right to be determined by certain Gens, rather than by a direct application of a Method to a particular situation. It seems to me, however, to be very nearly a vision of what morality ideally ought to be like, though I have doubts about Warnock's form of this vision. What troubles me about it is a conviction that a realistic morality and moral education, while not consisting entirely of a PSM, must include such an institutionalized and/or socially sanctioned system of rules along, perhaps, with other sorts of standards, ideals, or "values"—given such facts about human nature as were mentioned before. I think, therefore, that we must in practice choose between Brandt's type of view and Hare's, though not necessarily in their utilitarian versions.

VI

Thus far I have been discussing rather pure types of theories about the Method and its application. It is, however, possible to combine them in various ways, and it may be that such combinations are more adequate than any of the pure theories. One combination theory was presented years ago by H. L. A. Hart, P. F. Strawson, and J. O. Urmson;[12] according to them morality is or should be partly a matter of positive social morality and partly a matter of personal ideals, moral views, or principles. For them both parts of morality involve intermediate Gens that are not mere rules of thumb, but perhaps one could think of one part in genarian and of the other in actarian or situational terms. The most widely discussed recent combination theory, however, is that of John Rawls and D. A. J. Richards.[13] This adopts a rational contractor (or hypothetical social contract) conception of the original position (OP) and hence of the Method, and maintains that the Method is to be used to decide on principles, not to determine directly what is right in a particular situation (which is rather to be determined by reference to the principles), and that it is to be used to decide both on principles for individuals and principles for institutions. It could be that the principle of utility would be chosen by such rational contractors, both for individuals and for institutions, but the proponents of this theory argue that in fact it would not, and they see their Method as an alternative to the utilitarianism so widely adopted by other recent moral philosophers. In any case, they hold that the right action is the action that conforms to the principles such social contractors would agree to in the OP. They might also claim, though I am not sure they would, that such contractors would set up a PSM; at least they could argue that this is one of the institutions such contractors would devise or that, once chosen, principles for individuals or some of their corollaries should be embodied in positive social rules reinforced by internal and external moral sanctions. If so, then a PSM would figure in moral education; otherwise, not; in any case, moral education would presumably include (a) getting across the idea of taking a certain OP and of choosing Gens from this position, (b) teaching certain Gens as those one would choose from this position, and (c) fostering the dispositions needed to motivate one to live accordingly, e.g., a sense of justice.

In my opinion, some such non-utilitarian combination theory which favors having a PSM is the line we should take. With this comment I conclude my rather sketchy review of recent theories of morality and moral standards. My purpose has been to exhibit them as offering alternatives we might take in answering the question what we should do about the present situation with respect to moral standards, or, rather, in accordance with my proposal that we re-direct our moral philosophizing, as alternatives for reconceiving the moral education of society. At least I think I have shown that recent British and American moral philosophy has much to say that is interesting and constructive from this point of view.

Perhaps it has too much to say? Philosophers have sought out so many inventions! There are so many different theories! How can we choose between them? I have tried to do a little to guide our choice, but my discussion certainly has not been conclusive in favor of any one Method or of any one kind of theory about its application. However, there is more agreement between recent moral philosophers than shows up in what I have been saying. As Hare has pointed out, there are close formal similarities between some of the Methods; and, while there are, as he also says, marked differences of substance (e.g., some are act-utilitarian, some rule-utilitarian, and some non-utilitarian), there is a good deal of agreement about working moral standards, or at least a considerable amount of overlapping in the lists of Gens and Virtues. There can be important agreement, at least among those who give a central role to Gens other than as rules of thumb, whether they accept the idea of a PSM or not, even if their basic theories are rather diverse.

It is true that the views sketched have different implications for the form of moral education, if not for its content. Even about the form, however, it may be that philosophers can, if they take moral education as the focus of attention, reach a consensus sufficient to serve as a basis for a salutary program of moral education.

At this point my mind reverts to the old question of Plato's *Meno*: assuming that virtue (i.e., a grasp of moral standards and a devotion to them) is not innate, is it a matter of luck or divine grace, or can it be successfully fostered by some program of education? The best answer is that we need what Socrates and Plato were then still looking for, a theory of moral education, and that, having one, the only thing we can do is to try it out and see. As he must have known, Socrates' kind of evidence to show that virtue cannot be taught does nothing to prove that such an attempt, if we are serious about it, must fail. Of course, a full theory of moral education is not something philosophers can work out alone; psychologists, social scientists, and teachers must also do their part. But perhaps philosophers can help in an important way, even by discussing such rather theoretical issues as divide the various theories described above.

Can a salutary programe be mounted, even if we have the needed theory? Plato (later) thought it can be mounted only if philosophers become rulers or if rulers become philosophers. Perhaps it will be enough, however, for us to be educators to the best of our abilities. At least this would be enough if the rest of society were ready to make true something Protagoras said in reply to Socrates in another dialogue:

> ... everyone is ready to teach anyone justice and the laws ... all persons are teachers of virtue, each one according to his ability. You ask, where are the teachers? You might as well ask, who teaches Greek?[14]

What is necessary and probably also sufficient is that society itself become educative in accordance with a satisfactory moral theory. Is *this* a matter of luck or grace?

NOTES

1. See William K. Frankena, "Moral Philosophy at Mid-Century," *Philosophical Review*, LX (1951), 45–55.

2. R. M. Hare, "Value Education in a Pluralist Society," *Proc. of Philosophy of Education Soc. of Great Britain* (1976), p. 3.

3. See D. Z. Phillips and H. O. Mounce, *Moral Practices* (New York, Schocken Books, 1970); R. W. Beardsmore, *Moral Reasoning* (London, Kegan Paul, 1969).

4. M. Oakeshott, *Rationalism in Politics* (London, Methuen and Co. Ltd., 1962), p. 62.

5. J. Fletcher, *Situation Ethics* (Philadelphia, The Westminster Press, 1966), pp. 1–39.

6. For an earlier view that holds approximately this, see Adam Smith, *The Theory of Moral Sentiments*, 1759, Part III, Chaps. 2 and 3.

7. On an actarian view what is right or wrong in a particular situation is to be determined by an individual by a direct use of the Method (itself a kind of Gen), e.g., by the principle of utility. On a genarian view, this is not so, what is right or wrong is to be determined, at least sometimes, by reference to Gens of limited specificity that are stronger than rules of thumb but are determined by a use of the Method.

8. See W. H. Walsh, *Hegelian Ethics* (New York, St. Martin's Press, 1969), pp. 17, 77. For present purposes I include Marxists among Hegel's followers, as well as Walsh.

9. See e.g. R. B. Brandt, "Toward a Credible Form of Utilitarianism," in *Morality and the Language of Conduct*, eds. H. N. Castaneda and G. Nakhnikian (Detroit, Wayne State University Press, 1963), pp. 107–143.

10. See especially R. M. Hare, "Principles," *Proc. Aristotelian Society*, LXXII (1972–73), 1–18; "Ethical Theory and Utilitarianism," in *Contemporary British Philosophy*, Fourth Series (London, Allen and Unwin Ltd., 1976), pp. 113–131.

11. See *The Object of Morality* (London, Methuen & Co. Ltd., 1971).

12. See H. L. A. Hart, *The Concept of Law* (Oxford: Clarendon Press, 1961);

P. F. Strawson, "Social Morality and Individual Ideal," *Philosophy* XXXVI (1961), 1–17; J. O. Urmson, "Saints and Heroes," in *Essays in Moral Philosophy*, ed. A. I. Melden (Seattle, University of Washington Press, 1958), pp. 198–216.

13. See John Rawls, *A Theory of Justice* (Cambridge, Mass., Harvard University Press, 1971); D. A. J. Richards, *A Theory of Reasons for Actions* (Oxford, Clarendon Press, 1971).

14. Plato, *Protagoras* 327E.

MORAL PHILOSOPHY AT THE BICENTENNIAL

COMMENTS ON FRANKENA'S "PHILOSOPHY AND MORAL STANDARDS"

ABRAHAM EDEL

University of Pennsylvania, Philadelphia, Pennsylvania

There is a rising note of self-criticism among moral philosophers today, and the Bicentennial is an apt moment for reflection on how far ways of doing moral philosophy have prepared us for coping with the tasks posed by moral phenomena in the present period. The question is legitimate because almost all moral philosophies have assumed that the ultimate objective of their work is to guide moral decision. And to raise it in commenting on Frankena's paper is doubly appropriate. For one thing, as he tells us in the beginning of his paper, he had the job at mid-century of outlining where moral philosophy stood and what were its tasks—an outline which itself helped channel the energies of philosophers in a very specific direction. For another, in asking where we stand today, he has given us a rich study of some of the pure types or structures that have been found in recent moral theory and, by relating them to moral education, has put before us the question of what can be done to remedy the apparently widespread collapse of morality in our age. In essence, then, Frankena bids us search among and evaluate theoretical structures in morality as a prime task in coping with morality today. No clearer mandate could be given both for theoretical and practical direction. We have therefore to ask— indeed we cannot avoid asking—how adequate is an approach which tells us first to decide on a formal structure, second to use it in moral education, and third to hope for a consequent upgrading of morality.

That the approach deals with formal structures is clear enough. For example, Frankena talks of a Method (M), a moral point of view (MPV), an original position (OP) in the sense employed by Rawls, and considers whether there are general rules (Gens) of a subsidiary sort that operate between the highest rules and the particular. The tacit assumption of this methodology is that structural features are independently meaningful and, even more importantly, that we somehow independently decide which we want to employ in making moral decisions and in generating a positive social morality (PSM).

This conception of structure was imposed on morality in the mid-century through a sharp distinction between meta-ethics and normative or substantive ethics, as if the theoretical considerations of moral philosophy lacked any human purposive content either in internal detail or in external setting and as if they could be decided on purely logical and linguistic grounds. It was not, of course, without support in the previous history of modern philosophy—the Kantianism that elaborated categorial principles as necessary conditions of experience imposed as postulates on all experience; a positivist theory of analytic truths framed as commitments to generate formalistic structures; the sharp separation in logical and mathematical analysis between pure or uninterpreted systems and their interpretations or applications (the outcome of the development of alternative geometries); even the way in which ordinary language analysis in spite of its opposition to formalism treated the linguistic domain as a self-enclosed territory from which to extract structures by the thrust of example and counter-instance. Let us call this the *lordly* conception of a structure, not because it lorded over the dominant moral philosophy of the last few decades, but because structure is one sense or another established without responsibility to the content of moral phenomena, certified independently (just as the lord derives his powers by inheritance or the procedures of his peers).

There is a quite different way of conceiving structure that ties it closely to content. This is a *functional* conception. A structure is not made of different stuff: it is simply that part of the content which is elevated to a governing role for specific purposes, much as some persons are elected to do specific socio-political jobs. Others might have done them instead, and in any case the assessment of a structure is by its success in carrying out the jobs. Such a functional view of structure usually finds that what goes on in the structure has to be understood continually in close relation to the on-going content. Each field has to decide for itself how great the distance is to be between content and structure: there are dangers in staying too close to the ground as well as in flying off to the stars. It was Aristotle who first criticized the aspiration to mathematize ethics and he tried to tie it instead to biology, psychology, and the social disciplines. Perhaps the same criticism has not to be offered of the aspirations that issue from current vital theories of logic and language.

The lordly conception of ethical structures generates analytic difficulties of its own. For example, how do we decide among alternative structures? At times the choice of structure seems a voluntaristic preference on our or Frankena's part: it is almost as if we could consult Frankena's catalogue of types and make our selection. Only once in a while do we find a reason given: for example, that the absence of intervening Gens opens the way to opportunism and self-favoritism to which human beings are psychologically prone. But if we can appeal to a psychological truth for support in selecting a structure, why not to a social truth (that a certain structure will produce conflict or a predatory selfishness or social chaos), or to an historical truth (that certain structures enhance cooperative loyalties), and so on? The selection of structure becomes tied as a consequence to the whole range of moral phenomena and moral and social problems and its independence becomes only a relative and changeable one. A similar conclusion is suggested by the fact that profound moral differences may arise as readily within the same structure as between structures. For example, both a utilitarian structure and a natural rights structure have had conservative and revolutionary interpretations. In the former, the differences are associated with different lessons of history and different accounts of human nature and human social'processes; in the latter, with whether the rights that claim a natural status coincide or run counter to the set of established rights. It would seem plausible therefore that structures are themselves best understood in terms of the interplay of the demands of content, context, social needs, historical problems. If so, then the sharp distinction of meta-ethics and normative or substantive ethics was an undue formalism which is particularly misleading at the present moment when moral philosophers, because of the rapidity of change in our lives, can no longer ignore the pressure of moral problems. We see all about us how they are throwing themselves into bio-ethics, legal-ethical problems, and the rest, and while they do excellent work in making distinctions, they do not have a theoretical approach capable of coping with the full impact of these novel problems, nor do they attend to any feed-back on their theoretical ideas.

I do not mean that the distinction between meta-ethics and normative ethics was simply a mistake—in the sense in which Prichard entitled a famous article "Does Moral Philosophy Rest on a Mistake?" To say that it was a mistake would suggest that it involved a logical fallacy or a straightforward factual error. Rather it has to be seen as a *program* for moral philosophy to be tried out and to be assessed for its consequences in dealing with morality. Instead, it was offered as an obvious logical truth, and so became enshrined as a dogma. My point is simply that after a while—and three or more decades seems enough in the present case—we ought to recognize that the program has failed and try another. The new program is also to be judged not as a dogmatic truth but as a proposed way of doing moral philosophy that will prove more satisfactory in dealing with the problems that morality poses. No crash argument will do; we need rather the vista of jobs and experiments to be tried out.

The domain whose successful handling will judge our ethical structures is of course what is going on in our social and moral life itself. Frankena tends to see the field as one of moral decadence, the prevalence of immorality or indifference to morality in practice, and uncertainty, relativism, subjectivism and scepticism in theory. But perhaps this is looking at things from the point of view of past institutional patterns that are themselves undergoing transformation. Closer attention to actual efforts and aspirations suggests instead a vital upsurge in which there are not merely new answers to old problems but new problems as well. In the counter-culture of the 1960's there was a fundamental shaking of traditional patterns of the good, putting love and present consciousness against the puritan complex of work, striving for success and guilt at shortcoming. In the theory of justice there have been new ideas of equality and redistribution of resources, not as involving charity but as a basic attack on traditional concepts of meritocracy. (Rawls's argument that natural advantages do not of themselves constitute a ground for reward in its various forms is an indication of the extent to which this has penetrated theory.) New problems are best illustrated in bio-ethics, where the impact of new techniques and powers brought by the growth of knowledge and consequent technologies is evident. New problems are also reflected in the genuine changes that have taken place in our picture of our world and its possibilities. For example, there is the prominence of the idea of limits and the challenge to traditional concepts of endless growth, bringing into active focus the issues of over-population, pollution, depletion of resources—problems which the reports of the Club of Rome have over-dramatized. These have made a serious and practical moral issue of what we owe to future generations. There have also been shifts in our view of our relation to nature—for example, from conquering nature to cooperating with it. (Passmore's lecture—see p. 363 below—and the discussion that followed it brought these issues clearly before us.)

These few remarks may suffice to suggest that the phenomena in the moral field are not to be taken simply as deterioration or decadence, but as indication of a period of stress and transition resting on profound underlying material and social changes, and so as calling for active reconstruction. Now why has our dominant moral philosophy found it difficult to cope with such a situation? I suggest three defects: (1) It has been *ahistorical*, concerned with an eternalist picture and so not geared for change and reconstruction. (2) Its analytic approach, stressing linguistic analysis, has been too *piecemeal* and too *isolated*. (3) The dominant model has been *unduly individualistic*. Each of these requires consideration.

(1) Our dominant moral philosophy shows its *ahistorical* character throughout. It looks, in effect, for eternal unchanging once-and-for-all answers. For example, Rawls wants a once-and-for-all decision on the formula of justice. (Even where he makes profound changes in morality he seems to take it as the discovery of a correct answer.) Frankena asks us to choose between the structures. Actually, different ones might be appropriate for different areas of material or different complexities of life: why, for example, would it not be appropriate to follow utilitarian method in deciding on legislation and a different framework for a very personal decision? By this time, practically every other discipline has discovered that there is intellectual profit in diachronic studies of its material, but not moral philosophy. It is significant that neither Frankena nor Rawls reckons with what historically conscious moral analysis and ethical structures have in fact been developed—particularly Marx in European philosophy and Dewey in American. The neglect of Dewey's moral theory in contemporary America is a serious mistake which a Bicentennial reckoning of our intellectual capital should try to remedy.

Dewey's work in moral theory is almost the only one that has seen the task of ethics as fashioning intellectual instruments for reconstruction. It carries this motif into the heart of its theory, and does not leave it as an external application. Thus it defines a moral situation not in terms of conformity to the right (for when we know the right there is no moral problem, only practical problems of following or accomplishing it) but as one of decision when we are torn between different directions and do not know which should be followed. He reinterprets the concepts of good, virtue, right and obligation in this framework; they epitomize modes of evaluative decision among desires and interests, directions of character development, pressures of disparate claims, all of which arise from the cultural and historical problems that express human efforts to survive and give expression to our needs and natures. Morality is thus refined and developed with the growth of human knowledge and both conceptual change and corrigibility are inherent in the process. Of course in the nearly half-century of human experience since Dewey developed this moral theory there is much to change, but the reconstructive outlook is definitely at its center in a way which even other naturalistic theories of this century rarely achieved.

If moral philosophy is to help in the contemporary tasks of moral reconstruction it is not enough that historical questions and applications be added to pre-existent ethical theories themselves developed in an ahistorical way. The theoretical task that faces moral philosophers is the reconstruction of their theories so as to give due place in the very concepts and methods to the facts of time, history, and change.

(2) In criticizing our analytic approaches as *too piecemeal* and *too isolated* I do not mean to join the chorus that treats analysis as a whipping boy. Philosophy is centrally analytic but there are more and less adequate modes of analysis. If positivist modes were too formalistic, ordinary language analysis helped overcome that; but the latter—in its diverse Oxford forms—had an insufficient consciousness of what it furnishes as an outcome. In general, a linguistic-analytic approach tends to favor our current dialect and locks us into the meanings that contemporary language has already built in, and through that it locks in status-quo patterns. I do not derogate the sensitivity of diagnosis and description, a phenomenology of what is going on. But the structuring of the field may be inadequate and out of date.

Our analytic practice has been too fragmentary because we tend to deal with each term or each concept separately and too isolated because we stay in the realm of concepts. We do separate studies of liberty and equality and fall readily into controversies of liberty vs. equality as if the concepts, not the people with all their interests and problems in that historical-cultural situation, were engaged in the struggle. Similarly for the right vs. the good, or justice vs. utility. And so we are left with imperialist aggression of concepts and a ballet of bloodless categories grasping at primacy. Suppose, however, that we analyzed *whole networks* (not isolated concepts) and in terms of their mode of functioning with the subject-matter (not isolationist). We would then ask different kinds of questions which at present we ignore. For example: What concerns and anxieties of people of the time are being channelled through liberty, which through equality? What human needs are finding expression through aspiration for the good and what situations are seeking resolution through rights? Physicists did not hesitate to unify space and time to take care of problems that emerged in their subject-matter. Realistic political scientists will study the division of powers in the operation of a whole system, not seeking theoretical primacy for legislature or for courts or executives; they will want to know the role of the different checks and balances. In such a network-functional analysis we get both conceptual sharpness and conceptual functioning.

Earlier in our meetings, for example, Morton White gave us a beautifully subtle analysis of Jefferson's terminological changes in the Declaration of Independence to show a struggle of a conception of rights and of ends with different relations to the possible use of governmental power. It was this basic question of policy that furnished the meaning of the changes. White was dealing here with full conceptual systems, not fragmentary concepts. Suppose he had gone even further into the socio-historical picture and related them to the Jeffersonian and Hamiltonian programs for American development in the state of the country at that time. Would the outcome not have been an even richer understanding of conceptual content and conceptual functioning?

In this vein, current meanings become actors in a current drama. If a special interpretation of liberty has been locked into the central meaning of that notion and is discovered there by our present modes of conceptual analysis, then emerging demands are barred from finding expression in that concept and must invoke others. There is no reason why, for example, contemporary liberation movements of Blacks and women should not have been formulated as demands for an extension of liberty. But the latter is fixed in specific historical forms and analyzed in very particular ways, with built-in interests of established powers, so the liberation movements have to be channelled through the ideal of equality, and the struggle of older established and newly emerging interests is cast as liberty vs. equality. Similarly, today's preoccupation in moral philosophy is with utilitarianism vs. justice or some kind of rights conception. But once we look at it historically a different picture emerges. In many ways their struggle is like that of the legislature and the courts. Each rises to do the job the other is neglecting—as the legislature together with the president pressed for economic reforms in the 1930's while the courts tried to stem them, and the courts opened the door for civil rights in the 1950's, particularly in education, while the legislature was lagging. So too with the history of utilitarianism and its rival, the rights framework. Abstractly both are capable of reconstructive efforts: the public welfare concept pressed ahead in the 1930's while the rights concept was held in thrall by conservative property interests; but by the time of the post-World-War-II situation the rights concept had discovered that it could admit of new or emerging rights, and the UN Declaration of Human Rights was only the beginning of a militant rights ethic which no neo-Lockean ingenuity can now effectively stem. Perhaps the trouble with a utilitarianism today is that the greatest happiness of the greatest number is not enough; the exploited minorities also have to be taken care of. A systematic analysis closely tied to a study of socio-historical functions is required to show us how the same imperative job can be done in different ways; it will track down value-criteria arising directly in the analytic process that enable us to judge which intellectual tool in what context is doing the job more effectively.

The question of determining how such analysis is to be done and where it will lead when systematically developed is no easy task and offers no easy assurances. It requires as much work in moral philosophy in the next generation as the more limited analysis did in the last few philosophical generations. But I venture to predict that it will narrow the gap between our moral philosophy and the development of our moral standards.

(3) There remains the problem of continued adherence in our contemporary moral philosophy to an *unduly individualistic* model. This owes its vested position not only to two centuries or more of development in the western tradition but, today, to still-strong fears that to deal with social morality in any primarily direct way is to fall under totalitarian influence. Again, Rawls's elaborate schema of the original contract under a veil of ignorance and the establishment of moral rules and institutions from an initial individualist base is the best illustration of the continued force of the model. Frankena notes the view that morality is an institutional and social matter, not a personal business, but passes it by since

philosophers usually favor the individualistic view, and suggests that it is likely to mute individual moral initiative.

This antithesis of individual and social seems to me to be largely an ideological issue, in some respects a residue of the Cold War we-they outlook, even in theory. Perhaps its roots go even further back, to the developments of the past few centuries in which intermediate groupings—kin, familial, varieties of association—either broke down or lost their significance, so that in the moral consciousness there emerged the picture of the lone individual in the community of all lone individuals. And the growth of the state as the dominant organization of the group led to the assimilation of the social and the politically controlled. Liberty became dominantly conceived as individual rights against the state, and the idea of the social was tied to the organized group. It has taken us a long time to rediscover the wealth of other categories of human relation—for example, the sense in which the interpersonal is revealed in G. H. Mead's social psychology or in Martin Buber's ethical analysis of I-thou, or in contemporary strivings for the smaller face-to-face community.

In some way or other, at this present stage, moral philosophy has to emancipate itself from this welter of problems and leave the way of organizing its inquiries open to an empirical and almost experimental procedure, determining by concrete contextual considerations where it should approach a moral problem in a group manner, where in an individual manner. For this purpose I suggest that we take a leaf from the economists' distinction of micro-economics and macro-economics—a terminological leaf, for these concepts are by no means uniformly interpreted by them—and distinguish *micro-ethics* and *macro-ethics*. This is done without any assignment of primacy, and any claims of primacy have to be empirical, relative to specific respects and problems. For example, institution-building is a macro-problem. We write a constitution for a community, and we set up a system of insurance for a group. Problems of macro-ethics can thus be seen as problems for a group, under specific conditions and with implicit criteria of their resolution. Whether these criteria in turn can be derived from established principles of micro-ethics remains a matter of hypothesis; we do not, to take a scientific analogy, refuse to carry out a biological investigation because its phenomena and their study cannot be immediately reduced to the laws of micro-physics. If today it turns out that most pressing problems in moral reconstruction may fall under macro-ethics, it is not on ontological or on moral grounds (the familiar views of the "reality" of the group or the value primacy of the group) but simply because the present historical character of more and more moral questions requires institutional or social handling and cannot be resolved by individual choice or action alone.

There may prove to be theoretical windfalls as well from pursuing the contrast of macro- and micro-ethics. For example, some of the hard questions of ethical history may be significantly reinterpreted. Thus a Benthamite utilitarianism can readily be seen as a macro-ethical formulation, with practical indices (whether of monetary standard of living or of voting procedures) for determining social policies; only when applied in micro-ethics may it generate paradoxes and violate moral sensitivities by its verdicts. Similarly, Kant's universalization test may make more sense in institution-building than in personal decisions in micro-ethics. But more important, the distinction clears the decks for empirical treatment of categories of human relations. For example, the actual context of human life today may suggest that for moral purposes the division of rural-urban or even more that of national-global may be more important than that of individual-social. Certainly the national-global distinction is at the heart of the moral issues of distributive justice in ideas of a new economic order, as well as in the older more familiar problems of patriotism and international outlook. There is, of course, much to be done in developing the concepts of micro- and macro-ethics, and in testing proposed analyses on borderline issues, in formulating types of relations, as well as in taking care of possibilities of shifts in moral problems from one to the other. Like the network mode of analysis it will take a generation of intellectual labor at least. But from the beginning it will get us out of the impasse that the stereotype of individual-social has imposed on innovation in moral philosophy.

The Bicentennial is an appropriate time to recognize that the moral problems of our society have been intensified, that moral philosophy can make a genuine contribution to our national development, that it can do so by focusing on the demands for reconstruction in all fields, and that to gear itself for its tasks requires innovative reconstruction within itself. Most of all it must recognize that such inner reconstruction is called for by its own internal development. It is not being asked to abandon its work for service abroad. It is being challenged in terms of its own traditionally professed aims to do the jobs which it has always posed for itself.

PHILOSOPHICAL PROSPECTS FOR A NEW WORLD

JUDITH JARVIS THOMSON

Massachusetts Institute of Technology, Cambridge, Massachusetts

Some fifty years ago, philosophy was a rather quieter discipline. Philosophers argued with each other about whether there are any sense-data, whether there are any negative facts, whether this or that is a logical construction, and even the moral philosophers among them argued only with each other, and at that only about such matters as whether or not the good is unanalyzable. As *philosophers* know, metaphysics (by which I mean to include philosophy of logic and language) continues to flourish—indeed, it is arguable that metaphysics is the most exciting branch of philosophy nowadays. But as pretty much *everybody* knows who reads—what? *The New York Times? The New York Review of Books?*—philosophers have, in the last ten years or so, also been attending to matters wholly outside what would have been counted philosophy fifty years ago. The noise we make has markedly increased: philosophers are now addressing themselves to non-philosophers—they are now speaking to the very same concrete moral, social, and political issues which face all of us when we ask what we or others or governments should or should not do.

It is perhaps not *very* difficult to explain this relatively new engagement of philosophers with the going concrete moral, social, and political issues. There were developments outside philosophy: on the one hand, the Vietnam war, on the other hand, the growth of the civil rights and women's movements. And there also were developments inside philosophy: I have in mind in particular the death of positivism, which freed us from the need to be constantly defending the possibility of rational argument in ethics, so that we could then go on to try to produce some.

Whether it will last is another matter. Fashions come and go in philosophy. I *think* it will last. And it goes without saying that we all of us profit if it does. Training in philosophy is training in interpretation and criticism, and thus equips philosophers particularly well for the sorting out of issues and the critical assessing of argument which are so conspiciously lacking in so much public debate; and as the quality of public debate improves, so does the prospect of responsible decision-making.

But I said only that I *think* it will last. There seem to me to be two reasons for thinking it may not. In the first place, we have recently begun to see a shift in interest amongst undergraduates. Many graduate students are still actively interested in, and even writing thesis on, concrete moral, social, and political issues; but there has been a falling off of interest in such things amongst undergraduates. Five years ago an undergraduate course entitled "Contemporary Moral Issues" was standing room only; nowadays those who sign on have room to spread out and put their feet up. Where are all the bodies? Well, a good many are in courses on logic, a good many also in courses in theory of knowledge and philosophy of science. (I haven't meant to say that interest in *philosophy* has declined.) Moreover, a good many are in courses entitled "Bio-medical Ethics" and "Introduction to Legal Reasoning," and this has perhaps made the shift in interest I am talking about less easy to see. But of course the students enrolled in "Bio-Medical Ethics" are pre-meds, and the students enrolled in "Introduction to Legal Reasoning" are pre-laws; and I doubt they'd be there if they weren't. As we all know, the average undergraduate now is considerably more concerned about making a living than he was five years ago. Whether it's because of that, or because of something more subtle in the cultural air, at all events he isn't either intellectually or emotionally where we could expect to find him five years ago.

Now why should this shift in undergraduate interest be reason to think that the current engagement of philosophers with concrete moral, social, and political problems may not last? Well, perhaps it's obvious enough. On the one hand, it would be no surprise if we were affected by the interests of our audience—we live off them emotionally as well as financially. On the other hand, it's from amongst those very undergraduates that this "philosophy club" we all belong to will draw its future members.

But the second reason for thinking that engagement may not last seems to me considerably more interesting: it lies in the internal dynamic of the discipline. Many philosophers plunge into the public arena with enthusiasm. Fine. But what precisely do they bring with them? In the case of many, a battery of intuitions, and a dialectical skill in the use of them. That skill is, of course, just the skill at distinction-making and argument which, as I said earlier, we acquire in graduate school. But what about the intuitions? Unless you have a theory in your back pocket, the only way you're going to establish a moral conclusion is by way of argument from shared intuitions; and a battery of fresh intuitions which others instantly recognize as theirs too is therefore a *very* powerful tool. Nevertheless a moral philosopher can't go on for too long working (as it were) down from his intuitions without beginning to feel the need to work up from them to a theory which should connect, explain, and justify them.

No doubt many philosophers bring with them, not merely intuitions and skill at dialectic, but also theory—perhaps utilitarianism of some variety or other, or, more likely nowadays, some or other piece of Rawlsian theory. But then it is precisely the theory that their opponents take issue with. What I mean is that if you start a paper on (as it might be) what ought to be done about starvation in underdeveloped nations by saying you're going to assume this or that Rawlsian principle, your opponents will fasten on the principle, and dispute *that*, leaving the hungry to fend for themselves in a footnote.

I'm inclined to think, in fact, that the intense discussion of Rawls's *Theory of Justice* which we have been seeing in the journals is not due merely to the fact that it is so wonderfully big and rich a book; I am inclined to think that it issues in part from, simply, a hunger for theory. There has been so little of it! God must have loved the varieties of utilitarianism, He made so many of them; but many philosophers think a plague on all of them, and if you look back at the history of moral philosophy over the last fifty years, there isn't really anything else. No wonder the appearance of Rawls's book was so exciting an event!

So there has been, all along, a hunger for theory; and it is reinforced by reflection on our own use of intuition in public debate.

What will the theoretical work to come look like? Goodness knows. But one thing I think very likely is that much of it will show the effects of what I think is probably the most interesting and important development in recent moral philosophy, viz., the fact that moral philosophers are now talking to economists. Rawls's *Theory of Justice* plainly shows its effects; so does Robert Nozick's *Anarchy, State, and Utopia.* Economic theory lays a new range of problems before us, and new ways of thinking about familiar problems, and I think that no moral theory which purports to yield conclusions about group behavior will be unaffected by it. A similar development took place some years ago, with the appearance of Hart and Honore's *Causation and the Law*: moral philosophy was immensely re-invigorated by the fact that moral philosophers then began talking to lawyers. I think, myself, that the impact of economics on moral philosophy will in the long run prove more significant. But whether or not this is so, there is at all events *this* difference between the way in which economics has affected philosophy and the way in which law has: the lawyers drew our attention to cases, and thus to the concrete, the economists draw our attention to theoretical problems—abstract problems about distribution and economic justice generally.

I am sure that moral philosophers will never go back to talking *only* with each other. They are certain to want to remain on speaking terms with economists and lawyers, if not with non-philosophers generally. But there is something which I think will make some of them, anyway, feel the need to turn back into moral philosophy itself, for a closer look at it. I mentioned earlier the way in which the death of positivism liberated moral philosophers: they were freed from the need to be constantly defending the mere *possibility* of rational argument in ethics. Well, no one now holds the crabbed and cranky conception of language which was at the heart of positivism, and which constituted the threat against which ethics had to be defended. But there recently has appeared yet another threat to ethics, one which comes, not from within philosophy itself, but from outside it—I mean the one which comes from evolutionary biology. If it turns out that we have such moral beliefs as we do have because of natural selection, then *can* it be that we have, not merely moral belief, but moral *knowledge*? Many of us think we *know* that gratuitous harms are bad, and callous disregard for suffering indecent; we need to ask precisely how, if at all, the speculations of the biologists cast a shadow on our thought that we know. A similar threat from cultural anthropology has been lurking in the background for years, but years, but it has not, for one reason or another, been taken seriously by many moral philosophers; this new threat, I think, will be. In consequence, I hazard a guess that we shall be seeing more moral epistemology than we have seen lately.

Yet another room in which we may expect to see moral philosophers is the room marked "moral psychology"—I borrow the term from Miss Anscombe. Miss Anscombe argued some years ago that moral philosophy has suffered from the lack of a plausible account of the nature of intention and motive, wish and desire, pleasure and pain, and she was surely right. How on earth can we pretend to give an account of the conditions under which a man has acted well or ill if we have no plausible account of the ways in which his intentions, motives, wishes, and so on (as I shall vaguely say) "bear on" what he did?

Indeed, we stand in need of something deeper still, namely an ontology of action. Act utilitarians say that the question whether an act is right or wrong is the same as the question whether its consequences are good or bad—more precisely, whether its consequences are better than the consequences of any of the other acts open to its agent at the time. But what precisely are these "other acts" open to the agent at the time? What in fact is act and what is consequence? Suppose I kill a man by shooting him. If my killing of him *contains* his death as a part, then presumably his death is not a *consequence* of my killing of him; so are we to suppose that my killing of him was not so wrong an act as my shooting of him?—for his death was on any view a consequence of my shooting of him, and, as we like to think, deaths are bad things. On the other hand, how can my killing of him fail to contain his death as a part? Surely the killing is not over until the death is, and it is at best a hard saying to say that the death is a *consequence* of the killing. Act utilitarians have until relatively recently paid no attention to difficulties such as these; it is plain enough that they must be attended to if the theory is to have so much as a chance of being true.

Nor is it only act utilitarians who stand in need of an ontology of action. Whatever your moral theory, you must surely allow that moral assessment of an act turns in some way, and in some measure, on the alternative acts open to the agent of that act—and you too will therefore need an account of what counts as an "alternative act." Moreover, an act may be part of a series of acts, guided by a single intention; appropriate moral assessment of the series surely depends, at least in part, on appropriate moral assessment of the members of the series. But confronted with a man who is acting, how are we to carve what we see into discrete (or in-discrete) chunks, which should be the members of the series?

These past few years have been boom-time in that branch of metaphysics we currently call "theory of action." (The length of the current bibliographies on action is enough to make the eyes glaze over!) I am sure we can expect interest in action to continue for some time to come, especially in light of recent work on semantics generally, and in particular on the semantics of what Donald Davidsom called "action-sentences"—i.e., sentences such that in asserting them we predicate an action of a person. Many moral philosophers have a foot in both camps: while standing on one foot they do ethics, while standing on the other they do theory of action. I do not think there has as yet been sufficient attention paid to the question how precisely current work in theory of action bears on moral philosophy, in part, perhaps, because nothing is as yet settled in theory of action—the central problems remain open. But I am sure we can expect to see it in future.

Having already mentioned semantics, I feel free to mention yet one more room in which moral philosophers will probably be found, namely the room marked "deontic logic." Up to now, deontic logic has been the exclusive property of the logicians: most moral philosophers have regarded it with some disdain—the results have seemed meager and the problems uninteresting. But it seems to me on two counts that this situation may change. In the first place, the logic itself is likely to become richer as more linguists come to take an interest in it. In the second place, I think it likely that *some* moral philosophers, at any rate, may come to feel a need to attend to it. For my own part, what I should like to see at some time in the future is a full-scale theory of rights. As we know, a number of moral philosophers have of late taken to relying heaving on the notion of a right—Robert Nozick, for example, rests a political theory on it—but as we also know, the notion itself (as it were) hangs in mid-air. Now producing a full-scale theory of rights requires producing two things: on the one hand, an account of what we might call the *external* logic of rights (that is, an account of the ways in which ascriptions of rights are supported by reports about people's desires, expectations, and perhaps other things), and on the other hand, an account of what we might call the *internal* logic of rights (that is, an account of the ways in which ascriptions of rights support each other). Indeed, it seems to me that the internal logic of rights must come first. But what I am calling the internal logic of rights is a branch or sub-field within deontic logic; and it seems to me therefore that anyone who wants to produce a theory of rights will simply have to engage himself with it.

In sum, then, it seems to me that we may see in moral philosophy a turn away from the concrete towards the abstract—at any rate, towards the theoretical. I *hope* that philosophers will continue at the same time to attend to conrete moral, social, and political problems, and to address themselves to non-philosophers generally; on the other hand, I for one view the prospect of a turn to theory with no dismay—quite to the contrary, I look forward to the results of it with considerable interest and enthusiasm. It is a *very* good time in which to *be* a moral philosopher.

EDUCATION AND MORALITY

RICHARD T. DE GEORGE
University of Kansas, Lawrence, Kansas

The aims of education have traditionally and appropriately been derived from and related to a theory of knowledge, a view of human nature, and a consideration of society and of the individual's role in it. Contemporary American philosophers have dealt with all of these latter topics and some have recently addressed such practical issues as war and peace, abortion, medical ethics, reverse discrimination, and so on. But contemporary American philosophers on the whole have not turned their attention to the question of the general aims of education; and psychologists, sociologists and others have filled the gap. In the process the philosophic distinction between fact and value has been misconstrued in many educational institutions, undermining any commitment to values and generating a scepticism towards the possibility of attaining objective non-scientific knowledge. Confusion with respect to moral education on the one hand and politicization of the university on the other have been two of the results.

I

Education, in Aristotelian terms which are still relevant, has traditionally been concerned with developing the excellences that human beings are capable of realizing. It should help the individual develop his positive capacities for self-control, for fruitful social activity, for the enjoyment of cultural and intellectual pursuits—a task which Dewey rightly pointed out is never-ending. It involves providing the inspiration, the motivation, the knowledge, and the techniques the young need in order to develop their talents. In the language of an older tradition unembarrassed by references to values it involves the development of the moral and intellectual virtues. Better insight into psychology might help us achieve these aims more successfully. But the values have traditionally been articulated by religion, common sense, and philosophy—not by psychology or sociology or anthropology, which have been more

346

interested in describing values than in making or defending value judgments. What we to some extent lack is an articulation and defense of the moral and intellectual virtues worth pursuing in out time.

Whitehead in the *Aims of Education* takes account of the rhythm of the learning process from infancy through maturity, and some of his insights have received support from the work of Piaget and others. A failure of contemporary education in America—to the extent that it is a failure, and in many ways it is a success— stems not from a lack of new and appropriate ends, nor from a need for better psychological techniques to achieve those ends, but from the lack of a clear view of the importance of the moral and intellectual virtues. Too many have succumbed to a relativistic view in ethics, to a fragmentary view of knowledge, and to an uncritical acceptance of pseudo-science. They are reluctant to express or defend value judgments, and in education they shy away from mentioning, much less defending, the intellectual virtues. Reliance on techniques of education has led to a nascent science of instruction; there is no science of education. Instruction by machines is a facet of education whose time has come but education by machines is a contradiction in terms. For not only must facts be transmitted and mastered, but the student must learn what it means to know and learn, think and value from the example provided by the teacher who knows, masters, integrates, respects and lives by the facts he teaches. Education involves not only facts but values, an appreciation of culture, and an independence of thought. Independence of thought can be achieved only rudimentarily on the lower levels of education and becomes more central only later. But values cannot be separated from education at any point. If this thesis is correct, part of what philosophy can do for education is articulate the virtues and values of science, art, literature, justice, intellectual honesty, and so forth, which education should aim at developing.

Virtues are achieved by practice, not simply by learning precepts. Though both the moral and intellectual virtues are important at all stages of education, the lower grades are more properly concerned with the moral virtues, and the higher levels of education with the intellectual virtues.

In America the initial education of children, which begins at the moment of birth, is in the hands of the child's parents. The parents teach by caring for the child, helping him develop, talking to him, playing with him, and so on. As the child grows he learns how to do things and he also learns how to control some of his drives, how to treat and interact with other people. He absorbs some initial scale of values. Lawrence Kohlberg calls this the pre-moral stage[1] and Sartre notes it is the stage at which the child is fitted with the glasses of his class through which he sees the world.[2]

Now if we take seriously the aim of developing the moral and intellectual virtues of children and young adults and if their formal education is to help them discipline themselves and provide them with the foundation for their future and continuing education and development as adults, then, though the best means for achieving these goals is not yet known, we are not hopelessly lost. If we do not know exactly how some of the students who go through our schools become educated, there is no doubt that some of them do become educated. Similarly there is no doubt that many of them rise at least to Kohlberg's stage of conventional morality, despite their self-doubts and uncertainty on many moral issues.

Some of the difficulties of contemporary educational practice stem from the fact that inculcation of the moral and intellectual virtues is not recognized as a proper aim of education, and that in some ways the stages of education have been blurred with too little attention paid to the different sub-aims at each level. This lack of recognition stems from a mistrust of value judgments and a failure to see that human society contains within it moral imperatives, the observance of which makes many of its practices possible. Virtues are not value judgments added to living and to social practices; rather social life and practices are human ways of acting which involve value judgments.

The emphasis on moral pluralism in the United States has led many to accept moral relativism and has prevented them from recognizing the moral consensus which exists on a vast array of issues. Pluralism may be found on varying levels. At the most extreme level a radical or hard pluralism would consist of evaluative systems which were mutually exclusive and basically opposed both in principles and practices. A system which holds that murder and lying and theft are right and good is at variance with one which holds they are bad. The former might questionably be called a moral system, since its rules do not seem to be universalizable, and since they seem to preclude the possibility of any social life at all. But such radical pluralism and the relativism it might imply are not serious issues in the United States or anywhere else in the world. A Manson family may hold some such views, though inconsistently. All societies, however, internally agree on certain basic practices; these are called by some the structural similarities of all moralities. Nor is the existence of such similarities at all strange since the structures are part of the social practices in which humans engage in all parts of the world.

The frequently overlooked point is that there is an enormous amount of agreement in the United States (as well as elsewhere) about what is morally right and what is morally wrong. Some of this is expressed in law. But instances such as Watergate and the taking of corporate bribes have brought to the surface a moral consensus that goes beyond the law.

Moral pluralism on another level may emerge in disputes about particular practices—e.g., on pre-marital sex and abortion; or it may emerge on the level of principles, e.g., a religious set of principles vs. a utilitarian set vs. a Kantian set (though representatives of both of the latter claim compatibility with the former). Disputes on practices may result from viewing the same facts in the light of different principles or from viewing different facts. Much of moral controversy, as the emotivists have argued, stems from differences of fact. How such differences and how differences of principle are adjudicated in America depends frequently on the particular issues involved. Sometimes the differences are tolerated; sometimes the arguments on each side are weighed and a consensus emerges expressed in law.

For purposes of education, however, the large area of morality on which there is consensus is especially significant. Much of this is embodied in what Kohlberg has called conventional morality. Though conventional morality is not the highest stage from the point of view of personal responsibility and commitment, it should not be disparaged. For acting in accordance with it most frequently produces actions which are morally correct, even if they do not on the Kantian and some other views carry with them much in the way of individual moral worth. Since there is this large area of consensus, and since many of the moral norms and practices are necessary for social intercourse at every level, these practices are willy-nilly taught to some extent in the schools, which are social institutions. Respect for the rights of others, whether explicitly formulated or not, is to some extent necessary. Truthfulness, fairness, equality of treatment, honesty in one's work, willingness to take responsibility, promptness, diligence, cooperation with others, are all moral virtues which should be acknowledged and inculcated, not ignored or denied in a vain attempt to be value-neutral.

The individual is necessarily and intimately linked with his society. His self-development, therefore, cannot be separated from his society, the role he may eventually play in it, and the opportunities he will have in it. In a static peasant society the need for reading, writing and mathematical skills was frequently minimal and formal education was the exception rather than the rule. Moral education fell to the family, the church, and society at large. The skills needed in a contemporary post-industrial society to earn a living or contribute to the society through one's labor as well as to continue one's education through the opportunities available require reading and writing and basic mathematical skills. Knowledge of geography and some history seem to be other examples of socially agreed-upon skills. The moral education of children is part of their socialization. They should be helped to develop self-control, to master material, to fulfill assignments as well as to be considerate of others, to pull their fair share in cooperative endeavors, and so on.

Parents and teachers serve as the child's super-ego, setting down norms to which they expect him to adhere, reprimanding him when he violates them, until they become internalized. As Aristotle correctly noted, virtue is a habit and response to legitimate command and so obedience is an initial virtue necessary to the development of other virtues. Enlightened non-authoritarian control of the child by others helps the child grow in control of himself. Skinner and others have argued that all of us are in some way programmed and our actions conditioned by others.[3] Yet it is possible to distinguish manipulation, which is the directing or influencing of the actions of A by B for B's benefit, from the teaching of A by B for A's benefit. Moral education, if it follows the latter model, is not manipulation.

Moral education, moreover, may be by precept or by example, and is usually by both, if it is to be effective. Since the child starts with so little knowledge, he learns an enormous amount by believing what he is told, even if he does not understand why it is so or how such knowledge is acquired. The correct spelling of words, the grammatical use of language, the meaning of words, the adding of sums, the location of countries and cities, the facts of history can all be taught to and mastered by a child who believes and trusts those in authority—parents and teachers. The same is true in the sphere of morality. Morality in its broad sense can be taught by precept, but to be effective should be taught by example as well. There was good reason for the early American tradition of choosing prim and proper people as school teachers rather than the town drunk.

Even in a pluralistic society such as ours there is a community of values—conventional social morality—which can and should be taught; and unless some values are taught the child, he will never know or at least have difficulty learning how adequately to deal with them. This does not mean, however, that there must be a set of national values centrally drawn up and imposed. Rather, I would argue, the lower the school the more responsive it should be to home rules, to the local values and to local control. The lower the school the more need also for the development of self-control and self-discipline and the greater the need for both epistemic moral authority and exemplary moral authority.[4]

Many parents seem at a loss with respect to their own moral beliefs on disputed moral issues and some claim that in a pluralistic society morality has no place in the school. Such a view, I have already argued, fails to understand either the broad moral consensus necessary for any society to exist, or the Aristotelian notion of a moral virtue as involving self-control, control over passions, the rule of reason and the fruitful channeling of our drives. It also fails to understand that in a society in which there are legitimate moral disputes and differences the virtue of tolerance is a social necessity in some areas. Teaching morality by precept and example does not mean that answers must be given to all moral issues, that different views on some topics cannot be explained, that the imprecision of moral decisions cannot be made clear.

By the high school years mastery of basic skills should be, and in most cases can be, established. The scope of knowledge should be and generally is expanded, and the beginning of independent critical judgment can be developed. The emphasis on the moral virtues should therefore begin to give way to emphasis on the intellectual virtues.

II

If my view is correct, the difference between high school education and college and university education should be significant. College education can be and should be different in kind from high school education, with the emphasis being placed increasingly on what Aristotle calls the intellectual virtues. The moral virtues should be taken for granted. The legitimate role of authority is therefore properly restricted. The goal is or should be not so much to teach facts as to teach the theories which account for them and the reasons for holding them. A teacher by right should earn the epistemic authority given him by his students.[5] They may well be predisposed to acknowledging him as an authority and to believing what he says; but he should justify their belief and help them to rely less and less on their belief in what he says and more and more on the reasons he gives them for what he says. A professor should have something to profess and should be able to *do* philosophy, *do* mathematics, *do* chemistry as well as talk about them. He teaches by example as well as by word.

To the extent that the pursuit of knowledge at the college and university level is not just the accumulation of facts but their evaluation and subsumption under theory, the critical faculties of the student should be developed. Intellectual honesty, openness to new data, materials and arguments, rigor in thinking, willingness to follow a line of argument or thinking to its conclusion, the constant attempt to be objective are all facets of intellectual virtue which students should find embodied in their faculty teachers. The sub-aim of university education should be not only to learn facts but to learn how to assimilate them, integrate them, explain them, and defend one's findings and positions. Knowledge can be stored in books and on computer tapes. It is not merely stored but constantly tested, evaluated and integrated in the mind of a thinking person.

Just as the basic moral virtues and moral imperatives are not arbitrary but necessary for there to be a society, so the basic intellectual virtues are not arbitrary. They are closely related to the process of developing and transmitting knowledge, to the development of the kind of intellect capable of discovering it as well as capable of creative innovation. And just as with the moral virtues, the intellectual virtues are transmitted not only by precept but also by example.

The live model at this level, just as at the earlier level, is all-important. But the virtues exemplified are the intellectual ones. With the development of his critical powers the student *vis-à-vis* the moral virtues is able to rise to what Kohlberg calls the reflective level of morality where one can question the basis for the values he has previously held simply because they were taught to him, just as one can critically question the basis for the facts which were previously taught him. The institutions of higher learning are the places where the intellectual virtues should be found preeminently.

The values of the home and of conventional morality are here both assumed and questioned.

One of the frequent failures of universities in past decades was to lose sight of the intellectual virtues and of their importance to both the development and transmission of knowledge. The result in some cases has been the politicization of the university to the detriment of society. For if my argument is correct an enlightened, free society derives more social good from an autonomous non-politicized university which fosters and pursues the intellectual virtues than from a politicized one which it controls.

A university may be politicized in many ways, all of which involve the corruption or subordination of the intellectual virtues necessary for the transmission and expansion of knowledge. One way is by its making or taking some political end as its primary goal, either in theory or in fact. Thus, in the late sixties many students claimed that the universities had been politicized because they were taking as their implicit, if not explicit, goal the defense of the status quo by cooperating with the military-industrial complex, by providing docile white-collar workers for industry, and by serving as apologists for the existing structures of society. The aim of the radical groups on campus was therefore to politicize the university differently, i.e., by choosing different values, by using the university to bring about radical change, by making the campus the jumping-off point for anti-war and anti-establishment demonstrations, by entering directly into the mechanics of social change instead of simply discussing such change. To the extent that universities made either the defense of the status quo or the attacking of the status quo a primary end, they were and are correctly said to have been or to be politicized. There are two other ways of politicizing a university. One is by directly running the university by the decree of either the state or federal legislature which sets its internal policy or rules or interferes with its internal decisions. Another arises when there are internal factions within a university which decide on various aspects of university policy— whether they be graduation requirements or promotions and tenure or other similar matters—by power struggles based on vested interests. The factions may develop in departments or schools or lines may be drawn between faculty and students or between either group and the administration.

Different views of knowledge justify different kinds of universities. In their misplaced and misguided attempt to separate facts and values, many American universities have ignored the intellectual virtues and have become infected and politicized by what I shall call the "building-block" view of knowledge.

The building-block view of knowledge begins with naive realism, to which are added the assumptions that knowledge is not problematic and that the general lines of human knowledge are fairly well in place. What remains is to fill in holes or gaps, and to add on higher levels to existing knowledge structures. Knowledge is achieved by starting with experience, which is then analyzed and described. The various kinds of knowledge correspond to the various kinds of experience, and to these in turn correspond the various schools and departments in a university. Some areas have larger, better developed structures than others—i.e., they have more, and more tightly cemented, blocks of knowledge.

According to this view, college and university education are not different in kind from grade school or high school education. At the lower levels simplified blocks of subject matter are presented. At the college level a greater number of facts and more advanced blocks of knowledge are presented to students, and students are exposed to areas—e.g., of philosophy, psychology—to which they were not exposed earlier. Graduate school provides the opportunity for specialization in a particular field. But once again the knowledge communicated is simply more of the same kind of knowledge learned at earlier stages.

In such a university it is not unreasonable to expect professors to spend most of their time teaching, since the body of accumulated knowledge is so much greater than the contribution any one of them can make. Their teaching, moreover, since it consists of the transmission of blocks of knowledge, can increasingly be taken over by computerized techniques. Through their research professors may add a block or two to knowledge. More frequently they refine previously existing blocks, or by criticism uncover a somewhat defective block; or perhaps several professors in a series of articles and counter-articles finally succeed in roughly shaping a new block. They may also write the books used by teachers on the lower levels. Though they know how the blocks of knowledge in their own fields fit together, however, they individually and collectively have no grasp of the whole of knowledge; nor does their specialized knowledge reveal what education as a whole is supposed to accomplish, other than to prepare students either to become professionals of some kind or to find satisfactory jobs in society.

Since the building-block view of knowledge provides no guide to educational structure or ends, the job market becomes the guide to what students should be taught. The students in turn, using the same guide, come to demand increasing relevance in their courses. They wish, with good reason, to know what use a course will be in getting or keeping a job, or in advancing upward once they get a position. The schools within the university such as law and business have no trouble answering the question of relevance. Many of the departments in the liberal arts and sciences are harder pressed to do so, and attempt to gain relevance by emphasizing the contemporary aspect of their fields, or the current modes and fads. For their continuance depends on attracting students and generating credit hours.

Since the building-block view provides no unified account of what knowledge is and no unified view of what a university should be, a university can have as many departments as there are areas and as many professional schools as there are professions. Since the building blocks of knowledge from area to area are relatively independent, however, a university can pick and choose among departments and schools. The decisions about what departments and what schools are represented in a university are not a function of the nature of knowledge but of student or social demand or of the prestige factors a university chooses to pursue. This view both justifies the growth of multiversities which are unified only administratively and justifies non-academic administrators who decide what departments or schools a university will have, how money will be allocated, and so on. On the building-block view these are not academic but administrative matters.

Finally, the building-block view of knowledge adopts the fact-value distinction and allows only factual blocks into the knowledge edifice. Hence knowledge is said to be objective and value-neutral. If values are introduced—as they frequently are—their justification cannot be based on knowledge claims. In the end, the imposition of values—whether they be the entrenched social values of a society, or radical ones, or self-interested ones—tends to invite politicization of the university. If such politicization is not a necessary concomitant of the building-block view of knowledge, it is at least a common result.

The tragedy is that the building-block view of knowledge is popular folklore and does not represent knowledge as it should be pursued in a university. Analysis and description are certainly parts of the process of knowledge. The primary and insidious defect of the building-block view is that it reduces the process to these. The reduction results in a model which is a distortion of the nature of the knowledge which should and can be produced at a university and which should inform its functions and ends. The reduction is insidious in that it tends to distort the knowledge process in the university, to determine the organization of the university, and to preclude the university's fulfilling what could be a positive, unique, social function.

The building-block view of knowledge pays no attention to and has no room for the intellectual virtues. It ignores, if it does not deny, the unity of knowledge; it confuses the objectification of fact with objectivity; and it fails to leave sufficient room for the critical element in the knowledge process. The latter involves evaluation in the process itself, instead of superimposing it from the outside.

On the lower levels of education the *results* of the knowledge process together with social values should be taught; on the university level the *process* itself should be taught together with the intellectual values it requires. This involves taking a critical attitude toward the results of the process, integrating them, and evaluating the earlier assumed social values. The liberating aspect of such a pursuit of knowledge is that it can help students develop their perspectives. In the lower phases of education students learn about the world from the perspective of their own culture. In the higher phases they learn to see their culture in the perspective of the world. If one questions one's values and perspective, they may become better grounded and supported, or they may be found to be groundless and crumble, or they may be found to be partially sound and partially built on less-than-solid ground. Critical liberal education, therefore, does not necessarily reinforce, nor does it necessarily undermine, the social and cultural commitments of a society.

In the knowing process there is not simply analysis but also the construction of theories to account for uncovered or alleged facts; there is not simply description, but interpretation and evaluation of what is described. Research involves not only the finding of new facts and the addition of new blocks of knowledge but the raising of questions about how the new facts affect the old ones and how they change the whole. The research of a professor, consequently, can and frequently does lead him to see more deeply and perhaps differently into what he held before. This is why a professor who has something to profess and who continues to do research cannot be replaced by teaching machines. For they would have to be reprogrammed as frequently as he is—which is continuously.

The view of knowledge which I would defend, therefore, holds that knowledge as pursued and developed, preserved and transmitted at a university results from active encounters with reality and that its pursuit—like knowledge itself—should be objective, systematic, and unified. To call knowledge objective is to underline the fact that it is communal—shareable and open, and neither personal nor individual—and the fact that it is possible in some way to demonstrate or cogently argue for it. The claim of openness implies further that the knowledge sought is not secret. (Hence secret research either for government or industry is inimical to it.) Objectivity, moreover, should not be confused with the static building-block conception of knowledge according to which units are fixed, known, recorded, and transmitted. Objectivity involves critical, negative, creative thinking, a constant testing of what is known, and a constant evaluation of accepted fact and theory. This aspect of knowledge makes it inappropriate for those not actively engaged in its investigation to attempt to dictate what its content is or must be. This aspect also makes its pursuit sometimes conservative and sometimes radical vis-a-vis the conditions of the society in which it is developed. In itself the objective pursuit of knowledge is neither necessarily radical nor conservative, though its pursuit involves elements of both preservation and change.

If the nature of knowledge pursued by members of a university is systematic, this indicates that it is not their goal simply to collect facts but also to provide the reasoned theory which accounts for, interprets, explains, and makes sense of those facts. This is an *activity* engaged in by those within the university—both by those who profess the results of their intellectual work and those who are led through the process by their professors. The unity of knowledge represents the ideal of total knowledge which can be fit together. It is because of the unity of knowledge that it makes sense to have all the branches of knowledge represented in one place, housed in one institution, and transmitted simultaneously along several lines to the students who come there to learn. The ideal of the unity of knowledge, however, is an ideal which students cannot pursue on their own without the direction and example of faculty members who see beyond the boundaries of their specialties.

The intellectual virtues demanded by such a view of knowledge and the process by which it is achieved include a love of the truth and the willingness to follow an argument wherever it leads; the ability to withstand political, economic and other pressures to falsify or skew one's research and findings; the intellectual honesty to admit mistakes; the intellectual courage to criticize what is popular; and the desire for knowledge and wisdom for their own sakes as well as for the uses to which they might be put.

Industry, government and specialized schools can teach students what they need to know in certain careers or businesses. What university-substitutes do not provide, and what universities can provide students, are the benefits of what has been termed a liberal education. Education is liberating to the extent that it frees rather than binds individuals in their thought and development. They should not only receive exposure to a variety of fields in which to test their interests but they should also learn how to pursue and integrate knowledge so they can develop the intellectual flexibility necessary to adjust to changing conditions. A society, moreover, benefits from having a large number of liberally educated citizens who will be flexibly prepared to adapt to changing conditions, who will be able to participate in public affairs, who will be critically trained to question and to actively participate in their own governance. Not every society will want such people. But an open democratic society is especially in need of having a large body of such citizens to act as a counterweight to the exercise of power in government or in the economic or social realm.

Without a sanctuary for the pursuit of knowledge, free from restraints or limits or specific objectives set by government or business, the objectivity of knowledge is threatened. The university, if it is not politically controlled, can provide a forum in which theories and policies can and should be rationally examined, criticized, discussed and debated, thought about and written about without fear of reprisal or loss of position. We would not expect a company training program to teach its students how to radically criticize the company; but we should expect a university supported by public funds to teach how to radically criticize any and all aspects of society when appropriate. It is not and should not be the function of the university to directly change society, however, for objectivity demands a certain distance from the need for immediate practical decisions and action characteristic of politics and business.

This brief sketch of what a university *can* uniquely contribute to society and what the nature of the knowledge and intellectual virtues it pursues *should be* provides the basis, and so far as I can see the only basis, for claiming autonomy for the university. Autonomy can be claimed therefore, only to the extent that it pursues these ends. To the extent that it does not, to the extent that it loses its objectivity, tries to directly implement changes in society, or puts the vested interests of getting sponsored research funds or of generating more credit hour production above the goal of objectively developing and transmitting knowledge and of being a forum for open debate, it corrupts itself from within and can hardly expect to have its autonomy respected. This was all perhaps clearer in a less complicated age—before the university attempted to become a multiversity and before government contracts and grants were discovered to have post-facto strings attached to them.

The ideal of objectivity may seem to have clearest application in the realm of the arts and sciences. But the argument holds for the professional schools as well. If they are to be other than simply training grounds for particular professions which happen to be located together with other educational institutions, then they too must be liberating and not simply schools which produce the docile, well-trained product requested by law firms or hospitals or businesses. These latter can train people in their own institutions if they so desire; but there is no justification for the public's subsidizing such firms through education unless society receives in the graduates of educational institutions citizens who are liberated, critical, and able to function as a counterweight to governmental, economic and social power and pressure.

If my argument for a university's autonomy is correct, the reason for demanding lack of interference from those outside the university is that in matters of curriculum, requirements, promotion, and so on, the determining essential ingredient is knowledge, and that judgments in these cases should be made on the basis of the kind of knowledge properly preserved and developed at a university, especially by the faculty. Those within the university's walls are not necessarily any more intelligent than those outside its walls. But if those within are dedicated to and motivated by the preservation, development and transmission of knowledge, then their actions are in the interests of those outside its walls as well as of those within. The level at which a society supports its universities is dependent on the resources available, the number of students enrolled and many other factors. But whatever the level of funding, a society can only be expected to support without interference a university which is in fact dedicated to the objective pursuit of knowledge. How is society to know whether a university is dedicated and why should it trust its universities? The trust of society, I believe, must be earned and documented. In fact only if there is accountability is it reasonable for a society, which understands the benefits and necessity of having an autonomous university, to support it and to allow it its necessary autonomy. For only through accountability can it rest assured both that the university is fulfilling its function and that it has not in some way or other become politicized. Accountability, therefore, must not only be such as to satisfy society but should also operate to prevent the growth of factions and power blocs within the university. Accordingly, accountability should not only be hierarchical, but each section or portion of the university should be accountable to each other section below it, above it, and on the same level as it itself.

The university, if it wishes to be autonomous though publicly supported, should have nothing to hide from any portion of society. Each portion of the university should be academically accountable to the other portions in the sense that the work of each must be open for interaction with and evaluation by the others, thereby helping to enhance the quality of the whole. Those outside observers who wish to question or evaluate any portion of the university in terms of the canons of knowledge should be able to do so.

To evaluate the adequacy of the job the university as a whole is doing, those who support it, however, should realize its true end. To expect narrow or immediate relevance in all its aspects or an immediate payoff from its activities is to fail to appreciate the nature of knowledge and the meaning of either basic research or disinterested objectivity. They might gauge the success of the faculty's teaching by turning to the alumni: what is their attitude towards their university experience, their appraisal of the development of their abilities and talents, and their record of achievement? They might ask: to what extent has the university helped preserve and transmit the culture of the past and how is the university helping that culture to live and develop in the present? Has the faculty advanced and preserved knowledge—in what ways, how successfully and to what extent? Even more importantly those who wish to evaluate the university should ask whether it has withstood the political and economic pressures constantly threatening to subvert its primary ends. Has it accepted grants and projects which have taken its faculty away from pursuits to which it should be devoting itself? Has it served as society's critic and social conscience or has it simply gone along with whatever would bring it the most students, money and faculty?

Finally, the reply to the claim that the university is already politicized is that it need not be so. To the extent that it has been politicized, it should not be politicized differently, but depoliticized. If my argument has been correct, the need for change should be recognized by those within the university. Only if they reaffirm the pursuit of objective knowledge as their goal and guide their actions accordingly, developing and enforcing strict though informed canons of accountability, can they expect to have their autonomy respected and adequate support continued. This will not of course be enough. For they must also convince society once again of the need for the objective pursuit of knowledge and of the need for an open forum for discussion in all areas, whether politically sensitive or not.

To ask this is to ask for a place where collective self-knowledge may take place; and obviously not every society and not every member of society is ready to face up to the implications of such knowledge. A society can limit a university's ability to perform its appropriate functions, but it can only do so at its own peril, as I believe the instances of Berlin, Italy and Yugoslavia demonstrate. The alternative to autonomy is politicization. To accept or to develop politicization in a university may be practically expedient, but it entails giving up what makes a university unique and most worthwhile. Hence, if a university gives up the primary end of seeking objective knowledge, if it subordinates this to other ends, if it politicizes itself, then it forfeits the basis of its legitimate autonomy, and it does so at *its* own peril. For once internally politicized it will almost certainly be externally politicized as well.

Philosophy of education has fallen on bad days. Yet philosophy of education can, among other tasks, set realistic norms and ideals and defend them; it can uncover illegitimate uses and so abuses of authority in education; and it can help articulate and develop the moral and intellectual virtues necessary for the good life in present-day society. The importance of the development of a critical capacity in a democracy has been argued by Dewey and others. The importance of education for change is obvious in a society as full of changes as ours is. Adaptability is both a moral and an intellectual virtue we should add to our updated list of virtues.

The people of each society in each epoch face different problems from their predecessors. As we begin our third century we face a dynamic, changeable, unknown future. Our institutions need reexamination and our values need rearticulation. The ability to carry on an informed critical examination of issues and to distinguish, articulate, defend and appreciate values is a characteristic of the educated person. Our aim as educators should be to produce such people.

NOTES

1. Lawrence Kohlberg, "Stage and Sequence: The Cognitive-Developmental Approach to Socialization," in *Handbook of Socialization Theory and Research*, ed. D. Goslin (New York, Holt, Rinehart and Winston, 1969); Lawrence Kohlberg, "Stages of Moral Development as a Basis for Moral Education," in *Moral Education: Interdisciplinary Approaches*, eds. C. M. Beck, B. S. Crittenden, E. V. Sullivan (Toronto, University of Toronto Press, 1968); and "Moral Development," *The Journal of Philosophy*, LXX (Oct. 25, 1973). See also Jean Piaget, *The Moral Judgment of the Child* (London, Kegan Paul, Trench, Trubner & Co., 1932).
2. Jean-Paul Sartre, *The Words* (New York, George Braziller, 1964).
3. B. F. Skinner, *Beyond Freedom and Dignity* (New York, Bantam Books, 1972).
4. For a fuller discussion of these types of authority, see Richard T. De George, "Authority and Morality," in *Authority*, ed. F. Adelmann (The Hague, Nijhoff, 1974), pp. 31–49.
5. For the argument see Richard T. De George, "The Nature and Function of Epistemic Authority," in *Authority: A Philosophical Analysis*, ed. R. B. Harris (University, Ala., Alabama University Press, 1976), pp. 76–93.

PHILOSOPHY, TECHNOLOGY AND THE QUALITY OF LIFE*

JOHN A. PASSMORE

The Australian National University, Canberra, Australia

I propose to define technology somewhat narrowly—but in a manner which reminds us of, even if it does not precisely reflect, its etymology—as the application of science *(logos)* through artisan skill *(technē)* to the solution of practical problems. Most inventions, of course, are not science-based; they are what I should call "practitioner inventions," skill operating through trial and error rather than through the application of general principles. So, to take an instance, a developed theory of aerodynamics was stimulated by, not the source of, the trial-and-error invention of a workable aeroplane. Practitioner inventions are to be found in every society—the boomerang is a notable example—whereas science-dependent inventions are a peculiarity of modern Western societies, not coming to the center of the stage until the mid-nineteenth century. And whereas philosophy and practitioner invention have moved along independent paths, the relationship of philosophy to technology, to science-based invention, has been a peculiarly intimate one.

Not, of course, that philosophers have done the inventing. But they foresaw technology, lent their patronage to it, helped to create an intellectual atmosphere in which technology was seen as not only conceivable but eminently desirable.

Francis Bacon is a familiar instance. He was no scientist, no technologist. But he prophesied that human beings, by conjoining science with invention, could extend their government over the earth in a "great restauration," repairing the damage done by Adam's Fall, so that they would once again become masters, under God, of the world around them. Even more significant is the less familiar case of Bacon's near-contemporary Descartes, himself a scientist and the author of a philosophy much stronger intellectually, much better adapted to the technological revolution, than Bacon's.

What I have called "technology" Descartes called "practical philosophy." It marries the intellect of the scientist to the skills of the artisan. Traditionally, intellect and manual skill had been sharply disjoined. The intellect, it had generally been supposed,

363

should confine itself to the contemplation of the fabric of the universe, under the tutelage of that "queen of the sciences," theology. Such contemplation, in the still prevailing Platonic-Aristotelian system, was the highest life possible to mankind. The artisan, in contrast, was by his very nature one of the lowliest of human beings, working as he did with his hands, restricted as he was by his materials. That artisan and scientist should unite their forces in order to conquer the world by manipulating it with theoretical understanding—this was the revolutionary concept of their relationship which Bacon and Descartes shared.

No less revolutinary was Descartes's anticipation of what would issue from their marriage: "an infinity of arts and crafts, enabling us to enjoy without any trouble the fruits of the earth and the good things that are found there." "An *infinity* of arts and crafts," no longer then the limited, traditional crafts which every village knew. "Enabling us to enjoy without any trouble the fruits of the earth and the good things that are found there," where the traditional doctrine had been that the sweat of the brow was a perpetual, divinely ordained, punishment for Adam's sin and that "the good things of the earth" were available, in any range, only to those who had been ordained by God to rule—what David Hume once called "the gayer and more opulent part of the population."

But not only did Descartes, along with Bacon, promulgate this startling program for the transformation of the world in the interests of humanity, he developed a theory about the nature of that world which made its transformation look both possible and natural. On the one side, there was inanimate nature—including the human body—so mechanically organized as to call out, like any machine, for modification in the interests of greater efficiency and so malleable, so flexible, as to place within the range of human agents the power needed for that modification. On the other side, there were conscious minds, rational, potent, free, self-conscious. The paradigmatic natural object, for Descartes, is a piece of wax. When we melt wax, we do not destroy it, we transform it, altering its shape, its consistency, so that we can use it for human purposes. That is the spirit, Descartes thought, in which we should approach the world. Nothing need stand in the way of our subjugating it. We need not fear that animals will suffer as a result of our actions; for animals *cannot* suffer, they are mere mechanisms. We need not fear that we shall destroy the world, because that is impossible— matter is conserved. Inspired by the power-machines of the Industrial Revolution, nineteenth-century science was to think in terms of energy rather than matter, of a thing as a store-house of forces rather than as mere extension. That was to make the possibility of technological achievement even more obvious. But the fundamental step, certainly, was taken by Descartes.

Modern technology, however, is directed towards transforming not only inanimate nature and animal life—if, unlike Descartes, we distinguish the two—but, as Descartes does not allow, the very mind itself. In this case, too, the initiative was taken by a philosopher. The human mind, no less than a material object, is, so John Locke argued, like a piece of wax or, for he varied the metaphor in a way that makes the malleability of the mind even more conspicuous, a blank sheet of paper on which educators can write as they will. There is a direct intellectual pathway from Locke to brain-washing, even although Locke would have abhorred the fanaticism which employs brain-washing—or "re-education"—as its chosen instrument, a direct route, too, which terminates in Skinner's *Beyond Freedom and Dignity*, however much Locke would have been at odds with Skinner's conclusions.

But it is not only the friends of physical science, like Bacon, Descartes and Locke, who provided a metaphysical framework for technological innovation. The idealist movement which we associate with the name of Hegel and which had Marx as one of its more rebellious offspring rejected the metaphysics of a Descartes, as leaving human minds "homeless" in the universe, islands of consciousness eternally separated in an inanimate ocean. Equally, it condemned the metaphysics of a Locke for reducing the mind to passivity. But it did so only in order to carry the aggrandizement of mind to its highest level. Inanimate nature, in its eyes, exists only as something which is on its way towards being spiritualized—in itself it is "negativity." And the mind spiritualizes nature by gradually transforming it, making of it a place in which it feels "at home," surrounded only by what bears the mark of being a spiritual creation. Compared with the beauty of works of art, the beauty of nature is, for Hegel, as naught; "even a silly fancy," he once wrote, "such as may pass through any man's head is higher than any product of nature." Compared with cities, or a humanized country-side, primitive nature does not, in the fullest sense, so much as exist.

Marx described himself as a materialist, not an idealist. It might be supposed, then, that the concept of an independent nature would play a much more positive part in his thinking than it did in Hegel's. But if, as he saw his own achievement, Marx "stood Hegel on his head," this was not by denying that nature existed to be transformed; so much he continued to assume. The difference between Hegel and Marx lay in the fact that for Marx it is productive forces rather than "mind" or "spirit" which transform nature. This matters much less, for our present purposes, than the fact that for both philosophers nature is of no value until it has been transformed. That familar slogan—"the conquest of nature"—is nowhere more powerful than in the Marxist societies, whether Soviet or Chinese, for all that man is himself, for them, a natural being.

From this necessarily summary sketch, it will be obvious that philosophy can by no means wash its hands of the technological revolution, as none of its business. To a striking degree, it provided technology with its ideology, its view of the world, its moral outlook. Exactly how should philosophers react, now that technological development has proved to have such unexpected and actually or potentially disastrous consequences?

For philosophers in the Marxist tradition, the answer is obvious. If the technological revolution has brought devastation in its train, this is the fault not of technology but of capitalism. Capitalism cannot contain the new productive forces it has created. Once capitalism is abolished—and it is the philosopher's task, so Marxists would say, to help to destroy it—human beings can set about perfecting themselves and nature, with technology's aid. As a recent Czech-Soviet statement puts it: "The Marxist interpretation of scientific and technological progress proceeds from the key assumption that the objective course of history has now led to a situation where all the necessary means and opportunity are available for solving the major problems of human existence, and that this progress is not only a remedy for poverty, famine, disease and hardship but it turns the human quest for freedom, happiness, personal perfection and creative fulfilment into a genuinely attainable possibility."

When we look at the Marxist countries, however, we see no reason for believing that they have succeeded in so controlling technology that it serves only as a useful instrument in the passage towards "freedom, happiness, personal perfection and creative fulfilment." Quite the contrary: the doubts and hesitations we feel about technological development in our own countries are equally justified by the experience of the Soviet Union, except insofar as it has not yet attained to the Western level of affluence. Ecological devastation is not a peculiarly Western phenomenon. Neither, even more obviously, are the manipulation of opinion, the invasion of privacy, the emphasis on quantity rather than quality. Soviet scientists, like our own, are beginning to look with trepidation on advances in genetic engineering and nuclear warfare. As in our own society—China is trying to avoid this consequence, but at a heavy cost—Soviet scientists constitute a mysterious élite.

So it looks as if certain kinds of problems are inherent in technological development, whatever the political and economic system in which the development occurs. Of course, one can readily envisage forms of social organization which fall neither into the Soviet nor the "Western" pattern. But unless they prevent technological advance they are bound to suffer from the unexpected consequences of that advance, whatever their social system. Naturally, there will be differences in degree; the more affluent societies will make greater use of technology. Its effects, in consequence, will be more widespread and obvious. But at the same time, they are better able to afford the kinds of restriction and limitation which the growth of technology necessitates. I see no ground for believing that the effects of technology are of a different order in socialist states, or indeed in any other society which is committed to continuous technological development.

What facts about the world has the growth of technology brought forcibly home to us, to such a degree that we ought not now to take any philosophy seriously which does not admit them? I shall particularize only five, closely related one to another:

(1) A rationally planned system, deliberately designed to fit human needs, is not *necessarily* superior in all respects to a system which has gradually taken shape by a lengthy process of minute adjustments.

(2) Human beings do not necessarily acquire greater control over their surroundings by modifying them. Such manipulation may, indeed, increase their helplessness, either by generating natural or social forces which they do not know how to control or by making it easier for a few to establish a tyranny over the many.

(3) A technological innovation does not *simply* transform one material object into another. Nature is neither a passive "negativity" nor a plastic piece of wax, as the old stoic doctrine, influential throughout the centuries, that "matter lies inert, a thing ready for all purposes" implied.

(4) It is impossible to do one thing at a time. To act is to interact with an on-going set of processes, to set in motion more than we intend.

(5) Human beings can, in principle, so act as to destroy not only the human species but every form of life. Their continued existence is in no way metaphysically guaranteed by their rationality.

Unlike classical empiricism or Cartesian rationalism, idealism of the Hegelian sort is in large part comfortable with many of these principles. But it supposed that even if individual human beings constantly find their intentions frustrated by the "cunning of history" that very "history," nevertheless, would in the long run ensure man's victory over the world, his total spiritualizing of it. (Or at the very least, the conquest of nature by "Mind.") So for all its emphasis on unexpectedness, the final effect of idealism and its descendants was to make human beings, if not particular individuals, feel secure in their attempts to modify the world by the application of reason.

There is one philosophical tradition to which *none* of these principles need come as a surprise, whether in relation to inanimate nature or to society, a tradition powerfully represented in the United States and more particularly in the city of New York: that is naturalism. Naturalism, except when it has been corrupted by Hegelianism, totally rejects the view that nature is either a passive instrument of the human will or "mere negativity," of value only when it has been transformed. Naturalists are more than ready to recognize that human beings are dependent for their survival on the character of the biosphere. Nor are they surprised to find that technological transformations often produce quite unexpected consequences—that follows from the complexity and the inter-dependence of natural processes. The principle that "you can't do one thing at a time," that to make any change is to set further changes in motion, naturalists can welcome as an illustration of the connectedness of things. They are far from astonished by the view that neither nature nor history is "on humanity's side," that like any other species, the human species could die out, that its continuous existence, let alone its continuous progress, is not metaphysically guaranteed. They will not presume either that what is natural is inevitably superior to what is man-made or, on the other side, that it is inevitably inferior. In technology they will see one of the methods which human beings employ in their attempts to gain greater control over their surroundings. As one form of imaginative enterprise, they will welcome it, but not with the prior expectation that, as a rational enterprise, it is bound to create a better world. No doubt, many of its critics condemn naturalism as a bleak philosophy; it has nothing to promise us as a reward for merely being human. But it is far from hostile to love, to joy, to comradeship, to whatever, except false hopes, makes life worth living. And the consequence of persisting with systems of metaphysics which unduly elevate the status and prospects of the human being is likely to be bleaker still.

It is now not infrequently argued, of course, that naturalism is no protection against human destructiveness, that only if we think of plants, animals, landscapes as spiritual beings like ourselves, shall we ever persuade ourselves that they ought not to be degraded or destroyed. To take that view, however, is to reduce the concept of "mind" to so low a level—for one can scarcely argue that trees are capable of having intentions, of discussing, of taking responsibility, of inquiring, of creating—that the possession of mind no longer serves to mark out what calls for special consideration. Or alternatively, it is to fall back into mere superstitition, to ascribe suffering to a falling tree, or an intent to take vengeance to a river which poisons us as a consequence of its being polluted. Naturalism does not share these defects, provided only that it does not take a reductive form, a form in which it reduces to the level of "mere appearance" the distinction between what is, and what is not, human.

I am far from suggesting that philosophers should rummage in their historical attic for old clothes which might now serve as the latest fashion. A wholly satisfactory naturalism, which will do justice at once to the uniqueness of human beings and their communality, their uniqueness as creators of culture, as capable of participating in and being influenced by rational discussion, their communality as animals, constituents of a biosphere—such a naturalism has still to be fully articulated. And at every stage in that articulation it will have to face up to philosophical criticism. I *am* suggesting, however, that the now-discernible effects of technological change are in no way incompatible with naturalism— as they are incompatible with any metaphysics which thinks of nature as something which "lies inert, ready for all purposes," to be molded into whatever shape is in the interests of humanity, or which assumes that, for metaphysical reasons, the human species cannot be at risk, or which supposes, as in this case the idealists did not, that what we will to occur is what will occur, just as, and only as, we will it.

If the rise of technology, as I have suggested, presents a challenge to many familiar metaphysical systems no less does it present a challenge to traditional moral assumptions. There are those, of course, who would deny that anything whatsoever can challenge a moral principle. On their view, moral principles are eternally graven, whether in the human mind, the universe at large, or the divine will. But in fact the relationship between human conduct and moral principles is two-way, not one-way; the principles grow out of reflection on human conduct and changes in human conduct can demand their re-consideration. Certainly, they ought not to be too readily abandoned or modified; they represent a great deal of experience. But they are not, never have been, unmodifiable. What is there about our recent experience to suggest that their modification might now be called for?

Consider first the question of rights and their relationship to right and wrong. *Rights* has always been a troublesome concept, but at least we thought we knew who possessed rights—existing persons. But now we find it argued that posterity has rights, that the foetus has rights, that animals have rights, that even plants and landscapes have rights. These conclusions have arisen out of our gradual recognition that technological innovations can greatly influence the mode of life of our descendants, that the foetus is now subject to technological intervention, deliberate or accidental, that the continued existence of the biosphere, in its present form, is under threat as a result of our activities. That posterity, the foetus, animals have rights is sometimes taken to follow from the supposed fact that they have not only needs but interests, sometimes to be a consequence of the fact that there are ways in which we ought not to treat them. The philosophical question: "What are the conditions for possessing a right?" has come then to possess a new urgency, as also has the definition of interests and their relation to needs, and the determination of the logical relationship between such statements as "animals have a right to be well-treated" and "it is wrong to treat animals badly." We all now agree, unlike most of our predecessors until a relatively short time ago, that it is wrong to be cruel or callous in our treatment of animals; to accept that principle entailed breaking with the long-accepted doctrine that only relations between "intellectual beings" were subject to moral censure. But whether or not it follows that we must ascribe rights to animals or to foetuses or to posterity is by no means so apparent.

Then there are problems about *specific* rights as distinct from rights in general. Is there, for example, a right to privacy? If so, how far does it extend? In some countries, it is easy to buy electronic spying devices which enable the purchaser to listen to and record conversations held hundreds of feet away or behind a bedroom wall. These are bought and sold without any moral misgivings, advertised as enabling the purchaser "to find out what he needs to find out." Is the use of such devices an infringement of rights, or in some other way morally wrong? If so, on what grounds?

Again, it is often supposed that there is something describable as "the right to life." Yet the rise of technology has had as one of its more devastating consequences an overwhelming increase in population growth. Is there in fact a right to life? If so, what does the existence of that right prohibit—contraception, sterilization or only abortion and infanticide? How and where can the line be drawn? Medical science, too, has made it possible to keep many physical organisms alive which would once have died, physical organisms which have the bodily form, at least, of human beings— if, perhaps, mutilated human beings. Does it count as killing to withdraw medical support from organisms in which, let us say, the brain does not function? And if the brain, why not other organs?

These are only samples of the problems about rights and about right and wrong which the rise of technology have forced upon us. Others have to do with relative weighting. Our relationships to posterity have been altered by technological change; it is at least possible that as a result of the modifications we have introduced into the world, posterity will find itself impoverished. Perhaps, even, there will be no posterity. Should we reconsider the weight we have been accustomed to give to the interests of posterity, now that our powers in relation to it have so notably strengthened? Or to take another question which now constantly arises, how much importance should we attach to the destruction of a landscape when, by trying to preserve it, we create unemployment?

It would be obviously absurd, in the present context, to attempt to answer this quiver-full of questions. If in anything but a final fashion, I have tried elsewhere, in *Man's Responsibility for Nature*, to point to some of the considerations which will determine our answers to them. All that, for the moment, I want to insist upon is the range, the difficulty, and the novelty, of the problems technology has set for the moral philosopher.

A rather different set of moral problems arise out of discussions about "the quality of life." That is a newly coined phrase, but it has rapidly swept the world. Advertisers, with their inimitable capacity for vulgarizing, have taken it up; in the United States, we find ourselves assured that to improve the quality of our lives we need a more comfortable executive suite, in France that we need a more comfortable bed. But the phrase is no less prevalent in more serious contexts, for all, or perhaps just on account of, its obscurity.

Quality, as I have already implied in a passing reference, is in this context antithetical to quantity. The tendency of a technological society is to measure progress in quantitative terms. The Soviet Union's passion for statistics illustrates an enthusiasm for numerical superiority by no means confined to that country. But in the Western world we are gradually, if painfully, turning against that approach. When, nowadays, we are considering whether a freeway ought to be built, we are not content to be told how many cars will pass over it, what will be the average time-saving, how much it will cost. We want to know how it will look and what modes of life, human and non-human, it will weaken or destroy. These we think of as *qualitative* considerations; they relate to the character of our life rather than to the calculation of economic consequences.

The quality of our life, broadly considered, can of course be reduced or enhanced in a great variety of different ways. Our upbringing, the friends we make, the causes to which we attach ourselves—all of these and many other factors can profoundly influence, for better or worse, the quality of the life we lead. But as the phrase is now currently used, "quality of life" refers only to those forms of spiritual impoverishment or enrichment which flow from changes in our material surroundings, whether natural or man-made, surroundings which were once mainly categorized as something for human beings to exist within and work upon but which we now vividly apprehend as working upon us. So the French Ministry for *La Qualité de la Vie* concentrates upon the control of noise and pollution, the preservation and extension of green spaces, urban renewal, transport. For the most part, it casts technology in a destructive role, not of intent but as a consequence of the technologists' narrow concern with the readily quantifiable.

But has this distinction between the qualitative and the quantitative any real force? Many of the classical philosophers, influenced by the rise of mathematical physics, have encouraged us to believe that what we normally regard as qualitative distinctions are reducible to differences in quantity. If one life is better than another, so Bentham argued, this is only because it contains more pleasure and less pain. Pinball machines—slightly to modify his examples—are as good as poetry if they give as much pleasure to as many people. This is a doctrine very consoling to a technologically minded society, a society excellently adapted to producing bigger and better pinball machines but made uneasy by poetry. (John Locke once remarked that he did not understand why parents whose children showed some inclination to poetry did not at once do everything in their power to destroy that inclination.) For Descartes and his scientifically minded successors, all transformation, accurately considered, is a quantitative re-arrangement of matter or energy; Bentham is suggesting, in the same spirit, that social transformation is nothing but a quantitative redistribution of pleasure and pain.

To consider the general metaphysical doctrine first, we need to distinguish between the standpoint of physics, with its overwhelming interest in quantitative relationships, and our standpoint as human beings living, as it is now sometimes put, at the "ecological" level—in the biosphere in a particular society. At this ecological level, qualitative distinctions are of the utmost importance; quantitative distinctions matter only when they come to be perceived as qualitative distinctions, as when the quiet becomes noisy, the clean dirty, the varied monotonous, the busy overcrowded. (Modern "catastrophe theory," in contra-distinction from calculus, concerns itself with this type of transformation.) For this same reason we see as destruction, as the loss of desirable members of, or features of, the world around us, what, for the physicist, is only a change in the distribution of energy. Although its energy is no doubt conserved, a species which has been wiped out is nonetheless, from our everyday point of view, destroyed, as is a razed building or a lost liberty.

Nor are we consoled by the Hegelian doctrine that such destruction is but the lifting of the world of the spirit to a higher level, incorporating all that was valuable in the past in a new and nobler form. That the modern must, in virtue of its very modernity, be better than the old is far from being a self-evident truth; that destruction is only transformation is, at the level which now interests us, obviously false. Our emphasis needs rather to be on the fact that to transform is to destroy, to destroy, often enough, in a way which is absolutely final. And, certainly, we should always ask in detail what will be destroyed and what will replace it before we applaud "development" or "modernizing." Nor should we permit our demand to know that what will be destroyed to be answered in purely physical terms. To demolish an area of the city, to intersect it with freeways, to replace shops and houses with office-blocks, can be, as we have already suggested, to destroy not only property but entire ways of life. To be sure, we must not fall into the trap of supposing that if it is not always good, transformation must always be bad; we have had more than enough of such melodramatic oppositions in our political and social lives. Technology is neither to be hissed as the villain nor applauded as the hero. Like most of us, it is neither of these, or not all the time.

Necessarily involved in any critical examination of plans for transformation is a decision about what changes are to count as for the worse and what for the better. The answer of classical utilitarianism sounds easy, at least until we try to apply it in practice: we should do whatever will give most pleasure and least pain to the largest number of people. But, thanks to the growth of technology, we can now contemplate at the level of practical possibilities, a society in which pain can always be alleviated and pleasure is constantly available by hooking ourselves up to machines which stimulate the pleasure centers of the brain. Are we *really* prepared to take such a society as our ideal? Are we *really* convinced that the fanatical devotee of pinball machines is living as good a life as those who engage in a broad range of activities, each exercising a particular form of human virtue?

Recent discussions about the quality of life tend to assume a negative answer to such questions. They refer scarcely at all to pleasure; their emphasis is on the need for preserving and extending those features of our environment, natural and social, which help us to live lives which are varied, imaginative, enterprising, which encourage us to show consideration to others, to exhibit warmth and tolerance. John Stuart Mill's outburst— "better to be a Socrates dissatisfied than a pig satisfied"—falls upon ever more responsive ears as does his more general contention that the quality of our pleasures is all-important. But this, of course, still leaves the question wide open: How do we determine that one pleasure, one form of life, one kind of devotion is of higher quality than another? Is it mere élitism, to use the fashionable cant phrase, to suggest that there are qualitative differences between the life of the pinball player and the life of the poet? It is my hope that contemporary discussions of the quality of life will force Anglo-American moral philosophers away from their preoccupation with rights and duties, with forms of contract, to ask older and broader questions about the moral differences between alternative modes of living, about whether the Founding Fathers were right to believe that liberty was at least of equal importance to the pursuit of happiness, even if liberty brings in its train "divine discontent." I do not mean that philosophers should abandon deontological problems—indeed, at an earlier stage of this paper, I raised a set of questions about rights—but that they should spread their wings more widely. They might ask, for example, when discontent is "divine" and when it is mere petulance or a childish demand for everything, all at once, the simultaneous having and eating of cake. (If one cannot do only one thing at a time, equally one cannot do everything at once.)

If they undertake such tasks, should philosophers restrict themselves to formal analysis, to studies of what "it means to say," for example, that one pleasure is better than another? Many philosophers, especially in the Anglo-American tradition, have argued as much, and in consequence, that it does not fall within their province to write the contemporary equivalents of Mill's *On Liberty* or Locke's *Essay on Toleration*. Then whose province is it? One can understand why philosophers are reluctant to be thought of as moral preachers, as sages rather than as systematic thinkers. Systematic thinking is their specific virtue, thinking in a manner which is exceptional in its clarity, its exactness, its argumentative force. I should be the last to wish philosophers to give up such systematic thinking in favor of large pronouncements. But they need not entirely restrict themselves to systematic thinking about systematic thinking. There is no one else so well equipped, just in virtue of their capacity as systematic thinkers, to undertake that critical examination of ways of life which Socrates initiated. Sophistry did not die with Protagoras, the worship of power with Thrasymachus.

Philosophy, I have suggested, gave its blessing to technology. It can now contribute to clearing up the mess technology has created by re-examining the larger concepts, the wider principles, on which our culture depends. And more than a few philosophers are now engaged on that very task. It is no longer quite ridiculous, as it might have seemed to be but a decade ago, to look to philosophers, not indeed for instruction, but certainly for guidance.

NOTES

* For a fuller account of the topics taken up in this paper see my *Man's Responsibility for Nature* (London, Duckworth; New York, Scribner, 1974); "Attidues to Nature" in R. S. Peters, ed. *Nature and Conduct*, Royal Institute of Philosophy Lectures, Vol. VIII (London, Macmillan, 1975); "The Treatment of Animals," *Journal of the History of Ideas*, XXVI, 2 (April–May, 1975), 195–218; "Ecology and Persuasion" (*Proceedings of the St. Louis Conference of Legal and*

Social Philosophy, forthcoming) and *Science, Technology and Anti-Science* (Rutgers University Press, forthcoming).

NAME INDEX